MW00619339

Amalgamation Schemes

Amalgamation Schemes

Antiblackness and the Critique of Multiracialism

Jared Sexton

University of Minnesota Press
Minneapolis • London

Published by the University of Minnesota Press
111 Third Avenue South, Suite 290
Minneapolis, MN 55401-2520
http://www.upress.umn.edu

Library of Congress Cataloging-in-Publication Data

Sexton, Jared.
   Amalgamation schemes : antiblackness and the critique of multiracialism / Jared Sexton.
      p. cm.
   Includes bibliographical references and index.
   ISBN 978-0-8166-5104-7 (hc : alk. paper) — ISBN 978-0-8166-5105-4 (pb : alk. paper)
   1. United States—Race relations. 2. Racially mixed people—United States. 3. Interracial marriage—United States. 4. Race discrimination—United States. I. Title.
   E184.A1S563 2008
   305.800973—dc22
                                                                                    2008008574

Printed in the United States of America on acid-free paper

The University of Minnesota is an equal-opportunity educator and employer.

15 14 13 12 11 10 09 08   10 9 8 7 6 5 4 3 2 1

Contents

On the Verge of Race

There is a psychological phenomenon that consists in the belief
that the world will open to the extent to which frontiers
are broken down.

—Frantz Fanon, *Black Skin, White Masks*

It's never enough to shout long live the multiple.

—Félix Guattari, *Soft Subversions*

Amalgamation Schemes offers a critique of multiracialism in the post–civil
rights era United States. "Multiracialism" here is inclusive of the political
initiatives of the multiracial movement, the academic field of multiracial
studies, and the media discourse about "race mixture" in contemporary
culture and society. In this book, I consider both the implications of multiracialism for theorizations of race and its restaging of sexual politics in
the name of progressive social change. Against the claims of leading proponents, I find that the principal political effects of multiracialism are neither a fundamental challenge to the living legacies of white supremacy
nor a defiance of sexual racism in particular but rather the reinforcement
of longstanding tenets of antiblackness and the promotion of normative
sexuality. The former effect follows from the advancement of (sometimes
alternating, sometimes simultaneous) ideologies of colorblindness and multiracial exceptionalism, while the latter effect proceeds along with the promotion of a (sometimes implicit, sometimes explicit) repackaged family
values platform—extolling *bourgeois* virtues of domestic coupling, two-
parent childrearing, and the nuclear family unit. This ideologically restora-
tive work serves to counteract the overlapping critical interventions of

black freedom struggle, feminist movement, sexual liberation, and queer activism; and it is conducted under the protective metaphors of natural growth: an *extension* of civil rights advocacy and an *evolution* in the politics of antiracism.

Yet, if the impact of multiracialism is detectable across a range of political conflicts, its primary target is found nonetheless in historical formations of black community, taking aim at the singular antagonism that conditions "racial blackness" as social identity, structural position, locus of identification, and object of desire.[1] The declarations of multiracialism are grounded in a discontent with the theoretical status of the concept of "hypodescent" (Davis 1991), according to which convention the issue of interracial sexual reproduction assumes the status of the black, usually maternal, parent.[2] However, the objection to hypodescent is pursued only insofar as this rule of definition is detached from the antinomies of North American slave society. More precisely, a contradictory argument is forwarded that the rule is, on the one hand, autonomous and self-sustaining and, on the other, embedded in the system of racial slavery as its Achilles heel. At once, we are told that the "one-drop rule" of racial classification can be dismantled, de jure and de facto, without the least transformation in the social structures of slavery and that these structures are somehow susceptible to collapse through the redrawing or renunciation of the color line enabled by its suspension.

Because one of the most widely cited markers of historical distinction between Anglo and Latin American racial formations regards the respective rigidity/fluidity of their classification systems and their relative tolerance toward sexual encounter across the color line (Esteva-Fabregat 1995), this reckoning with a multiracial critical mass north of the U.S.–Mexico border is also involved in, and perhaps symbolizes, what some scholars have called "the Latin Americanization of U.S. race relations" (Bonilla-Silva 2004): a situation wherein a binary black–white model of race is said to give way to more a permeable and highly differentiated multiracial arrangement. One component of this change regards increased social acceptance of and participation in relationships of interracial intimacy and the official recognition of a self-identified multiracial demographic.

As such, this transformation demands reflection not only upon the effects it may hold for African Americans and the repositioning it portends for other people of color in the United States but also upon the dissemination of a racist culture fundamental to the legacies of Western modernity and the deeply uneven emergence of global civil society.

On this view, the enlargement of multiracialism can be more fully appreciated as an element of the regional integration of the Americas and the formation of a Pacific Rim economy, what we might call "the cultural politics of free trade agreement," wherein the United States seeks to win hegemony—and maintain political, economic, and military dominance—by incorporating to its own ends the trappings of an age-old Latin American crisis-management strategy. More broadly still, the politics of multiracialism can be taken as a component of the highly politicized contest over globalization insofar as race remains decisive to its unfolding: from the deregulation of financial markets and the privatization of the commons to the subjugation and displacement of labor and the reconfiguration of strategic military alliances. All such developments should be considered in light of a heterogeneous and countervailing black radical tradition (C. Robinson 2000) that not only contests the ravages of historical capitalism but takes to task the limits of its left-wing opposition as well. Its constituencies today operate at a remove from the mainstream of the anti-globalization movement, pursuing demands well in excess of the platforms of global justice: from the transnational movement for reparations for slavery to the emergence of black consciousness as a principle of political mobilization, social organization, and cultural production among Afro-Latino populations throughout the hemisphere. The groping solidarity evinced around the reparations controversy at the 2001 United Nations' World Conference Against Racism speaks directly to the former (McGreal 2001), while the recent formation of the Organization of Africans in the Americas as supplement to the official machinations of the Organization of the Americas is telling with respect to the latter (Minority Rights Group 1995).

With our context briefly sketched, I abbreviate the main objectives of the present study as follows:

1. To provide a critical overview of contemporary multiracialism from the emergence of multiracial studies in the 1980s to the federal race (and ethnicity) classification debates of the 1990s.
2. To highlight the relationship between sexuality and racial politics in general and interracial sexuality and multiracial identity in particular in hopes of reinvigorating debates that remain burdened by a set of archaic assumptions.
3. To challenge the conservative tendencies of contemporary multiracialism and confront the recruitment of the multiracial movement by right-wing political forces determined to undo the gains of the civil rights movement.
4. To revisit the history and significance of the one-drop rule of hypodescent, the central point of contention for multiracial critics and the improper name of a principle of mobilization within the centuries-long black freedom struggle.
5. To recommend a conception of nonbiological racial embodiment that disarticulates interracial sexuality from "miscegenation"[3] and resituates racialization in a field of power: a political ontology of violence rather than a specious genetic inheritance or a dubious phenomenology of perception.

While providing condensed introduction to salient points about the re-emergence of a self-avowed multiracial demographic in the contemporary United States, this study aims to problematize the prevailing account of civil rights and liberties and the various deliberations regarding antidiscrimination and affirmative action that have saturated its development to date. Important as these clashes have been, I argue that multiracialism, as it is framed by such debates, suffers from an assumptive logic that diminishes or conceals altogether the historicity of race and sexuality (Hodes 1999) and, more importantly, that displaces or disavows the protocols of violence that gird the twin pillars of U.S. social formation: racial slavery and genocidal conquest (Blackburn 1998). This is why the extensive, often anxious attention paid to the dynamics of race mixture within the popular fabrication of "*mestizo* America" (Nash 1999) is best understood as a confounded meditation on the possibility of multiracial democracy beneath the long shadow of "global white supremacy" (Mills 1998). To enter unselfconsciously into the fray of multiracialism in the post–civil rights era United States is to take for granted such democracy, whether it is claimed to be extant or nascent. Rather than accept this common frame of intelligibility, we might do better to disassemble the architecture of multiracial discourse, itemizing the elementary binaries through which it establishes its operative terms and uncovering the relations of force it obscures in the process.

The fêted turn toward multiracialism, or *mestizaje*, in the United States signals less the salutary force of a historic Latin American intervention than an articulation of otherwise progressive political, intellectual, and cultural movements toward competitive comparison with the enduring pressures of black liberation struggle.[4] What generates the affective intensity and symbolic purchase of multiracialism in the current conjuncture is the capacity of "American mixed race" (Zack 1995a) to both emulate and undermine—that is, to *caricature*—the cultural politics of Black Power rather than any propensity to elaborate the laudable contributions of the best of the black radical tradition. In this precise sense, multiracialism is a decidedly *post*–civil rights era phenomenon, taking its immediate tone and tenor from the "conservative restoration" (Shor 1992) of the last thirty years and partaking of the more recent advent of an "intimate public sphere" (Berlant 1997): conditions under which the political is *reduced* to the personal, confined to the pluralism of "lifestyles," and citizenship—or national belonging more generally—is increasingly adjudicated on the basis of one's moral integrity in putatively private affairs. Under these conditions, in the tendentious realm previous generations have known as "social equality," the problematic of interracial sexuality has resurfaced as a topic of national focus and global concern.[5] And it is in these terms that black community—assumedly beholden to a retrograde separatism and therefore *uninterested in interracial intimacy*—has been found wanting, to the point of criminality, in the project of "Building One America for the Twenty-First Century."[6]

As that which draws the line not only between white and nonwhite but also, more importantly, between black and nonblack (Yancey 2003), the legacy of the one-drop rule of hypodescent stands out within multiracial discourse as the fulcrum of historical distinction between a supposedly vestigial era of "racial dictatorship" (Omi and Winant 1994) and the dawning of an enlightened multiracial or nonracial democracy in the United States. As noted, it is also supposed to counterpose the racial formations of Anglo and Latin America where the latter provides a propaedeutic for the former. As a result of the vectors established by this spatial and temporal mapping, political struggle is located in the relative degrees of freedom afforded or secured apropos of racial definition and identification. On this account, freedom from the one-drop rule is construed artfully (because not without inconsistency) as freedom from the exigencies of being identified, or identifying oneself, with racial blackness. Modernizing the nation—at least that segment of the nation with the potential to be "more than black" (Daniel 2001) or simply to move "beyond black" (Rockquemore and Brunsma 2002)—and liberating it from the deadening weight of the past requires that the signature of its persistence (or perseverance or preservation) be effaced. In this light, multiracialism can be read, as suggested previously, as an element of the ascendant ideology of colorblindness (Hernandez 1998), but it is not thereby identical to it. Its target is not race per se, since multiracialism is still very much a politics of racial identity (one often enough holding up multiracial identity as exceptional and exemplary), but rather the categorical sprawl of blackness in particular and the insatiable political demand it presents to a nominally postemancipation society (Wilderson 2003).

In this precise respect, multiracialism solicits alliances with other political and intellectual efforts to go "beyond the black–white binary"— whether in the current campaigns for immigrant rights or the research agendas of comparative ethnic studies—efforts which, in many cases, have been shot through with an air of antiblackness (Matsuda 2002). In the register of contemporary racial politics, black identity appears as an antiquated state of confinement from which the "multiracial imagined community" (Stephens 1999) must be delivered; the negative ideal against which "the browning of America" (Root 1992a) measures its tenuous success. One discovers in this new-fangled admonition of runaway blackness traces of the criminalization and repression of Black Power that subtends the birth of Reaganism (Churchill and Vander Wall 2002). In the longer view, the "communal tyranny" (Kennedy 2003) imputed to the collective black personality in this context appears as a refraction of the pronounced fear of "black domination" that underwrites the history of white supremacist discourse: whether postbellum alibis for institutionalized lynching, segregation, and disenfranchisement (Hunter 1997) or the propaganda of "reverse discrimination" fashionable today—from "welfare queen" (Roberts 1998) to "coddled criminal" (Mauer 1999) to "affirmative action baby" (Post and Rogin 1998). Ultimately, it is consternation about being eclipsed by blackness that articulates multiracialism with the array of political campaigns consolidated under the heading of the New Immigration (Jaynes 2000) and links them collectively, and perhaps unconsciously, to political projects they might otherwise oppose.

Perspicacious scholars in the field of black studies (Gordon 1997; Makalani 2001; Spencer 1997, 1999) have already offered similar arguments, and I seek to affirm and extend their insights on this score. However, multiracialism also entails a sexual politics, and revising the history and significance of the one-drop rule is a necessary but insufficient response to its formation. This is the case because conceptions of the multiracial cannot help but imply a production of race in the field of heterosexuality, nominating, more specifically, the reproductive sex act as the principal site of mediation for racial difference itself. In this respect, not only does multiracialism conceptually retain a pernicious system of racial *breeding* (Zack 1993), a system that announces reproduction as the alibi for a more comprehensive regulation of sexuality, it also elides the politics of sexuality— its social production—especially with respect to processes of racialization (Bhattacharyya 2002). The latter is accomplished, in circular fashion, by presumptively confining the range of (interracial) sexual practices and the vicissitudes of (interracial) desire to a normative heterosexual frame, an interpretive gesture structurally required by the disavowed recourse to race-as-biological that notions of the multiracial put into play. In short, to the extent that one thinks of race as biological (e.g., genotype, phenotype), one thinks of race mixture in heteronormative and reproductivist terms. Put slightly differently, insofar as a figure of mixed race forms the backdrop for thinking interracial sexuality, the erasure of sexual encounter beyond or outside the heterosexual matrix is a fait accompli. Dislodging biological notions of race becomes, then, a condition of possibility for the queering of interracial sexuality (Warner 1999), including its disarticulation from the specter of miscegenation. If we grant Fanon's famous formulation, "the Negro symbolizes the biological danger" (Fanon 1967), then we can sense how black liberation in particular is potentially refashioned and revivified here as well.[7]

This is perhaps an ambitious exercise, considering the general reticence of multiracialism to engage the sexual domain, even within the limited purview of a normative heterosexuality. In seeking to gain moral distance from age-old racist fantasies of interracial sexuality as the realm par excellence of the perverse, the pathological, and the pornographic (Hernton 1988), the new multiracial consciousness eschews the sexual dimensions of racialization (and vice versa) in favor of axiological pronouncements on "love," "romance," "family," and "childrearing." One effect of this distancing from the sexual is to reinforce the imaginative quarantine of interracial sexuality to the margins of the public sphere: the political networks of the white supremacist movement and the political economy of global sex industries. Circulating uncomfortably between these marginal fields, interracial sexuality appears only at the extremities of a traitorous moral failure (for white supremacist ideologues) or an irreverent moral flouting (for captains of the sex trade). Both positions fortify a politics of sexual shame that has long animated racist culture, and both positions contribute to the longevity of antimiscegenation as a result. Interracial sexuality, figured in these terms, stands as a condition of possibility and a condition of impossibility for multiracialism.

Another effect of this quarantine is to render a discourse of race as a matter of personal identity despite pretenses toward politicization and the development of historical consciousness. This move concentrates the often diffuse hostility of multiracialism toward black community, a formation wherein the history of sexuality and the prospects for collective political struggle remain items of recurrent, if often truncated, public debate (Black Public Sphere Collective 1995). However, recovering sexuality for racial critique need not salvage dominant frameworks in the process (recuperating the contradictory "normality" of a "subversive" interracial heterosexuality would prove a Pyrrhic victory indeed). In fact, so much would not be possible unless and until race could be effectively dissociated from biology and breeding displaced as the privileged locus for the production of racial difference. Only in the wake of this disinterment could interracial sexuality be understood in its proper sense: a domain in which racial difference emerges as an effect of the power-laden approximations of pleasure and pain, a "mode of enjoyment" (Žižek 1989).

It is here that the two central aspects of the critique of multiracialism converge: to return historicity to race is to understand it as a production of bodily (not biological) difference at the nexus of violence and sexuality, where the heuristic distinction between the latter terms is often difficult to retain at the level of lived experience. That is to say, racial difference *issues* from direct relations of force—the scales of coercion—and it is only elaborated or *institutionalized* within relations of power—the scales of consent. What establishes race, what positions one within racial formation, is the relation one suffers and/or enjoys with respect to the state-sponsored social organization of violence and sexuality. Refocusing the historic violence of racial slavery as an "allegory of the present" (Hartman 1997), on the one hand, and distinguishing interracial sexuality from the heterosexual matrix of breeding, on the other, are indispensable steps toward a rethinking of race and mixed race appropriate to the contemporary scene. From this angle, *Amalgamation Schemes* seeks to repoliticize the unstable juncture of race and sexuality in ways that avoid the pitfalls of reification. Moreover, it works to de-sediment race and sexuality without jettisoning the body altogether, preserving a repertoire of critical terms for the future of black freedom struggle (and, as noted, a host of other overlapping new social movements). This book is driven by the intuition that, perhaps, in the historic frenzy of our requisite political resistance, we have yet to truly encounter the body, to learn precisely what it is or, rather, what it can do, to think creatively about its *becoming* rather than to pronounce upon its *being* (Massumi 2002). It is hoped, at the least, that the following commentary invites an unfamiliar rendezvous.

Frameworks

The present work is interdisciplinary to the extent that it draws conceptual resources from across the humanities and the social sciences, as most contemporary studies of race have found it necessary to do, however successfully. It is also transdisciplinary insofar as it finds an orientation within poststructuralism, an intellectual movement whose impact has registered throughout the academic milieu (Rapaport 2001). More precisely, a reconstructed psychoanalytic theory, or "psycho-Marxism," provides the single most important frame of analysis for my work (Miklitsch 1998). Of course, there is no single framework called psychoanalysis (much less in its intersections with Marxism), its status as a discipline is widely questioned, and the history of its various schools is contested perennially (Brooks and Woloch 2000). My appropriation from the field is selective and open-ended and seeks in no way to enter the larger fray. While I may demonstrate an affinity at times for Freud and Lacan and contemporary commentators like Žižek (1989) and Copjec (1994), I also bend the intellectual project of psychoanalysis to meet the needs of my own ensemble of questions, an appropriation that includes a certain rapprochement with historicism and deconstruction. The latter move is inspired by the pioneering work of Hartman (1997), Judy (1993), and Spillers (2003) as well as more recent contributions by Keeling (2003), Marriott (2000), and Wilderson (2003). Political and intellectual exigencies have pushed these authors to straddle the bright lines of academic division and fashion innovative linkages between the classic Marx–Freud couplet and other well-known figures of the postwar French intellectual scene, such as Althusser, Deleuze, Derrida, and Foucault. These various theoretical projects are opposed or incommensurable on some counts, and keeping them in productive tension is often unwieldy as a result. However, the ecumenical spirit of Fanon and Du Bois, both of whom exert their influence here, pulls otherwise incompatible modes of inquiry into a common horizon of concern. Fanon, in particular, proves deft at moving between the fields of philosophy, literature, poetry, and history or psychiatry, psychoanalysis, political theory, and anthropology—often in the matter of a paragraph. I am entirely unable to reproduce his deservedly famous style, yet his sense of intellectual freedom and professed methodological "dereliction" licenses, I think, a certain shuttling back and forth between disciplines, in and out of entrenched disagreements among theorists and critics. Returning to Fanon at different points serves to ground an analysis that might otherwise take flight. So, if this study cannot be considered a straightaway "psychoanalysis of race" (Lane 1998), it might still be termed, pace Spillers, a "psychoanalytics" of its culture and politics: cultural and political criticism that draws from the psychoanalytic archive, putting to work its concepts and operating within its broad intellectual sphere but guided by aims "beyond the couch."

Amalgamation Schemes is also situated, somewhat critically, in the field of comparative ethnic studies, which is to say it takes up questions of hegemony in contemporary formations of race and sexuality with a decided interest in how such investigation might enable social movements for radical change (Butler 2001). On that score, it is indebted to feminist and queer theory as well, particularly as they have been developed and deployed by black scholars and other intellectuals of color.[8] I am motivated by a concern for the intersections of race, class, gender, and sexuality, and I take for granted a number of insights produced by antiessentialist or social constructionist arguments (Ore 2003). However, I am not satisfied to simply bring such insights to bear on the matter of multiracialism in the United States. Rather, I work from a notion of race as neither a biological index of natural kind nor an illusion produced in culture (Shepherdson 2000). Nor do I take race to be simply a social fact or "a complex of social meanings" (Omi and Winant 1994). Of course, race does exist, in some sense, as a reliable social indicator of life chances and as a traceable chain of significations, but its political ontology exceeds the terms of sociological investigation and the operations of the symbolic order: it is, to try another phrasing, a "division of species" (Fanon 1963) effected and maintained by the technologies of violence and sexuality that underwrite the social formation, not a discriminatory manipulation of already existing bodily marks (Guillaumin 1995). Moreover, it is in the register of fantasy, a social category of psychic reality described by psychoanalysis (Burgin 1996), that this matrix of forces is most vividly staged and those obligatory "scenes of subjection" find their touchstones of coherence. In my view, race is "real" in a sense that distends the notion as found in Lacan. By thinking race through and beyond the register of the Real—toward what Spillers (2003) suggestively terms the "socio-nom"—we are able to understand better the place of sexuality in the production of racial difference. At the limits of signification—a limit that is both *historical* and *structural*—race and sexuality cohabit.

On that note, I introduce a guiding idea for the readings offered here: the inverse historical relation between white supremacy's tolerance for multiracial formations and the relative strength of black liberation struggle. When black resistance is thought by state and civil society to be effectively contained or neutralized, both practically and symbolically, the color line becomes considerably more fluid. This point is hypothesized from the strong correlations found in most historical treatments of "mulattos" in the United States in which one finds a relative relaxation and expansion of the rules of racial definition during moments of white supremacy's greatest confidence alongside a marked constriction of those same categories during moments of real or imagined crisis (Williamson 1984). Typically, that crisis takes form in the prospect of increased black freedom, that prospect is declared a violent threat to the white body politic (the res publica), and that threat of violence is infused with fears of a consuming, violating black sexuality.

When faced with the specter of violent black sexuality or sexualized black violence, white supremacy in the United States has consistently conflated blacks and mulattos through retrenched enforcement of the one-drop rule. That is to say, when blacks move against the structures of white supremacy, "mixed race" is revoked as a viable social identity and racial blackness is again understood as a broad spectrum. Under the system of chattel slavery, multiracial populations in the United States occasionally served as buffer classes between whites and blacks, both enslaved and free, and these multiracial populations often corroborated and collaborated with antiblackness (echoing dynamics prevalent throughout the slave regimes of the Caribbean and Latin America). However, the resurgence of white supremacy in the immediate antebellum period and, again, in the wake of Reconstruction pressed blacks and mulattos into a relatively common category and solidified, to large extent, their collective fortunes. Of course, this conflation did not necessarily ease and certainly never erased distinctions of class and color among blacks so defined (though it did *mediate* them), but its reappearance in the face of legal segregation and the institution of lynching was largely affirmed—not simply pragmatically adopted or cynically tolerated—by those formerly or otherwise considered to be "more than black." Rather than a naïve or pathological miscomprehension, the historical forms of black solidarity against which multiracialism does battle today is a complex political *identification* forged most clearly during the century between the circumscription of chattel slavery and the rise of Black Power—the era of Jim Crow. Contemporary multiracialism is enabled by the historical dynamic described previously. It unfolds amid the ebb of black political energies and the *resegregation* of the United States, which is to say a refortified antiblackness. The chief ideological or rhetorical difference between the discourse of the post–civil rights era and earlier contractions of the color line—the proslavery campaign of the 1830s and 1840s, the mobilization for southern "Redemption" of the 1880s and 1890s, the "massive resistance" to desegregation of the 1950s and 1960s announced by the infamous Southern Manifesto—resides in the ascription of determinate power: in the present, black community, rather than white society, is said to bear primary responsibility for cutting the border of race. To repeat an earlier point, blacks in this moment do not so much police the traditional boundary between blackness and whiteness as that which obtains between blackness and *everything else.*

Given this backdrop, my interrogation involves a second order of abstraction. In looking to the field of multiracial studies and the domain of multiracial identity politics since the early 1990s, I am interested in the ways that present-day authors interpret the extant scholarship on race and race mixture (i.e., their reading of the archive) and the arguments that they advance in response (i.e., their contribution to the archive). I do so less to mark advancements in the production of knowledge than to indicate several persistent continuities betrayed by recent perturbations in our understanding of race and race mixture. New historical treatments of anti-miscegenation, for instance, contend with prevailing accounts in the history of slavery and segregation, buttressing the problems of earlier projects even as they seek to revise and depart from them. Or, to take another example, new psychological studies of multiracial identity development steel themselves against the recurrent tropes of the "marginal man" or "tragic mulatto," but the scholarship generally fails to escape such entanglements, falling prey to longstanding blind spots. These are failures that return not because they are intellectually unmanageable but because they are fixed by libidinal investment. I elucidate the debates underlying this intervention in racial theory in order to focus the political ramifications involved, ramifications spelled out with sometimes surprising clarity in the pronouncements and proposals of multiracial lobbyists and advocates.

En route, I examine works gathered in several pioneering interdisciplinary anthologies as well as a number of influential philosophical meditations, political manifestos, historical studies, social scientific investigations, and autobiographical accounts—all of which can be considered keynotes in the formation of multiracial discourse. Because I am considering a wide range of writing, the authors engaged cannot be reduced to a party line and in some cases evince unadorned conflicts of interest. Nonetheless, what lends this discursive field its coherence—beyond the dense web of intertextual citations, the networks of political organizations and professional associations, and the standard (metropolitan, college-educated, middle-class) demographic profile of its constituency—is its obdurately unsophisticated understanding of race and sexuality and its conspicuously negative disposition toward what Fanon (1967) terms "the lived experience of the black." Building upon critical currents discernible at the margins of multiracial studies, currents that are both disruptive to and disavowed within the field, I identify the exclusions that remain vital to its reproduction. I am particularly interested in delineating how this discourse both rejects and reintroduces a biological notion of race; how it relies upon a pernicious simplification of the historic one-drop rule as it objects to its devastating politics; how it persists in mobilizing pathology as a term of aspersion for the world outside its camp in order to declare itself healthy and wholesome; how this moralizing displacement requires a sanitized—or anesthetized—sexuality within and across the color line; and how multiracialism premises its contribution to knowledge, culture, and politics upon an evacuation of the historical richness, intellectual intensity, cultural expansiveness, and political complexity of black experience, including, perhaps especially, its indelible terrors. In reading across these different types of writing and public address, I highlight how certain figures of blackness resurface in each instance of multiracial discourse and how such figures are generally made to serve as a foil for the contemporary value of multiracialism. The conceptual framework pursued throughout the book is designated *"critical mixed-race theory"* (Gordon 1997) as a means of keeping in mind the questions and concerns that drive the broader political and intellectual project of black culture critique, to which it is hoped that *Amalgamation Schemes* can offer some modest contribution.

Critical Mixed-Race Theory

The politics of interracial sexuality are fundamental to racial formation. Much more than a recurrent topic of debate or a persistent focal point of psychosocial anxiety, it is foundational for racial difference—the field for its production, contestation, and containment. In everyday conversation, this centrality is indexed in the ubiquitous queries about the race of one's intimate partners, the figures of one's fantasy life, the objects of one's aesthetic appreciation, and so forth. The standard repertoire of interrogation is at times more pointed for multiracial people themselves (Twine 1996), but only to the extent that their social positioning demonstrates the historical labor that strives to make the forms of racial difference appear as both normal and natural. In the last decade or so, the introduction of the multiracial movement and the proliferation of multiracial studies have brought this constellation of questions about interracial sexuality back to the forefront of public debate where it has in some sense always been. However, this reframing of the issue has exceeded the stated objectives of the movement's leading advocates and the academic field's leading scholarly voices. One cannot address the notion of multiracial identity without broaching a discussion of the politics of interracial sexuality, yet the intrinsic relation between the two has been a source of significant trouble for the political and cultural representation of this newly forged constituency. This trouble stems from the fact that in confronting the domain of interracial sexuality—as a material practice and a discursive formation—one is pressed to reckon with the social formation of white supremacy and antiblackness, the production and reproduction of the historic dividing line between humanity and "infra-humanity" (Gilroy 2000), the inside and outside of a racist polity, economy, and culture. This division is established through the demarcation of the black body and, as such, is both irritated by and dependent upon the volatility of negrophobia. In fact, these operations are coeval. Multiracialism respects these coeval operations to the extent that it allows them to escape from scrutiny.

But the distress so regularly provoked by interracial sexuality qua negrophobia is also deeply related to the "impersonality of desire" as it has been elaborated in psychoanalytic experience (Dean 2000), that is, its profound indifference to the powerful mythos of the individual and its unstable connivance with social categories of race, gender, and class.[9] This is one way to understand the strident individualism that characterizes the multiracial movement and its academic inscription: a disavowal of the structures of violence that have enabled and conditioned the historical development of white supremacist capitalist patriarchy (of which antiblackness is the ground floor) as well as the essentially disjointed, ill-fitting relationship between individuals and (their) desire. However, we should also take into account how the booming reclamation of (racial) identity and the anxious domestication of (interracial) sexuality in multiracial discourse function as defenses against equally impersonal forces of political economic restructuring coincident with the development of a post–civil rights era multiracial consciousness. In other words, multiracialism fabricates a provisional rendition of the social landscape in lieu of a more widespread failure of "cognitive mapping" (Jameson 1992a). Finally, within academic circles proper, the articulation of identity politics in the field of multiracial studies absorbs and defuses the radical revision of the subject of history in theory, research, and writing that has flourished since the 1960s.[10]

These points are discussed further, but suffice it to say at this point that "blackness" serves throughout as the master sign of intertwining forces of instability that together conspire to frustrate the aspirations of an esteemed neoliberalism: the waywardness of desire, the impersonality of the global economy, and the awesome intellectual estrangement provoked by "the cultural turn" (Jameson 1998a) among practitioners across the arts and human sciences. Blackness, as seen through the lens of multiracialism, ruins the propriety of sexual relations (by introducing the prospect of their vulgarization), hampers the prosperity of the United States in the global age (by demanding, at least, outdated "welfare state" policies), and impedes the development of "a fuller, more differentiated" discussion of race and racism (by insisting on an uncritical black–white binary framework or by pursuing an overly theoretical treatment of race that obscures the complex realities of racism) (Cho 1993, 196).

In pointed response to such conclusions, this study attempts to recuperate the critical potential of theorizing race and sexuality by presenting a meditation on what we might call "the general economy of racialization."[11] I do so through an engagement with the historical regulation of interracial sexuality in the United States and, more precisely, its post–civil rights transformation in the discourse of multiracialism. While the theoretical stakes of the project are broad based, aspiring to a level of abstraction and general application, its formal parameters are, as noted, fairly circumscribed. I argue that multiracialism is part of an attempt to symbolize and manage (without explaining, much less redressing) a crisis of social meaning lived through the knotted modalities of race, class, gender, and sexuality and their collective bearing on reconfigurations of the nation-state—a crisis experienced profoundly in and on the body (Lowe 1995).[12]

This multifaceted crisis is articulated to considerable extent through the specter of multiracialism and, for this reason, slates the latter for continued supervision. That is, because multiracialism operates by way of a historic double standard—endorsed when it does not involve blackness in significant ways, abjured whenever it does—it demands supple and discriminating techniques of administration if it is to mitigate the confusions of the day. What I hope to demonstrate in *Amalgamation Schemes* is that the moments of failure or impasse in the discourse of multiracialism, particularly the difficulty exhibited with respect to the matter of racial blackness, offer considerable insight into its political and libidinal economies. By reading symptomatically, we can identify the basic elements of multiracialism and perhaps go some way toward elucidating the "fundamental (social) fantasy" (Brennan 1993)[13] of the post–civil rights era in which it finds its principal coordinates. First, some introductory comments are in order about the concepts of race, racialization, and general economy.

The Racial Suture

Rather than providing a radical challenge to the racial order, the threat of miscegenation actually works—historically and contemporarily—in the service of white supremacy and antiblackness. This seemingly paradoxical relationship becomes intelligible through recourse to the psychoanalytic concept of "suture," a term first developed by Jacques-Alain Miller (1977) and disseminated in Anglophone academic circles through its appropriation in the field of film theory since the late 1970s (Silverman 1983). Suture designates the set of processes by which the effects of meaning, which is to say coherence and unity, are provisionally generated for a subject as it is inserted into, or represented within, the order of language amid the endless movements of signification. In fact, this provisional generation of meaning is coextensive with the intermittent production (or the alternating appearance/disappearance) of the subject insofar as the subject is a "speaking subject," a subject of language or, better, subject *to* language.[14] In the case of classical cinema, suture is bound to the construction of what Stephen Heath (1985) calls "narrative space." He argues that because film works with and through movement in the visible field, a structural difficulty arises as to how this potentially disorienting, shifting plane—the commotion on the screen, "the mobility that could threaten the clarity of vision in a constant renewal of perspective"—will function as a legible experience for any given audience. How, he asks, does one effect "the conversion of seen into scene" (Heath 1985, 36, 37) and contain that threatening mobility? For Heath, this is "the problem of composition" that vexes the cinema's logic of movement.

> The ideal of space remains that of photographic vision which brings with it the concern to sustain the camera as eye . . . outside process, purely looking. . . . The ideal, however, is a construction, the mobility required is still not easy, the shifting center needs to be settled along the film in its making scenes, its taking place; space will be difficult. To put it another way: mobility is exactly what is possible in film, complicit—the possibility of holding film within a certain vision, thereby "perfected"—and radical—the possibility of film disturbing vision, with which none the less it is immediately involved, historically, industrially, ideologically. (32–33)

We can see, at this early point, the strong resonance between the problem of composition in cinema, which is to say the problem of subject formation described by the processes of suture, and the internally conflicted obsessions of racial whiteness, the overriding historical imperative of U.S. social formation (Allen 1994, 1997; Martinot 2002). The mobility of the moving-image camera presents the possibility of both a construction of perfected vision (complicit, as Heath argues, with the hegemonic perceptual regime) and the irreducible difficulties of cinematic space (offering radical possibilities for a disruption of that regime, "the possibility of film disturbing vision"). Similarly, we might say that "the binary machine" of racialization (Deleuze and Parnet 1987)[15] enables both the construction of a putatively pure racial identity (i.e., the myth of whiteness) and the inevitable disruption of that racial identity through the intermixture of otherness. But what sort of disruption is at stake, that which is called for, *organized* in the name of unity or perhaps a more radical disturbance?

The relevance of this comparison exceeds the recitation of theoretical commonplaces regarding the differential nature of meaning: "any given term, concept, or cluster of terms and concepts cannot exist other than within a given conceptual chain or matrix" (Plotnitski 1993, 10). The point not to be missed in both cases is that the production of coherent meaning or a unitary image—whether at the level of scene, narrative, or social category—relies upon a certain restricted deployment or strategic marshalling of disunity, incoherence, and disruption: movement and space outside or beyond the frame. "The need," as Heath puts it, "is to cut up and then join together in a kind of spatial *Aufhebung* that decides a superior unity" (1985, 40). Stated differently, "It must be seen that the work of classical continuity is not to hide or ignore off-screen space but, on the contrary, to contain it, to regularize its fluctuation in a constant movement of re-appropriation" (45). Read back into the economy of racialization, this brief gloss on suture begs a crucial question: Amid the present celebration of a multiracialism that purportedly "represents a potentially radical disturbance of the smooth stability" of the white racial image, what are we to make of those related political tendencies that betray a "need for a systematic organization to contain it" (49)? If, after all, "whiteness is elaborated and defended *because* [and not *despite* that] it is perceived to be threatened" by the specter of interracial sexual encounter (Ferber 1998, 5; emphasis added), then the (disavowed) affirmation of interracial sexuality inherent to mul-tiracialism actually energizes white supremacy and antiblackness through the effects of its subversion, an indispensable component of its incessant propagation. In this respect, psychoanalytic theory reveals the dynamics of the racial suture, or what we might alternately call "the verge of race,"[16] urging us to think about means of critical resistance that break from the debilitating loop of repudiation and embrace.

Approached in this way, the turbulence associated with scenes of in-terracial liaison or figures of the multiracial body within the contempo-rary political culture can be understood as providing the pivotal grounds upon which the "racializing project" (Goldberg 1997) continuously repro-duces its closures and classifications. Far from functioning as the Achilles heel of racialization, miscegenation stands as the wobbly fulcrum of the racial formation, resource of its dreadful tenacity and fuel for its dreams of perpetuity. One of the tasks of this study is to consider the agonistic rela-tions between white supremacy, antiblackness, and the multiracial beyond pathology. In other words, "race mixture" will be considered a structural element of the fiction of race purity, and the concept of suture offers a help-ful backdrop to the inquiry. The double movement of suture—deploying movement or mixture to produce seeming stability or purity—calls atten-tion to a complex relation between "the give and take of absence and pres-ence, the play of negativity and negation, flow and bind" (Heath 1985, 54) in the production of image, scene, and narrative space. This "flow/bind" rhetoric aptly evokes the dynamics of a general economic approach through which our understanding of racialization in general and the operations of antimiscegenation in particular can be theoretically enriched.

Within the fields of African American and comparative ethnic studies, the sociology of race, and more recently, cultural studies of race, one is hard pressed to find a critical commentary that does not have something to say about the discourses and practices of antimiscegenation, about their virulence and persistence in the present, and about their centrality to the history of the United States (Bell 2000; Fredrickson 1981). However, most writing to this end is rife with inconsistencies that defy resolution or synthesis. Those that seem to achieve coherence do so only as a result of reductionism or unsubstantiated speculations about the motivations of social actors. Most commonly, these different theorizations of antimiscegenation bifurcate into two general positions. On the one hand, there are theorists who would characterize antimiscegenation as a political strategy integral to the maintenance of white social, political, and economic power (Fredrickson 1987; Myrdal 1962; Williamson 1984). This account would have us believe that the actual pronouncements of avowed white supremacists are ideological subterfuge for the political economy of whiteness. On the other hand, we find scholars who attribute the project of antimiscegenation to the preoccupations of an individual or collective white psychopathology (Kovel 1984; Stember 1976). In these cases, motive is sought in the fear, anxiety, insecurity, or repressions of the white imagination. In its crudest form, the latter approach argues that the whole of white supremacy is a projection of this more fundamental psychological complex (Spurr 1993).[17]

This conceptual polarization can be mapped onto other familiar binaries: private/public, sexual/political, psychological/sociological. Not surprisingly, we also note a theoretical preference in each position for either Marx or Freud or for some version of Marxist or Freudian theory. This begs the question, must the white supremacist taboo on miscegenation and the violence in which it obtains be represented as either superstructural or overdetermining? Must they be considered either a smoke screen for some more fundamental political economic project or an all-consuming fixation, either coldly calculating or blindly irrational? The aim of a more adequate critical theory of antimiscegenation is to avoid these twin pitfalls and assist the formulation of a new problematic.[18] In order to do so, it is important to consider what these two prevailing theoretical approaches hold in common across their divergences. In brief, these conventional positions render antimiscegenation as subordinate to some other, more primary agency, that is, as the instrumental rationalization of some other purpose. The method of this relegation can be stated concisely. On one account, antimiscegenation rationalizes a political economy in which the production and maintenance of the color line plays a functional role. As such, white supremacy and antiblackness suppress challenges to the capitalist mode of production under the guise of doing something else, such as preserving the integrity of the racial whiteness or defending the sanctity of white womanhood. On the other account, antimiscegenation rationalizes a psychic operation that cannot express and justify itself in its own terms. Thus, the threat of miscegenation serves as a red herring, a cover for a deeper psychic malady (e.g., repressed same-sex desire, contradictory desires for equality and hierarchy, a disavowal of common humanity) that, if exposed, would undermine the self-sufficiency, the naturalness, or the ethical consistency of white racial identity.

These positions are summarized in two richly provocative studies of race and sexuality from the twilight of the civil rights era that, despite their limitations, are too little discussed today: Calvin Hernton's *Sex and Racism in America* (1988) and Charles Stember's *Sexual Racism* (1976). Hernton declares: "When all is said and done about the reasons for opposing racial integration, the bottom line is invariably a superstitious imagining of the pornographic nature of interracial sex" (1988, xiv). Stember draws heavily from Hernton's work (and both, it bears mentioning, are deeply inspired by Fanon's *Black Skin, White Masks*) and, in his turn, notes:

> Most other theoreticians of race relations [excepting Hernton] have apparently discarded sex as an issue because they could see no great sexual loss to the white man in accepting integration. . . . It was therefore more fruitful

[in their view] to seek potential loss to the white man in other spheres if social and economic equality were granted—i.e., jobs, political power, and relative loss of status. (12)

There are other explanatory accounts that do not adhere strictly to the dichotomy between sex and political economy established here, but they are exceptional. Ferber (1998) and Daniels (1996), for instance, demonstrate that the obsession of white supremacist discourse with interracial sexuality quickly slides into paranoia about the pollution of the white racial stock, a process resulting in a universal "mongrelization" tantamount to genocide of the white population. In this sense, their researches suggest that the quest for race purity cannot be reduced to a reactionary psychological disposition. It is also preeminently a problem of social constitution from the point of view of a white, racist imagined community. If it is central to the dictates of identity formation, the purview of the psyche, it is equally about the materiality of social organization and the production of a human geography. More radical ambiguities mark the traditional conceptual split itself: what precisely is a "sexual loss," and how might it be distinguished from a "relative loss of status"? Considering this vagueness, it is no wonder that antimiscegenation continues to frustrate scholars who take it as an object of inquiry. In the caesura between these various explanations, the breakdown of their attempts to conceptually mirror one another, the question can be reformulated: what exactly is miscegenation that this puzzled theoretical practice must assume it as its undisclosed ground? If, in other words, we find ourselves undecided about the proper understanding of antimiscegenation—its pressure, source, aim, and object—perhaps it is because the historical forces under scrutiny demand, in the first instance, several incompatible understandings of the notion of miscegenation.

The *American Heritage Dictionary* defines miscegenation as (1) in general, the "mixture of different races"—from the Latin *miscere*, to mix, and the Indo-European *gen*, the genus or race; (2) in particular, "cohabitation, sexual relations, or marriage involving persons of different races." This blurred distinction between "mixture," on the one hand, and "cohabitation, sexual relations, or marriage," on the other, brings us closer to the confusion that hamstrings much thinking on the subject to date. It suggests that while common usage may suppose the conflation of definitions housed under this term, the delineation itself bespeaks a certain slippage that demands to be parsed. *Gen*, of course, is the etymological root for terms like *gene*, *gender*, and *genesis*—terms fundamentally related to the notion of *production*. However, *gen* is linked, in a subsequent entry, to adjectives like *general* and *generic*, an entry noting that "the central meaning shared by these adjectives is 'belonging to, relating to, or affecting the whole.'" That is, they share an antonym in the *particular*. A genealogy of "miscegenation" that revisits this obscured internal tension might understand it as a concept in which production is always in some sense a production of the general or generic. The marking out of "race" establishes itself, therefore, not only against the possible failure or absence of its production but also, more precisely, against its immanent deconstruction in and as particularity. Race, as a production of generality, is mixed or mingled with particularity from (before) the moment of its inception, its essential byproduct being a particularity ineluctably other than and inseparable from the general, a difference that inhabits it as a force of negation or unbinding. This particularity reveals the general term of race as irreducibly *miscible*, essentially capable of being mixed—indeed, from its first appearance, the general is *always already mixed*, if only because it inheres in a restless contradistinction to the particular as its most fundamental differential term. The form of this mixing bears a certain compulsory, if deeply historical, relation to racialized sexual encounter. Yet, as an in-mixing that is theoretically *prior* to the formation of the subject of race (not *subsequent* to its encounter with the empirical difference of two particularities), the interracial preoccupies the phenomenological domain of racialization. It gives the lie to the mythos of any autonomous racial designation but—here is the twist—only provided it returns to the nonidentical "origins" of the production of race itself and does not simply revel in the promise of the eventual dissolving of races conventionally understood. That is to say, the "event of miscegenation" (discussed in detail later) is a structural force of deconstruction, not a temporal horizon of political détente qua biological fusion. To the extent that antimiscegenation focuses on the defense of reified racial differences in a vain attempt to resolve the double bind of racialization, it will, by definition, refuse to settle into a coherent rationale.

Having glossed things this way, we are now able to say something perhaps counterintuitive about the more properly political relationship between race and race mixture. If white racial identity has a public reputation as a form of purity, then antimiscegenation is the mode of production for the value of whiteness (Tadiar 2003). Antimiscegenation is not the ideological defense of already constituted privilege or status or power; and it is not a psychic defense mechanism rationalizing, after the fact, the contradictions of a nominally democratic society, the anxiety of tenuous social identities, or repressed sexual desires. However, antimiscegenation is not the essence of white supremacy or antiblackness. Rather, white supremacy and antiblackness are fundamentally relational processes unfolding between antimiscegenation and its necessary failure. White supremacy and antiblackness, in other words, emerge in the interplay between miscegenation and the forms of resistance to it. An important claim follows from this reasoning: rather than establishing themselves in vulgar opposition to miscegenation, *white supremacy and antiblackness produce miscegenation* as a precious renewable resource, a necessary threat against which they are constructed, a loyal opposition, a double exposure. They rely upon miscegenation to reproduce their social relations; their relations are, in fact, this very reproduction.

Miscegenation is thus taken to indicate processes of mixing, meddling, or mingling between the general and the particular, between the ephemeral body of white universality and the strangely dense corporeality of its dark-skinned others, imagined as sprawling and overpresent, anonymous in their racialized particularity.[19] Antimiscegenation, as a result, is not so much a defense as it is activation, an agency or an aggression that is only inversely indexed in the savage violence attributed to the ontology of racial blackness. The unspeakable horrors that haunt the white cultural imaginary as properties ascribed to the black only veil the extravagance of racialization, bespeaking and covering over its utter *gratuitousness*. Antimiscegenation is not a convenient rationalization for some other instrumentality; it is a vital component of the creation of race ex nihilo, a social contraction articulated as the form of white identity. The search for the external causes of white supremacy and antiblackness and of the operations of antimiscegenation saves us from the more difficult, perhaps more disturbing, task of thinking through the formations of white supremacy and antiblackness in and of themselves. It saves us from thinking about the logic of a self-organizing system of violence without recourse to any political, economic, or psychological pieties. How might one think about an apparently simple imperative—the law of the color line—emerging from and working through social chaos and complexity?[20]

Affective Anomalies

This aporia is approached by Albert Memmi in a collection of his late work, *Racism* (1999), and it is the impasse at which his theorization comes to grief. "Racism," he writes, "is not simply of the order of reason; its real meaning does not reside in its apparent coherence. It is a discourse, at once both functional and naïve, that is called forth and maintained, in its essence and its goals, by something other than itself. To understand racism, one must address the real purposes at which it is aimed and from which it is born" (21).[21] Further,

> Racism does not limit itself to biology or economics or psychology or metaphysics; it attacks along many fronts and in many forms, deploying whatever is at hand, and even what is not, inventing when the need arises. To function, it needs a focal point, a central factor, but it doesn't care what that might be. . . . The reality of the situation is wholly beside the point; what is essential is that racism rests upon and functions as a kind of seesaw: the persecutor rises by debasing and inferiorizing his victim. (78–79)[22]

In Memmi's view, there can be no reasoned account of this debasement. The seesaw of racism is self-justifying, and it organizes the social order simply for its own sake, without regard for the "reality of the situation." "In short, racist reasoning has no secure foundation, is incoherent in its development, and is unjustified in its conclusions" (19). Crucially, this is because "the foundation of racism is not in reasoning but in affect and self-interest" (190). As a result, "a refutation of racism's formal arguments is wholly insufficient; one must strip bare the underlying system of emotions and convictions that structure its discourse and govern its conduct" (22).[23]

Racism has no secure foundation because it is incoherent, unjustified, and founded in affect, emotion, or conviction. Yet this underlying affective basis is systemic, structuring and governing for the entire racist complex, making it appear as intelligence, intention, and coherent formal arguments, indeed, as status quo. Racism only ever appears in *this* way; that is, it appears as what it is not, as something other than it is. It is essentially misleading, suggesting that the underlying affective system operates only to the extent that it does not appear as such. The key point is that all attempts to decipher the cause of racism from its forms of appearance are, as Memmi has it, "wholly insufficient." Contrary, then, to his own prescriptions for stripping bare what underlies these varied appearances, by Memmi's account, such efforts would only drive the real purpose of racism elsewhere, the elsewhere in which it always already resides. It is as if every attempt to discern the elusive core of racism, to approach its shadowy secret, drives it further from view. Indeed, racism does its most essential work in the shadow of the very attempt to explain it.[24]

The task facing the theorization of antimiscegenation today, an analysis that does not preoccupy itself with monitoring the rates of intermarriage or the numbers of U.S. citizens self-identified as multiracial, is how to think about it as a complex economy, both restricted and general. In *Reconfigurations* (1993), Arkady Plotnitski explains that "the *general* economy . . . relates to the material or intellectual production of excesses that cannot be utilized—*in principle*, rather than only in practice" (20; emphasis in original). In the present discussion, this nonutilizable excess can be considered a sign of the underlying affective system and the radical contingency of racism's central ideological factors at any given moment. We recall Memmi's warning regarding racism's formal arguments and its apparent coherence. These manifestations of racism, its forms of appearance—what we might call its restricted economies of meaning or its instrumental practices—are called forth by something else, something other that escapes definition, its evasive "real purposes." This something else is, in my view, a trace of the general economy.

> The general economy itself . . . relates the configurations it considers to the loss of meaning—a loss that it regards as ineluctable within any given system. . . . Classical theories configure their objects and the relationships between those objects as always meaningful and claim that the systems that they present avoid the unproductive expenditure of energy, containing within their bounds multiplicity and indeterminancy. The general economy exposes all such claims as finally untenable; it demands—and enacts—a different form of theoretical practice. (Plotnitski 1993, 4)

What is different in this theoretical practice is the relinquishing of a priori frames of reference and deterministic models of analysis; it is a nonreductionist, nonderivative analysis. To be sure, such studies are well underway in a number of fields of postwar intellectual culture. My interest is to marshal these insights for the study of a social issue that has been approached in particularly reductive ways to this point. What I sense is that investigations like Memmi's, among others explored in *Amalgamation Schemes*, point toward a possible reconceptualization of racism in general and antimiscegenation in particular. What his work intuits, but cannot formulate within its own terms, is the complex interaction between the general and restricted economies of white supremacy and antiblackness[25]—that is, an interaction through which the general is both productive of *and* dependent upon the restricted or particular. The dispersion of meaning thus gives rise to and unsettles its particular forms of appearance.

This much was suggested earlier with the statement that "white supremacy and antiblackness produce miscegenation as a precious renewable resource." We might now say more precisely that *miscegenation is a name for the imperceptible productivity of white supremacy and antiblackness.* Accordingly, antimiscegenation becomes the restricted economy through which miscegenation appears as a refracted, distorted image. "In a pre-logical or pre-theoretical sense, as distinguished from a pre-ontological sense, a general economy precedes any restricted economy; but it does not simply suspend the latter" (Plotnitski 1993, 22). Rather, the general economy points toward an excess of circulation, dispersion, expenditure—an excess of *energy*. However, "that the *excessive* energy is lost does not mean . . . that some [energy] *cannot be* utilized, via the production of meaning or value" (22; emphasis in original). In point of fact, "any general economy depends on restricted economies for its functioning" (15). Stephen Melville (1986) argues similarly: "There is no sense in which one can speak of a 'general economy' apart from its effects on or its refractions through the projects of . . . conservation given within the restricted economy" (80). Antimiscegenation is the reactive effect of the general economy of *racialization* as it is refracted through the restricted economy of *race*, the conservation of the races in and as images of a certain bodily legibility.

Race is a production of meaning or a form of value and hence operates as communication, an element of exchange. This is why Memmi (1999) describes its sociality so insistently:

> Racism is a cultural discourse that surrounds each person from childhood on, in the air one breathes, in parental advice and thinking, in one's streets and newspapers, even in the writings of people one is supposed to admire and who might be otherwise admirable. . . . Racism is a collective language at the service of each person's emotions. . . . It is a discourse formulated by a group that addresses itself to a group. (112)

Not coincidentally, the etymological roots of *race* link it to writing— to the scratch, the mark, the line. The general economy relates to the inevitable loss of this meaning or value, the going astray of the line of race as it verges on becoming something else. It highlights the continual functioning of a restriction or contraction—Heath's "problem of composition"—in relation to the proliferating "range of possibilities" accruing to, indeed exceeding, any categorical designation. What the general economy of race endlessly produces, then, is *bodies as images*—not images *of* bodies, but rather *living images* of race (Keeling 2001). Visual tropes may predominate in the image of race, but they do not exhaust its repertoire. Robyn Wiegman (1995) notes, for instance,

> The logic of race in U.S. culture anchors whiteness in the visible epistemology of *black* skin. Such an epistemological relationship circumscribes our

cultural conceptions of race, contributing above all to the . . . violent equation between the idea of "race" and the "black" body. (21; emphasis added)[26]

If, in the economy of race, whiteness is a form of money—the general equivalent or universal standard of value—then blackness is its gold
standard, the bottom-line guarantee represented by hard currency.[27] Of
course, just as gold has no intrinsic value as the foundation of a money
economy, in the economy of race, "bodies are neither black nor white" in
any strict sense (Wiegman 1995, 9). Beyond this, it is clear that "race in
Western culture is constituted as far more than skin" (23), signaling a dis-
comfiture of the visible within the logic of race itself; yet, that "skin color"
remains a metonym for race in the common sense indicates a general failure or refusal to engage properly with its convoluted logic. To wit: "The
move from the visible epidermal terrain to the articulation of the interior
structure of human bodies [in the late nineteenth-century United States]
extrapolated . . . the parameters of white supremacy, giving it a logic lodged
fully in the body" (31) and not just upon its surfaces.

However, "while the visible must be understood as giving way to the
authority of the invisible recesses of the body, to organs and functions," and
now, via genomics, to protein interactions, "the full force of this production
of racial discourse [is] nonetheless contingent on the status of an observer"
(31). An unsteady observer, it would seem, seeking out an obstinate invisibility that is "unwilling to betray its object"—an always receding or continually disappearing visibility, shrinking to infinity.[28] This strained, fantastic
relation of the observer "to the object under investigation [is] mediated
and deepened by newly developed technologies for rendering the invisible visible" (31), but such technologies can serve only as prosthetics of
disavowal. Among these visual technologies, we can count not only the
various cameras, lenses, and devices that produce the images of our visual
culture or the stores of specialized scientific knowledge but also the "optics"
of critical theory itself (Jay 1994). That is to say, if "the construction of
race is predicated on its obsessive performance" (Wiegman 1995, 9), then
this performance cannot commence; it is not called for if some "off-screen"
deconstruction is not similarly rehearsed. Race has to remain a problem—

threatened, imperiled—if it is to remain at all. To satisfy oneself with exposing it as an illusion of power or, anticipating later arguments, to live one's life in defiance of its stricture, is to risk, if it does not simply ensure, that one will become the screen of its renewed production. It is, in other words, to play one's part in the calculus—abstract and applied—that endlessly renders the black body image as the "anchor" of racial knowledge. If even a generous critique of multiracialism finds it implicated in the uncritical reaffirmation of the race through a "purification" of racial blackness, we can see how, at this lower frequency, its critical potential is compromised even more fatally. Multiracialism not only proves complicit with white supremacy and antiblackness but goes on in that respect to announce itself as avant-garde.

The Tableau of Mixture

Why address interracial sexuality in the United States as a social, political, aesthetic, or other category?[29] If we choose to focus our sustained attention upon it, to consider its significance, we risk joining company with the discourse of white supremacy and antiblackness, complicit with the terms of the pathological or the exotic. We risk, in other words, getting hooked or hung up, developing an obsession. Yet, to obsess over interracial sexuality can be more than a lurid preoccupation. It is, in fact, already more than that, far more, especially for the avowed white supremacist. To participate in a discussion under this heading, then, to read and write about what both enables and threatens our constructed selves, all of this relates us, unavoidably, to white supremacy and antiblackness, party to its storm of enjoyment, its fear and rage, its phantasms. But are we not indelibly situated within the discourse, held together and apart through its operations, oriented by its symbolic universe? This critical activity, as it were, grasps something essential to our social existence, digging in where we are, working (with) the stricture.

But if it is an understatement to claim that white supremacy and antiblackness are obsessed with interracial sexuality, then how can obsession function as an instance of understatement? What, precisely, is obsession beyond obsession? To obsess is already to be excessively concerned, to be fixated. Is there, then, such a thing as an excess of excess, an excessive excess, a fixation that is not a stalling out or disruption of normal movement but rather the index of an obscured and more fundamental trajectory? What characterizes the discourse of white supremacy and antiblackness is a certain superintensity of attention, an exorbitant single-mindedness concerning the centrality of interracial sexuality to all things. It lingers too long on the topic, looks and speaks too often, with too much passion, at scenes of "frenzied, interminable copulation" (Young 1995, 181). In fact, white supremacy and antiblackness seem to exist in large part *through* this prolonged activity, perhaps even *as* this very mode of watching, ranting, and brooding: white supremacy and antiblackness as surveillance, extraordinary vision, an unending meditation. To repeat: the obsession with interracial sexuality is far more than a preoccupation or a lurid fascination. It is an essential social and psychical process, a political operation of the first order. It is the proper occupation of the subjects of white supremacy. Without this obsession, there would be no markers of identity, no conceptual matrix to determine the bounds of race and gender at least. That is to say, we obsess necessarily over interracial sexuality to the extent that "white supremacist capitalist patriarchy" (hooks 1992) structures our social formation even as the stakes of this common obsession vary radically depending on who is in question, which subjects, where, and when.

Antiracist politics is challenged to devise responses to the obsessive structure of racialization if it is to mount a more effective intervention in the post–civil rights era. Liberal models of multicultural "unity-in-diversity" and conservative prescriptions for colorblindness have proved themselves to be as damaging to movements for radical social change as they are intractable as elements of contemporary political discourse (West 1994). Critics on the Left seem unsatisfied with the bleakness of these options yet at a loss for an alternative analytic framework. This is especially true with regard to matters of interracial sexuality:

> "Sexual politics" reduces the interracial to black self-hatred and white exploitation of social disparity. I chafe against the poverty of this politics. But . . . to point out the poverty of the politicization of the interracial is not

sufficient to render the interracial illegible as such. . . . Expose the myths, divest deceptively simple "identity politics" of its power, and salvage life from degradation, but the romance of socially constituted difference remains. (Cutrone 2000, 249)

Cutrone's comments do not fret over the supposed wrongheadedness of the "romance of socially constituted difference" and, in fact, seek a departure from this popular self-righteousness. "I wish to both enact and discuss the problem of racial reification," he writes. "Rather than struggle against racial objectification, I wish to work through it" (249). How would one develop political and theoretical strategies that precipitate a *working through* of racialization in the field of sexuality, a strategy that does not simply *repeat* the social constitution of racial difference? This is not a quest for transcendence but a move toward complex processes of negotiation within the horizon of the interracial encounter. That which must be attended to is the remainder of romance—the remnants or residue—that survives the exposure of its mythic foundations.

On this score, Stuart Hall seems to miss an important point of Robert Young's arguments in *Colonial Desire* (1995). Hall gives short shrift to the book in a rather off-handed comment about "the incredibly simplistic charge in Robert Young's *Colonial Desire* (1995) that the postcolonial critics are 'complicit' with Victorian racial theory because both sets of writers deploy the same term—hybridity—in their discourse" (quoted in Williams and Yousaf 1999, 85). I think it important that so flippant a statement was made by so grand a figure in the field of social and cultural theory, precisely because Young's arguments offer a serious, and seriously underappreciated, challenge to dominant currents in recent critical theorizing around race, culture, and identity. My reading of Young finds him far from arguing that contemporary cultural theory *merely* reproduces the signifying systems of colonial race thinking. Though he does give considerable attention to what is perhaps an unwitting, or unconscious, resonance between the racial logic of colonial scholarship and various positions taken in the fields of cultural studies and postcolonial theory of late, his book cannot, on those grounds, be dismissed as a haughty gesture of condescension. His major contribution is, I believe, more subtle and pertinent, and his insights may be disturbing because, frankly, they make our political and theoretical work more difficult. One of his governing theses is captured well in the following passage:

> The ideology of race . . . necessarily worked according to a doubled logic, according to which it both enforced and policed differences between the whites and the non-whites, but at the same time focused fetishistically upon the product of the contacts between them. Colonialism was always locked into the machine of desire. . . . As racial theories show in their unrelenting attempt to assert inalienable differences between the races, this extraordinary vision of an unbounded "delicious fecundity" . . . only took on significance through its voyeuristic tableau of frenzied, interminable copulation, of couplings, fusing, coalescence, between races. (180–81)

His point seems clear enough, though it is often passed over. The attempt to assert inalienable differences between the races, most notably those differences associated with sexual excess or degeneracy, "*only* took on significance" *through* the image of "copulation, of couplings, fusing, coalescence, between races." This indicates a shift of perspective that could and should have a transformative effect on the ways that "hybridity" or intermixture is thought about in the field of racial theory. Put simply, racial *differences* are elaborated out of the tableau of *mixture;* they depend on it for their articulation, their social existence, however tenuous and provisional. Hybridity, to reiterate an earlier point, serves as the *support* of difference rather than its antithesis or, in another vein, its source of deconstruction. Interestingly, Hall (1998) seems to acknowledge as much in another passage:

> The future belongs to the impure. The future belongs to those who are ready to take in a bit of the other, as well as being what they themselves are. After all, it is because their history and ours is so deeply and profoundly and inextricably intertwined that racism exists. For otherwise, how could they keep us apart? (299)

Precisely *because* of this impurity, this profound and inextricable historical intertwining, *because* of this togetherness, racism exists, not *despite* that fact. How else could it operate, and why else would it be, as it were, necessary? It seems that even by Hall's own reckoning, such prophetic statements about the impurity of the future might be tempered. Impurity and hybridity, in and of themselves, are no guaranteed challenge to the racial orders of white supremacy and antiblackness—such are their conditions of possibility.

Summary of Chapters

Chapter 1, "Beyond the Event Horizon: The Multiracial Project," reexamines the politics of multiracialism by reading key statements from the multiracial movement and the field of multiracial studies in light of the mid-1990s U.S. census classification debates, which provide its historical inauguration. I do this in order to specify further the antagonism between multiracialism and the remnants of Black Power attributed to the contemporary civil rights establishment. En route, I take seriously the more stridently conservative voices considered by other critics to be marginal to multiracial discourse, as it seems that their grounding assumptions are not disputed by the liberal mainstream of multiracial advocacy. Because multiracial discourse lodges no *substantive* claims about the injurious effects of black politics for its constituency, I argue that the politics of multiracialism is properly understood as a purely *formal* negation of racial blackness. In this capacity, it promotes a phobic imagery of blacks as an authoritarian political bloc that illegitimately determines the direction of federal policy making and the substance of the national culture—imagery that takes form in gender-specific ways and with overtones of profound sexual threat (i.e., reviving nineteenth-century tropes of the black male rapist and the black female seductress). Contrary to the received wisdom of its liberal-progressive opponents, multiracialism is not founded in the desire to exacerbate cleavages within black communities along lines of color and class. Less a classic *divide-and-conquer* strategy, multiracialism serves more as a rationalizing discourse for the continued and increasing social, political, and economic *isolation* of blacks. In this sense, I suggest that multiracialism arbitrates neoconservative racial politics as an indispensable libidinal accompaniment to an advancing neoliberalism that is itself oscillating between official (liberal) multiculturalism and the (conservative) posture of colorblindness.

While resurrecting the tenets of a long-debunked scientific racism, multiracialism renders any discernible black resistance to its dubious goals as a force of political *repression*. On this account, the historic demand for an affirmative and egalitarian revaluation of blackness in the face of its manifest negation becomes the paramount source of objectionable "un-American activities" like the policing of identity and the restriction of sexual freedom. Blacks are thus depicted in the multiracial imagination as a conglomerate anachronism, perpetuating disreputable traits of antebellum slave society and presenting a foremost obstacle to the progress of liberal society today: white supremacy in blackface, antiblackness turned upside down. But the assertion of a pernicious black racism relies for its rhetorical purchase upon an impossible merging of racial blackness with the power of the racial state. It is not simply asserted in this milieu that blacks can exhibit morally objectionable attitudes or even discriminatory behavior in the private sphere, but also that blacks have, as an outcome of the modern civil rights movement, commandeered the repressive and regulatory agencies of the federal government and, through such means, transformed the whole of the economy and society to their collective advantage. That is to say, blacks have *inverted* racial hierarchy—or *reversed* racism—to the categorical disadvantage of, primarily, whites, but also Asian Americans and Latinos. Multiracial people, so runs the story, are caught in the midst of this great transformation, suffering from the emergence of what I call "oppressive black power."

In chapter 2, "Scales of Coercion and Consent: Sexual Violence, Antimiscegenation, and the Limits of Multiracial America," I scrutinize the depiction of the history of interracial sexual violence that underpins the contemporary discourse of multiracialism in the United States and that illuminates key aspects of the tenuous conceptual framework assumed therein. I argue that the highly charged and largely convoluted contest over present-day representations of interracial sexuality and multiracial identity is bound up with long-standing theoretical discrepancies regarding the links between power and pleasure, agency and affect, subjugation and sexuality. Most pointedly, it involves a dispute over what constitutes consent in the field of racialized sexuality, under what conditions it might be said properly to exist or, alternatively, to be thrown into unrelieved crisis or rendered practically ineffective. As such, it is also by definition a commentary on the nature and effects of coercion and, crucially, the scale at which its consideration will be posed. At the center of this conflict lies the historical memory of New World slavery and, in particular, the key role of three centuries of codified antimiscegenation in its formation, development, and transformation. The questions under pursuit in this chapter are: How and why does the new discourse of interracial intimacy insist upon, perhaps require, the disavowal of the structures of (sexual) coercion at the heart of racial formation in the United States? And, in keeping with the central theme of this book, what does this impossible acknowledgment have to do with the deeply vexed attitude toward blackness betrayed by so many multiracial advocates?

In the literature of the multiracial movement, a forbidding truncation of historical memory—which supposedly bespeaks a crisis of faith and a failure of imagination—is spuriously ascribed to an atavistic black social psychology. To understand better this troubling ascription and to examine the function it serves in the present context, I provide a close reading of several historical accounts to emerge recently in the field of multiracial studies (Kennedy 2003; Stephens 1999; Talty 2003). Beyond a mystification of historical process and the dynamics of power, I also find that a feminist critique of gendered sexual violence is cynically deployed in these texts and done so along clearly racial lines. The insights of black feminist theory regarding the sexual violence institutionalized against black women before and after the Civil War are minimized or discarded, while the arguments of mainly white feminist authors, including many thought to be explicitly hostile to black political movements, are marshaled to establish a purported reversal of racialized power in the post–civil rights era, a claim that today black men, not white, represent the seat of an unbridled sexual threat to women (and men) across the color line.

Chapter 3, "There Is No (Interracial) Sexual Relationship," builds on the shift of perspective enacted in the preceding chapters. The objective, simply stated, is to reveal the idea of a "healthy" interracial relationship as an ideological lure in two senses: first, insofar as it is considered an arrangement unconnected to supposedly unhealthy liaisons (i.e., those structured in dominance), and second, as something like a *real union* of differentially racialized subjects or bodies. Again, the argument proceeds in two sections. In the first, I describe in more detail the ways in which multiracial discourse delinks interracial sexuality and mixed-race people. I do so by way of a discussion of several foundational texts in the field of multiracial studies looking closely at the architecture of their arguments. In the second, I look at the discourse on interracial sexuality itself across a number of equally popular texts in the field as well as some lesser-known critical essays in order to draw attention to the anxiety that obtains in each account and the various ways in which this anxiety is managed, disavowed, or, alternately, openly worked upon.

What I find here is that the depathologizing of the interracial couple that multiracial discourse seeks is accomplished *retroactively* by highlighting the soundness and healthiness of mixed-race people. The point is, of course, that the discourse conducts the debate on the terrain of *reproduction*, most often within the institution of the bourgeois family, and not that of *sexuality*. Since it is assumed that objection, criticism, and opposition to interracial couples (implied in this case to be heterosexual and reproductive) are based in large part on concerns about the children thereof, the creation of positive images of multiracial people is deemed to be something of an exoneration of interracial couples too. The interracial couple reenters the public sphere through the legitimization of mixed-race people, in the guise of loving parents and supportive family members. The project evinces, as a result, a stark resistance to discuss the sexual means and relations of (interracial) reproduction or, moreover, to disarticulate sexuality from biological reproduction and engage a critical discussion of the politics of interracial sexual encounter. In this sense, there is at work a certain *desexualization of race* and a *deracialization of sexuality*. This scission operates simultaneously within twin tendencies of the movement: the tacitly progressive fight against white racist taboo or ethnocentrism and the more clearly conservative affirmation of traditional family values and/or clean romance without the vulgarity of dirty sexuality. What remains consistent with the past is the utter inability to actually speak about interracial sexual acts in anything but the most extremely naïve or bawdy ways.

I draw the arguments of the previous two chapters especially into a discussion of the ideologies of antimiscegenation itself in chapter 4, "The Consequence of Race Mixture." Working along a logical regression, it examines how multiracial discourse (and, before that, the discourse of the civil rights movement that presumably spawned it) has constructed as its supposed opposition a simplistic image of white supremacist sexual taboo and, as is often the case, the chauvinism of insurgent nationalisms. I argue that critical theories of antimiscegenation to date have either contained complex political and historical processes by psychologizing them or have nearly evaporated questions of subjectivity, agency, and fantasy—in other words, psychic reality—by too rapidly socializing the issue. In place of this bifurcated conceptualization, I propose a general economic approach to the study of white supremacy such that antimiscegenation is taken to be only one component or dimension and wherein the politics of interracial sexuality is thought to cut across the various scales of racialization. I argue that a radical critique of interracial sexuality must take seriously the vicissitudes of desire in the formation of fantasies of racial difference, sexual union, and even the apprehension of the body as such.

To that end, I introduce the concept of "the event of miscegenation" and make a crucial distinction between miscegenation *as event* and miscegenation *as interracial sex acts* or *the presence of mixed-race people.* The latter, I suggest, are the lures produced by the paranoia of white supremacy, its racist reasoning, and predictably mirrored by its liberal opposition. Miscegenation, in this new sense, is what cannot be represented, conceptualized, or apprehended in either the interracial liaison or the multiracial body but rather is that which prevents either appearance from attaining a fixed and stable meaning, whether as object of aggression or desire. Here I am attempting to supplement what have come to be commonplace assertions of race as a social category. I am not interested in how the empirical history of sex across the color line or how the existence of people of mixed racial descent *in itself* might trouble the fantasy of pure races or discrete and rigid racial categories. Rather, I discuss in a more radical sense what I believe undermines and frustrates *that* fantasy of transgression, the fantasy of the subversive multiracial. In this chapter, I am interested finally in what wards against our thinking of interracial sex or mixed-race people as *things in themselves*. It is a critique of what Fanon (1967) refers to as the "psychological phenomenon that consists in the belief that the world will open to the extent to which frontiers are broken down."

Chapter 5, "The True Names of Race: Blackness and Antiblackness in Global Contexts," situates multiracialism within the field of globalization, a discourse and transformation that has gained consistency in the same historical moment. Here I argue that many of the concerns articulated in multiracial discourse within the United States are animated by the demands of globalization in political economy, political culture, and political geography. Taken together, multiracialism and globalization can be understood as largely compatible discursive formations, fellow travelers faced, in part, with a common predicament. This shared predicament can be understood as a confrontation with the radical limit of the New Immigration, the limit found in those populations whose full-scale exclusion schedules them for immobilization, containment, or elimination (Mbembe 2000). In my view, the emergent global apartheid, which primarily draws out of the picture the domestic black populations of the Americas (via the prison-industrial complex in the United States, ghettoization and displacement throughout the hemisphere) and the whole of sub-Saharan Africa (via structural adjustment programs), establishes the project of global civil society as uneven economic, political, and cultural integration along the East–West axis. The political economy and cultural politics of the AIDS pandemic—the grammar and geography of the greatest public health crisis in recorded history—have only solidified these tendencies—so much so that, to paraphrase Fanon, "whoever says AIDS says Negro," and vice versa. As such, the North–South imaginary proves itself misleading and insufficient to apprehending the present conjuncture (Doty 1996).

In this vein, I suggest that the qualitative difference between sub-Saharan Africa vis-à-vis the other regions of the global South is reflected

in the qualitative difference of black positionality in the U.S. racial formation vis-à-vis "the colors in the middle" (not black, not white). While the
discourse of globalization is consumed by the proliferation of mobility
(much like multiracial discourse lays emphasis on movement between and
across the borders of race), the supposed recalcitrance of immobilized black
populations is aligned with the outdated and marked as a primary hindrance
to the emergence of globality (Green 1997). As the New Immigrant is
brought into relation with the technologies of policing and imprisonment,
the transnational nonetheless sits in tension with the transatlantic, the
postcolonial with the postemancipated (Han 2006). In sum, the economy
of mobility is dependent upon, indeed intensifies, an economy of constraint
wherein disposable populations are systematically warehoused, eliminated,
or exploited in their raw state, without the mediation of variable capital.
In this despotic milieu, the black body moves primarily, in some cases only,
as spectacle, an image of capital, or what Gilroy (2000) calls "the planetary traffic in blackness." To conclude both the chapter and book, I recall
briefly the legacies of black radicalism in order to contemplate in summation the conditions of global apartheid and the difficulties engendered by
the politics of multiracialism. I claim tentatively that the structured isolation and "absolute dereliction" that characterize black positionality can
and should serve as sources of political inspiration, not impediments for a
political transformation. It may well be that the unavoidably global movement for black liberation in this moment is a precondition for the success
of any radical politics worthy of the name. The "globe-girding social movements" (Spivak 1999) presently challenging the triumphant march of capital neglect this point to their own detriment.

CHAPTER 1

Beyond the Event Horizon:
The Multiracial Project

Occultation of the conflicts of interest is gained in their reduction
from being struggles of highly complex matrices of power to
comprehensible categories of "natural" difference. The overbearing
motif of this occultation is the exclusion of the African from the
space of Western history, and the marginal inclusion of the
Negro as negativity.

—Ronald Judy, *(Dis)Forming the American Canon*

Contrary to commonly held beliefs and long-standing prejudices,
the mulatto world predated and conditioned what would later
become known as *mestizaje*.

—José Buscaglia-Salgado, *Undoing Empire*

The Racial Supernumerary

During the 1990s, the United States was home to an unprecedented
national conversation regarding the politics of recognition in the practice
of racial demography—not in pursuit of the conventional cordon sanitaire
that historically constitutes white communities, but for the express purpose of administering an inclusive, multiracial democracy. For nearly three
decades, the various federal agencies responsible for generating and reporting statistical data on race (and ethnicity) had been wrestling with the
designation of relevant differences when the belated, and rapidly belabored,
question of "diversity" exploded into public discourse, linked mainly to
the impact of mass immigration from Asia and Latin America and, sec-
ondarily, to the rising rates of interracial marriage since the late 1960s.
The significance of the latter trend was linked again to the issue that most

expert commentators eventually took to be the crux of the matter: a newly visible, self-identified "multiracial" or "mixed-race" population begging renewed consideration not only about its place in the new racial order but also about its impact upon the proper functions of race in the relations of state and civil society.

In 1996, *U.S. News and World Report* carried an article entitled, "Don't You Dare List Them as 'Other'," highlighting then current debates about the potential reconfiguration of the federal racial classification scheme to which the U.S. Census Bureau adhered. By the time of the article's publication, the immediate contest about the tabulation of racial data was already three years old. It took shape around a series of congressional hearings sponsored by the Office of Management and Budget (OMB) initiated in July 1993 in response to public criticism of the 1990 census schedule, and it would be provisionally concluded by the report of the Interagency Committee for the Review of Racial and Ethnic Standards in July 1997. The proceedings were spurred largely by Asian Pacific American and Latino lobbyists interested in retooling existing categories to include or detail previously unnamed groups within their respective bounds. Yet, it was the pressure brought to bear by multiracial advocacy groups that proved to be more contentious and lasting. Since the 1970 decennial survey, census form respondents had the option of choosing (or "self-reporting") one racial category or, failing that, checking the "other" box (prior to 1970, census officials designated racial categorizations based on direct, door-to-door observation). For many in the multiracial camp, this scenario was both unacceptable and symptomatic: unacceptable because it demonstrated the state's failure to accurately reflect vital information about a growing segment of the national population and symptomatic because it seemed to bespeak a general unwillingness in U.S. politics and culture to acknowledge the history and present of race mixture. Just months after the *U.S. News and World Report* ran its coverage of "the multiracial question," the House Subcommittee on Census, Statistics, and Postal Personnel arrived at the language ultimately used in the 1997 Interagency Committee report: individuals would be allowed to "check all [racial designations] that apply" on the upcoming 2000 Census form.[1] Thirty years after the U.S. Supreme

Court ruled unconstitutional all remaining antimiscegenation statutes in the case of *Loving v. Virginia* (1967)—culminating a three-century history of legal regulation and prohibition (Bardaglio 1999; Pascoe 1999)—the federal government had, so it seemed, belatedly codified multiracial existence, now recognized as the issue of *sanctioned* interracial heterosexual union.[2]

However, the dispute was never as straightforward as both the multiracial contingent and a largely sympathetic mass media reported it to be. That is to say, the five-year federal review of official racial classification did not symbolize an enlightened turning point in the short and beleaguered history of postwar civil rights legislation but rather was enabled by and contributed to a rightward shift in the discourse of racial equality that had been underway throughout the preceding two decades. This political faux pas relied on a fundamental misunderstanding of—or a refusal to understand—the nature of civil rights compliance monitoring, the purpose and function of federal racial classification (as redacted per the 1964 Civil Rights Act), and the various methods available for the collection and tabulation of data on race (and ethnicity). To that end, it is telling that the multiracial movement refrained from putting forth any substantive arguments regarding either a history of discrimination or a violation of the civil rights of multiracial people per se. Instead, the demand to alter the existing classification scheme was grounded in a nebulous "right to recognition," a pseudolegal claim buttressed by the specious contention that the physical, mental, and emotional health of the multiracial community, and the self-esteem of multiracial children most especially, hinged on this form of official acknowledgment.[3]

Rainier Spencer (1999), in a definitive treatment of the census debates of the 1990s, makes clear the distortion of historical mission sought by the multiracial lobby.[4] Although various segments of the national population have sought social validation by way of the decennial survey, there is no such thing as a right to representation under its auspices, and the census clearly has never responded in any direct way to the self-perceptions of the demographic units it constructs. In other words, the census is an unfaithful mirror. Its historical origins lie in the dual interests of the state to apportion congressional representation and to levy taxes, and its recent transformation, an institutional legacy of the modern civil rights movement, has added to these tasks assistance in the enforcement of civil rights legislation dating back to the federal interventions of the Reconstruction era (Skerry 2000). The current racial classification scheme was developed in the decade following the apex of the civil rights era (from the mid-1960s to the mid-1970s) in accordance with the latter objective—statistically tracking "progress toward racial equality" or the lack thereof—and any changes to its configuration must be based in such criteria. The multiracial intervention was thus fatally flawed on at least two counts. First, it failed not only to meet the criteria of relevance to civil rights enforcement but also even to present arguments to that end. Second, it demanded a change to the *standards* of federal racial classification when its overriding concern to create some statistical indices of race mixture was easily addressed by minor augmentation of the *questions* asked on the census schedule. Whatever data is gathered by the census must be filtered through the existing federal classification scheme in order for compliance to be measured. However, once this mandatory reporting is completed, the data can be retabulated in myriad ways, including approaches that would directly address the concerns of the multiracial movement to generate a revised racial profile of the national population. Given, then, that the error of the multiracial challenge to federal racial classification was glaring upon the most cursory review, the question remains as to why this coalition of advocacy groups would persist in a fundamentally misguided campaign over the better part of a decade.

The answer is found partly in the learning curve of its different players, none of whom could be considered politically savvy, much less expert, on the often arcane policies of the federal bureaucracy. Another portion is accounted for by the sheer zeal of the campaign's more vociferous personalities. The fervor that drove a small group of mostly white and middle-class professionals from a loosely affiliated band of support groups and fledgling student organizations into a highly visible media presence and, at least momentarily, an influential voice in the halls of Congress was characterized by considerable blindness to the broader implications of not only the various policy proposals under consideration but also the public commentary surrounding the controversy (Njeri 1997). This blindness was a major catalyst to the hostilities that arose immediately between multiracial groups and traditional civil rights organizations, such as the National Association for the Advancement of Colored People and the National Urban League, seeking to defend the existing system of civil rights compliance monitoring. It provided, as well, the basis of a schism between the liberal and conservative tendencies within the multiracial movement that eventually fractured the strategic alliance that had garnered attention in the first place. As those with greater sympathies for the wide-ranging goals of the civil rights establishment like the Association for Multiethnic Americans (AMEA) and the Hapa Issues Forum (HIF)[5] gained clarity about the potential obstruction involved in the desired modification of federal racial classification, they rescinded their support for the original joint proposal of the multiracial lobby—the formation of a separate "multiracial" category in place of or in addition to the "other" designation—and revised their position toward the multiple-check option that eventually prevailed, leaving the extant classification scheme intact (Spencer 1999).

Of course, this compromise disgruntled die-hard proponents of the separate multiracial category like Project RACE, A Place For Us National, *Interracial Voice*, and *The Multiracial Activist*,[6] a contingent that urged the adoption of a distinct multiracial designation as both a necessary step in the evolution of a "new multiracial consciousness" and, with no apparent irony, a prelude to the abolition of race-thinking altogether.[7] In the short term, this meant for them a concerted effort to dismantle the conceptual machinery for civil rights compliance monitoring, and the amendment of the new multiracial category was proffered as a proverbial wrench in the gears. The spirit of colorblindness was manifest well prior to the opening of the congressional hearings and soon attracted the attention of top Republican officials like then Speaker of the House and architect of the 1994 neoconservative manifesto, *Contract with America*, Newt Gingrich, who endorsed the multiracial category proposal and received in return words of public appreciation from, among others, Susan Graham, founder and former executive director of Project RACE, and Charles Byrd, founding editor of *Interracial Voice* (Rockquemore 2004).[8] Although Graham, Byrd, and their fellow travelers never confirmed or denied Republican Party affiliation, this willingness not only to enter marriages of convenience with the neoconservative movement but also to openly deride the legacy of the civil rights movement raised the ire of the traditionally liberal and Democratic civil rights establishment and, as noted, crystallized tensions within the array of multiracial organizations themselves. However, the tactical distinctions that surfaced between the left and right wings of the multiracial movement cannot, in my view, be maintained at the discursive level. Put differently, though the factions went their separate ways in the wake of the 1997 decision, they continue to share a discursive field, an organization of concerns, and a structure of feeling. The ideological discrepancy that provoked a fracas within the census campaign is belied by an overarching unity of purpose, and this disavowed correspondence between supposedly divergent political dispositions generates ambivalence and anxiety within the movement's enterprise, from its liberal mainstream to its reactionary margins.

To date, most sustained commentaries on "the politics of multiracialism" (Dalmage 2004) begin and end with this story, centering the ongoing debates about official classification in their treatment of the matter (Spencer 1997, 1999). Indeed, it is difficult to understand the emergence of multiracial identity politics without situating its relation to this highly publicized flashpoint. Likewise, the rapidly developing academic field of multiracial studies takes as its historic point of departure the struggle for official state recognition and often refers to its symbolic and material significance for its evolving project (Root 1992a, 1996b; Zack 1995a). However, as Kimberly DaCosta (2000) notes, "The attempt to obtain an official multiracial designation is a crucial dimension of an emerging politics of multiracialism. But the issues of census classification, and the collective action oriented toward it, is but one indicator of such a movement" (4). In her analysis, DaCosta evaluates "the social bases and implications of the multiracial movement," detailing the demographic, economic, political, and cultural contexts within which and "the various means (organizational and representational) through which a new social category—'multiracial'—is being made" (2).

The present study takes a cue from this important work in several ways. It takes seriously the caution of reductionism and seeks therefore to discuss aspects of multiracialism not directly pertaining to the federal classification policy debates.[9] It takes an interest in the social bases and political implications of multiracialism, particularly its ramifications on prevailing notions of race and racism in the United States. However, this study is more precisely concerned with how contemporary multiracialism either addresses or dispenses with questions of interracial sexuality inherent to its domain and, further, how that awkward engagement bears a relation to the combative statements about formations of racial blackness that otherwise mark the discourse. As noted in the introduction, multiracialism describes itself as the logical extension of the civil rights movement, but its effects have not proven salutary to the aggrieved constituencies, namely black communities, from whom multiracial advocates claim to have inherited the ethical mantle in the absence of any discernible mandate. What is more, proponents of multiracialism envision its relation to the watershed of twentieth-century black activism to be less one of *extending* its transformative capacity than of *superseding* its historic mission, a framing that interpolates an antagonism between an unrefined identity politics and the longstanding concerns of a beleaguered civil rights apparatus, the fading institutional trace of recent extra-parliamentary black political pressures. Their high-profile clash about the revision of official categories provides a condensed view of the political culture of race at the turn of the twenty-first century, and we discover there some of the most pressing themes of contemporary global transformations as well, embedded in a local quarrel too often and too easily written off to the peculiarities of U.S. racial formation. As a result, this conflict, which will undoubtedly continue despite the waning of its major partisan organizations, has failed to engage the Left as a political battle of worth. This disinterest should not, however, be read as a sign of the innocuousness or inconsequence of multiracialism. Rather, it indicates that key elements of its regressive ideological tendencies and, more to the point, its libidinal economy (or "affective formation") have resonated with more recognizably progressive political and intellectual labors. Together they contribute to a common unease about the remnants of black liberation and the prospect of radical black feminism in particular.

To that end, I am interested in "the field of *representations*, coextensive with politics" (Burgin 1996, 22) within which multiracialism fashions its theoretical object—race mixture—after the post-*Loving* inauguration of decriminalized interracial sexuality and the dawn of an ostensible "biracial baby boom" (Root 1992a). We should understand this politics of "representation" in at least two ways: first, "representation as 'speaking for,'" as in politics," and second, "representation as 're-presentation,' as in art or philosophy." Gayatri Spivak (1988) has demonstrated that "these two senses of representation—within state formation and the law, on the one hand, and in subject-predication, on the other—are related but irreducibly discontinuous . . . [marking] differences between the 'same' words" (275). Within the ambit of multiracialism, this critical discontinuity is lost to conflation, covered over as the processes of representation are effaced in favor of a supposedly self-evident product. The multiracial movement (as a project of political representation) and the field of multiracial studies (as a project of scholarly and literary re-presentation) recapitulate similar procedures with respect to an anticipated multiracial populace—as, respectively, a subject of representation and an object of knowledge. That is to say, each instance organizes itself around the interpretation of the multiracial as a sign, or trace, of interracial sexuality insofar as the latter is thought to be a positive threat to the racial status quo. The liberal critique engendered by these twin phenomena aims at the amendment of individualized sexual morality and the reform of privatized racial etiquette. A dichotomous alignment is thus drawn: on the one hand, racism with antimiscegenation; on the other, antiracism with the affirmation of an unsullied interracial sexuality, epitomized by the romantic ideal of "love across the color line" (Peiss and Horowitz 1996). Cast in these terms, political struggle, including struggle about sexual politics, is personalized and reduced to opinion.

Welcome as may be the attenuation of the legal regime of antimiscegenation in the United States, to assume that "global white supremacy" (Mills 1998) or what Gordon (1997) more fittingly calls "the antiblack world" is undermined by the proliferation of now permissible race mix-ture and the correlated growth in multiracial self-identification requires, at the very least, gross historical amnesia and acute political naïveté. Rad-icalizing the politics of multiracialism, if it be possible, entails going beyond the celebration of multiracial people as "the best of both worlds . . . the solution to centuries of racial discord" (Spencer 2004, 106) or the living extension of a tedious antiessentialism (Dalmage 2004, 6). Even the latter point is too generous, since multiracialism, in point of fact, wards against antiessentialism and represents instead a reification of biological notions of race (Goldberg 1997). It is our task to demonstrate how this reification of race—insofar as the concept of mixture relies logically and rhetorically upon a purity concept—is linked as well to a naturalization of sexuality, including questions of interracial desire. But what most pointedly solicit the critique developed here are the specific consequences that multiracial-ism presents for the half-life of antiblack racism. If multiracialism reinforces the idea of biological race in general, it does so by negatively "purifying"—which is to say *quarantining*—racial blackness in particular as the center-piece of a vaster re-racialization of U.S. society in the post–civil rights era (Martinot 2002). After resurrecting the tenets of a long-debunked scien-tific racism, multiracialism then renders black resistance to its dubious goals as an intransigent, unthinking force of political *repression*. The historic de-mand for an affirmative revaluation of blackness in the face of its manifest negation becomes, on this count, the paramount source of objectionable "un-American activities" like the policing of identity and the restriction of sexual freedom.[10] Blacks are thus depicted in the multiracial imagina-tion as a conglomerate anachronism, perpetuating disreputable traits of antebellum slave society and presenting a foremost obstacle to the progress of liberal society today: white supremacy in blackface, antiblackness turned upside down.

The assertion of a pernicious black racism relies for its rhetorical purchase upon an impossible merging of racial blackness with the power of the racial state.[11] All arguments about the supposedly overbearing pres-ence and persuasion of blacks in the United States—from the popular cul-ture industries to the mass media to the court of public opinion—hinge upon this social fantasy. In other words, it is not simply asserted in this milieu that blacks—much like their white or nonblack counterparts—can exhibit morally reprehensible attitudes or even discriminatory behavior in the private sphere toward those deemed racially other. It is also claimed that blacks have, as an outcome of the modern civil rights movement, commandeered the repressive and regulatory agencies of the federal government (hence the renewed hue and cry of "state's rights!") and, through such means, have transformed the whole of the economy and society to their collective advantage. That is to say, blacks have *inverted* racial hierarchy—or *reversed* racism, to cite the common phrase—to the categorical disadvantage of, primarily, whites, but also Asian Americans and Latinos. Multiracial people, so runs the story, are caught in the midst of this great transformation:

> Multiracial people experience a "squeeze" of oppression *as* people of color and *by* people of color. People of color who have internalized the vehicle of oppression in turn apply rigid rules of belonging or establishing "legitimate" membership. The internalization of either/or systems of thinking operates even between communities of color, such as Asian American and African American. (Root 1992b, 5)

Although it would seem from this passage that communities of color, much like the unnamed white community that is historically instantiated through "the vehicle of oppression," are all equally culpable of oppressing multiracial people with "rigid rules of belonging or . . . 'legitimate' membership," it is clearly black communities that present the gravest perceived danger on this score.[12] In fact, the latter, darker term of this oppressive "squeeze" not only defines the multiracial experience as *different from* a "monoracial"[13] black experience but also—in direct contrast to Root's guiding metaphor—explains why multiracial people are, rather, located *beneath* "monoracial" blacks (not in "the land of 'in between'" [Root 1992b, 7]) in "the hierarchical interpretation of differences," *the most oppressed*, "the final 'other' in a complex of power moves" (Sandoval quoted in Root 1992b, 5). We might flesh out Root's central claim in this way: "multiracial people experience a 'squeeze' of oppression *as* people of color [historically oppressed by white supremacy] and [as multiracial people, in particular, who are also oppressed] *by* [monoracial] people of color [which is to say, black people who have commandeered (internalized *and* applied) 'the vehicle of oppression'].”[14] Hence, the populating of this discursive landscape with worrying, hallucinatory images of black depravity: corrupt black public officials—hucksters, blowhards, imposters, liars, and petty lords; undeserving black beneficiaries—affirmative action babies, coddled criminals, and welfare queens; and, perhaps most paradoxically, vicious black police, a "racial border patrol" (Douglas 2003). This swarm of figures in black has as its upshot an imaginary world of black oppression, or what I would call "oppressive black power," of global proportions—not the oppression *of* blacks by others ("primarily, whites, but also Asian Americans and Latinos") but the oppression of others *by* blacks.

If the range of this alleged epochal shift in the racial distribution of power remains hazy in the common sense, it finds consistency in dogmatic pronouncements about the dominance of a "black–white binary paradigm" over all discussions of race and racism, justice and equality, rights and privileges, politics and public policy in the United States. Whatever else may preoccupy partisans of multiracialism, all can agree, without benefit of even the most rudimentary definition, that the issue at hand "is *not* just about black and white." This perfunctory popular appeal, despite its professed commitments to decenter whiteness and build progressive coalition with blacks, serves only to dislodge sustained discussions of the conditions of black existence and the political possibilities of radically transforming the structures of antiblackness. Again, not because black politics has *proven* to be detrimental to any multiracial constituency whatsoever—recall that, when granted a coveted congressional audience, the multiracial movement refrained from substantive arguments regarding either a history of discrimination or a violation of the civil rights of multiracial people per se—but rather because it is simply asserted that black politics *must* be detrimental to any multiracial constituency whatsoever. The politics of multiracialism is, then, properly understood only as a purely *formal* negation of blackness. Substantive arguments grounded in structural analyses are jettisoned by reference to an archive of anecdotes in which fielding hostility—or even questions—from blacks is elevated to the status of political oppression, regardless of the actual relations of power involved.[15]

Contrary to the received wisdom of its liberal-progressive opponents, multiracialism is not founded by the desire to exacerbate divisions within black communities along lines of color and class. It is driven neither by attempts to introduce a wedge issue that might facilitate a statistical reduction of the national black population nor by attempts to interrupt civil rights compliance monitoring. These are likely byproducts of its political intervention, and they are often noted as objectives among the right wing of the multiracial movement, but I suggest that they do not represent the motive forces of the wider social phenomenon. Rather, multiracialism augments the neoconservative discourse of "reverse racism" that has taken root since the late 1960s by promoting, in novel ways, the image of blacks as an authoritarian political bloc that illegitimately determines the direction of federal policymaking and the substance of the national culture. Far from a strategic offensive deploying classic divide-and-conquer tactics, it is more appropriately understood as a rationalizing discourse for an ongoing "American Apartheid" (Massey and Denton 1998) or an inchoate preemptive strike for a nascent resegregation (Frankenberg and Lee 2002; Logan 2002),[16] which is to say the continued and increasing *isolation* of blacks without state and civil society. Seen in this light, multiracialism arbitrates neoconservative race politics as an accompaniment to an advancing neoliberalism that is itself oscillating between official (liberal) multiculturalism and the (conservative) posture of colorblindness, twin aspects of what David Theo Goldberg (2002) calls "the façade of racial dispersal" (5).

> Racist states have undertaken to deflect resistance by *indirection*. Contemporary states have sought thus to dissipate the normative power of critique in two related ways. On one hand, they have rerouted rightful anger at the homogenizing exclusions of racist states into circuitous ambiguities and ambivalences of "mere" racially characterized, if not outrightly colorblind, conditions; and on the other hand, they have pursued superficial appropriation through uncritical celebration of the multicultural. (5–6; emphasis added)

This explains, to some extent, why the political dissension, organizational weakness, and theoretical confusion of the multiracial movement or the dearth of intellectual rigor in multiracial studies do not in any way diminish the historical significance of multiracialism. Its appeal to the "circuitous ambiguities and ambivalences of 'mere' racially characterized . . . conditions" is predominantly affective, which is to say it is "prelogical" or "paralogical" (Fanon 1967, 154–59), and its official rhetoric does not so much articulate the interests or illuminate the position of any particular nonblack group (i.e., the New Immigrants, the white middle and working classes, or even multiracial people themselves) as much as it rehearses the phobic annulment of the "rightful anger" of blacks and the "normative power of [black] critique." It is, in other words, a political theater for the acting out of a repetition compulsion, the staging of ritual loathing, an ardent refusal to be addressed by, and therefore *implicated* in, the historical force of black rage, the insatiable demand for black reparation, or the inconsolable melancholy of black suffering. As the color line of the twentieth century is swiftly transformed into "the new black/nonblack divide" (Yancey 2003) of the twenty-first, it is this collective antipathy toward the lived experience of the black that tenders the possibility of any nominally post-racial rapprochement. Whether characterized as an expanded and refashioned whiteness (Warren and Twine 1997) or a selective multiracialism (Lind 1998), this portentous shift, so vital to the "browning of America," discloses the uneven and uneasy camaraderie obtaining in the culture of antiblackness.

Refounding the Republic

Like their Republican sponsors, the multiracial movement's most vocal spokespersons have attempted to attach an initially liberal "critique of racialism"[17] to various planks in a neoconservative platform clearly opposed to the progressive trajectory of the modern civil rights movement and its radicalization under the heading of Black Power.[18] As mentioned previously, the battle of/for identification that multiracialism enjoins initially featured two broad-based and opposing organizational alliances, both claiming the moral and ethical high ground and both offering what was, to their minds, the most viable antiracist public policy. That these contending forces shared political terminology, forms of mobilization, and venues of public expression demonstrates that the antiracist imperative instituted during the civil rights era has registered widely on the social landscape, but because its ameliorative effects have been absorbed by the mechanisms of bureaucratic state reformism and the monotonous discourse of media punditry (Omi and Winant 1994), the form and substance of antiracism remain the stakes of continued struggle. What, then, have been the principal terms of dispute?

We have already learned that leading figures in the multiracial movement have identified the network of African American political organizations as the chief barrier to the empowerment of multiracial people and the acceptance of the interracial intimacy they are thought to index. The nature of this barrier is named as a form of black "reverse racism," and its genesis is explained, as it were, by imputing to the collective black personality an irrational adherence to the one-drop rule or hypodescent rule of racial designation.[19] Multiracial advocates suggest that this new "racism from below" constitutes less a counterpart to than a successor of a residual regime of white supremacy ("racism from above") in an ill-named "squeeze of oppression" that characterizes the contemporary multiracial experience. That is to say, it is suggested that the racism of blacks toward self-identified multiracial people, and toward nonblacks more generally, has become not simply dominant but hegemonic—a structure of unwarranted enmity and illegitimate political power eclipsing the historical centrality of white supremacy. The force of black racism, or oppressive black power, has become, as a result, the proper object of antiracist activism today. To be more exact, this new oppressive black power is figured as an *internalization* of white supremacy (its rules of definition, codes of conduct, and overall frame of mind) that amplifies its effects insofar as it is now projected against victims who are more vulnerable and less powerful than blacks were once thought to be. This represents a historic transfer of Root's tidily phrased "vehicle of oppression," a surrender of arms—the ways and means of racial power—to new rulers more dangerous and less accountable than the old.

The alarmist historical review that we have just glossed launches the politics of multiracialism and is found readily in all of the published works considered for the present study, but it was articulated with a particular alacrity, and acrimony, from the steps of the Lincoln Memorial in Washington, D.C., on the occasion of the first annual Multiracial Solidarity March (MSM). Held July 20, 1996, the MSM brought together over two dozen multiracial organizations, including many of the major participants of the contemporaneous census hearings prior to their eventual rift, in order to announce to an international audience the historic arrival of the multiracial movement. "Never before has there been an attempt to offer the perspective of racially mixed people on racial issues, but that blessed day has finally arrived," declared Charles Byrd, MSM organizer and *Interracial Voice* founding editor, in his keynote address. Crucially, the articulation of "the perspective of racially mixed people on racial issues" against a presumed historical obscurity proceeds from a signal desire for *secession*.[20] Byrd (1996) continues:

> We are no longer invisible, and "mixed-race" should never have been viewed merely as a "subset" of "blackness." That is patently absurd, is hypodescent-driven, and it ignores other mixed-race individuals not of the black/white variety—such as hapas, mestizos, metis, creoles and latinos. Identifying all individuals of mixed-race as black is nothing more than a lustful embrace of the mythical concept of white racial purity, and proponents of such an ideology are essentially in bed with the slavemaster. We reject the notion of white racial purity, and we affirm the right of otherwise self-determined individuals to identify as they see fit—not as others would force them to identify. Hypodescent, the inheritance of only the lowest status racial category of one's ancestors, also known as the infamous "one-drop rule," is no mere "curious quirk." It is an integral aspect of American racism, and it could not—did not—survive and does not survive today without the complicity of many of its victims. This is unacceptable and must end.

In an earlier note, I remarked upon the reduction in multiracial discourse of hypodescent to the "'infamous' one-drop rule." The point not to be missed here is that the critique of hypodescent is thereby restricted to its unique application to blacks in the United States. Further, because it is claimed that the one-drop rule is "an *integral* [rather than, say, a dispensable] aspect of American racism," any defense of its operations becomes tantamount to sustaining racism *tout court*. That is to say, without the survival of the one-drop rule, American racism as such would simply disintegrate, and absent continuing enforcement by blacks (and their allies), the one-drop rule could not survive as a foundation. It is somewhat unclear who Byrd intends as the "victims" of the one-drop rule here—many of whom he charges with "complicity"—but it is safe to assume that they are multiracial people narrowly defined rather than the broader population historically marked by racial blackness. The aim of his exhortation—"this is unacceptable and must end"—is, then, to embolden or, at the very least, to chastise "those of mixed-descent [who] would meekly tag along" with blacks, prompting them, in an act of "sanity" and the exercise of an "inalienable right," to break ranks with a community—and, more importantly, a political leadership—that has lost its bearings. To be sure, it is the reputed waywardness of black politics that licenses the multiracial intervention, an intervention carried out in the name of a return to a betrayed ideal. Thus, for Byrd, "it is *not* the mixed-race community that is 'distancing' itself from 'color' [i.e., blackness] but quite the reverse." He expands his point as follows:

> The black community in general and its political leadership specifically that I see in 1996 are not the same that I observed in 1966, and the change has not been for the better. Thirty years have produced tremendous changes, as the black leadership today is more separatist-inspired and too often exhibits the same racist mentality of the long-standing white power structure.

According to this rather unoriginal formulation, Byrd avers that the laudable integrationist message of a centrist civil rights movement lead by a colorblind Martin Luther King Jr. was abruptly supplanted in the late 1960s (1966, to be exact, the year in which "Black Power" was first popularized as a political slogan) by the adolescent, loudmouthed militancy of a "separatist-inspired" faction. By fecklessly usurping the leadership of the noble grassroots movement that earlier and more reasoned civil rights activists had built, Black Power squandered the political capital of its predecessor, souring heretofore favorable public opinion and spurning the largesse of the majority of white America.[21] For Byrd, the moral conscience of the American nation was right to be as offended, if not more so, by Black Power—a movement of "black racists" exhibiting "the hate that hate produced"[22]—as it had been by Jim Crow segregation and racial slavery in the antebellum period. The *offense* of black racism was (and is) compounded by the peculiar expectation that blacks would adhere to a higher ethical standard, given a presumed sensitivity to their own unearned suffering. The *threat* of black racism was (and is) compounded by the peculiar expectation that blacks would exact vengeance to a higher standard of brutality, given a presumed insensitivity to the unearned suffering of others. The same "all-American" egalitarianism, demonstrating its repugnance toward the racial oppression of blacks under white supremacy, at once ensured the success of the civil rights movement (and the abolition of slavery before that) and demanded consistency when it was found that similar *attitudes* ("the same racist mentality") were taken up by black people themselves.

Interestingly, among the principal political casualties assigned to these "tremendous changes" is that they allowed white America to "avoid both identification with black people and the job of bettering this nation" (Byrd 1996). Whereas "identification with black people" once provided a necessary condition of possibility for "the job of bettering this nation" (the latter being synonymous, in Byrd's text, with "the cause of justice for black Americans"), it now represents, as a result of an entirely unexplained turn of events in the last generation, a positive barrier to such grand pursuits. In other words, due to an undisclosed and perhaps incomprehensible ideological departure from the "transcendent nature" of the civil rights movement "after the assassinations of Malik El-Shabazz [Malcolm X] and Martin Luther King Jr.," "the black community in general and its political leadership specifically" have suffered from massive but altogether self-inflicted *disidentification*. In standard fashion, Byrd describes this fated departure as a "turn toward Afrocentric nationalism," which for him stems from a pathological or "pathetic" embrace of "separatist ideology," an embrace driven in its own right by fear or greed or a quest for self-aggrandizement. Conventional separatist ideological commitments (whose hallmark is belief in the myth of white racial purity) demand a continued subsuming of multiracial people under the heading of racial blackness, which is why the pathetic commitment of blacks to post–civil rights era separatism—the bizarrely figured *black* defense of *white* racial purity—is determined to be the ultimate source of proscription for multiracial people's "inalienable right" to self-identify.[23]

Yet, for Byrd, the true *perversity* of black separatism (or Afrocentric nationalism) lies not in the fact that blacks are found mimicking or identifying with their historical oppressors (a defensive psychological response that is predictable as per the "hostage syndrome" [Root 1996b, 5]) but in the fact that blacks have attempted to arrogate the right and to assume the power to aggress their oppressors, as it were, to assault them, and to do so by way of a particularly *sexual* violence. Byrd announces his diagnosis on the authority of A. D. Powell, an amateur historian, who, according to Byrd, captured the oddity of this collective insolence in her discussion of the notion of "ethnic rape." Powell writes,

> Throughout history many nations and ethnic groups have tried to forcibly assimilate others. The English tried to assimilate the Celtic nations of Ireland, Scotland and Wales. The Castilians tried to assimilate the Basques and Catalons. The government of Turkey says there is no such thing as a Kurd, only another variety of Turk. Black Americans are one of the few cases of a subordinate ethnic group thinking it has the "right" to commit the ethnic "rape" of conquerors. American Indians, Asian-Americans and others might inappropriately claim some mixed people but they do not generally go into a towering rage over the thought of losing the "blood" of their "white" rivals.
>
> The "one drop" advocates should be told that they have no right to commit racial or ethnic "rape," telling others that they will be taken against their will. They have no right to "rape" either the living or the dead—"blackening" the names of people who were not "black" and never claimed to be (Jean Toomer, Alexander Dumas, Alexander Pushkin and numerous others

subjected to "kidnapping" when they are dead and unable to defend themselves). Anyone who says he wants to "unite" with you and will do so whether you like it or not is a rapist. Ethnic rape can be just as real and demeaning as sexual rape. (Powell quoted in Byrd 1996)

One cannot but notice that, in its haste, Powell's account fails to address the fact that in the history of racial formation in the United States, black Americans have not been targeted by white Americans for forcible *assimilation* but rather for forcible *exclusion* (from the captivity of the chattel regime to the myriad institutions of de jure and de facto segregation). What we learn nonetheless is that the idea of blacks reversing or inverting the racial order of white supremacy—in an exception that proves the historical rule—is something of a stratagem. This is the case not only because it dissimulates the matter of force—the determinant relations of power that would warrant the use of an adjective like *subordinate* in the passage above. More important is the performance of an elision wherein whites (the "conquerors" or "'white' rivals") are violated *through* the experience of multiracial people "taken against their will," an assault in which the denial of racial whiteness at the site of mixture metamorphoses from the banal, official state of *disinheritance* authorized by white supremacist law and custom to an overtly sexualized, criminal scene of *abduction*, a "blackening . . . just as real and demeaning as sexual rape," driven by the "towering rage" and necrophilia of villainous blacks (raping "either the living or the dead").

In this light, we do well to reconsider with special attention Byrd's claim that "blackening" multiracial people "is nothing more than a lustful embrace of the mythical concept of white racial purity" and, further, that "proponents of such an ideology are essentially in bed with the slavemaster" (Byrd 1996). However strange it may seem, in the multiracial imagination, it is a "lustful embrace," a *liaison* between (freed) blacks and their (former) white slave masters that, in the same instance, fortuitously permits and forcibly precludes psychological integrity qua legal entitlement— "the heart of one's self-esteem" as one's "inalienable right" to self-identify (Byrd 1996). In the terms of this strained metaphorical transfer, the sexual *assent* of the former is thus the sexual *assault* of the latter. In chapter 2, we see that this sacrificial formula is reversible. For now, suffice it to say that in its most public expression, the mounting political pressure to self-identify as multiracial, to cease "meekly [tagging] along" with the dominion of the one-drop rule, is shot through with the singular urgency of sexual self-defense, a movement organized on the premise—or pretext—of "rape" prevention and support for an untold number of "survivors." Beyond the expanded set of victims vulnerable to the putative menace of lascivious blacks, what makes multiracialism an augmentation of the negrophobia typically accredited to white supremacy is the variation it seeks in the functions of female gender. In the new dispensation, it is not claimed that the patriarchy "defends" the sanctity of a sexually endangered population of women so much as it is suggested that the entire constituency occupies a quasi-feminized position—a renovated tragic *mulatta*, "the translation of the 'she' to the 'we,' of everywoman to everyone" (Massumi 1993, 24)— but one which does not prevent "her" from withstanding the advances of a hypermasculine black mass, "a more or less imaginary attacker" (Fanon 1967, 155).

Most studies of multiracialism to this point have either refrained from accounting for the likes of Byrd (or Susan Graham, or James Landrith, founding editor of *The Multiracial Activist*) or relegated them to an embarrassing right-wing periphery of an otherwise liberal multiracial movement (Spencer 1999). This analytical sidestep complements an equally common reluctance to discuss the political mobilization of a multiracial constituency and the academic theorization of multiracial identity as components of the broader "conservative restoration" (Shor 1992). However, there is more than a family resemblance between the sensational diatribes of Byrd and his contemporaries and the more moderate stances of, say, the liberal AMEA, the oldest and perhaps most influential multiracial advocacy organization in the United States. The same could be said about the intellectual contributions of the liberal philosopher Naomi Zack (1993) (who renders all racial identity as a pathological, existential "passion") in relation to the even more problematic work of sociologists like G. Reginald Daniel (2001) (who lapses into romantic racial essentialism in the promotion of an egalitarian ideal of a cultural and biological "synthesis" between blacks and whites) and Kathleen Korgen (1999) (who erroneously suggests that growing biracial identification in the United States is a sign of the increasing irrelevance of racism and, hence, of black identity), and, again, to the fallacious historical writings of Randall Kennedy (2003), Gregory Stephens (1999), and Stephen Talty (2003) (who together rewrite the institution of racial slavery as a valuable forum for interracial intimacy and mutual recognition).[24] What traverses this range of published opinion is a shared belief that racial blackness, in and of itself, inhibits or disables multiracialism and, for this reason, that those who remain black-identified require the most severe pedagogy.

From this angle, we find cogency in the fact that Byrd and his cohort deploy political rhetoric that associates racial blackness with "malicious intentions" and "malefic power" (Fanon 1967, 155). That is, it seems *necessary* for prominent figures in the multiracial movement to summon publicly the terrifying specter of the black rapist as a means to indict "black community in general and its political leadership especially" for the denial of race mixture and the promotion of a mythical concept of white racial purity, policing sexuality and personal affiliation in ways equivalent to or worse than the "longstanding white power structure." Such utterances, repeated time and time again, become vital to the legitimization of an otherwise untenable political program animated by the aggressions of neo-conservative colorblindness and neoliberal multiculturalism.[25] The baleful figure of a raging, lustful black mass abusing unassuming and unprotected multiracial persons, "either dead or alive," inhabits the movement's political imagination as a projection of its own belligerence, a hallucinatory alibi for its complicity in fomenting "the new black–nonblack divide."

Here I depart respectfully from observations made by Njeri (1997) and Spencer (1999) regarding the motives of a Susan Graham, who, when confronted with evidence of the trouble caused to civil rights compliance monitoring by a separate multiracial category or, in another vein, the inherent insult of claiming that a black social identity is debilitating to the mental and emotional health of multiracial people, feigned incomprehension and simply subordinated such concerns to the otherwise discredited interests of the multiracial movement for "accuracy in naming." I say that I am departing from the more charitable interrogations of Njeri and Spencer because both authors find that the hardline tendencies that Graham represents are the result of inexperience in the political arena. After examining the relevant literature and observing the major political developments on the multiracial front since the early 1990s, I do not see how it can be maintained that the movement leadership is naïve. In point of fact, a disregard for longstanding and well-founded popular black political concerns has characterized the movement for well over a decade and was made only more patent in 2003, long after the lessons of the census debates (1993–1997) were known. Project RACE, *Interracial Voice*, *The Multiracial Activist*, and A Place for Us National all publicly endorsed the failed California State Proposition 54, the so-called Racial Privacy Initiative, sponsored by the stridently conservative Republican front man, Ward Connerly, as part of a national antiaffirmative action campaign roundly criticized by civil rights leaders across the country.[26] Moreover, the framing of the one-drop rule as the effect of outmoded black-authored—or, at least, black-enforced—race rules is commensurate with the more familiar discourse of "angry white males" generated about the Reagan and Bush administrations, an insistence that the liberal platform of the Great Society (and the New Deal before that) is a masked totalitarianism founded on massive capitulations to the political demands of "parasitical" blacks (S. Robinson 2000).[27] A permanent charge of contempt, and the fraudulent historical narrative required to sustain it, is thus inscribed in the discursive touchstones of multiracialism, evident in its founding documents, as we shall see in a moment.

The discourse of multiracialism begins with a displacement of the concern for battling racism by a concern with "the theoretical status of the concept of race" (Winant 2000), a point made similarly by Heather Dalmage (2004), who notes that "the [multiracial] movement is complicit with white supremacy as seen through claims to color blindness and by the acknowledgment of racial divisions without the acknowledgment of racial hierarchies" (6). Indeed, our discussion to this point indicates that the ethical evasion of antiracism (i.e., acknowledging divisions without acknowledging hierarchies) is a necessary condition of possibility for multiracial politics. This obligation was revealed, quite practically, during the census debates examined previously. When the historical mandate of the civil rights establishment finally registered among the liberal wing of the multiracial movement present at the congressional hearings, the result was ruinous: the initial proposal for the stand-alone multiracial category was abandoned, and a compromise proposal (to "check all [racial designations] that apply") was pursued in lieu. The right wing of the movement was thus correct in its outrage at this concession to the status quo, for it forfeited entirely the "subversive" import of multiracialism, its promise to "[challenge] generally accepted proscriptions and prescriptions regarding intergroup relations" (Root 1992b, 3). However, the "proscriptions and prescriptions" at stake in this challenge were not, and never have been, the boundaries of racial group membership in general, as the liberal credo of the multiracial mainstream would suggest, but rather the possibility of a *political* "identification with black people" that made practicable the intervention of the civil rights movement, and eventually Black Power, as a progressive response to antiblackness in the postwar era. Multiracialism, to recast our earlier claim, is a tendency to neutralize the political antagonism set loose by the critical affirmation of blackness—the impossible claim to black humanity (though not necessarily a black humanism) in the face of its manifest negation—an affirmation, moreover, that holds open the only genuine possibility for a comprehensive escape from racialization in the historic instance.[28]

Multiracialism suffers from this conundrum: wanting to condemn identification with racial blackness as the source of social crisis, seeking to locate a politicized blackness as the barrier to a postracial future, while affirming "mixed-ness" in ways that reinforce and expand notions of racial purity *and* the concomitant hierarchies of value that underwrite white supremacy and antiblackness. This is why the reclamation of whiteness, or more precisely, *nonblackness*, is elevated to the status of a virtue, a sign not only of mental and emotional well-being (openness to diversity, within and without) but also of moral rectitude (tolerance for difference and commitment to reconciliation) (Daniel 2002). It is more than contradictory that this bid to recuperate whiteness—an intrinsic component of reclaiming, usually in the covering language of *ethnicity* or *culture*, the totality of one's multiple "heritages"—occurs in the same moment that whiteness is interrogated by a range of critical inquiries inspired by the exemplars of twentieth-century black intellectual history (Delgado and Stefancic 1999). In the process, two operations are executed: one, blackness is negatively *purified* insofar as mixed-ness and blackness are strictly demarcated; and two, whiteness, whose purity remains intact, is *revalorized* by a people of color contingent flying the banner of antiracism, awarding themselves the proper legacy of the civil rights movement. The yield is threefold: first, an ironic denunciation of black political formations advanced *in the name of* the preeminent modern black political formation; second, a deceptive moral defense of whiteness as something equivalent to the (still unavoidably racialized) *ethnicities* or *cultures* of nonwhite immigrants and American Indians; and third, a comforting internment of political struggle within the terms of *personal identity*.

It should be emphasized here that the political containment strategies of multiracial discourse cannot be relaxed by a more reflexive or enlightened politics of multiracialism. They are the *logical* effects of its fundamental orientation and its driving impulses. In *Race and Mixed Race* (1993), the most sophisticated argument on behalf of multiracialism to date, Zack explains: "The necessity for a critique of customary racial designations comes from the logical breakdown of the biracial schema against the fact of the existence of individuals of mixed black and white race" (6). For Zack, an epistemological objection to the method (or "schema") of racial categorization, its failure to meet the criteria of consistency, is what drives the enterprise, not an ethical objection to the injustice of racism and/or a political desire to challenge it. On closer scrutiny, however, we learn that the catalyzing concern for *inconsistency* is, in fact, ancillary to a more elementary criticism regarding the *falsity* of "customary racial designations," a status that ipso facto renders them ethically compromised: "The general thesis of this book is that black and white racial designations are themselves racist *because* the concept of race does not have an adequate scientific foundation" (3–4; emphasis added). And, so it seems, for no other reason. The political import of this initial formulation obtains in the implication that were the concept of race to enjoy "an adequate scientific foundation," its deployment as a principle of organization for "societies structured in dominance" (Hall 1996b) would no longer be considered racist and therefore would enjoy immunity before the ethical dimensions of radical critique: from the abolitionist ideal of human emancipation to contemporary notions of social justice. Just above the cited passage, Zack writes,

> It has been acknowledged for a long time that there are racial problems concerning black people and white people in the United States. And there has been a shifting spectrum of moral, political, social, and legal argument about how whites ought to treat blacks, as well as a less visible but equally unstable spectrum of views about how blacks ought to react to whites. *This book is not about either one of those spectra.* (3; emphasis added)

For multiracial advocates, it is not the structural conditions of racial slavery or the history of racial segregation but "the fact of the existence of individuals of mixed black and white race" that spurs their political and intellectual endeavor, be it the development of a "philosophy of antirace" or the promotion of a "new multiracial consciousness." There is a tension, however, between the "necessity for a critique"—to be implemented "with all deliberate speed"—and the brute defiance, the unthinking blurring of boundaries, the embodied conceptual challenge generated by racially mixed people by dint of their corporeal existence, their emerging presence or *physis*. Where the former task entails the possibility of confrontation, if only intellectual, the latter involves an entirely passive transformation, consisting only of the knock-on effects of "love's revolution" (Root 2001).[29] Root, to take another instance, writes,

> The presence of racially mixed persons defies the social order predicated upon race, blurs racial and ethnic group boundaries, and challenges generally accepted proscriptions and prescriptions regarding intergroup relations. Furthermore, and perhaps most threatening, the existence of racially mixed persons challenges long-held notions about the biological, moral, and social meanings of race. (1992b, 3)

Or again:

> The emergence of a racially mixed population is transforming the "face" of the United States. The increasing presence of multiracial people necessitates that we as a nation ask ourselves questions about our identity: Who are we? How do we see ourselves? Who are we in relation to one another? . . . Resolving the [national] identity crisis may force us to reexamine our construction of race and the hierarchical social order it supports. (3)

Others have established how the representation of a multiracial population in the United States as "emergent" is predicated on a disavowal of the complex history of intermixture in the Atlantic world and a corollary denial of the normative, present-day "hybridity" of African Americans (Makalani 2001). It is also clear that the mere "presence [or existence] of racially mixed persons" neither "defies the social order predicated on race" nor "challenges generally accepted proscriptions and prescriptions regarding intergroup relations," precisely because race mixture has been incorporated in the production of racial knowledge and racial order from the colonial era onward. As mentioned in the introduction, fantasies of mixture as well have been central to the articulation of racial theory throughout the social universe erected by European colonialism and its neocolonial afterlife (Young 1995). So, if multiracialism's "critique of the customary racial designations" proves to be not only inadequate but also preempted, then what, if anything, can be gleaned of the relation between this chimerical reexamination of "our construction of race," about which much ink has been spilt, and the fate of "the hierarchical social order it supports," about which we find either curious silence or official disinterest?

Declaration of Independence

Here we must look to the pseudoconcepts of race and racism on which the multiracial movement and the field of multiracial studies have drawn. To illustrate, we can consider two political manifestos published in close succession at the height of the census debates and that effectively express the premises of multiracialism. Our first example is titled "Declaration of Racial

Independence" (Douglas 1997), composed by Nathan Douglas, a delegate of the Interracial Family Circle to the congressional census hearings and a regular *Interracial Voice* contributor. The Declaration lists twelve "truths" meant to guide the multiracial struggle for self-identification against what he cryptically terms "racial hostility." I quote it here in its entirety:

1. Race is a subjective biological construct which is an inaccurate predictor of capabilities or attitudes.
2. People deserve to be treated with dignity and respect, regardless of their alleged race.
3. Original intent notwithstanding, any government classifying its citizenry by race perpetuates racism.
4. The "One Drop Rule," which declares everyone with any "black" blood to be a member of the "black" race, is a myth which could be equally misapplied in other racial directions. "One Drop" is false and devoid of merit.
5. Racial pride bestows worth based upon race. Real worth stems from individual achievement, as well as the love of family and friends.
6. Racial loyalties are a threat to human rights. Socially responsible allegiances must transcend racial categories.
7. Based upon existing evidence, it is reasonable to believe each of us is a distant descendant of primitive human beings originally inhabiting Africa. In this sense, we are all Africans.
8. Every "centrism"—be it Afrocentrism, Eurocentrism, or otherwise—is counterproductive. We are what we are, due to the interaction of multiple peoples and cultures throughout history.
9. The sins of our ancestors or contemporaries are not our fault, including slavery and other acts of racial bigotry. The only guilt we need feel is for the wrongs we have personally done.
10. It is natural and normal for members of different racial groups to love each other, marry each other and have children. People have done so from the beginning. And the offspring from these unions are neither one race nor the other—they are multiracial.

11. Parents bear the primary responsibility for breaking the cycle of racism. We should teach our children to judge others by character, not race.
12. Racism exists among all populations. We must challenge racism wherever we find it.

Despite the gross convolution of the text, a diacritical reading of its statements allows us to tease out an implicit political stance. In so doing, we gain greater insight toward the discursive formation of multiracialism.

It may assist our efforts to aggregate the pronouncements of the Declaration into thematic clusters in order to parse the various positions assumed with respect to race and racism, among other things. The first cluster (statements 1, 2, 4, 7, and 10) relates specifically to the ontological status of the concept of race but has embedded within it a secondary commentary on its ethical value as well. Although there is no logically required connection between the two assertions (ontological and ethical), the latter is nonetheless *rhetorically* dependent on the former, much as it was for Zack in our earlier discussion. That is to say, the ethical significance of race, or more precisely its *insignificance*, is derived from its ontological falsity; however, its falsity is designated in contradictory ways. On the one hand, race is demoted to an entirely subjective interpretation of nominally "objective" biological traits (statements 1, 2): subjective because such traits function as an "inaccurate predictor of capabilities and attitudes," or what Douglas alternately terms "character" (statement 11). This point is extended by the claim that "dignity and respect" ought to be afforded nonracially, which is to say according to "real worth" that can be arrived at objectively by the measure of one's "capabilities and attitudes," "character," and "achievement." However, it is not without consequence that the content of all such terms is undisclosed. We might ask, capable of what? Exhibiting which attitudes, what sort of character, under what circumstances? Achieving what, according to whom, in what spheres, and to what effect? And so on. In the absence of any specifications, we are left to assume the commonsense criteria of a mythic capitalist meritocracy, but not without complications arising from the formal inclusion—or rather co-optation—of a critique of race and racism.

This is why, on the other hand, race is rejected or subject to disproof on strictly biological grounds (statements 4, 7, and 10). Where race is affirmed as biological at the opening of the document, it is determined to be irrelevant to questions of worth, dignity and respect. However, Douglas is not satisfied to disconnect race from "capabilities and attitudes" and goes on to disassemble even the conventional understanding of race as discrete biological categories of human being. The divisions are not hard and fast, we are told, because a history of mixture has by now blurred the boundaries in question ("people have done so from the beginning") and/or because any racial division of the human species is completely illusory in the first place, given the lie by a common (i.e., nondifferentiated) ancestry reaffirmed by the findings of physical anthropology ("we are all Africans").[30] These two propositions are in direct competition, displaying a basic indecision or equivocation about the admission of human divisions under the heading of race. Douglas is stating, in other words, *both* that biological racial differences did and do exist but have diminished by a history of mixture dating back to time immemorial *and* that biological racial differences never existed in human history and still do not exist today. More importantly, this halfhearted disproof of biological race is undercut by its own recourse to biology when designating the supposed reality of race mixture, past and present. In fact, the problem that this oscillation institutes—claiming that race *is* and *is not* a fact of biological data—seems to be indispensable, a conceptual doubletalk that makes room for the simultaneous discrediting of race-based politics for blacks and the promotion of race-based politics for the multiracial contingent. The logical leap between the rejection/retention of racial biology and the subsequent bid for the wholesale privatization of antiracism relies on the belief that *because* race is superficial, it is an invidious term of distinction when utilized within state policy or social custom.[31]

This rhetorical misdirection can thereby approve the conservative political prescriptions gathered in the second thematic cluster (statements 3, 6, 9, 11, and 12) with the hard-won moral force generated by the social movements against slavery and segregation. In this way, the legacy of the liberal-progressive intellectual efforts (i.e., the debunking of scientific racism) that underwrote the litigation and political mobilization that culminated in the modern civil rights movement is called upon to sanction the retreat of the state from any and all race-conscious remedies, including the compliance monitoring of Fourteenth Amendment civil rights legislation, the initiatives of affirmative action, voter redistricting, et cetera. More importantly, a strict political quietism is advanced with respect to "systemic racism" (Feagin 2006), since the issue of racism is whittled down to the scale of the domestic estate and the moral training of children by their primary caretakers. The bridge that sutures the conceptual demotion of race to the promotion of laissez-faire, colorblind public policy is the forced association between "racial pride" or "racial loyalties" and some nebulous "threats to human rights," an association that confuses and conflates the historical and political specificities of racial identifications. The threats to human rights that scholars and activists attribute to the centuries-long development of Eurocentrism are manifest. Afrocentrism, however, is neither an intellectual mirror image nor a symmetrical political match to its European counterpart (Bernal 2001). (The collective position of blacks in the global political and libidinal economies would have to be completely transformed before such judgments might even be entertained.) Nonetheless, for Douglas, the social contract ("socially responsible allegiances") should bypass racial considerations altogether, presumably toward the scale of the *species* (although the nation-state seems for him an acceptable point of group identification, often standing in place of humanity). Or else it must dissolve altogether in the adjudication of *individuals* where "achievement" can be granted "real worth" and the "guilt" of "the wrongs we have personally done" can be redressed. "We are all just human" becomes "we are all just individuals."

It is at the scale of the individual that prescriptions for "political" action are finally pitched. The stakes of these prescriptions are brought into sharpest relief in Douglas's decree of universal absolution for the history and legacy of racial slavery (statement 9). He writes: "The sins of our ancestors or contemporaries are not our fault, including slavery and other acts of racial bigotry."[32] All "we" are responsible for, according to Douglas, are our immediate actions, "the wrongs we have *personally* done." Yet, in the reduction of political life to individual decisions, we are left without an explanatory framework for the persistence of the structures of racial inequality. We are simply assured that if they exist at all, then others ("our ancestors") constructed them in the distant past and others ("our . . . contemporaries") reconstruct them in the present. In this sense, we are excised from historical context into positions of categorical isolation from which we make decisions and enjoy privileges (or disadvantages) in strict proportion to "our capabilities and attitudes." If Douglas's document is indicative of the broader ideological field, we see that multiracialism is not so much a *political* movement (in the vein of the progressive antiracist struggles it mines for rhetorical elements) as it is a *moral* crusade (in the vein of the neoconservative patrons it continually disclaims). Of course, like that of its Republican backers, this program is thoroughly political, and its principal ramification is to undermine the *legitimacy* of collective efforts for progressive and radical social change, specifically those populated by "the black community in general and its political leadership especially." In this respect, the wishful historical quarantine of racial slavery and its relegation to a mere "[act] of racial bigotry" are not merely sloppy writing or hasty deflection correctable by a more careful editing process or more patient deliberations. They are structural effects of the architecture of multiracial discourse, a presupposition of the multiracial project.

I do not draw out these very noticeably conservative political commitments to add fuel to the opposition of the liberal civil rights establishment (my dissatisfaction with the latter's antiradicalism and gradualist doctrines of reform are taken up in later chapters). What I am exploring, rather, is *how* the discourse of multiracialism articulates neoconservative race politics through the defensive nomination of its phenomenal experience—what Root calls "multiracial phenomenology" (Root 1992b, 10)— and does so in general conformity with the larger policy prescriptions of neoliberal economic restructuring. This conservatism is not lost on what may be the most vital, and therefore most contentious, point of the Declaration, a thesis affirmed across the movement and reiterated throughout the academic field: "It is natural and normal for members of different racial groups to love each other, marry each other, and have children. People have done so from the beginning. And the offspring from these unions are neither one race nor the other—they are multiracial" (statement 10). Not only does this statement undoubtedly reinforce the notion of biological racial differences that Douglas alternately claims do not exist, but it also enshrines a naïve, pretheoretical conception of colorblind desire.

The aim of this defense of interracial love, marriage, and reproduction, however, is, ironically enough, to fortify a *denial* of interracial kinship—that is, to block or interrupt the "patently absurd" association of multiracial people with racial blackness. Because the disassociation of multiracial people from racial whiteness is historically intractable, the description of "the offspring of these unions" as "neither one race nor the other" is an artifice, a means of more subtly declaring that "'mixed race' should never have been viewed merely as a 'subset' of 'blackness'" (Byrd 1996). The Declaration of Racial Independence does not concern independence from racial categories altogether or even the desire to identify "other than monoracially" (Byrd 1997), only an escape from designation as black. Not unlike the incendiary comments of Byrd and Powell discussed earlier, this drive for a distinction-by-right from blackness sounds a disturbing resonance with the musings of the contemporary Far Right. Indeed, the very phrase "declaration of racial independence" was coined several years earlier by noted white supremacist Richard McCulloch in *The Racial Compact* (1994), one of many texts he has authored since the early 1980s to elaborate his philosophy of "racial preservationism" against an emergent "multiracialism" ("the ideology or system of beliefs and values which favors a multiracial social condition"). Here is the relevant passage:

> The Racial Golden Rule asserts the right of every race to racial freedom through racial separation and independence. To secure racial freedom and separation it respects the requirement of every race for its own exclusive racial territory or homeland, its own independent and sovereign government. It declares for every race the freedom to follow its own path, to control its own life and existence, to determine its own course of development and to pursue its own happiness and evolutionary destiny. It is *a declaration of racial independence*, freedom and diversity, holding it to be self-evident that all races

were created different, and have *a right to be different, to be themselves*, with equal rights to life, liberty and the pursuit of their own happiness. (emphasis added)

McCulloch and the Föreningen för Folkens Framtid (FFF), a Swedish neo-Nazi network that once promulgated his writings in defense of a supposedly endangered "Nordish race," would certainly include the multiracial movement among those political forces promoting the threat of "racial nihilism." But it is not without consequence that these otherwise opposing ideologies share a certain fundamental disidentification. As one moves across the U.S. political spectrum from the narrow white nationalism of the reactionary Far Right to the more inclusive colorblindness of the neo-conservative center Right, one finds an increasing willingness to expand the boundaries of whiteness in a process of "racial redistricting" (Gallagher 2004) whose only conditional limitation is the exclusion of racial blackness.

I return to the idea of "natural" and "normal" interracial love, marriage, and reproduction in the following chapters. It is only necessary to note here that this popular belief is beholden to "heterosexual libidinal determinism" (Zantop 1997, 137) whereby heterosexual orientation, the objects and aims of desire, and the conceptual framework of racialism are reified in a fantasy of untrammeled *Eros*, "the [natural] selection of taste" (Vasconcelos 1997, 32), that at once insists upon and ignores the political formation of the color line. It suggests that interracial relationships, particularly, as we will see in the present case, those between white men and black women in the antebellum scene, have developed in the abstract or under conditions of mythic equality. Perhaps predictably by now, we can identify this rhetorical gesture as one that flattens relations of power and, more pointedly, offers retroactive justification for racial slavery in the name of Cupid's arrow—"the acknowledgment of racial divisions without the acknowledgment of racial hierarchies" (Dalmage 2004, 6). To call such "unions" to question, to examine their underlying relations of power, is, on this view, to contend with love, to belittle it, and so to become a partisan of hate, an agent of *Thanatos*. The animus of white supremacy is thus reassigned to the animus of black supremacy, the sine qua non of multiracial discourse. The ideological inversions and reversals enabled by this determinism are discernible in another manifesto of the multiracial movement, one circulating with great currency in its precincts. What, after all, is a Declaration of Independence without the supplementary protections afforded by a Bill of Rights? No proper "revolution"[33] would be complete without these twin pillars of the social covenant.

Bill of Rights

Maria Root's canonical "Bill of Rights for Racially Mixed People" (1996b)[34] illuminates most powerfully the political sensibilities of the multiracial movement and the theoretical bearings of multiracial studies. To be sure, Root stands at the epicenter of multiracial discourse, the preeminent founding figure of its public reputation. The better part of her famous proposal, much like Douglas's lesser-known Declaration, is given over to delineating the basic right to self-identify, in different ways at different times, without adherence to familial obligation, social convention, political exigency, government mandate, or historical precedent. It also suggests, as an extension of the right to self-identify, that multiracial people can and should be allowed to maintain "loyalties" to more than one *ethnic* group.[35] However, this right to multiple loyalties is never explicated by Root. The reference to "loyalties" and the claim to maintain more than one at a time suggest that these "ethnic groups" experience objective *conflicts of interest* based in a "hierarchical social order" (Root 1992b, 3) and not simply a diversity of customs, rituals, religious beliefs, social outlooks, political orientations, and so forth. If this is indeed the case, as Root otherwise acknowledges, are there not times when multiple loyalties are simply *impossible* to sustain, particularly if we remain in the domain of *race* and not take cover under the pacified heading of *ethnicity?*[36]

On this note, it seems fitting that this right is formulated in the positive terms of *loyalty*, since it offers a misleading comfort to all parties involved that the affirmation of multiracial identity is not, as it were, a *betrayal*. But again, because racial whiteness *already excludes* multiracial people, and so cannot be betrayed in any case, the racial group that has voiced the loudest concerns about multiracial identity politics in this regard is the racial group with the most *inclusive* criteria of classification, namely, African Americans. How, then, might the upbeat tenor of Root's Bill of Rights change if it were recast as the right to commit "disloyalty" or "treason" or "treachery" to the mightily imposed "racial patriotism" of blackness? To do so would, I suggest, reveal the open secret that simultaneously enlivens and embarrasses the multiracial movement: not only an objectionable push for distance and distinction from racial blackness but also a necessary disregard toward the hard-won juridical gains monitored by the civil rights establishment and an obligatory disdain for any future black political activity.

The last statement in the document reads: "WE HAVE THE RIGHT not to engage in racially-limited partnerships and friendships."[37] In standard fashion, the delimitation of intimacy is framed in the absence of sustained consideration of racial hierarchy and, as a result, begs a crucial question of address. Against what particular limitations—institutional arrangements, social conventions, or legal statutes—is the right asserted? Antimiscegenation laws were challenged as a component of the broader opposition to Jim Crow pursued by black movements from Reconstruction to the civil rights era, so to reject the limitations produced by the exclusions of white society under the new banner of multiracialism would prove redundant. Like the right to multiple loyalties, the equal-opportunity rhetoric of this claim is belied by the unidirectional nature of its intervention. Dispensing with the double negative, we can say that the right to engage in racially *unlimited* partnerships and friendships is a right reserved against the "rigid rules of belonging," the limits on identification and affiliation enforced by black communities suffering from an internalization of the "vehicle of oppression" (Root 1992b, 5). The limitations enforced by whites against multiracial people as a precondition for the enjoyment of exclusive access to racially mediated (social, cultural, or real) capital, a means to secure greater life-chances in a hierarchical social order . . . all of this is trivialized. To wit: why would one need to exercise the right *not* to horde the resources attached to one's partnership or friendship? The key point here is not so much the narrowing of political life in the Bill but rather the continuity of the form it takes. Clearly modeled after the U.S. Bill of Rights, which sanctioned white supremacy and the institution of chattel slavery, the "Bill of Rights for Racially Mixed People" seeks to authorize the upward (or perhaps diagonal) mobility of those for whom being multiracial "doesn't necessarily make [them] 'all black, all the time' in society's eyes," those for whom "there is a considerable degree of uncertainty over just how 'black' [they are]" (Lewis 2006, 5). And it does so by assiduously avoiding an engagement with the ongoing struggles against racial inequality of those who are, in society's eyes, "all black, all the time," including whatever cultural politics might be imagined to counteract the devaluation of racial blackness over the better part of a millennium. In fact, the phrasing of Root's Bill works rhetorically to bolster the sense of black identity as a state of lack or insufficiency, and, barring some escape, a state of *confinement*. The only meaningful limits imposed on multiracial people are thus the limits imposed by blacks, not whites—the limits presumed to be *inherent* to blackness as such.[38]

In this light, what is put forth within the multiracial movement as attempts to guarantee "inalienable rights" for an invisible and socially marginalized population is understood from within the civil rights establishment as a disquieting commentary on the bleakness of black identity and an impediment to the ongoing struggle against white supremacy. Jon Michael Spencer argues this last point at length in *The New Colored People* (1997), the first critical monograph on the multiracial movement:

> In the United States, where blacks are in the minority, we need to count every black or part-black as black. So, while whites, with their majority status, hunt down, identify, and discriminate against everyone with that "one drop," the greater number of blacks resulting from the "rule" makes it more difficult for our oppressors to maintain the institutions of discrimination. This is no doubt the reason that doing away with the one-drop rule has never been on the civil rights agenda. . . . It has been by our numbers and unity, both a result of the one-drop rule, that we have made strides in attaining civil rights in this country. (73–75)[39]

Although Spencer overstates the impact of "our numbers and unity" on the history of black freedom struggle in the United States (black movements may have been widely supported at times, but they have never, or at least not yet, attained to a Gramscian "nation-popular" status), his contention remains both pertinent and persuasive. Still, multiracial advocates like Root, Byrd, Graham, and Douglas would render this political strategy as a psychological problem, a sign of damage or injury, the passive internalization of "the same racist mentality of the longstanding white power structure."[40] What multiracialism continually dismisses in so doing is the black community's evidently *critical* appropriations of the one-drop rule, a refusal to acknowledge that "blacks chose to wield race for their liberation by nurturing a sense of common identity and then fashioning unified social and political action" (2). What this demonstrates is that the parameters of racial blackness have long been in question for those subjected to it, those who would, in turn, subject its fluctuations and ambiguities to creative and instrumental manipulation. Even if blacks could not quite choose the terms of engagement—racialization being, above all, an *imposition*—they have of necessity made attempts to resignify or reinscribe such terms, underscoring their status as violent political fabrications. So, by representing multiracialism as a progressive claim for social change against the reactionary demands of blacks for maintenance of the status quo, advocates endorse the delusional, inverted worldview in which the oppressive power of racism is generated from the ground up, propagated by blacks, its prototypical targets, rather than by whites, its prototypical agents.

When the history of racial formation is returned to the discussion, the restriction of multiracial identification ostensibly imposed by blacks (via the one-drop rule) hardly seems an objective record of fact. Neither is it a clear injustice to multiracial people in any case. If black people have understood the one-drop rule to be a confining historical problem, it is because whites, in the service of political and economic dominance and the cultivation of a mythological supremacy, have violently regulated the coercive interracial sexuality of the racist social order "in the form of the color line that separated whites from those of mixed origin" (12). The one-drop logic of the color line was never opposed by blacks ("mixed" or otherwise) on the exclusive grounds that it denied some biological or genealogical truth of identity. Rather, it was understood to determine the material conditions of black existence under white supremacy, and it was challenged en route to securing legal protections, pursuing political participation (or separation, as the case may be), contesting foreclosure or divestment of property, escaping poverty, mitigating exploitation, fleeing mob violence, and so on.

That multiracialism psychologizes any black communal employment of the one-drop rule as a criterion of social intelligibility and/or political mobilization indicates a general callousness toward the history and present of black freedom struggle. It has the effect of depoliticizing and dehistoricizing what is an undeniably political and historical phenomenon. This callousness is highlighted by the lip service paid by many multiracial advocates to the ethical question of solidarity with "the black community in general and its political leadership specifically" while they actively distance themselves from racial blackness and denigrate progressive black political efforts along the way. Francis Wardle, executive director of the Center for the Study of Biracial Children, asks rhetorically: "Are we [multiracial advocates] a threat to Blacks and their continual struggle? We don't believe we are. We believe we are strong supporters and advocates. . . . We belong on the same side" (quoted in Spencer 1999, 40). This remark is characteristic of the "good intentions" caveats featured regularly in multiracial discourse, disingenuous pronouncements whose function is to place sole responsibility for solidarity in the hands of blacks (since the multiracial camp absolves itself *through* its glibly stated desire for collaboration) while foreclosing negotiation about terms of coalition that have been established *unilaterally*.

What such discomfiting words of "support" studiously fail to address, however, are the *structural* changes put into play by the social construction of multiracial identity. That is, "what many multiracialists are really asking for, if not demanding," despite pronouncements to the contrary, "is for mixed-race people to be accepted as a race apart from both the parent races—a race that would be called 'multiracial'" (Spencer 1999, 35). Put slightly differently, marking the "distinction between . . . multiracial people on the one hand and members of socially designated racial groups on the other . . . is the *raison d'être* of the multiracial identity movement" (93). Given the historical definition of racial whiteness as a state of purity, such that to be deemed multiracial is already to be deemed *nonwhite*, multiracial identification is more accurately described as an assertion of distinction from "monoracial" people of color. Given the unique history of the one-drop rule, multiracial identification is, to recapitulate, a nonwhite differentiation from "monoracial" black people in particular. Rather than simply reinforcing the circumscription of whiteness in pursuit of the conventional cordon sanitaire that historically constitutes white communities, solidifying the boundaries of blackness becomes the quintessential ambition for the politics of multiracialism.

Because racial blackness throughout the Americas has variously encompassed the mixture of African, European, and indigenous derivation—that is, because "black" can also be "multiracial"—to speak of "multiracial blacks" is something of a redundancy. Yet, "rather than acknowledge the highly heterogeneous Afro-American population as entirely multiracial, advocates of a federal multiracial category *distance themselves* from the Afro-American group in order to *distinguish themselves* from it" (95; emphasis added). As Byrd's inflammatory rhetoric seems to suggest, the quest for "distance . . . from the Afro-American group" is fraught with no small amount of terror, "a terror mixed with sexual [horror]" (Fanon 1967, 155). Cecile Lawrence, a contributor to Zack's anthology, *American Mixed Race* (1995), asks urgently: "Where is the black hole into which the non-'black' ancestors of these people get sucked?" (26). Here one is, again, overwhelmed by blackness, "taken against their will." But far more frightening than the specter of a menacing hypermasculine black rapist committing acts "just as real and demeaning as sexual rape" is the trope of an irresistible cosmic black maternal body: a region of distorted space-time with a field of gravitational attraction so intense that its escape velocity exceeds the speed of light. Once across the imaginary surface of the event horizon, the point of no return, one is crushed by its infinite density, sucked into its abyss, cast into a great black void—shrouded by *absolute* invisibility, immobilized by the boundless dilation of time.

Blackness is again attributed malicious intentions and malefic power, but now as a pulverizing, centripetal force of nature, a fantasy of the monstrous feminine that complements and perhaps eclipses its notorious

masculine counterpart. That such recurring statements are sanctioned—
or even considered stirring—from within the parameters of respectable
multiracial discourse is profoundly revealing.[41] Far from the ravings of a
lunatic fringe, this imagery seems to be symptomatic of a phobia shaping
the entire political culture, an aggression toward racial blackness inherent
to the single-minded *rejection* that sustains multiracialism across its assorted
research methodologies and academic disciplines, petty factional disputes
and minor variations in political leaning—a rejection of hypodescent reduced to the one-drop rule, to be sure, but only as the screen memory of
a more primeval definition. Turning to the historiography of multiracialism, the grand mythology that buttresses its claims in and on the present,
we must follow a regression to a universe predating the advent of the post-
Reconstruction culture of lynching and the rituals of sexual punishment
aroused by the charges of "ethnic rape" levied previously. What we find,
finally, is the resurrection of an earlier, antebellum meditation on interracial rape—not the alleged violation committed by the black male freedman
against the virtue of white womanhood but rather the institutionalized
sexual coercion of the enslaved black female by the white male master of
the house, "high crimes against the flesh" (Spillers 2003, 206) vindicated
by the discourse of ruinous black female seduction: "the black hole into
which the non-'black' ancestors of these people get sucked"—*partus sequitur
ventrum.*

CHAPTER 2

Scales of Coercion and Consent: Sexual Violence, Antimiscegenation, and the Limits of Multiracial America

The black American has been mostly freed from one part of being black in America: coercion. . . . Increasingly, African Americans live in a world of post-black possibility. . . . Choice has defeated coercion.

—Stephen Talty, *Mulatto America*

The experience is decisive. The Negro learns that one is not black with impunity.

—Frantz Fanon, *Black Skin, White Masks*

The questions posed today by the politics of multiracialism in the United States reconfigure what previous generations from Reconstruction onward have known as "social equality," and this is so to the extent that multiracialism returns the matter of interracial sexuality to the center of public discourse. Yet, it does so obliquely, through disavowal and deflection. In chapter 1, we saw that multiracial advocates consider African Americans in the post–civil rights era, particularly the native-born black population, to have become, by strange twist of fate, a community of latter-day segregationists prey to a retrograde, separatist nationalism that has allowed them not only to abandon the "transcendent nature of [Martin Luther] King's movement" but also to supplant "the long-standing white power structure" (Byrd 1996) in its role as the principal enforcer of the color line. Blacks in the multiracial age reveal themselves to be, as a result, not simply "self-segregated" but, contrary to the phobic fantasy of black lasciviousness, disinterested in interracial intimacy.

In fact, it would be more accurate to say "in addition to" this phobic fantasy rather than "contrary to" it, for there really are two interwoven impressions at work here. On the one hand, blacks are said to be forcing themselves on the multiracial community, acting damagingly possessive of multiracial people, jealously and unjustly controlling multiracial identifications and affiliations—*public* acts considered in the discourse to be protected by *privacy* rights. Proponents have described this social and political process in extremis: in its masculine form, as an imposition "just as real and demeaning as sexual rape" (Powell quoted in Byrd 1996) or, in its feminine form, an absolute pulverization by the strongest, most incorporative force in the universe, a "black hole" (Lawrence quote in Spencer 1999, 94). One the other hand, blacks are said to be refusing the spirit of multiracialism altogether, denying or begrudging membership in the black community to multiracial people through the application of "rigid rules of belonging" (Root 1992b, 5) and, the focus of the present chapter, rejecting the sexual overtures of white America on the preposterous grounds that they somehow concern—in the present—the relations of racial slavery.

On this last point, multiracial discourse presents a curious interpolation in the historiography of early North America. The contest over contemporary representations of interracial intimacy and multiracial identity is bound up with discrepancies regarding the relations between power and pleasure, agency and affect, subjugation and sexuality in the past. Most pointedly, it is a dispute over what constitutes consent in the field of racialized sexuality—sexuality "structured in dominance" (Hall 1996a)—and under what conditions consent might be said to exist properly, to be thrown into crisis, or to be rendered virtually ineffective. As such, it is also a commentary on the nature of coercion and the scale at which its consideration will finally be posed. At the heart of this conflict lies the historical memory of New World slavery and, in the Anglophone context, the centrality of three centuries of antimiscegenation statute to its formation, development, and transformation. The questions under pursuit, then: how might the refashioning of "race mixture" in the present conjuncture extend the range of racist power even as, or perhaps because, it changes its complexion? In concocting what is already a Whig's history of interracial intimacy in the United States, why would multiracialism go on to deny, against the weight of overwhelming evidence, that structures of coercion *never* were constitutive of the racial formation? What might this artful—and logically unnecessary—denial have to do with the uneasy ethical authorization of the multiracial project described above? Why, in other words, is a story about the progressive liberalization of U.S. society insufficient?

We shall see that contemporary multiracial discourse returns in patterned ways to the southern states of the colonial and antebellum periods, revisiting and revising the primal scene of sexual encounter between master and slave—white man, black woman—in order to find there not a tale of terror but a tale of romance. This propitious return to the origins of New World interracial sexuality, at the point of greatest difficulty, is cast as an intervention on the pessimistic reduction of historical complexity afoot in popular and scholarly culture, a pernicious folklore that has hardened over the years into tracts of myth and stereotype. Beholden at present to this debilitating superstition, the "real" history of interracial intimacy must be delivered by the envoy of a new multiracial consciousness. But if our thinking a propos of this history has forfeited all dynamic movement, it is not, here and now, any longer a problem of white supremacy and anti-blackness. Quite the opposite, the forbidding truncation of memory—which reveals itself, in this rendition, as a crisis of faith and a failure of imagination—is located squarely within an atavistic black social psychology. In response, the task of politicos in the multiracial movement and scholars in the field of multiracial studies takes on the character of corrective "surgery" (Root 1992b), its methods running the gamut from orthopedics to electroshock therapy.

Stephens

What, then, is the distorted image of interracial sexual encounter to which black community finds itself enthralled, so long after the dawning of a new, post-*Loving* era? To address this question, we can look to several recent historical accounts published in the field of multiracial studies. These "new multiracial histories," as I will call them, reiterate strikingly similar arguments whose net effect is to contravene "pessimism." More specifically, they take aim at black feminist critiques of sexual politics in the history and historiography of racial slavery in order to undermine their signal contributions to knowledge. In our first example, *On Racial Frontiers: The New Culture of Frederick Douglass, Ralph Ellison, and Bob Marley* (1999), cultural critic Gregory Stephens charts a history of the "repressed" interracial dimensions of U.S. culture and society through extended meditation on several iconic figures of mixed black–white racial "heritage": Frederick Douglass, Ralph Ellison, and Bob Marley. These figures are reassigned from their previous reputation as heroes of black history to a new standing as "integrative ancestors . . . who can be claimed by more than one ethno-racial group" and who, in their own lifetimes, demonstrated "multiple allegiances *in which no one group is either centered or excluded*" (x, 7). Stephens describes his endeavor as an alternative to viewing the history of our present in the simplest of terms, a tendency particular to certain "colored" parties and that regards the nature of power relations within the matrices of race, class, gender, and sexuality. More precisely, it regards the reach of power, its absoluteness, its uniformity, and its capacity to totalize zones of contact. Importantly, the text is written in direct response to a collective disposition displayed symptomatically in the U.S. college classroom, the site of so much hope (or despair) for the future. In recounting his experience as an instructor at the University of California in the late 1990s, Stephens writes dismayingly:

> In California, as in the larger world, demographic shifts and multiple networks of economic and cultural exchange are *leveling out the long period of European dominance.* Some people, terrified of that change, try to protect a privileged position for European people and culture. *Others* seem terrified of a world without a European/white "other" against which to define themselves. . . . Conventional wisdom has it that our educational texts are still relentlessly Eurocentric, an opinion [my own] students voice reflexively. And yet almost all of them have emerged (in California, mind you) from a "reaction cycle" in higher education which has *inverted* previous racial mythologies. These students have absorbed a worldview in which a binary opposition between an oppressive white center, and marginalized "people of color" who

occupy heroic "sites of opposition," is so complete that *historical interracial relations short of rape and genocide are unimaginable.* (6; emphasis added)

Here we have, in template, some of the central postulates of multiracial discourse: (1) the supposed demise of global white supremacy or attenuation of antiblackness and the concomitant empowerment of blacks—twin developments miraculously devoid of *struggle;* (2) the shift in attention from white *retrenchment* to a purported black *resentment;* (3) the translation of *skepticism* regarding the prospects of social change into a *refusal* to believe in its very possibility; and (4) the reinscription of this refusal as active *resistance* to change, often with regressive implications for politics and policy. In this schema, it is black people in particular who prove guilty of such charges (hence the singular need to reimagine erstwhile giants of black history as "integrative ancestors"), even if ramifications for people of color more generally are occasionally mentioned. In examining the unwillingness or inability of white supremacy's chief targets to allow for an existence beyond its dominion and, more to the point, to accept inspiration from nominal exceptions to the rule, multiracial discourse produces what is, in effect, a study in the psychopathology of the oppressed. What remains inexplicable—or what is simply explained away—is *the problem of black consent*, a point that incurs discomfort not only for the slaveholder of old but also for proponents of the crisis-ridden project of U.S. nation-building in the post–civil rights era. Thus, what at first seems to be an exploration of consent in the sexual domain, a study of antebellum *interracial sexual politics*, proves to be freighted with cumbersome questions of consent in the broader political field, a field in which a *politicized interracial sexuality* today looms large. As a result, the inquiry—which often looks to be an inquisition—serves to obfuscate rather than to clarify the scalar relations between differing levels of coercion and consent.

On first blush, Stephens would seem to argue that people of color in the post–civil rights era are merely lagging behind the times, unable to recognize the true advances that "demographic shifts and multiple networks of economic and cultural exchange" have wrought to their collective benefit. Put this way, the need would be only to acknowledge the shift in conditions under which "interracial relations," in the broadest sense, now transpire. Whereas "rape and genocide" may have monopolized the realm of "interracial relations" during the "long period of European dominance," in the contemporary context of "leveling out"—characterized by a "reaction cycle" of militant black resistance—a broader spectrum of relations is enabled. Any demonstrable reluctance to appreciate this world-historical transformation is attributed to a pervasive (we might say "equal-opportunity") fear, one cutting across social divisions otherwise etched in stark contrast by the color line. "Some people," presumably whites, "protect a privileged position for European people and culture" in the face of gains made against "European dominance" by the new social movements in a process we have generally come to understand as racial "retrenchment" (Crenshaw 1988). "Others," presumably blacks, find themselves "terrified of a world without a European/white 'other' against which to define themselves." The latter fear—the fear of blacks to live in a world *without* European dominance—constitutes the focus of Stephens's scholarly attention and attempts to present itself as the logical correlate and ethical equivalent of the former—the fear of whites to live in a world *without* European dominance. If the leveling out of European dominance is both a welcome change (and an undeniable fact)[1] and the redoubled efforts of those committed to preserving it represent only a "residual" or "vestigial" conservative countertendency in need of further challenge, then it is the fear of change demonstrated by those others on the opposite end of the binary that actually retards the very leveling out that most directly benefits them, at least in the material sense. In other words, if the adherents of white supremacy and antiblackness present only a lingering defense against their relative loss of collective power, then the reticence exhibited by blacks toward that same historical reconfiguration is held to present a greater, indeed *hegemonic*, threat: as Stephens says, the position "achieves an instant legitimacy."

There are several sleights of hand at work in this construal, not least of which is the gainsaying of the structural power of white supremacy and antiblackness and the renewed vigor with which many of its dimensions are being reconstructed at present (Bonilla-Silva 2003). We have noted, as well, that there is scant evidence to support the notion that black people are, as it were, "terrified of a world without a white/European 'other' against which to define themselves," evidence whose absence is compensated for by a selective reading, at times a baldly willful misreading, of the critical literature, examples of which are addressed in this chapter. It is important first to note the *conceptual* problem inherent to any assertion of equivalence between what are elsewhere called positions of oppressor and oppressed or dominant and dominated, a conflation that insidiously rewrites "difference-in-and-as-hierarchy" (Spillers 2003) as difference without relations of power. (This conflation, as we have already seen, often takes the form of a rewriting of "race" in the more amiable, though no less problematic, terms of "ethnicity" or "culture" [Omi and Winant 1994].) Given the veritable library of eloquent and erudite research published on the topic in the past generation alone, one would think it quite clear that the trouble posed by white supremacy and antiblackness is *not* one of simple self-definition, a banal politics of identity formation. This is the case not only because *self*-definition has been the historic prerogative forcefully arrogated by the European/white (who has, in fact, served as the minor term, the defining other to no one) but also because of the structural inequalities that have made such arrogation possible, the disjuncture between the claims of established power and the claims of those it continually dispossesses.

That being said, the present quarrel seems to have less to do with the welfare of blacks after the leveling out of European dominance than with the standing of whites, or perhaps nonblacks more generally—that is to say, their prospects for *moral* deliverance from historic culpability. The genius of this reckoning, however, lies in its surrogacy. The issue of white deliverance is broached under the rubric of "the interracial" in a pathetic (as in "affecting" or "moving") defense against defamation from all quarters "regardless of color." But since it has been established that European dominance has leveled out, the ostensibly universal imperative is lodged particularly against the rancor of those others of the European/white, which is to say blacks. The recovery or resurrection of the interracial is, in this way, proffered as an evolutionary historical schema driven by a developmental psychology, maturing from an early state of conflict and division (in which blacks remain fixated while whites increasingly transcend) to a state of cooperation and "synthesis" (for which our "integrative ancestors" and others living "on racial frontiers" are especially well disposed). The issue thus remains contemporary, a challenge to the *current* sentiments of blacks, but not without expanding to mitigate the *historical* impression of how bad things were, back then, "in slavery days." The latter is a much more difficult undertaking, of course, given that even the neoconservative movement, while touting the splendors of colorblindness and the obsolescence of affirmative action policies or civil rights enforcement more generally, will concede, however disingenuously, that the state of the union was, once upon a time, less than ideal. It is curious that in a quest to recover the moral rectitude of whites in the post–civil rights era, the multiracial project does not simply cut its historical losses, attempt to gain distance toward the past, and proclaim the arrival of a new and improved whiteness freed from the old-fashioned evils of antimiscegenation. It does this much of the time, but that fact only contributes to the awkwardness of its attempted historical demolition.

The following passage from Stephens is typical of the displacement in multiracial discourse from a containment of the historical critique of (and opposition to) white supremacy and antiblackness to the reinscription of such critique (and opposition) as the pathological rejection of interraciality:

The sheer terror which many American intellectuals exhibit toward the prospect of being called optimistic or utopian about race relations is a psychosocial phenomenon that is "ripe for the picking." This discourse seems to be driven by a belief in white racism as a sort of biological inheritance. Those who declare for the "permanence" of (white) racism and the impermeability of the Racial Divide acquire an instant legitimation: they assume that they have, and are widely assumed to have, the weight of history on their side. People who consider themselves progressive (or radical) wind up in a reactionary position quite similar to white supremacist thought: resistance to, repression of, and pathologizing of "interracial life"—the denial of the very possibility of an interraciality which residents on racial frontiers have adopted by choice. (15)

Stephens forcibly aligns the cause of the interracial with optimism regarding the passing away of white racism (an optimism not only of the will but also of the intellect) and seeks to establish pessimism or cynicism (terms deployed not to describe but to deride radical critique) on that score as the effective reincarnation of white supremacist thought.[2] Again, Stephens's formulation is characteristic of the politics of multiracialism; however, in order for him to make such a claim, several basic contentions must be held entirely beyond question.

First, the argument regarding the "permanence of (white) racism" is driven by a belief in "racism as a sort of biological inheritance." Stephens never proceeds to make this argument by returning to either the text from which the phrase is glossed (Bell 1992) or the field of academic inquiry—critical race theory (CRT)—in which it is situated. The footnote in which CRT is addressed, and summarily dismissed, reads: "Claims for the 'permanence' of racism that *infer* a theory of white racism as a biological inheritance. . ." (239n11; emphasis added). And it is accompanied by citations of works by Derrick Bell, Andrew Hacker (who is not a CRT scholar per se but whose work is cited by those who are), Lani Guinier, and Mari Matsuda. Although an overview of the field of CRT is beyond the scope of the present study, suffice it to say that were Stephens to actually present a *reading* of the scholarly enterprise he writes off, he would find his point untenable. As such, it is sustained only by assertion.

Second, pessimism toward the demise of white supremacy and anti-blackness implies in some way a belief in or an argument for "the impermeability of the Racial Divide." In fact, it does not, and for at least two reasons. First, there is no necessary relationship between the two postulates (because the Racial Divide can be permeable while white supremacy and antiblackness remain robust) and, additionally, the second claim (re the impermeability of the Racial Divide) is deeply ambiguous in its own right. That is to say, it is unclear whether this ascribed imperviousness is put forward by the authors in question as descriptive (i.e., the divide *cannot* be breached) or as normative (i.e., the divide *should not* be breached). More to the point, Stephens fails to indicate where or how those purportedly pessimistic scholars of race and racism under scrutiny actually deny (i.e., commit a descriptive failure) or render monolithically pathological (i.e., issue a normative judgment) the pervasive "crossing of the color line" that he hopes to document in his own study. To insist on this point, then, is to reduce the complexity of a diverse critical project, to evade rather than to engage the questions and concerns raised therein. It is, moreover, to issue pejorative allegations about the intellectual effort that cannot be supported in the text.

Third, arguments regarding the "permanence of (white) racism" rely on mere assumptions rather than solid historical ground. Again, even a cursory review of the writing published under the auspices of CRT (or ethnic studies, a field that Stephens caricatures in neoconservative parlance as "oppression studies" and "ethnic cheerleading") would make clear the error of this point. In fact, the scholarly work that Stephens groups under the ill-famed banner of pessimism—because such work understands racism in its structural dimensions and across its astonishingly long historical trajectory—is largely consistent, substantiated, and persuasive, far more so than Stephens's counterargument, which proceeds by obvious leaps of logic and substitutes epithet for evidence.

Fourth, and finally, there is no way *both* to recognize *and* to interrogate "the interracial" other than through recourse to the nomenclature of pathology; in other words, one cannot think critically about the ways that "interracial life" is structured by relations of power without denigrating multiracial people or interracial sexuality as such. On that score, we must mark the distance between the phobic relation to interracial sexuality (particularly sexual contact with blacks) that characterizes white supremacy and the well-founded fear of systematic interracial sexual violence found in a certain black common sense. If the urgency born of the latter fear tends to animate (or even dominate) the analyses of race and sexuality developed by black activists and intellectuals, it hardly stands as evidence that blacks fear "interracial life" as such, or, if it is feared by blacks, that it is feared *in the same ways* and *for the same reasons* that whites (or other nonblacks) do. Even if it were the case that blacks did fear interracial life in the same ways and for the same reasons as whites, it would only suggest that blacks share a common phobic relation to blackness, a condition otherwise known as negrophobia.[3] From that angle, the problem is not one of "racialism" in general, as Stephens would have it, but one of antiblackness in particular.

Having outlined the arguments that Stephens foregoes in order to collapse pessimism toward the permanence of white racism with both a theory of racism as a *biological* property of whites and a "resistance to, repression of, and pathologizing of 'interracial life,'" I now want to highlight what seems to me his central concern. We find it housed under the sign of "multiracial redemption" and the boundless role this term plays within the thematic of historical progress: from "interracial" to "multiracial" to "transracial," onward to the telos of "postracialism" or "nonracial democracy" (1, 3, 6). For Stephens, the subjects of his study, our "integrative ancestors," are of utmost importance today because (1) they stand as paragons of an ongoing and much-needed black freedom struggle and (2) they stand as paragons of an ongoing and much-needed black freedom struggle who articulated "a vision which, although focused upon the theme of 'black liberation', insisted that black freedom could only be achieved through the more inclusive project of multiracial democracy or multiracial redemption" (64; emphasis added). Black liberation is, then, worthy of its name only when it reaches beyond itself; the value of the struggle is its potential to become something else. In itself and for itself, black liberation is a moribund political project. My interest is not to debate the merits of Stephens's contention about this troika's collective social vision. To that end, Stephens's interpretation betrays a deep familiarity with these luminaries of political, literary, and cultural history. Rather, I am asking after the *uses* to which such historical revision is put in the present; the *position* of enunciation from which it is produced and, in turn, helps to fashion; the possible *audiences* of its lines of address; and the political *initiatives* that it enables or disables.

To that end, we might ask a few preliminary questions about the logical implications of his grounding terms. To begin, we note that *On Racial Frontiers* is framed—from cover to cover—as an intervention on contemporary racial discourse. As several of the esteemed reviewers note in the endorsements gracing the back cover of the paperback edition: "Stephens's book provocatively challenges the pieties of today's identity politics. . . ." "This is a bold work of cultural studies. . . ." "*On Racial Frontiers* is daring. . . . Gregory Stephens breaks new ground. . . . Readers will come to think differently . . . they will be challenged to reconsider their own relations to race." What is the context and rationale of Stephens's intervention, its raison d'être? What is the nature of such "pieties of identity politics," those conventions of thought and feeling and practice that are to be challenged, taken to task? What, in other words, defines the boldness and daring of the text, and how or why is such an evaluation of his project offered as commendation?

We already have a sense of things, but let us look in more detail. As noted, Stephens establishes himself at the outset as an analyst of "American intellectuals" (and the students they supposedly indoctrinate—he speaks at several points of students "regurgitating" "racial mythology" [5]), specifically those working in the fields of ethnic and cultural studies. As such, he endeavors to present an alternate history of "race relations"—what he calls a "complex history of racial ambiguity" (6)—and a commentary on a "psychosocial phenomenon" through which "people who consider themselves progressive (or radical) wind up in a reactionary position" (15). In addition to historical scholarship, then, this work is also an attempt at political judgment, a remapping or reconfiguration of the political spectrum insofar as race produces distortion in our critical assessments. This judgment is twofold: it entails, on the one hand, a reevaluation of erstwhile progressives (or radicals) as reactionaries and, on the other, a reevaluation of erstwhile reactionaries as progressives (or radicals). In the process, Stephens suggests that one's true political location, at least with respect to "race relations," is determined not by one's relation to white supremacy and antiblackness or to black liberation struggle but by one's stance on "interraciality," that is, whether one contributes to its repression or its liberation qua recognition. Thus we are introduced to the murky relationship between interraciality and what Stephens, following philosopher K. Anthony Appiah, calls "racialism":

> The debate about "race" is often polarized, in public sphere discourse, in such a way that those who insist that racialism should be resisted "regardless of

color" will be beaten about the head with something called "history," and accused of being naïve, if not reactionary. This context has impressed upon me the need for a truly historicized identity politics: the need to move beyond action–reaction cycles, and towards a synthesis: a reenvisioning of his-story as our-story. This is not to erase the history of "race," or the endurance of racial formations. But it is an insistence on the need to understand that our very conceptions of "race" grew out of interracial contexts—and most specifically, with the *repression of the interracial*, in order to construct racial privilege. The notion of racial privilege has roots in white supremacist thought, but it is increasingly used now *across the spectrum*, whether in overt or covert form. (1–2; emphasis added)

The polarization of this debate, its construction as a binary between "those who insist that racialism should be resisted" and those who beat them about the head, will be left intact by Stephens. In fact, it will prove indispensable to his arguments, both logically and rhetorically. Before addressing this point, however, let us pause to consider several things. We see, for one, how it is that Stephens positions himself and his intellectual progenitors as beset ("beaten about the head . . . accused") and, further, how this condition of being under siege is both understandable and undeserved. That is to say, Stephens concedes that race exerts a historical force, and that "racial formations" endure, but insists nonetheless that he and his cohort are neither naïve nor reactionary for resisting racialism "regardless of color." In fact, he maintains that his endeavor is actually *more* sophisticated, indeed *more* progressive, than those who would cast aspersion in his direction. For those who would make false accusations or browbeat the critics of racialism with a mythologized history reveal themselves to be habitual collaborators in "the repression of the interracial" and, according to the same logic, therefore committed to "the notion of racial privilege"—a generalization or, rather, because white supremacy is in decline, a confiscation of white supremacist thought. Ipso facto, to undo the repression of the interracial, to recover it for the history of consciousness, is to contribute to "the troubling of racialism" (3), to undermine the stanchion upon which the concept of race is built, and in that spirit, to ferret out "racial privilege" wherever its notion might be found hiding, "whether in overt or covert form." Yet, while this nominally nonpartisan investigation authors a general warrant in search of covert racialism, it is clear that what must be "troubled" or "resisted" in the name of "the interracial" is the notion of *black* racial privilege.

The analytic license granted by the notion of covert racialism is supplemented by the fact that racialism as such is never defined in Stephens's study. The footnotes that follow upon its introduction point, as expected, to the work of Appiah (1993), but a working definition is curiously deferred to those who might be ambitious enough to consult the bibliographic material in detail. Of course, Stephens's use of racialism may be perfectly consonant with Appiah's formulation, and in the broader scheme of things, it seems clear that they are, to large extent, fellow travelers, theoretically and politically. However, it is not simply the lack of rigor in Stephens's conceptual framework that concerns me at this point (though see below on this point). Rather, I mention the indefiniteness of so central a term in his study—and its complete obfuscation when appearing incognito (i.e., as a "covert form")—in order to discuss rhetorical strategy. From the start, Stephens's argument follows a circular itinerary: racialism is asserted to be at the root of the problem of racial privilege that black liberation struggle (and antiracism more generally) seeks to challenge, and therefore, racialism is its proper target of political criticism; yet, because racialism is never directly conceptualized, it can be used interchangeably with pliable notions like "the repression of interraciality," and if found guilty of such repression or its proxy (pessimism), black liberation can thereby be *turned against itself.* Squaring the circle, then, one can assert that black liberation is true to form if and only if it exhibits the requisite optimism toward its aims and objectives, if and only if such optimism is derived exclusively from the promise of interracial life, whose recognition entails, by definition, an entirely contradictory ratification and repudiation of racialism—seeing race *in its mixture* only to not see racial difference at all, a claim that is belied by its own assumption of the prior purity of race.

Yet, if "the sheer terror which many American intellectuals exhibit toward the prospect of being called optimistic or utopian about race relations is a psychosocial phenomenon that is 'ripe for the picking,'" then Stephens seems nonetheless incapable of pulling it from the proverbial branch. It is suggested that "this discourse seems to be *driven by a belief* in white racism as a sort of biological inheritance," but there is a rather transparent breakdown in the hypothesis. The discourse of pessimism about "race relations" (or "cynicism about interracial relationships" [239n10]) exhibits terror toward "the prospect of being called optimistic or utopian"—that is, the relation between terror and pessimism; one discourses in a pessimistic register as evidence of a palpable fear. Yet, this discursive-affective complex (Stephens's "psychosocial phenomenon") is, at root, "driven by a *belief*." However, the belief in question, Stephens's forced association notwithstanding, is not specific to the proper *location* of white racism but rather, as is suggested by Stephens in the following sentence, to its supposed *permanence*. At this level, we find a possible explanation for the terror that Stephens finds on wide display. The "prospect of being called optimistic or utopian" would suggest a betrayal of a deeply held belief, or more precisely, it would evidence an extant crisis of faith about which one is either unaware or unwilling to admit.

Such a reading is supported by Stephens's earlier claim that many people of color "seem terrified of a world without a European/white 'other' against which to define themselves." It seems supported by the following statement as well:

> One must take seriously the psychological realities of students who are often deeply invested in "racial" definitions of personal and collective identity. . . . An upsurge in voluntary segregation (or ethnic self-affirmation) is probably an inevitable consequence when national identities are writ on such a large scale [considering the massive population and vast territory of the United States]. "Racial" identity can be an attractive alternative when national identity is too grand to grasp, or has been written off as "the white man's country" to begin with. (6–7)

One should not be led astray by the rapid oscillation between the mention of difficulties attendant to U.S. national identity supposed here to be inherent to its geographical expanse ("writ on such a large scale," "too grand to grasp") and those attributed to more contingent and subjective factors ("written off"). Regardless of the problems that this formulation presents, it makes a consistent overall point: *"racial" identity stands in for national identity*, whether that national identity is unattainable or undesirable, where both explanations suggest a psychology operating at too small a scale, better known as small-mindedness. It seems that race identity stands in for nation as its improper substitute—a proxy marking a thwarted imagination—since it is qualified here by scare quotes, whereas national identity—difficult though it may be to achieve or accept—clearly is not. More to the point, in both cases, it is people of color who either fail or refuse to attain "Americanness" that is there for the taking provided one has the aptitude or fortitude to take it. Hence, "voluntary segregation" enters as the uncomplicated underside of "ethnic self-affirmation." Yet, for all of this, it does not seem that "ethnic self-affirmation" is the target of Stephens's critique; nor is it the continued or resurgent segregation of people of color in its new voluntary mode. Continuing along the early pages of his study, we find a more telling delineation of the problem at hand:

> I write from within an era and a geographical space in which changing demographics has radically shifted the nature of this debate. . . . But whereas tensions in Europe have centered on the exclusion, or assimilation, of nonwhites, among younger Californians, the tension has often centered on whether or not to "allow" whites to participate in multiethnic coalitions. This tension derives from a racial mythology, widely taught with institutional support, in which whites are portrayed as collective oppressors, and "people of color" as collective victims. (Although this can be read as tongue-in-cheek, it is barely a parody of the level at which this mythology is often regurgitated by students). (5)

Of course, "tensions" in California, as in the United States generally, have also centered on "the exclusion, or assimilation, of nonwhites," rendering the contrastive "whereas" immediately flawed. However, the effect of contrasting tactical debates about the terms of coalition among young progressive political activists with the reactionary racial adjudication of citizenship in "Fortress Europe" (Gilroy 1991) is to equate the frustrated ambitions of whites in the United States to "participate" to their liking in the political (and eventually social, cultural, and sexual) lives of black people with the plight of postcolonial immigrants displaced to the metropole. This metaphoric transfer resonates with the aforementioned slippage between Stephens's designation of racialism as a pernicious ideology and his otherwise inchoate campaign against "racial privilege." It has the effect not only of rendering Stephens's project equivalent to political struggles against neocolonialism but also of drawing them into a common orbit, identifying them as the same cause. The correlative effect is to identify the racist convulsions of an embattled European white supremacy with the wariness or reluctance of black activists to affirm the value of interracial encounter with whites.

But even this remains within the terms of mystification that Stephens's text advances. If we look again at the quote just cited, we see the core of the issue, the source of the "tension" that his synthetic approach seeks to resolve: "This tension *derives from a racial mythology*, widely taught with institutional support, in which whites are portrayed as collective oppressors, and 'people of color' as collective victims." Is this "racial mythology" another way to speak the name of "racialism"? Is it synonymous with "the repression of the interracial" mentioned at earlier points? This answer would seem to be both yes and no. Yes, to the extent that Stephens considers this all part of the same psychosocial phenomenon to be challenged, debunked, and disappeared. No, to the extent that the pivotal discrepancy at the heart of the concept of the interracial reveals itself now in plain view. As the various passages under consideration demonstrate, by Stephens's own account, the recalcitrance of blacks toward an affirmative politics of the interracial is *not* cut from the same cloth as the historical project of white supremacist antimiscegenation. The latter is bound up with mythologies of racial purity too well known to warrant rehearsal here (more on this in later chapters). The former, however, does not require notions of racial purity but rather centers itself on issues of domination and hierarchy and resistance to or transformation of both. More to the point, the former focuses on the systemic negation of the will and value of the dominated under the reign of white supremacy and antiblackness, while noting, at all points, that "miscegenation"—whether considered in the sexual field or the sphere of culture—is in no way incompatible with the maintenance of its structure and the extension of its violence. Indeed, it has been shown that "interracial life" has been essential to the construction of white supremacy and antiblackness not through crude and straightforward repression or denial but by way of a complex regulation and management (Moran 2001).

Despite recurrent commentary on the racial or cultural purism of blacks, I submit that Stephens is actually uninterested in such debates. Or rather, he takes interest in them only insofar as they serve as proxy for another issue that never fails to return to the surface of the text. Recall his earlier statements: "These students have absorbed a worldview in which a binary opposition between an oppressive white center, and marginalized 'people of color' who occupy heroic 'sites of opposition,' is so complete that historical interracial relations short of rape and genocide are unimaginable" (6). This is a statement about purity ("a binary opposition . . . so complete"), but the purity is not racial or cultural; it is political and ethical. Thus, the key terms are not "white" and "people of color" but rather "oppressive" and "heroic." What is at stake is the nomination of whites as oppressive. In the closing section of the book, Stephens writes of his young multiracial daughter beginning to learn of the history of racial slavery in the Americas and drawing an "association of whiteness with cruelty" (224). His daughter asks: "Does Dad own slaves?" And, more generally, "White people are bad, right Mom?" Stephens waxes pedagogic in response:

> How do you teach a child about the injustices of slavery, without painting all whites as being guilty of the atrocities of this system, or portraying all blacks as its victims? Is it possible to teach this history without forwarding the tendency to think in black and white, or divide the world between whites and "people of color"? When I hear questions about slavery and its legacy, from either my child or my students, I have two thoughts. I think that it must be important to know that, at the height of slavery, only 10 percent of whites were slaveholders. And I simultaneously think of the voices of students

I have heard at Berkeley, who said that they did not want some white teacher trying to tell them that things were really not so bad, after all. So, I know that there is no correct way of telling this integrative history. And I know that, in this era, it is usually not possible to separate the message from the messenger. (225–26)

"*It must be important to know* that, at the *height* of slavery, *only* 10 percent of whites were slaveholders." What would such knowledge do? Is such a statistic supposed to diminish the centrality of slavery to the foundation of the United States, to its polity, its legal system, its economy, its culture? Why, in other words, is this ratio important, indeed *necessary*, to know? With this—a statement on behalf of whites, not a comment on the position and condition of blacks—Stephens summarizes a more expansive point made in the first chapter of his study: "Just how small this slaveholding elite actually was may surprise us, given the endurance of *Gone With the Wind*–type images of Southern life, and the stranglehold that slaveholders had on national policy for almost a century. . . . In the late antebellum era, only about 10 percent of Euro-Americans owned slaves. What was the attitude of the other 90 percent? This was of course the audience which abolitionists sought to 'convert.' We need to know something about their historical interactions with Afro-Americans" (35–36). We do, in fact, know quite a bit about these "historical interactions"—including the *structural relations* between, and not just the *attitudes* of, blacks (slave and free) and whites (slaveholding or not, including the abolitionists)—rendering the feint of historical scarcity and the novelty of Stephens's contribution on that score mistaken at best, disingenuous at worst. It is worth quoting further his sketch of antebellum and colonial history as it serves as a model reiterated by other scholars examined later:

> This history of non-elites is not so easy to describe in black-and-white. The
> further back we look in American history, in fact, the lower the percentage
> of slaveholders becomes, and the less distinction we find between blacks and
> poor whites, who often came to the Americas as indentured servants. In the
> colonial era there was extensive economic, cultural, and sexual exchange

among poor blacks and whites. The existence of interracial alliances, and elite attempts to destroy these alliances, is an old story. . . . Elite whites often tried to stop or limit interracial interaction, and not only of a sexual variety. . . . Some of the most restrictive laws against interracial congress seem to have been passed either in reaction to or fear of . . . multiracial rebellions. The strategy, writes [historian Edward] Morgan, was to "separate dangerous free whites from dangerous slave blacks by *a screen of racial contempt.*" (36)

However, the "old story" about racialization as an elite attempt to destroy "interracial alliances" through a divide-and-conquer strategy has since been revealed as a racial mythology in its own right, a narrative that attempts to minimize the scope of white supremacy and discount the formative nature of racial slavery for the entire white population, across its class divisions (Martinot 2002). Yet Stephens's point is not simply to redeem or recover a history of solidarity-in-rebellion, an interracial alliance that might yet make common cause against the "long-standing white power structure" (Byrd 1996). Rather, he is, in the final analysis, at pains to debunk "stereotypes" about the slaveholding elite itself insofar as the history of that elite implicates white people in general and white men in particular:

[Regarding the antebellum era], racial mythology and the evidence do not always match. Significantly, most Southern miscegenation took place in cities and towns, not on plantations or farms, as Eugene Genovese emphasizes. Such interracial relations often began as a form of concubinage, but court records show that they sometimes evolved into a more permanent character. We have, even more importantly, the testimony of ex-slaves themselves, which indicate a range of behaviors in antebellum miscegenation: from white men violating black women, and selling their offspring into slavery, at one end of the spectrum, to a surprising number of white men who engaged in lifelong partnerships with black women, and who recognized, nurtured, and freed their offspring. Our view of this issue is slanted by a selective history that has been transformed into racial mythology, and then projected back on to history. As a result, stereotypes that all sexual relations between white men and black women are a form of rape have continued to the present day. . . .

Just as evidence of historical attraction between white women and black men has been largely tuned out [Stephens claims that "substantial numbers of white women and black men came together of their own free will" (37)], our view of relations between white men and black women have been reduced to a myth of original sin—a collective rape which caused a national stain, a racial guilt which can never be washed away. A more balanced view would acknowledge that sexual relations between whites and blacks almost always took place under unequal power relations, but on a spectrum. . . . And one must concede that, at the far end of the spectrum from rape, there were some interracial relationships that grew out of, or led to, love (38).

Within this spectrum, "rape," "violation," and "concubinage" are awkwardly counterposed to "relations . . . [of] a more *permanent* character," "*lifelong* partnerships," and, of course, "love." But the temporal criterion distinguishing the latter from the former can only collapse upon consideration that concubinage is a relation of "a more permanent character," even a "lifelong" one, and, further, that rape or violation need not be short-term or solitary events. Moreover, one cannot miss the terribly euphemistic description of enslavement as a "partnership" or the related reference to "love" as if its presence somehow cancels or suspends "unequal power relations."[4] Perhaps it does in the mind of the dominant given that Stephens is interested here in a "range of behaviors" or "attitudes" and emotional states *among slaveholding white men.* This shift of critical emphasis from the *structural* to the *empirical* and a shift from the *consent* of blacks (and black women in particular) to the *desire* of whites (and white men in particular) disguises a conceptual framework and an ethical orientation and enables the insolvent discussion into which Stephens draws his readers.

Among other things, the insolvency has to do with questions of scale. For instance, how does Stephens define "a form of rape" under the structures of racial slavery? How does his account determine the mutual consent of the parties at hand? Are we to conclude that blacks (whether enslaved or "free") were not in the British colonies or the antebellum United States or the New World more generally "of their own free will"; that they were not enslaved or, later, barred from the institution of citizenship or systemically terrorized by state-sanctioned violence "of their own free will"; were not in residence in this or that city or town "of their own free will"; on this or that plantation or farm "of their own free will"; under conscription as the object of property of this or that white person "of their own free will"; were not subjected by law to the scrutiny of any white person whatsoever as to their whereabouts "of their own free will"; but that, at the end of the day, they still enjoyed the legally binding and socially effective capacity to make a *meaningful* decision about whether, or on what terms, "sexual relations" would proceed between them and any white person whatsoever—elite or nonelite; rich, poor, or otherwise? Under such conditions, deliberations about the presence or absence of "mutual attraction" seem grossly beside the point, and assertions regarding "the very possibility of an interraciality which residents on racial frontiers have adopted by choice" (15) strike the reader as equally incongruous. Such deliberations or assertions require the bracketing out of social existence, shucking the materiality of history in favor of a transcendent and essential humanity that might announce itself *despite* the circumstances. Stephens speaks of relations between blacks and whites as if *both* parties involved were the self-possessed citizen-subjects of liberal democracy, interacting under the terms of the social contract rather than the terms of a fundamental inequality, a "racial contract" for which *there is no outside* (Mills 1998). The recourse to "mutual affection" dispenses with the political struggle to radically democratize the exclusive *conditions* of consent and contract guaranteed to propertied adult white males and installs in its place a patriarchal family romance.

By these means, Stephens's work contemplates an evasion of the ethical implications of this historical legacy. This evasion or extrication takes cover under the terms of contested cultural property and the racial designation of bodies in dispute. However, the pressure of the political dilemma underpinning the discussion about essentialism, authenticity, territoriality, purity, and so forth—from race to culture and back again—is never lost. The "instant legitimation" that Stephens spitefully ascribes to those "who declare for the 'permanence' of (white) racism"—and the foolishness of those who agree with them—redounds with this historic pressure, a force that is not felt simply because it can be assumed or asserted but because it has been demonstrated through painstaking intellectual labor against the weight of continued official denial. Amid Stephens's analytic commentary is thus a persistent return of the theme of multiracial redemption, attached as a rider on the moral high ground of black freedom struggle. In its distinction from "black liberation," "multiracial redemption" concerns finally the redemption (the deliverance or the rescue or, crucially, the *emancipation*) of whites: released from the association with "cruelty," absolved of their "racial guilt," acquitted for the crime of "collective rape." That blacks withhold such redemption is, on Stephens's account, experienced by whites as a form of oppression (i.e., their "exclusion" from political participation, the "divestment" of their [cultural] property, the "policing" of their social lives) *by way of* the "repression" of the existence of multiracial people. Bound by "a pain and anger rooted in the belief that black people have never 'gotten their due'" (34), blacks in the post–civil rights United States are, according to the author, ruthless, unforgiving, and bitter—a pathological resentment that discloses itself *through* the rejection of otherwise obvious empirical realities of racial and cultural fusion.

Yet, for all of the talk about the social benefits of reviving "integrative ancestors," evolving from a "selective history" (or "his-story") to a more balanced view ("our-story"), Stephens offers little in the way of recuperation for the history and heritage of white supremacy as something that whites and blacks (and perhaps others) can and should claim together. There is no mention of racial slavery or the institution of Jim Crow or the formation of the urban ghetto as an interracial "(co)creation" from which we might learn valuable lessons about "the true interrelatedness of black and white" in order to seek guidance here and now or to find inspiration for the future. Passing reference is made to the ways that truncated "oppositional thinking" supposedly "prevents those [diasporic Africans] who helped build the structures of modernity from claiming their rightful (co-) ownership" (23). But the thrust of Stephens's intervention is *not* to show Euro-American modernity just how black it really is. He is not, in other words, attacking pernicious myths of cultural or racial purity on the part of the white imagination. That project is assumed to be a fait accompli, the inevitable and well-nigh seamless effect of a multiracial history of black liberation from the bonds of white supremacy (from abolitionism to the modern civil rights movement). Given, then, the relative success of black claims to "(co-)ownership" within "the structures of modernity," the proper targets of criticism today, according to Stephens, are those elements of black community that cannot or will not accept the salutary truth of this mutual implication. His biting assessment:

> The most virulent opposition to the notion that people of mixed race can carve out an identity that is neither black nor white is now coming from Afro-Americans. Mixed-ethnicity children who do not have a black parent are not subject to the same "One Drop" rule, but for those with a black parent, there is often intense pressure to "cleave to the black," and accusations of racial betrayal if the individual chooses not to choose to be "only black." Surely it is a significant irony that, one century after Euro-Americans were trying to write mulattos out of existence, the repression is now coming from Afro-essentialists. It seems we are witnessing another instance of the construction of the "racial" out of the denial of the "interracial." (33)

It is all too easy to bog down in the wrong argument here. One could, for instance, argue that whites are, in fact, still largely opposed to the affirmation of multiracial identity or note that white acceptance of multiracial identities is conditional upon mixed-race people *not* claiming to be *white*, thereby leaving its mythic purity intact. Or one could demonstrate that contrary to Stephens's suggestion, black public opinion regarding multiracial identity is not particularly hostile, a point borne out even by Stephens's sources. One could cite, for example, the many contemporary studies that consistently find blacks far more accepting of interracial relationships and marriages or the wealth of historical evidence that finds black community to be the place where "people of mixed race" in the United States have largely made their home, to say nothing of the widely recognized "mixedness" of the black population itself. In short, one could make the case that denial of mixture has not historically been a black problem but a white one (Gordon 1997). This would all go toward disproving a spurious claim, but it misses entirely the point of its articulation.

Stephens is suggesting that in questioning the motive force and political trajectory of multiracialism, blacks *now* enforce the same "One Drop"
rule that whites *once* adhered to—a hundred years ago—but have since
collectively abandoned. That is, we are witnessing the emergence of a new
system of oppression, "the construction of the 'racial' out of the denial of
the 'interracial,'" not in addition to white supremacy but *in place of it*. However, the telling insistence that this regime change represents "a significant irony" undermines Stephens's entire diagnosis. For what lends this new
dispensation its irony is the fact that the agents of the current "denial of
the 'interracial,'" "Afro-Americans," were previously the targets of "antebellum antimiscegenation." That is, Stephens here implies that antimiscegenation is a historic component of white supremacy and antiblackness,
not an autonomous repression of mixture that blacks and whites might
commonly endorse on equal footing. If blacks were "now" to take up the
position occupied by whites "a century ago," they would have had to invert
the social order completely, reversing the terms of its "unequal power relations." For Stephens, it is enough to imagine it as to prove it. Nonetheless,
whatever pseudo-theories might be spun by "Afro-essentialists"[5] about
the imperative to maintain a mythic racial purity or cultural integrity in
the face of increased social intercourse—post–Jim Crow era—with whites
(and perhaps other nonblacks), the *political* questions embedded in any black
hostility or skepticism toward the new multiracial consciousness remain
unaddressed, whether they be published by professional black critics or
voiced in the pedestrian terms of common sense. It is not that such questions are simply dismissed or ignored but that their force is contained,
their significance disavowed as the critics—the messengers—are deformed
and distorted beyond recognition. We have seen how Stephens handles
this impasse, but he is not alone in his efforts. Let us consult another notable
text in the cul-de-sac in order to tease out some of the finer points of this
technique of prevarication.

Kennedy

Randall Kennedy's *Interracial Intimacies* (2003) is one of only a few book-
length treatments in the field of multiracial studies to date that addresses

interracial sexuality at any length. Among those, it commands perhaps the greatest authority not only because Kennedy is a well-credentialed academic—professor at the Harvard Law School and author of several critically acclaimed texts—but also because he is, to my knowledge, one of the first black scholars in this generation to pen a sustained argument advocating what he terms "a cosmopolitan ethos that welcomes the prospect of genuine, loving interracial intimacy" (35). This is not to say that other black intellectuals have not also welcomed "the prospect of genuine, loving interracial intimacy." Indeed, to declare for such has been one of the hallmarks of the black struggle for civil rights from at least 1787 onward (Birnbaum and Taylor 2000). Rather, I am suggesting that Kennedy's text is distinguished from other black critical commentary on the topic by the fact that Kennedy's text ascribes a determined opposition to interracial intimacy (or "repression of the interracial") to the very same black radical tradition that has often been its greatest proponent. Much like Stephens before him, the supposed opposition of those Kennedy appraises is more the effect of an unsustainable framing of debate than an honest and accurate portrayal of an articulate position circulated in the black public sphere.

On that score, consider that just prior to the description cited above, Kennedy offers quite different shorthand for his welcoming, cosmopolitan ideal: "one that evinces negligible attachment to inherited racial solidarities." We must add, of course, *any and all* "inherited racial solidarities," as this ostensibly equal-opportunity, colorblind neglect of racial solidarities is meant to arrest the historic black critique of white (supremacist) racial solidarity with a boomerang attack on black (egalitarian) racial solidarity. His opponents on this count, all of whom are black, are slotted into what he calls a "pluralist" camp "that encourages personal and communal identification along racial lines." Since the subject of interracial intimacies is broached in Kennedy's study for the task of "sorting out the type of racial community we really want" in order to "test uniquely the contours of our deepest beliefs and intuitions, fears and hopes about race, race relations, and the American future" (33), his positioning of opponents with respect to this cosmopolitan–pluralist divide involves stakes of considerable proportion: nothing less than national destiny. If, for Kennedy, "personal and communal identification along racial lines" leads inexorably to the terrors of "racial idolatry and racial authoritarianism" (35), in contradiction to the American credo, then pluralism becomes for him not only politically retrograde or morally reprehensible but also, as we saw in chapter 1, a source of un-American activities. However, Kennedy, like Stephens before him, can manage such pressurized connections only so long as the definition of operative terms—hastily drawn from David Hollinger's (2000) neoliberal treatise—gains no precision and the logical contortions that subtend his argument remain fully uncontested. And, like Stephens before him, a return to the antebellum era constitutes both the vestibule of his meditation and the point where it promptly founders on the interracial sexual territory between white men and black women.

In commenting on interracial sexuality in the early United States, Kennedy's task is not that of the historian. In this respect, he fails either to contribute new evidentiary material or to develop a novel interpretive schema for reassessing the available archive. Rather, Kennedy seeks to dispute the historical record in order to contest certain contemporary "misunderstandings" regarding the nature of interracial sexuality, particularly relationships between black women and white men within the slave estate. The source of misunderstanding is found in the work of several noted black feminist scholars, including the early writings of Angela Y. Davis (1981) and the more recent intervention of Saidiya Hartman (1997), work which, on Kennedy's gloss, holds that "there can have been no such thing as sexual intimacy between a black enslaved woman and any white man—a slave owner or overseer or even a mere stranger—because mutually desired sex requires *choice*, a power denied to slaves by bondage. According to this view, slavery created an extreme dependency that precluded the possibility of chosen as opposed to unwanted sex. As a result, *all* of the sex that took place between enslaved women and white men constituted some form of sexual assault" (Kennedy 2003, 41). Kennedy agrees that "mutually desired [by which he means consensual] sex requires choice," which is to say simply that he acknowledges that consensual sex requires consent. What he attempts to refute, at least initially, is the claim that consent was foreclosed by the conditions of slavery, correcting for its inattention to detail while chastising the unnecessary bleakness of its conclusion. We shall see that Kennedy not only caricatures the analyses of said black feminist critics but also, in lieu of a counterargument, bypasses altogether the inconvenient obstacles presented by their scholarship.

Because the complications of interracial intimacy—what Hartman calls the "inextricable link between racial formation and sexual subjection" (1997, 85)—cannot be convincingly countered within Kennedy's approach, the recourse to detail that is his wont undergoes a breakdown, pulling the disheveled argument into a naïvely empirical register that must discount structure (what Kennedy otherwise terms "constructive force" or "the totality of the circumstances" or, simply, "duress") in order to compose itself. Before demonstrating this, I want to highlight how, in the absence of any valid historical argument grounded in the appropriate evidentiary claims and in light of the resultant short circuits, Kennedy's position reduces to moral exhortation forwarded under the cover of academic finding. Demonstrating how Kennedy's rationale fails is a relatively straightforward task. The more difficult question to answer is, what is it about the "pessimism" of black feminist scholarship on the sexual politics of racial slavery that Kennedy, like his intellectual cohort, finds intolerable, so much so that he is willing not only to assert that the conditions of white supremacy and antiblackness have diminished of late sufficiently to disarm the gloomy view of interracial sexuality engendered by slavery (a sexuality sans intimacy) but also to insist that "even within these power differentials [of the slave regime], genuine affection characterized some sexual relationships between Black women and White men" (2003, 531fn11)? Why, to paraphrase Stephens, *must it be important* that we find "genuine affection" at this site of extremity, amid this organized violence, under the terms of this institutionalized brutality? Why, moreover, does the quest to discern interracial intimacy in the historic instance consistently proceed from a displacement of the structural dimensions of racial slavery, the very dimensions that hold the focus of much black feminist inquiry (and a good deal more black criticism otherwise uninformed by any feminist sensibility)? If interracial intimacy must be declared *in opposition to* the conditions of enslavement, *despite* their supposedly "deadening influence," then how is the former conceptualized in relation to the latter more generally?

In response to the last question, we examine several comments from Kennedy's opening chapter, "In the Age of Slavery." As noted, Kennedy is at pains to counter the claims of a certain black feminist history regarding the "extremity of power" exercised by the slaveholder and "the absolute submission required of the slave" (Hartman, quoted in Kennedy 2003, 532fn11). He is, in other words, attempting to demonstrate, or at least to speculate upon, the *limits* of the slave system's power of domination. Beyond this limit—whose locus proves frustratingly obscure—the agency of the slave herself was, we are told, able to affect significantly the conditions of captivity to alternate ends. Kennedy, in other words, proffers a narrative in which evidence of *agency* (evidence, that is, confirming an *assumption* of agency), however circumscribed or practically ineffective, is taken as a sign of *resistance*. More properly, this is a narrative of *resistant affection*, an insistence that the dehumanizing social order of racial slavery was unable to achieve its ultimate goal—"the absolute submission of the slave"—because it could not overcome the irresistible force of affection between men and women, "regardless of color." When all is said and done, a human is still a human, as it were, and the family romance of normative heterosexuality persists "even within" hierarchies that preclude for the captive all of the recognizable (social, political, economic, cultural, legal) trappings of "human being" in the modern sense. Here is Kennedy:

> The slave system *failed*, however, to perfect the domination that [Judge Thomas] Ruffin envisioned. It *failed* to bind the slaves so tightly as to deprive them of all room to maneuver. It *failed* to wring from them all prohibited yearnings. Slavery was, to be sure, a horribly oppressive system that severely restricted the ambit within which its victims could make decisions. But slavery did not extinguish altogether the possibility of choice. (43)

We might ask, what is the minimum ambit of decision making? What sort of system, if not slavery, would bind one so tightly as to deprive one of all "room to maneuver"? Need a system of domination be "perfect" in order for it to be legally binding or socially effective or politically determinant? Need the captive body be deprived of *all* room to maneuver for the situation to be considered one of extremity? Need the yearnings of slaves be wrung entirely from them for their prohibition to be considered a constitutive element of life? At what point does the quantitative measure of the slave's bondage become difference of a qualitative sort? What precisely is the "choice" available under slavery, and is it one worthy of belaboring, one whose sphere of influence is to be considered newsworthy? To put a finer point on it, why is the *categorical* discrepancy refused between the free and the enslaved, or more specifically, between the slave and the slaveholder? Is such refusal not tantamount to denying the very existence of slavery as a system that produced *slaves* rather than free people whose freedom was simply "severely restricted" or whose power was simply "severely limited" or who simply faced "difficult situations"? Kennedy continues:

> Bondage severely limited the power—including the sexual power—of slaves. But it did not wholly erase their capacity to attract and shape affectionate, erotic attachments of all sorts, including interracial ones. In a hard-to-quantify but substantial number of cases, feelings of affection and attachment between white male masters and their black female slaves somehow survived slavery's deadening influence. The great difficulty, in any particular instance, lies in determining whether sex between a male master and a female slave was an expression of sexual autonomy or an act of unwanted sex. The truth is that most often we cannot know for sure, since there exists little direct testimony from those involved, especially the enslaved women. (44)

The inability to quantify the "number of cases" or, indeed, to "know for sure" anything about them does not prevent the author from considering them nonetheless "substantial," and the paucity of direct testimony,[6] "especially [from] the enslaved women," does not stop the author from extrapolating wildly about said "feelings of affection and attachment" between them and their "white male masters." In fact, it is the void in its place—the great historic silence—that enables both the reiteration of longstanding alibis for white male sexual violence—what Hartman (1997) discusses skill-fully as the "ruses of seduction"—and the projection of this newfangled, though no less menacing, story about a maverick interracial intimacy that, almost undetectably, undermines the injunctions of white supremacy, serving not only as a sign of *agency* for enslaved women but a moment of their *resistance* as well. Their "sexual power" is expressed as the "capacity to attract"—and "somehow" to manipulate—the erotic attachments of white male slaveholders.

There is here an unsubtle shift in terms: agency is not in itself subversive; indeed, the entire slave system derives, in large part, from the agency of the enslaved (its capture, manipulation, redeployment, etc.) (Chandler 2000). Agency may be resistant or complicit or both, and it may or may not have practical effects in the world; all of this can only be determined contextually. Much more troubling than Kennedy's imprecision here, however, is his entirely uncritical suggestion about the "sexual power" of slaves. Is not one of the principal conceits of power to suggest that though the dominant may monopolize power political, economic, and social, the dominated nonetheless enjoy a wily aptitude for "getting their way" by other means, namely, the *ars erotica* of seduction? Is not one of the most pernicious elements of the proslavery discourse that the "attractiveness" of enslaved black women presents a threat of corruption to civilized white manhood and/or an internal guarantee against the excesses of state-sanctioned violence reserved for white slaveholders? The same quality that served as temptation was also, or alternately, taken to be that which would forestall the descent of slaveholding into unrestrained brutality, an essential rationalization for the upholding of white (male) impunity toward blacks, whether enslaved or nominally "free" (Hartman 1997).[7] Finally, was not the suggestion that enslaved black men might have the power to seduce white women (whether free or, in earlier periods, indentured) one of the prime alibis for the construction of regulatory or prohibitory statutes around interracial marriage and sexual relations from the seventeenth century onward (Bardaglio 1999)? In each case, the focus on the "sexual power" of slaves was undoubtedly a displacement of the *organized* violence consistently required of captivity and, further, a dissimulation of the *institutionalized* sexual power of slaveholders in particular (whose authority not only foreclosed the possibility of prosecution and militated against the extralegal reprisals but also contributed immeasurably to *their* "capacity to attract and shape affectionate, erotic attachments of all kinds." The asymmetry here approaches the incommensurable—how, after all, would a slave go on to "court" a master? How would such an exercise in self-objectification, supplementing structural availability with an affirmation of "willingness," rightly be called power?). This is no less the case simply because for Kennedy the "sexual power" of slaves is something to honor or celebrate rather than to fear.

Inconsistency is endemic to Kennedy's formulation. First, there is a world of difference between, on the one hand, "feelings of affection and attachment," however they may be described or accounted for, and on the other hand, the determination of "whether sex . . . was an expression of sexual autonomy or an act of unwanted sex" in any particular instance. Such feelings between parties may or may not have been present, for whatever duration, in whatever distribution, and they have no bearing on whether "sex" was "unwanted." In short, "desire" or "affection" does not equal "consent." More crudely still, wanting sex, as it were, or even participating in it, is not synonymous with permitting it or agreeing to it. Thus, that slaves were able to "attract and shape affectionate, erotic *attachments*" is of no consequence as to whether they were able to refuse (or allow or initiate) sexual encounter in any practically meaningful (i.e., legally codified and socially sanctioned) way. One is a question of "feelings," the other a question of the capacity for "consent." Beyond that, though, it is entirely debatable, and appears unlikely, to what extent the enslaved was able to shape "affectionate, erotic attachments" in ways that might designate an effective agency even in matters of the heart and mind. As Hartman (1997) demonstrates throughout her work, the captive body was, as an effect of its constriction and its dispossession, available for all manner of figuration and fantasy.

Quite aside from the question of consent (which we return to momentarily), Kennedy has no evidence whatsoever—it is not even scant—to substantiate his claim that "feelings of affection and attachment *between* white male masters and their black female slaves *somehow survived* slavery's deadening influence." It can only be conjecture if, as is the case, he is at an absolute loss—or feels no need—to substantiate this point from the evidentiary record, whether considering the legal documents left behind by white male slave owners or, more importantly, the testimony of enslaved black women. (Especially in the latter case, his evidence would have to contravene the vast majority of slave narratives that do exist and whose incisive commentary is strategically bracketed or disfigured beyond recognition in Kennedy's engagement, a gesture that recurs in the literature of multiracialism, as we will see again shortly. On this note, Stephens's nominal recourse to the testimony of ex-slaves, mentioned earlier, is no more founded. His "evidence," were he to consult it, would go overwhelmingly toward corroborating a quite different contention. Yet even in those instances where sources suggest that "affection . . . between white male masters and their black female slaves" was at play, they do not—and perhaps cannot—account for the way that gross power imbalances shaped or generated or sustained such feelings.)[8]

If Kennedy cannot speak for the enslaved black female regarding sexual encounter with the white male, and if she cannot speak for herself, of whom and for whom does Kennedy speak? The reversal of perspective is stunning:

> We can be sensitive to the plight of enslaved women, however, and still acknowledge that consensual sex, prompted by erotic attraction and other mysteries of the human condition, has occurred between subordinates and superiors in even the most barren and brutal settings. Evidence of consensual sexual intimacy within the confines of bondage is found in the unusual solicitude shown by certain masters toward slaves with whom they had sex and by whom they sired children. Freeing a slave mistress or the offspring of such a union, acknowledging paternity of or assuming financial responsibility for a slave's children, marrying a former slave—all of these are potentially telltale signs of affection. (45)

Consent within confinement: absent immediate interpersonal physical force, the *brutality of the setting* has, for Kennedy, no bearing whatsoever on the nature of sex. Truly a mystery of the human condition! In this manner, the question of *consent* on behalf of black women under slavery (which is too hard to establish anyway) are politely abandoned (we are, after all, "sensitive to the plight") in favor of excursus on the *affection*—the mental and emotional state—of slave-owning white men. The trouble with Kennedy's study would be acute if it stopped at this patent dislocation of black women's consent, evoking in order to expel black feminist contentions from the frame of analysis and refuting their critical purchase by merely rejecting their terms. And while we should not be altogether surprised that the subsequent argument begins to falter straight away, the unmitigated non sequitur that stands in for an answer to the disavowed black feminist interrogation pushes Kennedy's labors even more clearly outside the realm of intellectual endeavor, sterling credentials notwithstanding. "Evidence of consensual sexual intimacy . . . is found in the *unusual solicitude* shown by certain masters." Since it is the explicit task of the passage to show evidence, it is only appropriate to ask precisely what "consensual" means at this point of Kennedy's study. That is to say, if "consensual sex" can be determined *unilaterally*, as a show of kindness or concern on the part of *one*, the largesse or benevolence of the *dominant* one, then there seems little in the way of mutuality or reciprocity left in the concept. What is more, the "evidence" cited to establish the scandalous point—to wit, some masters were caring—can be accounted for by any number of motives (e.g., manumission for social, political, economic, or moral reasons), hardly "telltale signs of affection" or "unusual acts that probably betokened some variety of tender attachment" (46).[9] No matter, the point, and the desire it suggests, are taken.

Seen in this light, we are led to query whose interest is served—what desire is at work—in discovering "consensual sexual intimacy" (a telltale redundancy in Kennedy's terms, I think, since he defines "intimacy" as "mutually desired sex") where it cannot be substantiated, even within the brackets of the empirical? Which is to say, why does the author *insist* on its presence despite the lack of evidence and the claims (which are now rigorous scholarly findings) of black women? Why, to return to our guiding question, does it seem altogether insufferable to admit that, as Hartman (1997) avers, "the extremity of power and the absolute submission required of the slave render suspect or meaningless concepts of consent and will" (81)? Moreover, is there not, somewhere in this focus on the slave's supposed "sexual power," a potential resonance between the discourse of seduction dominant in the nineteenth century southern United States and the multiracial discourse of the twenty-first? Hartman writes: "In the case of slave women, the law's circumscribed recognition of consent and will occurred only in order to intensify and secure the subordination of the enslaved . . . and deny injury, for it asserted that the captive female was both will-less and always willing" (81). How might the "circumscribed recognition of consent and will" in the discourse of multiracialism also serve to intensify subordination, past and present, however unwitting this complicity might be? If it can be asserted that enslaved women (or men) can exercise consent—"choice"—with regard to the sexual politics of captivity, why not suggest that the same degree of consent was operative in "choosing" to work, to rise in the morning or return to the quarters at night, to serve dutifully for forty years or to rebel in the face of certain death at first opportunity? In fact, this is precisely Kennedy's conclusion:

> Slavery was, to be sure, a horribly oppressive system that severely restricted the ambit within which its victims could make decisions. But slavery did not extinguish altogether the possibility of choice. It was that possibility which endowed slaves with moral responsibility then, and which renders them susceptible to moral assessment today. It is precisely because they made wrong choices, albeit in excruciating circumstances, that slave informants who betrayed other slaves can appropriately be condemned. Similarly, it is because enslaved rebels made right choices in difficult situations that they can now be applauded. (43)

Hartman (1997) writes at length of the "burdened individuality" foisted upon former slaves as the "fruits" of emancipation, a conception of moral culpability that facilitated the virtual restoration of chattel slavery's social and economic relations and eventually many of its political and legal conditions, a hegemonic discourse of explicit criminalization that shifted responsibility for the degraded position of blacks (and whatever troubles faced by whites as well) away from the racist state and the institutions of white civil society. It seems that Kennedy would extend this interpretive framework to the *formal* conditions of enslavement as well. Although we tread on dangerous ground in so saying, the notion of moral responsibility for or moral assessment of the enslaved, much like the concepts of consent or will, are rendered suspect or meaningless. From what position can one rightly judge the conduct of a slave, and by what moral criteria? To ask this question is not to endorse the paternalist abolitionism whose proponents "excused" the "immorality" of violent slave rebellion as an effect of the slave's de jure and de facto exclusion from society (e.g., a "savage" means of rebellion for "savage" people). This latter discourse contributed to the symbolization of civilization/savagery in ways that compounded the violence of slavery by reinforcing the hypocritical ethics of white civil society, promoting the naturalness of white claims to the seat of moral judgment (Sharpe 1993). My point is pitched elsewhere. In my view, it is not the morality of the slave that warrants consideration (there is a forum for such debate among the enslaved, not the free) but rather the injustice—or the immorality—of the slave system. To do otherwise is to substitute moralizing for political analysis.

To applaud "enslaved rebels [who] made right choices in difficult situations" is not only to condemn, by contrast, "slave informants who betrayed other slaves" but also to condemn *all other slaves* who did not partake in forms of rebellion recognizable to this moralizing posture. Included in this second group would be "most slaves," who "given the stark, often lethal, punishment meted out for open rebellion . . . *acceded in varying degrees* to the sexual exploitation imposed upon them, their kin, and their loved ones" (Kennedy 2003, 168; emphasis added). How, after all, can one "accede," which is to say *consent*, in "sexual exploitation that is *imposed* upon them, their kin, and their loved ones"? Gathering together Kennedy's different comments on slave agency and the moral culpability it involves, a logical and rhetorical parallel presents itself wherein the applause glibly afforded the presumptively male "enslaved rebel" (glib because the center-right political cast of Kennedy's analytic framework could not support the enslaved rebel's counterpart in the present) mirrors the strange veneration for the figure of the affectionate, sexually consenting female slave. On the other hand, the condemnation reserved for "slave informants" and that vast majority who accede "in varying degrees" to their degraded moral lot echoes in the perfunctory compassion offered to those innumerable black women (Kennedy says the number is "uncertain") who suffered the "depredations" of sexual assault narrowly defined under slavery.

The conceptual dichotomy regarding the *alternations* of agency gives rise to a moral binary in which the *sympathy* formally extended to black women beset by institutionalized rape under chattel slavery is underwritten by an inarticulate but discernible *contempt*—a compassionate contempt. This produces ambivalence in the image of the raped black female slave, who at once must be considered praiseworthy, to the extent that she resists the "depredations" of slavery through self-defense, and embarrassing, to the extent that her "sexual power" is negated: enslaved women enjoy a reputed "capacity to attract and shape affectionate, erotic attachments of all sorts, including interracial ones," but not, it seems, the capacity to repel or refuse them. Resistance to slavery appears only as that which transforms the mental and emotional state of white male masters—thwarting their desire for enslavement—not that which concerns itself with the welfare of the enslaved. Kennedy is very close here to the double binds of nineteenth-century rape law as it applied to *free white women*, whose resistance (which is to say "virtue") registers only as the most demonstrable physical defense, a defense meant to thwart the assailant's *desire* to rape and not simply his attempt (Block 1999). Because the idea of the sexually *consenting* black female slave is celebrated as *resistance*, a tenacious historical pressure is exerted on the class of enslaved black women to have had the *capacity* to consent, that is, to *have been consenting*—by way of her desire or feelings of affection—so that the "stereotypes" that surround (her sex with) white men can be avoided in the present. The desire of the enslaved black woman for the white male master is presented as proof of slavery's incompleteness as a system of domination, its failure to achieve its ends absolutely, a sign of its limits or, better, of a heterogeneous force of resistance producing those limits by its very operation.

For things to have been otherwise suggests an unbearable historical legacy—"the triple burden of enslavement, racism, and sexism"—indeed, "conditions that are harrowing to contemplate" (Kennedy 2003, 174). Too harrowing to contemplate and, it seems, too harrowing to take seriously into account.

Kennedy's work travels a peculiar itinerary, evincing a staunch determination to reach its destination regardless of any obstacles it might encounter. Where he begins his narrative in consideration of the agency of the slave—recovering not only its existential presence but also its historic efficacy—he then quickly, and without announcement, slips into speculative discussion about the affections of the master. Such affections are then supposed to indicate the *value* of slave agency, its *capability*, insofar as affection on the part of the master shows up in the form of the occasional instance of manumission and/or transfer of property across the color line. In this way, it was the agency of the slave to influence the affections of the slave owner, case by case and not en masse, that constituted the limit of the slave system, since forms of open rebellion or other forms of resistance were prevented, preempted, or severely punished. Of course, all of this discounts the fact that manumission or inheritance remained by definition the *prerogative of the master*, thereby reinforcing, not subverting, his power and authority and required, if the slave's agency was to be effective, that she successfully seduce the master or, in more pleasant tones, win his heart and mind. That she may have done this deliberately or unwittingly seems to be beside the point, namely, that *seduction was the motive force of slave agency* and is, according to the scholars, to be taken seriously as a check on the otherwise unmitigated power of the slaveholding class (and whites more generally insofar as race and legal status were isometric). At work here, then, is a disavowal of the structural violence of the institution of slavery, operative within an analytic framework that jumps wildly about the question of scale. When pressed as to where and at what level we are properly to think through the relations of power between master and slave (or between blacks and whites more broadly), this approach replies that so long as we consider the encounter on small enough a stage, that is, so long as we suspend consideration of the "barren and brutal" conditions of bondage, we can say nearly anything about it we wish.

This much is made clear in both Stephens and Kennedy; both authors summarily dismiss points made repeatedly by black feminist scholarship. For instance, in a critical reading of then-current historical work on U.S. slavery, particularly the canonical work of Eugene Genovese (1976) (whose curiously romantic perspective—curious only because it departs so basically from his otherwise Marxist conceptual framework—on antebellum interracial sexuality is, in many ways, resuscitated by the multiracial histories of today), Davis (1981) countered the problematic tendency to read sexual encounter between black women and white men (and, with rather divergent dynamics, between black men and white women, to say nothing of same-sex interracial encounter) through the lens of the social contract, deploying a terminology of consensus unequipped to address the situation. Genovese (1974) opined as follows:

> The tragedy of miscegenation lay, not in its collapse into lust and sexual exploitation, but in the terrible pressure to deny the delight, affection, and love that so often grew from tawdry beginnings. . . . Many white men who began by taking a slave girl in an act of sexual exploitation ended by loving her and the children she bore. (419, 415)

Here is Davis's (1981) well-known reply: "There could hardly be a basis for 'delight, affection and love' as long as white men, by virtue of their economic position, had unlimited access to Black women's bodies. It was as oppressors—or, in the case of non-slaveowners, as agents of domination—that white men approached Black women's bodies" (25–26). Though we are approaching redundancy by this point, it bears repeating that Davis is speaking quite precisely in *structural* terms, using a language of what is today called *positionality* (Awkward 1995) in order to demonstrate why Genovese is so off-base in his musings. She notes, in other words, that there is no *material basis* for the formation of the mental and emotional states that Genovese seemingly mourns, no objective conditions in which something like "authentic" "delight, affection and love" could develop, assuming we understand these terms to be optimal under conditions of substantive or even formal equality. Davis is not at all interested at this point in the subjective dimensions of white men's existence (i.e., their thoughts and feelings, their beliefs, their ideological subscriptions) but rather underlines that "by virtue of their economic position," they could not but approach black women as "agents of domination," regardless of any individual wishes or motivations. As noted previously, Hartman (1997) extends this analytic point considerably in her own work, discussing in great detail not only the economic but also the legal, political, social, and cultural dimensions of this structural positionality under white supremacy. Yet, despite the force of this broad scholarly intervention, the new multiracial history persists in reviving or prolonging this nostalgia for the interracial intimacy of slavery à la Genovese and other, less esteemed company.[10]

Kennedy's dismissal of structure is evident, and Stephens balks similarly in his turn. Neither takes seriously either the testimony of enslaved black women or the contemporary commentary of engaged black feminist intellectuals. What might happen, then, if the multiracial project took up study of Harriet Jacobs's (under the nom de plume Linda Brent) *Incidents in the Life of a Slave Girl*, for instance? How might such an encounter upset or frustrate the drive to uncover consent *within* confinement or derail the search for the furtive desire between master and slave? Interestingly enough, both Kennedy and Stephens do cite Jacobs in passing, but neither offers extended readings. That task is taken up by journalist Stephen Talty, whose *Mulatto America* (2003) extrapolates even more stridently the logic of their earlier arguments.

Talty

Like Stephens and Kennedy before him, Talty takes as his primary objective the refutation of a troubling black feminist critique, and Davis again serves as the representative foil. Better said, it is the disposition of the analysis that dismays Talty, what are taken to be overtones of pessimism toward the emotional capacities of whites in general and white men in particular. In his treatment of interracial sexuality in the antebellum United States, he writes,

> Most of the relationships between southern black men and white women [in the colonial era] appear to be consensual; once you enter the 1800s, those

relationships became increasingly dangerous for both parties. The record with black women and white men, however, is much murkier and more controversial. Some pro-southern historians in the early decades of the 1900s argued that black women initiated most affairs as a sought-after badge of superiority; though affairs did sometimes bring gifts and status, the argument is touched with the leftover image of the black succubus. Others argue that all interracial relationships under slavery were de facto rape, pure and simple. Angela Davis staked out this line over thirty years ago when she wrote that it was "as oppressors . . . or agents of domination that white men approached black women's bodies." (2003, 62)

Talty attempts to soften this view by claiming (again, without substance) that contrary to such apparent bleakness, "the old South was a world of [interracial sexual] relationships ranging from the brutal to the sublime" (63). One cannot miss the resonance here between Talty's "world of relationships" (ranging from "the brutal to the sublime") and Stephens's spectrum of relationships (ranging from "rape" to "love") discussed earlier. Kennedy is in step as well, referring as he does to those "hard-to-quantify but substantial number of cases" in which interracial intimacy "survived slavery's deadening influence." (Genovese precedes both when he contrasts sexual "exploitation" to "love" in his own work.) We have seen how it is that Stephens and Kennedy counterpose incompatible terms in lieu of more persuasive, or logically consistent, arguments. That is to say, they argue that *all* sex between white men and enslaved black women was not coerced because, as they claim, *some* of the white men (whether masters or not) cared for or fell in love with these same enslaved women. We have seen that evidence for this non sequitur is unavoidably compromised. Talty adds to the problem in his turn. Even when considered prima facie, *brutal* and *sublime* do not exist on some sliding scale or range or spectrum. Rather, they speak to discrepant dimensions of interracial sexual encounter.

The brutality of sexual encounter between the free and the enslaved is not, for instance, experienced *by the free* but *by the enslaved*, an unavoidable component of the permanent violence, the systemic terror that *is* captivity. Moreover, this brutality can be broached in both subjective and objective terms (Judy 1993). The experience of the sublime is restricted, as in the authors previously mentioned, to that of the master and not because evidence is scarce with respect to the experience of the slave. Rather, it is primarily an effect of Talty's overriding concern with the subjective transformations of the free white male master class, changes of heart he considers to be subversive and renegade. More plainly, his concern is with the salvation or redemption of white men in the face of history *as a result* of these changes of heart. "In many cases, Davis's assessment is correct: white men approached black women as soldiers approach the women of their enemy [or, to use a more apt metaphor, as slave masters approached their slaves]. But what were the *consequences* of these relationships? There is, in fact, evidence that in a substantial [number] of cases the *[white] men were converted* to a new view of black humanity" (Talty 2003, 63; emphasis added). For Talty, the only "consequences" of these "relationships" that matter, even when the suffering of black women is contemplated, are those that hold for white men.

I want to underscore that Talty is *not*, like Stephens and Kennedy, merely interested in asserting that "love" or "genuine intimacy" between whites and blacks under slavery produced a "flash of recognition" across the color line that "*resulted* in a new, dissenting view of American society" (xiv). We have had great occasion to see the problems with this position already. Incredibly, Talty goes so far as to suggest that even the "instances" of unambiguous brutality that shape sexual relations between master and slave—empirical acts of rape—yield constructive results for the one inhabiting the position of dominance, the slaveholding rapist. In order to claim as much, Talty glosses Jacobs's narrative as the illiberal prelude to a sustained and violent misreading:

> When she reaches puberty, Harriet immediately claims the attention of the master of the household, Dr. Flint, now well into his fifties and portrayed by Harriet as a sly and volatile obsessive. He probes her reactions for an opening and follows patterns that would today identify him as a classic batterer. . . . But Jacobs's hatred sharpened her pen; she captures Flint in exquisite detail. If you look at her portrait closely, the image of a monster slowly

dissipates and is replaced by something that is more mercurial, almost affecting, and in terms of his treatment of Jacobs, much more reprehensible. Dr. Flint was in love. . . . Clearly, he does not want this to be rape; he doesn't see himself as a beast. (65)

One must keep in mind that Talty is attempting to show why it is that interracial relationships between white men and black women under slavery were not "de facto rape, pure and simple," a fact that would have to be established by accessing even the minimal testimony of enslaved women and situating such testimony within the totality of the circumstances in which it was offered. Yet, even when looking to such testimony, here put forth by Jacobs with eloquence and detail, Talty has no difficulty inferring—against Jacobs's own telling of the incidents in *her* life—what it is that Dr. Flint experienced in *his* volatile obsession and, by doing so, to intimate to the contemporary reader that slave masters, even the most terrible, were not, in fact, the monsters we imagine them to have been. In abandoning the structural analysis "staked out . . . over thirty years ago" by Davis (1981), Talty persists in redeeming the character and the conscience of the slave master, a rapist, a "classic batterer." What matter is it to the repeatedly discarded black feminist critique that "Flint was in love," that *he* did not want his sexual encounter with Jacobs to be marked by coercion, or that *he* didn't "see himself as a beast"? Are we meant to adopt the "delusional and obscene" perspective of the antagonist here, in spite of the protagonist's "reasonable" first-person narrative in this landmark abolitionist text? What is involved in the retrospective attempt to see something "mercurial, almost affecting" in Flint, something that Jacobs, in her proximity, was apparently unable to appreciate?

Talty continues: "Seeing that he will have to coax Harriet along, Flint treats her as a delicious child, to be coddled and then seduced, little realizing that he is being changed by his own approach" (66). How is he being changed by this approach, changed in his attempts to coax and seduce a "delicious child"?

Sex and a display of his own power are clearly not all he wants. Flint has been wounded by Harriet's confession of love for another; for him, this is a romantic crisis. . . . He is trapped in an unplayable role as the hated master. For Flint, the irony must have been acute: Southern society has given him complete license to regard Harriet as a piece of chattel and to use her like one. But he can't quite do it. The fact that she is a thinking, feeling creature with individual strengths and vulnerabilities, her own stubborn desires, has risen before his eyes like some horrifying apparition. For any reasonable observer and for Harriet, of course, this is no romance. Flint's "love" is delusional and obscene, a far worse scenario for Harriet than the normal terror the typical master would engage in. His affection is her bad luck; if only Flint *weren't* so human! (67)

By Talty's own account, Jacobs (and "any reasonable observer") could not regard the relationship as a romance (whether it registers as "sublime" we are not told), a statement that I take to mean that she does not consent in it, even at this severely circumscribed scale. Yet, Talty speaks, without irony, of *Flint being trapped*, "trapped in an unplayable role as the hated master." He speaks, as well, of Jacobs's inherent humanity (her "thinking, feeling," her "stubborn desires") as a curb against the "complete license" bestowed upon Flint's position in a slave society. However, it is not the inability to use Jacobs wantonly that plagues Flint, since his ability to do so is extant even if occasionally it is foregone. Rather, what torments him is the inescapability of his *dominance* over her, which is also to say her condition of bondage. If Flint wants for anything at all in this scenario, it is the extension of his own power over Jacobs's "stubborn desires," an extension that he cares to know nothing about, wishing to direct her desire, to guarantee it, while maintaining the "delusional and obscene" idea that it is freely given.

None of this should appear anomalous, however, since it is characteristic of the psychology of domination, "the pattern of the classic batterer": insisting that she wants it, forcing her to want it, punishing her for not wanting it, feeling tormented over this conundrum, and so forth. More importantly, it represents the unfulfilled quest for the *hegemony* of the slaveholder, the evolution of his power beyond the naked use of coercion to a more encompassing winning of consent.[11] For Talty, these internal fluctuations on the part of the master are salutary. In the dark corners of the *master's* mind we find prefigured the moral critique of slavery pursued by the international abolitionist movement, spontaneously operative in protopolitical form within the erotic attachments of enslavement itself, affections that "*resulted* in a new, dissenting view of American society."

> Flint's society-damaged brain is fighting for control with the part of his mind that now sees Harriet all too clearly. When he raises his arm to strike her, it is a response that American culture has almost managed to hard-wire into him—this is how the majority of masters have been taught to control their chattel for decades. It is as instinctive as pulling his hand from a hot stove. But the arm freezes and then falls to his side, useless; a new conception unknown to most of his class is short-circuiting his rage. This deep confusion is what these particular relationships introduced to the society before the abolitionists popularized the purely moral approach to slavery: an internal, dissenting voice powerful enough to counteract primal emotions. (68)

Perhaps there was little need for abolitionism or the cataclysm of the Civil War. Perhaps the legal institution and the political economy of slavery would have fallen of their own accord, undermined from within, if only more such enlightening "sexual contact" between masters and slaves, a conversionary form of sexual assault, had occurred. Talty sees in the sex between masters and slaves, especially that between white male and black female, the glimmering lineaments of a path leading, however errantly, out of the dark days of yore toward the relative light of our present malaise.

> Flint's torments suggest that sexual contact often brought white men face-to-face with the realization that the chattel under their command was not the half-child, half-savage of southern legend. Sartre once said that there was "an aura of rape and massacre" in all relationships between master and slave, but he missed *the second sight that so many of these unions gave to the masters.* Sometimes that revelation led to far harsher treatment than indifference would have brought, as was the case with Harriet. But when one considers that a significant portion of southern slave owners engaged in sustained

relationships with their female slaves, one must conclude that there was a transfer of intimate knowledge. (69; emphasis added)

"Flashes of recognition," "second sight" for the master (Du Bois rolls in his grave!): sometimes yielding *harsher* treatment for slaves even as the master is transformed *for the better*. For this are we to celebrate or take some solace? Or, in a more reasoned and well-established manner, are we simply back where others have already taken us, scouring around in the archive for evidence of "sustained relationships" between masters and slaves as some verification of intimacy supposed to run *counter* to the white supremacist order of things? Even if we were to put the evidentiary problems aside for the moment, are we to take the longevity of the "relationship" between master and slave as some transparent commentary on its kindheartedness? Even if we were to bracket out the violence, exploitation, and abuse *inherent* to captivity (all of which throws the notion of "relationship" into crisis)—that is, if we were to consider not the violent *institutional* context of enslavement, which the master must no less uphold at every turn, day by day, but rather the narrower matter of *personal* violence, exploitation, and abuse (e.g., empirical incidences of rape, sexual violence, emotional abuse) (Davis 1999)—can we not still conceive of "sustained relationships" characterized by violence, exploitation, and abuse at that level? Can we not, moreover, *presume* as much given the gross unevenness, the utter asymmetry of power, the characteristic impunity of white men (and white women) in relations between master and slave?

Taken overall, the historical case for "interracial intimacy" (Kennedy); for "interracial relationships that grew out of, or led to, love" and were adopted "by choice" (Stephens); or, going back to our intellectual progenitor, for "sustained relationships" marked by "delight" and "affection" (Genovese), specifically with regard to enslaved black women and white male masters, is flimsy at best. Bear in mind that this is the case even when taken on the dubious terms established by the scholars in question. When considered from the vantage of structural relations of power, or structural positionality, as elaborated by Davis (1981), Spillers (2003), and Hartman (1999), among others, the argument for even a marginal or exceptional interracial intimacy (meaning not simply extensive proximity or familiarity or contact but "consensual" or "mutual desired sex") becomes at least misplaced. However, when judged at this larger scale, it is not unfair, given what we have demonstrated thus far, to regard the argument as vacuous or, worse, as outright fraudulent. The analytic facade—wherein an untenable assertion is forwarded under pretense of scholarship, in lieu of evidence or rigorous argument—suggests the operations of a collective desire impervious to or unconcerned about contradiction or rational foundation. The situation therefore begs a number of questions: if the new multiracial histories cannot actually offer a cogent or plausible *argument* about the power and presence of interracial intimacy under slavery, then what exactly is their aim? If they cannot be taken seriously as historical works in their own right, and if they do not even cursorily engage, much less advance, developments in cultural theory and criticism—in fact, they retard the project—what purposes do they serve?

Conceits of Complexity

We can begin by asking what interpretive framework they promote. Talty urges tellingly: "If we can turn back in history and *resist* treating these relationships as Marxist battles between historical forces and *resuscitate* the relationship between Flint and Harriet *as it really was*—a battle of minds and souls in which each party came to an exquisite understanding of the other—we *recover* a more complex idea of the antebellum world" (2003, 74; emphasis added). His language is reminiscent of Kennedy's contention that "interracial intimacy, as we have seen, bloomed on occasion even in the era of slavery, and thus even in the least nurturing of soils" (2003, 69). The "deadening influence" of slavery, that ostensibly passionless and barren land, is coupled here with the supposed crudeness and simplicity, the lifelessness, of a Marxist analytic while the enhanced "complexity" of the multiracial lens is matched with the "exquisiteness" of the similarly resuscitated interracial relationship. This proposal gestures not only toward a prestructuralist sensibility but toward a view that is strikingly presociological, and, in its jettison of the critique of political economy, explicitly pre-Marxist as well.

One should not be misled, then, by any citation of critical scholarship from the twentieth, or even late-nineteenth, century in the multiracial literature. Instead, the writers considered thus far rely only on the austerity of pretheoretical speculation, journalistic narrative convention, and, it must be said, more than a few projections of whimsy onto the historical record. How, after all, can one describe in good faith the relation between master and slave as "a battle of minds and souls" that yielded for "each party" "an exquisite understanding of the other"? Are we to think that slavery may have been a "horribly oppressive system" but, alas, despite that horror, produced a wonderful insight, tenderness even, between parties who might otherwise remain coldly distant from one another or perhaps simply estranged? That it provided, moreover, some bizarre medium for socializing, created a valuable cultural exchange, or an unlikely matchmaking, and that, for these reasons, we could and should find some obscure encouragement in the slow but inevitable triumph of the heart's kindness or the mind's reasonableness over the residual evil of a less enlightened, less caring time? In this schema, "society" or "American culture" takes the rap for all that is bad in the world, while the individual—specifically the "spirit of humanity" enshrined in his or her heart and mind—serves as the essential source of redemption, nurturing the forces of reform and reconstruction: indeed, the seed from which the real curative, intimacy, blossoms. Thus, being true to oneself, as it were, becomes synonymous with a righteous outlawry and just rebellion—a "quiet revolution" (Root 1992b).

Perhaps it goes without saying that as a result, the avant-garde of "political" struggle is located at the scale of individual resistance, where the latter is recognizable only as the pursuit or affirmation of interracial intimacy. The net effect of this interpretive framework, with its romantic assumption of individuals beset by the world, is a construction of sexuality as an autonomous sphere of human activity, a strictly private arena counterposed to the supposedly external world of constraint, a world motivated by unjust political and economic imperatives. Racism begins "out there" and works inward with varying degrees of success. And since racism in the multiracial historical literature is an outgrowth of "racialism . . . regardless of color," the pursuit or affirmation of interracial intimacy becomes *the* path to social reform and reconstruction, against *any and all* detractors. But since the naysayer here and now is paradigmatically *black*, the true antiracist tack, whose spiritual inspiration draws from the unacknowledged agency of the slave, sets itself against the alleged inability or refusal of contemporary blacks to accept the grand legacy of their own ancestors.

Regarding the new multiracial histories, we must ask not simply whether these accounts are accurate (which question has preoccupied us so far) but also, more importantly, what interests, broadly conceived, are served by recovering or rather *inventing* such an alternate historical account in the present? What current exigencies and social anxieties buttress this broad-based discursive enterprise? What is the political utility of the new historiography of race mixture in the post–civil rights era United States? When the unsustainable historical argument is presented, what is the contemporary point to its bald assertion? To that end, what must be bracketed out, deemphasized, and diminished? What must be highlighted, glossed over, understated, or simply left out of the account? Finally, what does it mean that the historical arguments of multiracial discourse regarding the flowering of interracial intimacy under slavery systematically fall apart? Does the frailty of its most basic goals—forgiving an "original sin," acquitting a "collective rape," cleansing a "national stain," absolving "racial guilt"—undercut its assault on the "virulent opposition" of "black community in general and its political leadership specifically" toward the new multiracial consciousness? How might it at least challenge its self-appointed status as a progressive antiracist campaign, the logical extension of the civil rights movement?

In his genealogy of sexuality in the modern West, Michel Foucault (1990) writes sardonically of the "speaker's benefit," the gratification that accrues to the position of one who defines "the relationship between sex and power in terms of repression." I modify his comments slightly to highlight their relevance for the current study:

> If [interracial] sex [or interracial intimacy more broadly] is repressed, that is, condemned to prohibition, nonexistence, and silence, then the mere fact that one is speaking about it has the appearance of a deliberate transgression.

A person who holds forth in such language places himself to a certain extent *outside the reach of power*; he upsets established law; he somehow anticipates the coming freedom. . . . We are conscious of defying established power, our tone of voice shows that we know we are being subversive, and we ardently conjure away the present and appeal to the future, whose day will be hastened by the contribution we believe we are making. Something that smacks of revolt, of promised freedom, of the coming age of a different law, slips easily into this discourse of sexual oppression. Some of the ancient functions of prophecy are reactivated therein. Tomorrow sex will be good again [or for the first time]. Because this repression is affirmed, one can discreetly bring into coexistence concepts which the fear of ridicule or the bitterness of history prevents most of us from putting side by side: revolution and happiness; or revolution and a different body, one that is newer and more beautiful; or indeed, revolution and pleasure. (6–7)

The "ancient functions of prophecy" reactivated in contemporary multiracial discourse are not unrelated to the promises of sexual revolution discussed by Foucault. As noted in chapter 1, the multiracial project draws rhetorical elements from the civil rights movement and Black Power, on the one hand, and the feminist and sexual liberation movements, on the other, but its appropriation is highly selective, steadily sifting out notions of collective effort for *radical* social change in order to retain only the isolated libertarian impulse. Bourgeois individualism recast in this way acquires the patina of a beleaguered cause, the struggle of the resilient minority or, alternately, the post–civil rights era majority, silent no more. The "quiet revolution" advanced by the multiracial movement augurs "happiness," "pleasure," and "a different body," but these fruits are to be reaped as forms of "public," state-sanctioned multiracial identity and not as achievements in the "private" domain of interracial sexuality.

It is difficult to say whether the contemporary articulation of multiracial identity politics requires the historical sanitation of the recent scholarship or vice versa. In either case, the outcome is a reactionary rewriting of history such that the perpetual "state of emergency" heralded by Benjamin (1969) in his famous thesis on the philosophy of history is again rendered exceptional and the particular urgency of the black radical tradition is vitiated, redirected toward consensual courses of parliamentary action. Multiracialism maintains that what once was a marginal phenomenon, that is, interracial intimacy, has now, through its evolutionary force, become a mainstream development. Accordingly, the structural arrangements that rendered such "sexual contact" taboo or impracticable are passing away with the sureness of historical inevitability or, at the very least, the probability of a demographic trend. This sanguine view relies, in large part, on a reification of white supremacy in some prior institutional arrangements alongside a hypostasized demise of those same historic forms. It also understands the struggle against antiblack racism to be one of clearly progressive or regressive developments (within which a society moves "forward" or "backward") rather than, for instance, a complex antagonism unfolding in a structured field of power relations exhibiting tremendous capacity for *reconfiguration* in the service of continued dominance (Grossberg 1992). Multiracial politics takes white supremacy and antiblackness to be rigid formations of power and misinterprets them as a set of crusty prejudices, bad ideas, or irrational fears that are either defeated or upheld.

As noted, the pivot for overturning the white supremacist social order is, for multiracial advocates, the one-drop rule of hypodescent and the stigma of interracial sexuality it suggests. The one-drop rule and the stigmatizing of interracial sexuality are not the same thing, however, and to treat them as such is to commit to a conceptual conflation. This is part of the reason why multiracialism has nothing of value (and often nothing at all) to say about interracial sexuality, a point demonstrated in subsequent chapters. Multiracial discourse assumes that in defending the right to be recognized as multiracial, it has spoken the last word about the politics of race and sexuality as well. This confusion is embedded in a larger refusal to work through the historic consternation about interracial sexuality. As it insists upon an unexamined universal stance in support of interracial intimacy, multiracialism refuses to countenance that interracial sexuality is not the same problem for whites (or, for that matter, Asians, Latinos, and American Indians) as it is for blacks. The fact of this racialized discrepancy vis-à-vis sex across the color line seems rather banal to even the

casual student of history, but it is consistently lost in the multiracial shuf-
fle, thrown out as so much internalized racism—accession "in varying
degrees"—on the part of blacks.

Returning, then, to our earlier point—the reduction of antiracist
politics to an individual affirmation of interracial intimacy—there is an
insidious double inscription of black agency at work in the new multiracial histories. Blacks are said to exercise agency in the historic instance
and are celebrated as such when and if they embrace whites—or rather, in
a reversal of prerogative, when whites embrace them—as "lovers" under
racial slavery, but they are castigated for being in thrall to the ideology of
white supremacy whenever they speak critically in the present case about
the power, sexual or otherwise, of their own or their forebears' agency. The
latter meditation is taken to be a self-defeating denial of black power and,
moreover, a forfeiture of black responsibility. One is, then, an ideological
dupe to the extent that one does not take up the multiracial banner—wav-
ing Talty's "mulatto flag"—and one is a lover of freedom and a free lover
when one embraces it. This is, of course, a classic ideological gesture and
accounts for much of the language of "truth," "reality," "admission," and
"acceptance" that the multiracial contingent brings to bear against the
"racial mythology," "denial," and "falsehood" of the various policies and
political projects it contests. It runs a line as well through the association
of multiracialism with the trajectory of a world-historical development and,
what is taken to be the same thing, the resuscitation of a more authentic
U.S. national identity. Noted historian Gary Nash writes, "The blending
of races is not un-American; it is being American" (1999, vii–viii). For blacks
to query the multiracial *ethos*—an *ethos* demanding belief in its "historical
engineering"—is to impede the business of nation-building, to refuse its
advances and solicitations, posing problems for the *manufacture* of consent.[12]

To this end, it is not quite correct to say that multiracial discourse
is interested in the valorization of interracial sexuality for its own sake,
regardless of context and consequences. Such would seem to be the case
considering the gentrification of sexual coercion under slavery through
which Stephens's euphemistic "love . . . under uneven power relations" or
Kennedy's Orwellian consent-in-confinement is outdone only by Talty's

sentimentalist musings on the sublime edification of enslaved black women's normative sexual availability (Davis 1999) for white male slaveholders. However, the diffuseness of a moral system that understates or dissembles about the structures of sexual violence underwriting slavery in order to sing the praises of interracial intimacy when white male interracial sexual violence is under consideration becomes uncannily focused when the issue of black male interracial sexual violence claims its attention.

In a chapter entitled "Race, Racism, and Sexual Coercion," Kennedy—after concluding, finally, that the testimony of enslaved black women does not tell us *anything* of substance about the nature of interracial sexual violence[13]—writes pointedly about the recent case of a black male U.S. Army drill sergeant convicted of a series of felony charges, including various counts of sexual assault against white female subordinates. The 1997 case of Delmar Simpson was one in a string of "army sex scandals" in that decade, the majority involving black men and white women and considered by some media commentators to be the most important military legal controversy since the My Lai Courts-Martial in 1970. Referring to Simpson as "the most notorious" defendant, Kennedy cites these cases because, among other things, they involved intimations of racism in both the prosecution of charges and, to lesser degree, the media frenzy that grew up around it.

While condemning the defense's attempt to "[play] the race card" (2003, 213) in its arguments, Kennedy relates a crucial detail of the trial proceedings in an easily overlooked footnote. There the author chafes at the apparent baseness of Simpson's defense strategy, which attempted to undercut the allegations of white female plaintiffs through recourse to the patriarchal legal tradition that would discredit their characters and ascribe to them a sufficient measure of agency—the practical capacity to discern and to decide the terms of sexual encounter—in order to cast reasonable doubt on any claims to nonconsent. Such statements about the plaintiffs' understanding and willingness within the disputed situation were rebutted by the prosecution's successful evocation of the legal principle of "constructive force," a move that broadened the operative definition of rape in the case at hand. Kennedy notes,

Simpson's attorneys argued that most of the rape charges should be dismissed because references to force or threats of force were missing from the trainee's own accounts of the alleged crimes. According to the Uniform Code of Military Justice, a rape conviction requires proof of sexual intercourse "by force and without consent" [citation omitted]. The presiding judge in Simpson's case ruled, however, that the requisite force need not take the form of immediate or threatened physical violence; in his view, proof of "constructive force" would suffice. *Constructive force would consist of a totality of circumstances that, taken together, constituted duress.* The judge ruled that in Simpson's case, a jury might find that such force had been used. Drill sergeants, the judge stressed, "commanded so much authority over trainees—ordering them where to eat and sleep and how to act—that they were like parents" [citation omitted]. Unsurprisingly, Simpson's attorney strongly objected: "Do we have law that has become so paternalistic that now [women] don't even have to say 'No'?" Frank J. Spinner [of the defense] asked rhetorically. "Are trainees so ignorant that they can't distinguish between a drill sergeant telling them to run up a hill or lie down on a bed?" (208–9; author's note, emphasis added)

One can detect the disdain of Kennedy's reporting here in his use of the word *unsurprisingly* to describe the objections of Simpson's attorneys who are, after all, *required by law* to zealously defend their client (Kennedy could have described the objection, for instance, as "dutiful" or even "effective"). What would appear a mere sidebar about the Simpson defense strategy gathers its full force from the general principle Kennedy gleans from the case. Simpson's case is presented by Kennedy as an example of the ways that a supposed hypersensitivity to the racist prosecution and persecution of black men in the history of the United States, particularly the mass hysteria generated by allegations of sexual crimes against white women, has lead to a perversion in the heart of contemporary legal culture, producing substantial miscarriages of justice.

In other words, because so many black men have been subjected to railroad trial, fast-track imprisonment, death penalty, or lynch mob, the policing and prosecution of black men has become squeamish, granting black men, at least in the eyes of the black community, a veritable license to rape. Kennedy comments: "Demonization and its consequences have in turn prompted many blacks to regard allegations of black-on-white crime—particularly sexual crime—with great skepticism; some refuse to condemn black criminals even when their guilt is patent" (198). Or again: "Excessive anxiety over the image of the black man continues to trigger the suppression of any full and open consideration of rape" (206). Kennedy considers this refusal to condemn "black criminals" to be a moral failure of "many blacks" who, on this account, are captive to a racial mythology that would hold all charges of interracial sexual crime against black men to be simply false (complementing, perhaps, "stereotypes that all sexual relations between white men and black women are a form of rape").

Kennedy suggests that the failure to publicly condemn "black criminals even when their guilt is patent" is evidence of an uncritical belief in either their innocence (which I have heard we are supposed to *presume* until proven otherwise, "beyond a reasonable doubt") and the veracity of their acquittal. En route, he must assert that "guilt is patent" in cases in which verdicts rendered were sharply disputed within the juries *and* within the court of public opinion precisely because the evidence of guilt was doubtful and, often enough, contaminated. More to the point, Kennedy fails to contemplate in his harangue the possibility that, to cite the main example, "many blacks" believe *neither* O. J. Simpson's defense (they may not even care about it) *nor* the purported fairness and legitimacy of a racist criminal justice system, a system explored at length in Kennedy's own previous work (1998). That said, it seems Kennedy is more interested here to join the chorus of those proclaiming the injustice of O. J. Simpson's "getting away with murder" (or Delmar Simpson's attempt at "getting away with rape") in order to decry the grave societal dangers enabled by the "skepticism" of "many blacks" toward "allegations of black-on-white crime." Kennedy judges the danger to be most severe for white women (as the balance of examples indicates and as befits the thematic focus on interracial sexual coercion) and, on this conclusion, endorses the deeply problematic writings of white feminist scholar Susan Brownmiller (whom Kennedy incorrectly—outrageously—aligns with the "womanist" intervention of black writer/theorist/activist Alice Walker). Brownmiller's inflammatory position (criticized several times over by a generation of black feminists, including Angela Davis) regarding black men's so-called racial defense of sexual violence is reproduced by Kennedy, but now under the banner of improving the prospects for a colorblind interracial intimacy rather than enabling feminist political movement.

Black women figure in Kennedy's discussion of black male sexual violence, but as in his discussion of white male sexual violence, their scant treatment serves as foil for the spirited critique of black men's sexual violence and, along the way, those black women who forgo legal recourse against the former, what he calls "a pathetic, regrettable response" (2003, 207).[14] Not only the briefness of the encounter but also the curious historical periodization at work suggests this reading: the narrative of white male interracial sexual violence focuses almost exclusively upon the era of chattel slavery and virtually ends with the Jim Crow era, as if the issue dissolves with the rise of the modern civil rights movement. He states that "the bitter history of white-on-black sexual aggression continues to *reverberate* in our own time" (180; emphasis added), but it is not regarded as a contemporary social issue except insofar as "the powerful emotions it has generated" still hold considerable sway over our interpretation, or rather *misinterpretation*, of events. In this regard, the central dynamics of the post–civil rights era are illustrated for Kennedy by two episodes: the 1975 case of Joan Little, a young black woman acquitted of murder charges for defending herself during a prison term against the sexual depredations of a white male warden, and the 1987 Tawana Bradley affair in which a black female teenager alleged abduction and rape by a group of white men in a highly controversial criminal case that was eventually dismissed after grand jury review. For Kennedy, the first case signals the arrival of legal deliverance for black women, a historical overturning of the institution of white male sexual impunity and black female sexual vulnerability under the criminal code. The second case, on the other hand, signifies the troubling effects of a communal bitterness. In Kennedy's estimation, the widespread support that Bradley's spurious charges enjoyed among a "broad cross section of African Americans . . . regardless of the facts" (181–82) points to the presence of debilitation, unhealed historical wounds: "Her lie attained vitality, even in the glare of exposure, because *real* racially motivated sexual violence has been visited upon black women for centuries without adequate redress or even acknowledgment" (182). For all the apparent sympathy,[15] however, he demonstrates impatience for such collective resentment and reprimands its injurious effects: "The facts of specific cases, however, *do* matter. They matter even when they inconveniently complicate stories that at first seem starkly simple" (182).

Emotional anachronism on the part of blacks promotes not only crude and reactionary political rallying around the issue of interracial sexual violence. It fosters as well a cynical relation to the rule of law more generally, a relation whose inconsistency is held together by a subscription to the moral duality of the color line: on the one hand, a crippling disbelief in the virtues of criminal prosecution combined with a sense of unqualified (rather than presumptive) innocence whenever the accused is a black male and, on the other, an insistence upon unqualified guilt requiring disregard for the facts of the case, including the verdict rendered, whenever the accused is a white male. We cannot but recognize in this depiction the inverted image of white supremacist jurisprudence. The point not to be missed is that the compensatory mirroring of patriarchal white racism by blacks is entirely unwarranted—"excessive" in Kennedy's words—out of sync with, if not in pathological denial about, the progressive developments that characterize the post–civil rights moment. The criminal justice system no longer functions according to this tyrannical logic. Rather, the ideological mainstay that describes the legal mechanisms of white male supremacy, namely, the a priori distribution of guilt along the racial fault line, is today primarily or, at least, most dangerously perpetuated by blacks. But if the assumptive logic of black male supremacy is now being promulgated in many quarters, Kennedy is not interested in its ramifications for black women, despite the occasional passing reference to recognized names (e.g., Crenshaw 1995). His solidarity with black women and his references to black feminism in this regard are instrumental.[16] Above all, *Interracial Intimacies* is concerned with arbitrating black criticism, whose relentlessness we are growing increasingly tired of and about whose archaism we are increasingly perplexed. It is keen to dispute any proposition in which whites are thought to take the rap for things that are, as it were, no fault of their own. It is a barbed rejoinder against what Kennedy, alerting us to the insurgency, determines to be "effective mau-mauing" (398).[17]

Unlike his earlier insistence on the omnipresence of black consent (however "restricted" or "limited"), these comments are meant to be a historic argument, marking out a transition or transformation in the vectors of racial reason: "For many other Americans, especially whites, the specter of the white man as racially motivated rapist resides safely in the past and has been superseded by a different, more contemporary, and hence more frightening image: the black man as racially motivated sexual criminal" (182). Kennedy's appraisal is matter-of-fact. Its fatuous tenets are not subjected to criticism, its supposed novelty is not interrogated, its implication in the tropes of violent racist fantasy (whose dreadful implications Kennedy himself outlines in subsequent pages) is disavowed. In so doing, Kennedy upholds the historical projection, apologizing for those "many other Americans, especially whites" who today find themselves, like their forebears, fascinated by this "more frightening image."

There is one new dimension to this longstanding public ritual. Guarded by other blacks' skepticism toward the charges they might accrue and emboldened by a distorted popular history of violent interracial sexual encounter—both of which are now supposed to have *infrastructure*— the contemporary threat of unchecked black male rape is not, as it largely has been, limited to white women. Bad enough, white women have apparently lost the guarantee of redress, legal or extralegal, a loss suggesting for Kennedy both the end of Jim Crow lynch law—"It is a datum of some note that at the end of the twentieth century, in one of the most highly publicized sex-crime trials in American history [re: Delmar Simpson], a military jury sided with an African American male against a bevy of tearful white female complainants" (213)—and the advent of black male impunity before the law. In fact, the two points overlap to the point of identity. Worse still, white *men* are also vulnerable to black male sexual violence today and, ironically, in the very institutional space that for "the black community in general and its political leadership especially" represents the *continuing* antiblack racism of the criminal justice system, one responsible for, among other things, the erosion of hard-won civil rights and liberties: the prison-industrial complex. Kennedy writes,

> The cases described above all have involved black-on-white, heterosexual, male-on-female rape. But men also rape men. Black-on-white, male-on-male rape occurs often in prison. Again, all manner of motivations spark criminality of this sort; sometimes interracial rapes stem from evil motives or impulses that have nothing to do with race. A substantial proportion of interracial rape encountered in jails and prisons, however, is attributable at least in part to racial sentiments. In investigating the motivation behind such assaults, researchers have been told by some black perpetrators of sexual violence that "now it is [whites'] turn" to be dominated. Explaining the racial dynamic of rape in the prison in which he was incarcerated, one Negro inmate remarked, "You guys's been cuttin' our b[alls] off ever since we been in this country. *Now we're just gettin' even.*" (184; emphasis added)

In prison, under conditions of civil death,[18] the castrating patriarchy of white supremacy has its racial hierarchy inverted—avenged, in fact—by the conscious, systematic manifestation of black men's license to rape white men, echoing the legal exemption that some black men are, at least periodically, granted in the free world against white women. One can readily note that such assertions about the rapaciousness of black men in prison and the extreme sexual vulnerability of incarcerated white men are obsessively reiterated in the literature of avowed white supremacist organizations, and it would take little effort to recognize the common rhetorical strategies—and political preoccupations—at work in each case (Daniels 1996; Ferber 1998). We need not conflate the two projects, however, to consider the implications of the more genteel discourse. The larger point of Kennedy's discussion of black-on-white sexual violence is that black people do in fact have various degrees of power in the post–civil rights United States and, as a result, can engage in *acts* of racism, can even *institutionalize* them, and, finally, are responsible for such recently established power. In all, this oppressive black power—rolling down from the historical agency of the enslaved—endows blacks with culpability and opens them, individually and collectively, to moral evaluation. The latter designation is at the heart of Kennedy's enterprise, an objective that becomes clear in his brusque "proof" for the actuality of black racism:

> The logic that holds here [in the "mistaken, albeit influential, line of thought that holds blacks incapable of engaging in 'racism'"] is that racism is a product of power and racial prejudice, that blacks are devoid of power, and that therefore, by definition, they cannot be racist. This theory is faulty on a variety of grounds, one of which is empirical. *Blacks do, in fact, exercise power in American society.* Collectively, to be sure, they exercise far less of it than whites, but *that is not the same as having no power at all.* As politicians, business leaders, personnel directors, admissions officers, judges, police officers, prosecutors, and jurors, blacks clearly exercise *substantial discretion that is often unreviewable.* But ordinary, even quite lowly, people also have *the capacity to wield power in their day-to-day lives.* The obscure man who is relatively powerless in many situations can, in a blink, reveal himself to be *rather powerful in relation to others* whom he is in a position to hurt. For at least a moment, every rapist is powerful in relation to his victim. It is simply untenable to claim, then, that blacks and other discriminated-against people of color have *no* power. And because blacks, like all responsible individuals, have *some* power, their moral hygiene, like everyone else's, warrants close careful attention. (207; emphasis added)

The empirical rhetoric of Kennedy's ultimate claim is undercut by the institutional or structural rhetoric found in the opening of the passage. Whereas he begins by noting the ascendance of blacks to positions of nominal institutional authority (i.e., politicians, business leaders, police officers, prosecutors, jurors, etc.), he then proceeds to discard all such figures of collective black "empowerment" ("substantial discretion that is often unreviewable") and returns to an atomized discussion of "ordinary, even quite lowly, [black] people . . . the obscure [black] man who is relatively powerless in many situations." While he approaches an admission that there are people who are *structurally* disempowered ("relatively powerless in many situations"), Kennedy speaks, nonetheless, of this same (black) man being *in a position* to hurt others. More to the point, this "obscure (black) man," the prototypical rapist, is "*powerful* in relation to his victim" regardless of her or his power in "many [other] situations." Although we cannot expect otherwise from Kennedy's conceptual framework, his notion of power reveals itself here to be vapid. It renders meaningless questions of scale and the functions of institutions and social structure or what Kennedy earlier called a "system," all of which he reduces to mere "situations." For Kennedy, power can be described as inequitable participation in institutional functions in proportions "far less than whites" but nonetheless creating "substantial discretion that is often unreviewable" *or* brute physical strength by which "every rapist is powerful," assuming of course that rape always proceeds, as the Uniform Code of Military Justice would have it, by way of "immediate or threatened physical violence." It is significant that Kennedy returns here to a restricted conception of rape, indicating the sort of "power" that can be seized "in a blink" and held only "for a moment." Were this not the case, his earlier arguments about the absence of "constructive force" in sexual relations between white male slaveholders and enslaved black women would begin to unravel. If we read the two arguments side by side, this is precisely what occurs.

We have already seen that Kennedy is capable of affirming the validity of the legal concept of "constructive force" in the case of the black male drill sergeant accused of sexually assaulting white women subordinate to him in the context of military authority. The judge in that case found, to Kennedy's apparent approval, that the *structure* of authority between drill sergeants and trainees gives rise to a "totality of circumstances" that, taken together, "constitute duress." It is, in other words, a *relation* in which the solicitation of sexual favors or any other sexual advance on the part of the superior can be understood as *essentially* coercive, not contingently so. Kennedy would have the court find in favor of the plaintiffs on these terms— which it did, contra to Kennedy's concern about black male impunity— despite the ambiguity of the circumstances and despite the relative degrees of freedom, which is to say the limited agency the plaintiffs enjoyed. Yet, in considering the case of enslaved black women, Kennedy disallows this same perspective in the face of his own description of enslavement as *more oppressive* than imprisonment ("slaves were even more vulnerable than inmates to sexual exploitation") and beyond analogy to any situation of contractual employment in an all-volunteer military (45). This glaring inconsistency in the terms of analysis suggests, to my mind, a scholarly project guided by something other than the drive for clarification that Kennedy claims in the opening sections of his study. The *only thing* that remains consistent in each of Kennedy's interventions is the judgments they render about the "moral hygiene" of blacks. Where he seeks to mystify the situation of white slaveholding and ransacks the historical record in search of evidence for something other than interracial sexual coercion, he casts doubt on the otherwise cherished presumption of innocence for black men accused of sexual crimes, liberally citing dubious source material to substantiate his claims about imprisoned black men on the sexual warpath of racial revenge against vulnerable white male prisoners. More broadly, he mischaracterizes black community as unconcerned about justice and public safety, an allegation that is, at bottom, about a collective disregard for the protection of whites against sexual violation by the "frightening" male members in its ranks.

In fact, an apprehension about unchecked black male aggression is apparent in all authors discussed in this chapter. When examined as a fundamental aspect of the project of white male supremacy, revulsion toward interracial sexuality (let alone its violent regulation) is calmly and briefly criticized as matter of course, while the deliberations, the inner torment and turmoil, of even the most viciously racist white men (and not a few white women) are explored at length in the name of erudition, peppered with assurances that optimism about a white "cosmopolitan ethos," past and present, is well founded. However, when the respective skepticism of blacks is discussed, what should be taken as a complicated and ambivalent *questioning* is instead construed as outright hostility, some unthinking and prejudiced rejection, especially in the case of black women. On this note, multiracial discourse reaches fever pitch, and an alternating current of contempt and pity invariably rises up. Stephens (1999) writes, for instance, that "hostility towards interracial couples by black women writers is widespread and generally uncriticized, considering that similar attitudes would be roundly condemned if voiced by whites. . . . My sense is that this phenomenon is pervasive" (270n127).

Under what circumstances and by whom "similar attitudes would be roundly condemned if voiced by whites" is hardly self-evident. More to the point, the suggestion that blacks and whites voice "similar attitudes," even when they bear a family resemblance or approach verbatim repetition, sidesteps the historical and political question of *enunciation*—not only *what* is said (as if meaning were inherent to words in some literal guarantee) but also *who* is saying it and from *where*. Because this reckoning is evaded, the authors at hand can charge blacks with immunity for sordid acts that whites purportedly could not execute, immunity that takes its most troubling form as black women's "pervasive," "uncriticized" hostility to interracial sexuality, their collective nonconsent. Thus, the gendered ratio of black people's collective malfunction in relation to interracial intimacy has black women loudly refusing it and black men violently destroying it, both cases involving their own specific type of corruption, disgraceful and indefensible components of a problem of transnational proportion.

Conclusion

The new multiracial histories focus most intently on the political capital of black "moral hygiene," that is, the extent that blacks at the turn of the twenty-first century are deemed beyond reproach while whites are subjected to undue criticism, condemned, as it were, by a collective responsibility for the past actions of the slaveholding elite—a small group that, we are told, actually displayed moments of noteworthy tenderness, "flashes of recognition." We have seen that this intellectual project proceeds only by eviscerating structural analyses, arbitrarily applying or withholding an incoherent set of evaluative criteria, and bending the historical record, at times grossly, to suit the evidentiary demands of the present purpose. These methodological gestures should be considered laughable in the present-day humanities and social sciences and even among better journalists. But if otherwise respected intellectuals must perform such gymnastics to pursue the task, then why would they contort themselves in these ways to voice the desired moral scrutiny? Why claim, against all reasonable indicators and against good sense, that blacks escape criticism, "exercise substantial discretion that is often *unreviewable*," or enjoy some moral carte blanche? If Stephens, Kennedy, and Talty are interested in doing something other than reiterating the amorphous perils of unchecked black behavior, tending always toward "criminality," then with regard to what specific social and political issues are blacks to be held accountable today?

We have already glimpsed an answer: the issue to be established, that which must be established through reprimand, the charge confirmed by its punishment, is the problem of black racism, an *oppressive* black power. Though such concerns are not new to political culture in the United States, the cast of the American dilemma has shifted in key ways. In the domain of multiracial discourse, the specter of black racism against whites is not broached directly, it is not reducible, in other words, to the prevailing discourse of "reverse racism," but rather it is addressed *obliquely* as a component of black hostility toward interracial sexuality and multiracial people. This twist is essential to the rhetorical purchase of the current denunciation of "black community in general and its political leadership specifically" because it becomes a challenge issued by "people of color" who, it is supposed, are neither white supremacist nor antiblack. The figure of tragic race mixture remains in force, as the pathos of melodrama that shoots through the discourse, to return to Fanon (1967), provides affective cover for the "paralogical" nature of its grounding claims. Stephens, again, states:

> *The most virulent opposition* to the notion that people of mixed race can carve out an identity that is neither black nor white is now coming from Afro-Americans. Mixed-ethnicity children who do not have a black parent are not subject to the same "One Drop" rule, but for those with a black parent, there is often intense pressure to "cleave to the black," and accusations of racial betrayal if the individual chooses not to choose to be "only black." Surely it is a significant irony that, one century after Euro-Americans were trying to write mulattos out of existence, *the repression is now coming from Afro-essentialists.* It seems we are witnessing *another instance* of the construction of the "racial" out of the denial of the "interracial." (Stephens 1999, 33; emphasis added)

In multiracial literature, the polarity of racism in the post–civil rights era has shifted such that "the repression" of mulattos is "now" coming from "Afro-essentialists" (standing in for a broader black community) and no longer from whites, just as the overriding threat of interracial sexual violence no longer resides with white men—and it was never as bad as we imagined it to be—but now with black men (Spencer 1999).[19] Blacks are now judged the most virulent opposition to the multiracial project and that opposition judged to be merely "another instance" of the violent protocols of racialization marking the history of U.S. white supremacy and antiblackness. Because it is assumed that whites pose no "virulent opposition" to the "cosmopolitan ethos" of interracial intimacy, the final destination of this critique is the problem that the construction of black racial identity poses for the national project and, beyond that, for emergence of global civil society. To repress or deny, or to offer political criticism of, the interracial—it all amounts to the same thing—is to impede the creation of *true* national community (whether Talty's "Mulatto America" or Nash's more hemispheric "*Mestizo* America").

Multiracialism attempts to establish, by dint of assertion and repetition, against the historical record and the bulk of contemporary scholarship, that blacks are the prime antagonists of multiracial people and interracial couples today; that such antagonism is wrongheaded, unprincipled, and unfounded; that it either produces or threatens clear patterns of discrimination; and that all of this constitutes a form of racism more dangerous, reprehensible, and pressing to people of conscience than an abiding antiblackness. In essence, the multiracial intervention argues not only that its concerns are an extension of, and therefore equivalent to, those of historic black freedom struggle and that if the terms *black* and *multiracial* work at cross-purposes today, it is the former term that is in the wrong, but also— its most insecure and hence most vociferous point—that multiracialism is not, in itself and for itself, a discourse and a politics of antiblackness. This is the point of transit between the debate regarding the history of interracial sexuality under slavery and the dispute around contemporary interracial relationships and multiracial identity politics. If the knot of controversy cannot be undone at its source, then the present effort to manufacture black consent for "Multi-America" (Reed 1997) will remain frustrated by an unwarranted holdout.

The multiracial strategy is a difficult one, however, because the force of history continues to interject, reminding all who would listen that blacks demonstrate an entirely understandable reticence toward the political celebration of interracial sexuality. If black people have rejected stigmatization as *the* threat to the white body politic in defense of their right to "social equality," the sexual field has not thereby presented itself as a straightforward terrain of progressive struggle (Hammonds 2004; Mercer 1994). The field of sexuality has been central to the violent production of racialized difference in the crucible of modern slavery. In this sense, interracial sexuality for the black personality has not so much been a matter of simple exclusion or repulsion or loathing by whites as one of forced intimacy, suffocating overproximity, invasive familiarity, an uninterrupted and unsolicited *closeness*. The structures of white supremacy not only enabled the intrusion of white fantasies into the black *imagination* but, more important, ensured that black *existence* would be ensnared in the dream work of white communal protocols—from dawn to dusk and dusk to dawn.

If the history of black subjection in the New World is marked by seemingly eternal measures of political, economic, and social segregation—barred and banned from the most valorized institutions of state and civil society while trapped, "overrepresented," in the most miserable—the *psychic* and *sexual* incorporation of blackness by whites has nonetheless been equally relentless (Lebeau 1998). Because the black has been arrested, immobilized beyond the dynamics of the dominant public sphere—*taken*—rendered an object outside the historical development of proper subjects, she exhibits a mercurial figurative capacity, a medium of exchange enabling the psychic life of white power, facilitating the practical and fantastic dimensions of its sexual economy. Racial slavery gives rise to the question of the body's propriety: not only disputed claims to the products of its labor or the forms of its expression, but also its enjoyment, its desire, and the whole range of its imaginative powers. The *ethos* of slavery, the ideological and affective matrix of the white supremacist project, admits no legitimate black self-defense, recognizes no legitimate assertions of black self-possession, privacy, or autonomy. Living in a permanent state of theft, seizure and abduction order the affairs of the captive community. Structural vulnerability to appropriation, a perpetual and involuntary *openness*, is the paradigmatic condition of black existence in the modern world, the defining characteristic of antiblackness.

Given this, one can see why leeriness about expressions of "interest," "curiosity," "borrowing," or "sharing" from groups historically immunized against perpetual servitude by procedures of epidermal reading recurs so regularly in the cultural and sexual politics of black resistance. In fact, it is astonishing that recoil is not the dominant posture, surprising, in other words, that black history has been marked so prominently by a spirit of tremendous generosity, an ethics of inclusion, a willingness to connect across the color line—politically, culturally, or socially—on whatever terms of humanity are available. It is a truly amazing aspect of the historical record that black people have managed to foster such a catholic disposition in the face of unremitting domination, exploitation, and appropriation from friends and foes alike, though we must add immediately that any such "hospitality" emerges not simply despite the circumstances but also because it is compelled by them, a *compulsory hospitality*. Of course, some think any affirmation of cross-racial attachments is mere foolishness for blacks, and at many points it does appear unfounded, a capitulation to greater power or, at least, a perplexing appeal for recognition. Still, hesitating about or even spurning coalition or collaboration, refusing to relinquish "ownership" of culture, politics, even of body, is neither the symptom of black people's unreasoned passion nor the abandonment of their better principles. More likely, it is an indispensable property of encounter under conditions of severe and organized brutality, a term of negotiation put forth by those who survive, even if the procedure is rarely, if ever, respected.[20] The ire that typifies contemporary multiracial discourse is thus bound up in profound impatience about *negotiation* with black community over the history of its formation and reformation. That is to say, multiracialism wants simply *to lay claim*, by right of force, to erstwhile figures of blackness, and they want to hear no questions, and certainly no lasting protest, from blacks about the matter. They want, in short, to redefine *unilaterally* what or who was once considered "black" as what or who is now "multi-racial." Beyond the incipient *dispossession,* however, this politics of identity also involves an act of monumental *imposition:* rather than an exploration of interracial contact zones or the peculiar nonspace of the borderland, multiracialism represents an obdurate demarcation of the territory of racial blackness itself.

Here blackness is defined of necessity as the *negative residuum* of the interracial encounter, left over and distilled, the difference subtracted not only from the mythic purity of whiteness but also from the sanctified "im-purity" of the multiracial contingent. On this score, the multiracial camp would like to disentangle its incorporation of figures of "false" blackness from its inevitable expulsion of figures of "true" blackness, an annexation that is at the same time a distancing. Distancing *through* annexation: this is a differentiation installed by the new border, the new color line, the definition given to that which is not taken in and cannot be included under any circumstances. The disputed territories of race and culture therefore mark a displacement of another controversy, another point of difficulty, another source of consternation: *the re-racialization of blackness.* Multi-racialism refuses negotiation about redrawing the color line at the limit of a condensed black body, a refusal that is predicated upon the divestiture of anything resembling meaningful black title, the repudiation of some-thing we can only inadequately call black authority. It is a cancellation of legitimate black claims to anything desirable or valuable, including voli-tion. To grant such recognition would require a moment of deference to a black deliberative process, an unthinkable exposure to—and a partial dependence upon—the autonomous considerations of black people, to beg the question of permission. Racial formation in the United States is his-torically founded upon consensus that any movement in this direction, any relinquishing to the vicissitudes of black desire, to say nothing of assent to black guidance or leadership, however slight or fleeting, leads immedi-ately and inexorably to a total reversal of racial hierarchy, producing "in a blink" a universe of oppressive black power, commonly considered to be a fate worse than death and one certainly more fearsome than supremacy of the white (or other) variety. The force of this nightmare weighs down as a continued insistence on the *isolation* of black people and a popular inability to concede a space of black negation, that is, the right of the one or the many to say no to a proposition or to revise its terms of engagement. Of course, all of this also serves to deny to blacks the ability to say yes—that is, consent that carries objective value. This is the double bind that multiracial discourse produces for any black response, a situation in which black consent is simultaneously *demanded* and *refused*. We will not take yes for an answer because we cannot take no for an answer.

The historical paean to the interracial is, in the first and last instance, about attenuating the real and imagined disinterest of blacks toward its prospects in the present. Further, it is about consolidating continued access for nonblacks to those few slim spaces of *relative autonomy* (not "purity" or "authenticity") that blacks have appropriated for themselves through sheer perseverance over the last century and a half of organized and unorganized struggle. This is why in nearly every instance of multiracial critique we find claims about the damaging *fallacy* of black cultural or political or geographic *ownership* and the resultant *delusion* of black people's supposed *territoriality*. It is asserted in these accounts that blacks can go nearly anywhere today, do or say nearly anything, and generally find themselves impervious to criticism, degradation, and aspersion, let alone systematic or structural violence: "choice has defeated coercion" (Talty 2003, 239).[21] Even when a lingering antiblack racism is admitted, it is minimized in a scheme that cheers the fading of black freedom struggle *against white supremacy and antiblackness* in order to make way for the new multiracial struggle *against black community*, the reputed bastion of "monoracial ideology" or "binary thinking."

But because the discourse of multiracialism discourages anything resembling materialist analysis, its ramifications for political struggles around race, class, gender, and sexuality can only be stated ambiguously, when they are not entirely obscured. We are asked to participate in its tacit affirmation of a bourgeois political geography produced by the uneven patterns of both integration and resegregation in the post–civil rights era (Massey and Denton 1998). We are asked to look away from its inability to offer viable *alternative* models for antidiscrimination and civil rights enforcement, let alone broader notions of social change, political trans-formation, or economic restructuring.[22] We leave unresolved, as well, its duplicity regarding race-based mobilization, its fondness for a reconsti-tuted U.S. nationalism, and its uncritical endorsement of late capitalism. As to the *symbolic value* of the claim to distinction, distance, or difference from racial blackness—whether one says "neither/nor" or "both/and"—we are offered patronizing reassurance, indignant denial, or cold indiffer-ence. This critical difference affords its designees great liberties: not only advantageous complicity in the domination of blacks but also the eroti-cization of participation in or proximity to dissimulated sexual impunity.

CHAPTER 3

There Is No (Interracial) Sexual Relationship

> There is no neutral symmetrical sexual relationship/exchange,
> undistorted by power. . . . If we subtract from sexual rapport the
> element of "asexual" (physical, financial . . .) coercion, which
> distorts the "pure" sexual attraction, we may lose sexual attraction
> itself. In other words, the problem is that the very element which
> seems to bias and corrupt pure sexual rapport . . . may function as
> the very phantasmatic support of sexual attraction—in a way, sex as
> such *is* pathological.
>
> —Slavoj Žižek, *The Plague of Fantasies*

In the previous chapter, we explored the assertion within multiracial discourse that consensual sexual relations between white male slaveholders and enslaved black females allowed genuine interracial intimacy to flourish under the regime of chattel slavery in the antebellum United States. We found the assertion to be not only unsupported on its own terms but also entirely misplaced given the questions at hand—an ethical evasion of the foreclosure of black female consent under the conditions of enslavement, as detailed by a number of noted black feminist scholars. Further, the peculiar historical demand for black female *sexual* consent in relations with white male slaveholders symbolizes for multiracial advocates a broader problem of *political* consent from the captive community and its descendents for the project of multiracial democracy up to the present moment. The objective of the current chapter is to reveal the notion of healthy interracial relationships advanced within multiracial discourse as an ideological lure insofar as they are considered to be disconnected from supposedly unhealthy interracial liaisons and, beyond that, a real union of differently raced subjects. I demonstrate that this fiction of wholesome interracial relationships requires their desexualization, a gesture that requires, in turn, a distancing from racial blackness—rhetorically, politically, geographically. Blackness is transformed concurrently from a site of victimization to a source of perpetration and liability. To that end, I support the following hypotheses:

- There is no *interracial* sexual relationship: the political inflection and social valorization of intimate interracial relationships and the related publicizing of multiracial identities reifies schemes of racial categorization, reimposing notions of racial purity to substantiate claims of sexual transgression and racial mixture.
- There is no interracial *sexual* relationship: in its quest for a sanitized circuit of interracial reproduction, multiracialism elides interracial sexuality, a conceptual quarantine promoted in moral register. Sexual practices are barred from consideration, desire as an element of the interracial relation is disavowed, and the complex interplay of race and sexuality is disciplined.
- There is no interracial sexual *relationship*: multiracialism refuses to countenance the fissure between the intermingling of racialized bodies and the social-symbolic effort to mediate racial antagonism at the levels of sexual practice and identity formation. Also lost is an examination of the presumed integrity of the bodies in question. Revealed instead is a libidinal body more expansive and more fragmented than that self-contained organic unit demanded by the standard "subject" of liberal humanism implied by the discourse.

My interest in this discursive formation does not involve discussions of interracial sexuality as a social problem. Rather, my concern here is, as announced in the introduction, to address the *problematic* of multiracial discourse, to provide a symptomatic reading of its unconscious epistemological stakes and its inarticulate affective structures.

Multiracialism in the post–civil rights era United States is marked by a split political–intellectual project, turning on specific tensions between the symbolic deployment of race and sexuality. On the one hand, we find a desire to go further into the terrain of racialization, a pornographic operation, as it were, that seeks to "'reveal all there is to reveal,' to hide nothing, to register 'all' and offer it to our view" (Žižek 1992, 109). Regarding this impulse, it seems the problem with racialization is not so much the devastation of its political and economic functions, its centrality to contemporary relations of power, as it is the imprecision or inconsistency of its designations, its unwillingness to recognize by its own logic the "monster" it has created, to grant a proper name. The monster, the ghost in the racializing machine, is, of course, the figure of race mixture, and the principle concern of multiracialism emerges as a question of accuracy, or better, *honesty*. It is argued that current classification schemes, both official and unofficial, efface the reality of contemporary race mixture, denying the very existence of "racially mixed people in America" to the latter's express detriment. Multiracial scholars and activists consider the damaging effect of this systemic denial on several levels, though mostly in the terms of psychological development. Without proper recognition by the state and the institutions of popular culture, multiracial people are denied the right to a legitimate *self-identification.*[1] Other proponents suggest the necessity of proper recognition for the purposes of empirical research on the multiracial population in the areas of health care, employment, education, and housing—the typical domains of civil rights compliance monitoring. Here the guiding suspicion is that multiracial people may experience group-specific forms of discrimination or suffer from undiscovered problems of epidemiology.[2] However, none among either the largely white, middle-class, college-educated leadership of the multiracial movement (Williams 2004) or the academic field of multiracial studies has ventured to *argue* that interracial couples or multiracial people—not least their immediate constituency—suffer *particular* forms of exploitation, disenfranchisement, or oppression unaccountable by established forms of racism, especially antiblackness.[3]

The political purchase of properly recognizing "American mixed race" is to exert a deconstructive force on racialization itself. It is presumed that fixed and stable categories are necessary to the functioning of racialization and that the acknowledged presence of the multiracial *mutatis mutandis* disorders the undertaking. The trouble is well advertised, and its purported effects resonate in critical contexts outside the limited purview of the multiracial movement or its academic counterpart. Cultural theorist Lola Young (1996b), for example, explains apropos of the figure of the mulatto: "If 'race' is an ontological symbol, how does the 'mulatto' fit into or disrupt the power of racial categories? These 'almost white' subjects . . . are figures that embody racial liminality, occupying interstices between the terms black and white, Negro and Caucasian, other and self. Thus, the 'mulatto' subject disrupts the normalization of the divide between blackness and whiteness" (92). The general weakness of this argument can, I think, be granted at this point in our discussion. That is to say, drawing attention to the permeability of racial borders or rendering visible the embodiment of "racial liminality" does not necessarily render racial categories suspect, but rather it is structurally required by the process of racial suture.

There can be no claim to "the multiracial experience" without the attendant affirmation of racial purity, that is, without entrenching the very founding fiction of racialization that multiracialism means to subvert. This conceptual dependence is inscribed in the disconcerting neologism *monoracial*,[4] deployed by multiracial activists and scholars in attempts to distinguish themselves from those other racial subjects with whom they quarrel or coalesce, whatever the case may be. As such, there is no *interracial* sexual relationship that does not resurrect the same racial frontier it purports to transgress or transcend. Beyond this first counterdiction, though, I want to introduce another consideration that will resurface repeatedly in this chapter. In many ways, the question of the scientific validity of race, while ultimately unavoidable, is of secondary importance here. What matters preeminently is the ethical stance against white supremacy and antiblackness, a stance that is not reducible to a critique of racial essentialism. Albert Memmi (1999) comments in this regard:

> There are no pure races, nor are there even homogenous biological groups. Were there any, they would not be biologically superior. Were they biologically superior, they would not necessarily be superlatively endowed or culturally more advanced than others. Were they that, they would not have any

God-given right to eat more than others, to be better housed, or to travel in better conditions. They could certainly decree such conditions for themselves, and impose them, but then neither justice nor equality would be found among them. . . . Racist reasoning has no secure foundation, is incoherent in its development, and is unjustified in its conclusions. (19)

I do not wish to spend more time rehearsing these points. Let us leave this to one side for the moment and turn our attention to the other side of multiracialism's split political–intellectual project, a resistance inherent to the collective effort.

"A Great Example of a Relationship"

There are two resistances here, and they cohere in the faith that the normalcy of multiracial people retroactively legitimizes the interracial sexual relationships from which they issue. Once again, the gesture is split in its function. The first resistance is marked by a desire to purify the interracial relationship either by not talking about it at all or by talking about it politely, especially in its sexual dimensions. Talk of interracial sexuality is jettisoned in order to clear space for the articulation of a multiracial identity that is not overshadowed by or reduced to the aftershock of its sexual prehistory. This line of defense comes in the face of well-worn racist treatises on the immorality and unnaturalness of interracial sexual relations, typically attended by paranoid fantasies of (white) racial annihilation. Accordingly, multiracial children are attributed the stigmata of tragedy, marginality, and pathology, casualties of a racial war in which they are supposed to be trapped between camps. Versions of this popular historical account are found readily in the major anthologies published thus far (O'Hearn 1998; Penn 1998; Root 1992b, 1996b; Zack 1995a). What is most important about this historical narrative is that multiracial people are, as the story goes, damned by a certain racialized original sin, doing penance for the evils of the sexual transgressions of their forebears. As such, their identities are burdened or stained by a debased scene of inception.

From the vantage that locates the "spurious issues" of interracial sexual reproduction as the ultimate targets of antimiscegenation, multiracial people are ideally positioned to refute claims made, for quite different reasons, by both white racists and "ethnic chauvinists" in their respective oppositions to race mixture.[5] This refutation is most often rendered as the "coming to voice" of the multiracial subject or the reclamation of a previously scorned multiracial identity. The *doxa* of rebuttal runs as follows: *All* interracial couples are not pathologically motivated, or worse, poor and uneducated, derived from and/or relegated to the margins of society. *All* interracial couples are not obsessed with racial difference, motivated by a pornographic racial fetishism, sexual perversion, or the self-hating desire to escape the confines of their communities of origin. In addition to this, *all* multiracial people are not banished from the comforts of identifiable racial communities, destined to roam the hinterlands of social exclusion, suffering the psychological strain of unresolved ambiguity. *Many*, perhaps most, multiracial people have found ways to creatively manage their multiple situations, building in some way from what is misnamed a Du Boisian "double consciousness." The more prevalent terms used to describe such "achievements in identity": "social fluidity," "cognitive flexibility," "situational manageability," "environmental adaptability," and a generally "diplomatic" disposition.[6] Pouring over the interdisciplinary literature by and about multiracial people and interracial relationships, one is assured that multiracial people and interracial couples, *for the most part*, can and will navigate the treacherous racial terrain of the contemporary United States. In its brighter moments, multiracialism offers insights as to how the broader national population—the less fluid, less flexible "monoracial" majority—can enjoy the internal "defeat of racism" that interracial couples practice and multiracial people embody in their everyday lives. This is what Root (1992b) suggests with the notion of "mini-revolutions" against the racial order.

The branching narrative of resistance offered above does not do justice to the vexed discursive relations between race and sexuality in the politics of multiracialism. The depathologizing of the interracial relationship is attempted *retroactively* through the health of multiracial people, restricting the debate about antimiscegenation to the terrain of *reproduction*, most often within the institution of marriage, rather than of *sexuality* irreducible to "breeding" and the dynamics of the two-parent nuclear family. In this sense, the discourse is formulated in dialogue with the white supremacist obsession with "mongrelization" in both its liberal/conservative (i.e., "What about the kids, won't they be confused?") and reactionary (i.e., "What about the kids, won't they be degenerate, sterile, unintelligent, and dangerous?") modes. More to the point, multiracial discourse prides itself on being a definitive response to so-called ethnic chauvinists in both their more compassionate (i.e., "What about the kids, won't they be confused?") and hostile (i.e., "What about the kids, won't they dilute an endangered racial stock and dissipate an embattled cultural heritage?") objections. Since it is understood by multiracial advocates that criticism of or opposition to interracial relationships is based in large part on concerns about potential offspring, the creation of positive images for multiracial people is, in circular fashion, taken to be an exoneration of interracial relationships as well. The interracial relationship has to await the legitimization of multiracial people before it can enter the public sphere as a renovated family affair in the new and respectable guise of loving and capable parents a generation removed. In this representational strategy, there is a resistance to discuss the means and relations of sexual reproduction, to disarticulate sexuality from biological procreation so as to engage a discussion of the politics of interracial sexuality. In place of this critical discourse, we find a *desexualization of interracial encounter* and, as we will see in a moment, a *deracialization of sexual encounter.* This scission operates within the nominally liberal fight against a receding white supremacist taboo and the ascendant restrictions of "Afrocentric nationalism" (Byrd 1996) as well as the more obviously conservative promotion of traditional family values and romance against the corruptions of "vulgar" sexuality. What remains consistent with past iterations is the utter inability to speak about interracial sexuality with anything but naïveté or bawdiness.

Interracial sexuality is a necessary condition for multiracialism—there may be interracial sexual relations without multiracial offspring but no multiracial offspring without interracial sexual relations (new reproductive technologies, including surrogate pregnancy, in vitro fertilization, and the current experiments with human cloning present ramifications too complex to broach here, but they do not escape the field of sexuality simply because they introduce new forms of mediation).We must then ask how the specter of interracial sexuality haunts the political project to the extent that it conjures a realm of the unspeakable. One is hard pressed to imagine a politics of multiracialism reduced to people involved or interested in interracial relationships. Without the moral anchor of multiracial people, especially young children, multiracialism experiences difficulty distinguishing its prime objectives from those of, say, international mail-order bride services or the global pornography and sex tourism industries, paramount examples of the contemporary "commodification of Otherness" (Fung 1991, hooks 1992, Lee 1998, Meng 1994, Mercer 1994). Interracial sexuality is that moment in the circuit of reproduction that multiracialism occludes for fear of bogging down in the quagmire of stigma and ulterior motive. The parameters of interracial sexuality are inhabited, but its substance is removed from view. In the rare moments when multiracial discourse addresses sexuality at all, it is in attempts to endorse a "sexuality of the heights" over and against a "sexuality of the depths."

In his book-length treatment of the collaborative work of Gilles Deleuze and Félix Guattari, Philip Goodchild (1996) provides a helpful summation of what they theorize as desire's principal modes of investment—height, depth, and surface. A "sexuality of the depths" would be most closely associated with the sordid carnal pleasures that multiracialism is at pains to renounce. This is "a sexuality of bodies and their interpenetrations, usually focused on genital contact, the sole aim being physical enjoyment. . . . It often leads to the serial investment in various bodies" (Goodchild 1996: 80). Though it is perhaps interesting to discuss interracial sexuality on this level, I am not arguing that indulgence of this sort would lead the multiracial politics into more liberating directions, despite the promises of interracial pornographers and the prognostications of some sex radicals.[7] One can see how such an approach reinforces discourses of sexual exoticism. I am less interested in prodding multiracial advocates to talk about or cultivate a sexuality of the depths than in pointing up how the disallowance of this mode of investment serves the construction of multiracialism's asexual persona.

A sexuality of the heights, according to Goodchild, is "a sexuality . . . that aims to re-create the moral ideals of the oedipal family or the subjectified couple, founded on promises, principles, and mutual expectations." He expands:

> The aim is to isolate and protect the sexual drives from all forces of corruption and destruction. Here, loyalty to a single object of desire, including an obligation to abide by often unspoken contracts and implicit expectations, is of greater significance than the kind of person or object desired. (80)

This is the good interracial relationship retroactively substantiated by the robust multiracial subject. There is no trace of pathology here, no lustful attraction, no fascination, no fetishism, no evidence that power has irreparably damaged the relationship. This is true even in those cases where it is admitted that a titillating sense of racial difference was initially at work (though always in early stages that are subsequently outgrown) (Mathabane and Mathabane 1992; Reddy 1996). How do we gauge the apparent contradiction between this rather conservative understanding of interracial relationships and the liberal mission to transgress boundaries, break ranks, and violate traditional expectations of racially bound community? Goodchild explains: "The sexuality that is constituted around the transgression of laws, taboos, and standards of purity is no less a sexuality of the heights than those which follow a moral ideal" (80). In fact, transgression has become multiracialism's own moral ideal. In this sense, the contradiction gains consistency by simultaneously downplaying the importance of racial difference ("loyalty . . . is more important than the kind of person or object desired") and valorizing border-crossing couples as pioneers of a purportedly antiracist moral ideal. This is the second sense in which there is no interracial *sexual* relationship. Multiracialism claims not to be about interracial sexuality where its sexual acts are associated with the depths. It is, rather, about love, romance, family, and trust where these ideals are associated with the heights of racial harmony—it is the elevation of the interracial relationship up and away from the low areas of the body, the putative site of racism's pernicious effects.[8]

Formulating a rejoinder to such counterarguments is a difficult matter, largely because the voices articulating "the multiracial experience" and the many interracial couples responding to the expected charges with narratives about "the triumph of love over prejudice and taboo" have produced an *affective* closure, in part an effect of the rhetoric of "immanence" they deploy to those ends.[9] How, then, are we to think critically about the politics of interracial sexuality in the discourse of multiracialism in the current conjuncture?

The Soup of a Relationship

Calvin Hernton (1988) introduced the concept of sexual racism in his classic 1965 text, *Sex and Racism in America*. With it he tied then prevailing sentiments of antimiscegenation to the social structures of antiblack racism.

> Bad feelings and bad acts against interracial associations are part and parcel of the sundry acts of terror and violence that are presently perpetrated against black people in our cities and suburbs and on our college campuses. This violence is but a blatant manifestation of the more "hidden" racism that seethes just beneath the surface of contemporary American society and pervades every institution and every facet of our world. I want to emphasize that racism is an uncanny hatred. It infects not merely the economic, political, and social spheres but the most intimate sexual feelings and behaviors of our lives. . . . Racial hatred demands . . . emotional involvement with the biology of black people. The first focus of racism is the physical body. . . . Racial hatred, then, is carnal hatred. It is sexualized hatred. To the extent that racism itself is alive in America, the sexualization of racism is a *fait accompli*. Whether directed against blacks or some other racial group, sexual racism, moreover, is the most degenerate and perverse form of sexual turn-on. . . . This perversion . . . seems to be inherent in racism itself. . . . Negative, pornographic, inflammable emotions toward sexual relations across the color line are as American as God. (xii)

Thus, "when all is said and done about the reasons for opposing racial integration, the bottom line is invariably a superstitious imagining of the pornographic nature of interracial sex" (xiv). I quote this passage at length only to outline the "social problem" against which the authors discussed in this chapter are struggling. In this way, Hernton's polemic prefigures much of what will be said in the name of multiracialism more than twenty-five years later. Early in the text, he waxes romantic, extending the terms of dispute for his successors:

> People who trespass across race and sex barriers are *fugitives* in American society. . . . They appear to be forever in flight—psychological flight and geographical flight. . . . They are constantly irritated by their sure knowledge of being "oddities" in a sexist and racist culture. These stigmata—of being fugitives and outcasts from society—bring interracial couples together as kindred souls who desire love and companionship far more than mere sex. (xviii)

The desire to eradicate sexual racism by affirming "love and companionship" has produced questionable results at best. It is our task in this section not only to see if we might pose a challenge to sexual racism but also to interrogate as well the ostensible opposition—"love and companionship" versus "mere sex"—wondering if, in thinking we have surpassed the situation, we may have entangled ourselves more thoroughly within it. We return to Hernton's fugitives later in the chapter.

In her essay "Eating the Other," bell hooks (1992) tells of an afternoon encounter with "a group of very blond, very white, jock types" on the streets of New Haven, Connecticut, adjacent to the Yale University campus where she was teaching at the time. Once within earshot, she realized that these young white men were discussing "plans to fuck as many girls from other racial/ethnic groups as they could 'catch' before graduation." "They 'ran' it down," writes hooks. "Black girls were high on the list, Native American girls hard to find, Asian girls (all lumped into the same category) [and] deemed easier to entice, were considered 'prime targets'" (23). This anecdote is offered as the first in a series of examples through which hooks discusses the contemporary "commodification of Otherness" at the site of "racialized sexual encounter." As she describes the situation,

> Mass culture is the contemporary location that both publicly declares and perpetuates the idea that there is pleasure to be found in the acknowledgement

and enjoyment of racial difference. . . . Within commodity culture, ethnicity becomes spice, seasoning that can liven up the dull dish that is mainstream white culture. Cultural taboos around sexuality and desire are transgressed and made explicit. (21)

hooks refers to this development as a revival of longstanding modernist interests in the "primitive" with, she adds, a "distinctly postmodern slant."

For white boys to openly discuss their desire for colored girls (or boys) publicly announces their break with a white supremacist past that would have such desire articulated only as taboo, as secret, as shame. They see their willingness to *openly* name their desire for the Other as [an] affirmation of cultural plurality (its impact on sexual preference and choice). Unlike racist white men who historically violated the bodies of black women/women of color to assert their position as colonizer/conqueror, these young men see themselves as non-racists who choose to transgress racial boundaries within the sexual realm not to dominate the Other, but rather so that they can be acted upon, so that can be changed utterly. Not at all attuned to those aspects of their sexual fantasies that irrevocably link them to collective white racist domination, they believe their desire for contact represents a progressive change in white attitudes towards non-whites. They do not see themselves as perpetuating racism. (24)

It was suggested by several authors criticized in chapter 2 that a substantial number of white male slaveholders in the antebellum period *also* saw themselves as "non-racists who choose to transgress racial boundaries within the sexual realm not to dominate the Other, but rather so that they can be acted upon." Given this intergenerational accord, what might be novel or "postmodern" about the practices of sexual transgression hooks discusses is not the attempt to "break with a white supremacist past" but rather to rewrite it entirely as an evolutionary tale of repressed interracial intimacy maturing into an open declaration of desire for the other, a declaration whose reverberation in the post–civil rights era is dampened only by black feminist critics like hooks. I want to extend hooks's analysis in order to draw attention to a strategy of crisis management that seems to qualify the bold new pronouncements she rightly criticizes as complicit with "collective white racist domination." What requires further discussion is the question of complicity itself and its relation to a critical resistance that hooks finds painfully lacking in contemporary culture.

To pursue this space of inquiry, let us look to some of the rich testimonials that multiracial studies have delivered to bookstores in the last decade or so. I begin with Jane Lazarre's (1997) reflections in *Beyond the Whiteness of Whiteness: Memoir of a White Mother of Black Sons*. The book is a critical memoir—at times lucid and insightful—about the politics of race, class, and gender that structure her interracial marriage—a white woman married to a black man—as well as her ongoing role as a mother to two black-identified, multiracial sons. In the first chapter, she asks urgently, "How can I escape the weight?" For Lazarre, this is *the* question. We will encounter it several times over in our present discussion and shall find that a great deal is expressed in this one brief plea. I quote here at length:

> How can I escape the weight of this so recent history [of racial slavery] when a Black woman who does not know me encounters me on the street, at a meeting, or party, obviously attached to a Black man? I feel neither guilt nor regret nor any sense of personal defensiveness for my choice of a husband. An obsessively self-conscious person, I am very clear about the deeply rooted origins which tied me for life to this person, and these roots are unquestionably more defining than racial or cultural differences. And of course, I know many Black women who are not bothered by white women coupled with Black men in particular cases. . . . But there is also a social context and history to any personal decision or act.
>
> I go to a party honoring a good friend who has recently been promoted to an important position. He is Black. His wife is white. I know these two people well and, as with my own marital history, I know they fell in love with each other as individuals. I even know them well enough to think I can begin to imagine the specifics of spirit and personal history that drew them to one another. I do not doubt the complete authenticity, the humanity beyond race, of their attachment as I never doubted that same authenticity

in my nearly thirty-year attachment to Douglas. Yet, as I wind my way through the crowded party, held in a splendid apartment on the upper west side of Manhattan, full of progressive leaders in government, social agencies, the arts, I see numerous "interracial" couples, all Black men and white women. There are Black women there too, of course, and they seem to be with Black men or on their own. My personal experience, however unique, is also part of a historical process, a broader narrative framing my individual story, not completely defining it nor even, perhaps, substantially changing it, but touching it, affecting it. We do not exist outside of history, our lives uncomplicated by what came before. (7–8)

That the violent history of racial slavery is described as a "weight" bearing down upon the author is indicative. "Personal experience," "spirit," "authenticity," a "humanity beyond race" operate at the core of existence: all are sharply contrasted to the historical *externality* of race. As is the case across the literature of multiracialism, race is demoted to the level of framing narrative in relation to some more immediate and essential "individual story." Depicted as a glancing blow across the deep origins of this intimate connection, racial difference neither defines the relationship nor even "substantially [changes] it."

One is tempted here to invoke Derrida's (1970) provocative comments, offered in quite different circumstances, regarding the assumptive logic of structuralism. In the following passage from his famous essay, "Structure, Sign, and Play," he recapitulates:

[The concept of] structure—or rather the structurality of structure . . . has always been neutralized or reduced, and this by a process of giving it a center or referring it to a point of presence, a fixed origin. The function of this center was not only to orient, balance, and organize the structure . . . but above all to make sure that the organizing principle of the structure would limit what we might call the freeplay of the structure. . . . The center of a structure permits the freeplay of its elements inside the total form. . . . Thus it has always been thought that the center, which is by definition unique, constituted that very thing within a structure which governs the structure, while [itself] escaping structurality. . . . The concept of a centered structure is in fact the concept of a freeplay based on a fundamental ground, a freeplay which is constituted upon a fundamental immobility and a reassuring certitude, which is itself beyond the reach of freeplay. With this certitude anxiety can be mastered, for anxiety is invariably the result of a certain mode of being implicated in the game, of being caught by the game, of being as it were from the very beginning at stake in the game. (247–48)

The structure of the interracial relationship is organized by a principle of "authenticity" that Lazarre posits but fails to describe—"humanity beyond race," roots supposed to be more defining than what we can call the freeplay of racial difference. The freeplay of the structure—the disturbing historical effects of racialization, its relations of power—are held within a certain orbit, structured and subject to the metaphysical organizing principle of "spirit," governed by the ground of "humanity." But what is at stake in the endeavor to distill the true love of the interracial relationship from the pollutants of power, of race and sexuality, from those subtracted elements of pathology and pornography? To identify, that is, the stable center that might offer a reassuring certitude in the face of the vagaries and vicissitudes of race? Can the unidirectional relation between the center and its outside be maintained? Are these terms, in fact, discrete categories of social existence, one subordinate to the other? Do they exist on some sort of continuum? Or are we faced here with a case of mutual implication, a certain hybridity or categorical permeation? If, to augment earlier statements, racialization is a fundamental condition of possibility for multiracialism and the postmodern culture of transgression it affirms, how is it that the image of racialized sexual encounter, *the freeplay of the structure*, menaces the political project? It seems that without the moral anchor of "true love" (analog to and guarantor of the thriving multiracial child), multiracialism experiences difficulty defining itself against the image of interracial sexuality "which is responsible for all the conflicts that may arise" (Fanon 1967, 169).[10] Racialization is therefore addressed as a component of attraction in attempts to display its marginality, its containment, its pacification.

Race, which includes the way someone looks and acts, is just one factor in choosing a mate. It is kind of like the spice in soup. If we eat the spice alone it is overpowering and unhealthy. If we add the spice to soup it makes the soup so much better. The soup of a relationship is a mutual love and respect of the inner person. If we dispense of the soup we are left with nothing of value. (Barrymoore n.d.)

So writes Vincent Barrymoore, Dallas-based environmental engineer and webmaster of the Asiaphile homepage.[11] Describing himself, pro forma, as an "equal opportunity dater," his Web site is nevertheless "designed to explore and celebrate Asian/Caucasian dating" in particular. He explains:

One reason I made this page is because the Internet is loaded with Asian Women porn sites. This propagates the notion that Asian women with White men is a deviant relationship based on a fetish (hence my taunting moniker Mr. Asiaphile). Certainly there are some sick relationships out there. Some of them are interracial, some are not. I do not believe that an Asian woman with a White man is inherently deviant. . . . This page is partly here to make fun of myself. The name "Asiaphile" is meant as a tongue-in-cheek way of laughing at all those who would make a big deal out of dating Asian women [unlike those who would, say, dedicate an entire webpage to the issue— author's comment]. However, there is a more serious side. . . . If the Internet and media continue to feed images of Asian women as loose women, they may generate an even larger market. In other words, [white] men will act the way they are expected. So we, Asians and whites alike, must stand firm and not let the media define our attraction, but rather let us shape the media's image.

The heroic notion of standing firm against the technologies of stigmatization is representative of the new racial–sexual boundary crossing. The project of the growing multiracial literature is to shape the public image of interracial relationships and multiracial people in contradistinction to the marketable products of a racist and sexist commodity culture. Root (1997) expresses similar regret about the forces of commodification ("based on a fetish") that subtend racialized sexual encounter in the age of globalization. Whereas Barrymoore offers a call to arms against the international pornography industry, Root laments the proliferation of international mail-order bride services.

> Unfortunately the bride order industry has changed cross-cultural and cross-national marriage from a romantic event to a suspect catalogue business in which the Philippines is the largest supplier of international brides via this industry. . . . Denigrating stereotypes of Filipinas as exotic, childlike, subservient and gold-digging maintain an attitude that dismisses the validity of a majority of these relationships and the children from them. (85)

However, the "romantic event" Root refers to here is a shorthand for the numerous marriages between Philippines-based U.S. military personnel, primarily white men, and local Filipinas (among whose number Root's parents are counted), a phenomenon whose promise she initially tempers for its imperial premises: U.S. conquest and military occupation, the ongoing globalization of capital, overlapping structures of "imported" and "domestic" patriarchy, and so on. Yet when Root turns her attention to the more recent mail-order bride industry, she laments, without transition and with more than a hint of nostalgia, the displacement of the aforementioned "military marriages" (so named because the wives are incorporated into the U.S. military community, granted U.S. citizenship, and often take up residence stateside) by this emergent "suspect business." She does not see these twin developments as being intimately related but rather takes the latter to be both eclipsing and disgracing the former.

How are we to understand this critical reversal? Is this desire to cleanse the interracial relationship, to mark out a distinction between multiracialism proper and the supposed pollution of a commodified, pornographic pathology not the same chauvinistic reasoning, the same categorical prophylaxis that the multiracial movement and its academic cohort seeks to undermine? What are we to make of this effort to throw out the dirty water—the suspect business, the sexuality of the depths—while saving the healthy baby—the valid romantic event, the sexuality of the heights?

Why try to purge the interracial encounter of these unwanted elements? Are these not the very characteristics of the white supremacist ideology that would mandate an ethics of racial purity, the puritanical obsessions of fundamentalist movements in general? Is this not the very line of reasoning, the same logic of exclusion that stalwart defenders of the racial order have offered to justify realigning racial categories to accommodate nagging processes of hybridization only to *maintain* their boundaries? In the common sense of the United States, blacks are people who are, *for the most part*, identifiable as black—as convention runs, blacks can be mixed and still be black, this being the whole point of the present debate. Whites are people who, *so far as we can tell*, are not black at all. For present purposes, we might say that invalid, degraded interracial relationships are those that base themselves, *for the most part*, on racial and sexual stereotypes. Meanwhile, the true and proper interracial relationships are those that, *so far as we can tell*, are not suspect in this way—those that are, in a word, *passing*.

Notably, the statements made in defense of interracial relationships over and against the white supremacist taboo, the aspersions of "Afrocentric nationalism," or persistent associations with global commerce, must always be qualified. It is never asserted that *none* of the relationships in question can be characterized by disreputable exoticism or racist fascination or market considerations. Indeed, the previous quote from Root is just one example of multiracial advocates being continually forced to disavow—to recognize and to deny—such supposed aberrations. It follows, then, that the argument is based on the assumption that there is, as the pernicious saying goes, some truth to the stereotypes. Unable to produce an absolute refutation of the charges levied against it—as if that were the point—multiracialism instead celebrates the arrival of a critical mass or the achievement of a safe distance. The subsequent argument promises that, *for the most part*, the relations in question are healthy and the identities of any children thereof are sound. Most importantly, it insists that the very terms of this debate—healthy/unhealthy, moral/immoral, and so forth—are entirely acceptable, that this battle to legitimate the movement from *within* the Manichaean perspective of white supremacy and antiblackness is, in fact, the correct one. Perhaps, as Barrymoore says, race is an empty shell, valueless. Nonetheless, it is, by this account, still considered to be something unbearable if it is not mediated by or diluted in an amorous solution. "A little racial difference gives flavor to a relationship," he suggests. "But *it should not be the whole relationship*. A relationship based *solely* on race is like eating raw garlic . . . overpowering, unfulfilling and kinda gross." We are stuck within this polarization, between just a little and far too much, left with no specific commentary on the proper degree of racial difference for this so-called soup of a relationship. No guidelines or detailed instructions, no references to any suitable measures, just an appeal to intuition, to wholesome feelings, a flavor that we should, it is assumed, simply recognize without ever having been educated in exact terms.

Suspect catalogue businesses, such as the mail-order bride service, invalidate and undermine otherwise romantic events. The pornography industry gives otherwise decent relationships a bad name. Too much racialization, too much commodification, or too much sexualization, which is to say too much valuation on the market, devalues a relationship according to other, supposedly nonmarket considerations. Bear in mind that this is the position of the *advocates* of multiracialism and not its critics. Recall Memmi's observation: "What is remarkable is that these disparaging [racist] myths, whether funny or not, always devolve into the same basic themes: money, power, and sex, which reveals the preoccupations of the ones who impute the myth" (1999, 52). It seems, perhaps unsurprisingly, that these are also the preoccupations of those refuting the myth as well. The racist and sexist preoccupations of white supremacy and antiblackness—that the wrong balance of race, sex, power, and money spoils a relationship—have been refurbished *as* the discourse of the multiracialism. A constant line of denunciation functions as the proof of its respectability, its maturity, and its confidence in defending true love against corruption, successfully warding off perversion and pathology. And the categories of perversion and pathology themselves escape question as they are displaced further down the line in a gesture of reassurance to the reigning moral order. According to multiracial advocates, there are, in fact, perverted people in the most pejorative sense of the word. There are, in fact, sick interracial relationships. All of the relationships are not valid; some are invalid. However, they claim, *we are not among them*, and moreover, we have no pretense of solidarity with those other cases. In *Crossing the Color Line*, Maureen Reddy (1994) poses the question: "Whose interests are served by the attempt to portray *all* interracial relationships as pathological" (13; emphasis added)? She answers with certainty: white supremacists. We might now rephrase the question as follows: whose interests are served by the attempt to portray *some* interracial relationships as pathological?

Jonathon Zimmerman (1999) dramatizes these interests in a historical survey of black–white relationships among 1960s U.S. Peace Corps volunteers in Africa. There he specifies the world against which the interracial couple must position itself and the tactics of such a positioning. Musing wistfully on the hypothetical displacement of four full centuries, he writes: "But for America's own 'history of oppression' . . . no cause prevented blacks and whites from living—and loving—together" (515). Of course, "but for America's own 'history of oppression'" there would be no blacks and whites to live—or love—together in the first place! The theoretical edifice that has grown up around the concept of racial formation has persuasively demonstrated that blacks and whites, as racialized human populations, were and continue to be constructed as such by the incommensurability of their relative social and political positions. They are known only by their historical antagonism and not as some benign form of naturally occurring difference. Were the latter the case, race would again become essence. It would also suggest that the hostility and derogation inherent in the structures of white supremacy and antiblackness could be neutralized, all things held constant, such that blacks and whites could somehow "all just get along." What is the point, then, of this imaginative exercise? As we shall see presently, the desire to counteract racial oppression is desultory, for the coveted racial harmony does not become possible, on the ground, except through the displacement of the "domestic" antagonism to another level of social organization, in this case, through the spurious incorporation of black Americans into the structure of U.S. imperialism. Perhaps it goes without saying that such a gesture intensifies white supremacy and antiblackness even as it reconfigures them. Zimmerman begins:

Whites transferred many of their fears and anxieties about black Americans onto Africans: Africans were sexually promiscuous; Africans lusted after white women; and Africans would use racial blackmail to corner their prey. . . . Against this backdrop, black–white Peace Corps romances must have seemed fairly innocuous: whatever worries whites felt about dating black Americans, they paled next to the far more stringent taboos against sex with an African. . . . They were hardly eager to promote interracial dating or marriage among volunteers. . . . But they made it clear that romance with foreigners was even worse, flatly warning one group of female trainees to "stay away from African men." Women—especially white women—well understood that "black Peace Corps volunteers were safer than the black males over there." Only in Africa . . . would either race of Americans feel truly safe to love the other. (518)

He continues:

[In the United States], secret and shameful feelings of inferiority, like the ever-present threat of physical violence . . . often poisoned American interracial relationships. . . . In Africa, however, the senses of danger and inferiority both melted away. . . . Similarly, blacks found, white volunteers tended to discard their own sense of racial privilege when they left home. . . . In a new and often strange environment . . . black and white volunteers were less likely to replay their old conflicts than to discover their "many commonalties"—including an attraction to each other. . . . [And] after the initial thrill wore off . . . white and black volunteers came to share the African view of interracial sex: it was "no big deal." Indeed . . . volunteers seemed to be "losing [their] perspective on skin color"—and loving each other without regard to it. By contrast, volunteer romances with Africans were often rife with acrimony. (520–21)

Again, it is the external casing, the situation, or the context of the interracial relationship that disables it, a relationship that in another social and historical location could work precisely by fading into the quotidian: "no big deal." It is implied by this example that interracial relationships function best when they are *not* critically discussed, subjected to analysis or inter-rogation, when they are *not* considered suspect. The interracial *relation-ship* is supposed to do its work "in the background," though "the African view of interracial sex" did nothing to safeguard Africans, or their coun-terparts in the United States, from the racist projections of white Amer-icans that managed to accompany the latter "losing [their] perspective on skin color." When the veiled work of the relationship, the hidden labor that holds it together, is brought to our attention, we are left to throw our hands in the air, defer the answer, or look the other way. Interracial rela-tionships work best when they are not brought to question, when they are not understood to be "implicated" (in Derrida's sense), that is to say, some-thing other than natural, innocent, spontaneously occurring, or, when these terms cannot be maintained, at least *manageable*.

The mythology of the recuperated interracial relationship betrays itself when the vacated acrimony generally characterizing the black–white axis in the U.S. racial formation reemerges with respect to local Afri-cans. More accurately, it is *transferred*, maintained and rearticulated along the African–American axis by utilizing the same binary structure—civilized–savage, restrained–promiscuous, honest–deceitful, and so on. Thus, the constructed commonalty between black and white Americans is, at a geographical remove, strictly homologous to the social bond that allows the racist communities of white supremacy and antiblackness to cohere in the United States. But it only pretends to be an extension of that bond. Black and white Americans become *legitimately* attractive to one another, at this level, because they are, in the parlance, not the "niggers" that Africans are supposed to be. We might say that so long as U.S. blacks are "de-niggerized" (Fanon writes poignantly of "denegrification"), the relationship among "Americans" is rendered permissible. An impossible process: blacks dissociated from blackness at the height, no less, of the modern civil rights movement, the dawn of Black Power! (The latest absur-dity from a country that produces decaffeinated coffee, sugarless choco-late, fat-free doughnuts, etc.).

In sum, interracial relationships are corrupted from the outside by the forces of racism and, when this is not the case, they can and do function "normally." However, racism begins and ends in an emotional involvement with the black body. The essence of racism is located in the obsessive attention fixed upon the black body, its imputed sexuality, and the immorality of those who would risk an encounter with it. In this way, racialization and sexualization are inextricable. In order for interracial relationships to be "valued in this culture and society" and "triumph over prejudice and taboo," the relationship itself must be desexualized and, in a precise way, deracialized, which, as we have seen, requires a distance toward and denigration of blackness. This is not to say that no acknowledgment can be given to racial difference within multiracial discourse but rather that this recognition is oblique and muted, subordinated to the more defining features of the relationship *as such*. Race-as-spice, in itself overpowering and sickening, is permitted so long as there is sufficient soup to contain and direct and dilute its potency. Race may sit at the table so long as it does not take over the show, dominate the scene, and convert it into the obscene pornographic display we know all too well. That is, so long as a relationship between humans is at hand and not one between blacks and any others, which is only to say, finally, so long as it is *not an interracial relationship at all*.[12]

In this light, we discern a pivotal discursive function in the fashioning of interracial sexual encounter in the post–civil rights era. The "superstitious imagining of the pornographic nature of interracial sex" is, contrary to common sense, not what prevents healthy interracial relationships from flourishing, tarnishing their public standing. It is, rather, the very thing that enables them to be conceptualized in the first place. In other words, *racism is not an obstacle to interracial intimacy but its condition of possibility*. This is so in much the same way that the transference of white American racial anxieties onto Africans enabled their interracial romance with U.S. blacks in the Peace Corps to gain respectability and even a degree of heroism. Without the "suspect business" of the mail-order bride industry denounced by Root, the countless interracial pornography Web sites chastised by Barrymoore, or the historical legacy of racial slavery bemoaned by Lazarre, there would be no points of reference by which to judge genuine interracial intimacy worthy of celebration. This is the particular enjoyment of the healthy interracial relationship, one that is dependent on the very things it endlessly combats—a relationship that does not and cannot exist *as such*.

In the introduction to the second edition of *Sex and Racism*, Hernton (1988) writes:

> The taboo against interracial sex of any kind is alive and thriving in America. I am now prepared to state—as I was not when I first wrote this book—that interracial sex will never be more than tolerated in America; it will never be desired and valued in and by this society and culture; it will only be exploited and employed for pornographic titillation. Only a preponderance of interracial sex relationships or larger numbers of them throughout the population will humanize our behavior toward such relations. This . . . will never happen. (xviii–xix)

It is unlikely that Hernton anticipated the emergence of multiracialism (though he does detect the ascendance of hooks's postmodern "commodification of Otherness"). Nonetheless, we recognize within his requiem the longing for a fit and sound interracial relationship that multiracialism now promises to cultivate. His deeply felt pessimism, his resignation, leads him to conclude that such relations "will never be desired and valued in and by this society." Yet, without sharing in his remorse, we reconsider the costs involved in the seesaw of this societal valuation and respond to the point: we hope *not*.

"The height falls back upon the depth"

In thinking further about the difficulties of this process of failed differentiation between healthy and unhealthy interracial relationships within the discourse of multiracialism, let us consider arguments made in another context by Slavoj Žižek (1997) regarding the desire for a wholesome national identity purged of violent, intolerant nationalism.

> It is deeply wrong to assert that when one throws out the nationalist dirty water ("excessive" fanaticism), one should be careful not to lose the baby of

the "healthy" national identity—that is to say, one should trace the line of separation between the proper degree of "healthy" nationalism which guarantees the necessary minimum of national identity, and "excessive" (xenophobic, aggressive) nationalism. . . . In the matter of national identity, one should also endeavor to throw out the baby (the spiritual purity of the national identity) in order to reveal the phantasmatic support which structures the *jouissance* of the national Thing. (62–63)

This prescription can be transposed to prompt a new and unsettling look at the fantasy of commodified interracial pornography and multiracial pathology, connecting it not only to the paranoia of the racist imagination but also, scandalously, to the political imaginary of multiracialism itself.

What is suggested, then, is a rethinking of the relationship between the normal, official workings of political struggle in the public sphere (the vaunted sexuality of the heights) and the shadowy realm of its obscene, perverse underside (the disavowed sexuality of the depths), between official desire and "true" desire. Rather than positing the latter as a corruption of or deviation from the former, or worse, its opposite, we might think instead of how the underside serves as the *support* of the public face. This is not simply a point about the differential production of meaning that I have stressed in other parts of this study. Beyond the banal fact that officialdom establishes "legitimacy" in contradistinction from the "illegitimacy" of its designated others, we are dealing with something more radical. Multiracial advocates are not only constructing their political identities by differentiating themselves from the bad objects of interracial pornography and racist hatred and fear, thereby prolonging their own conceptual dependence upon them. What is more, the demarcation between self and other, much like the boundaries of racial categorization, cannot be maintained except by persistently effacing its defining criteria. After all, how can we determine the presence or absence of such contaminants, a contrary condition of purity or health, or relative degrees of each? A comment from a progressive student publication at the University of California reiterates this interpretive difficulty, recalling the delicacy of Barrymoore's culinary arts. In an article interrogating the timeworn topic of "racial fetishism" in relationships between white men and Asian women, the co-authors write:

> Just to be clear, it is not necessarily the . . . relationship that is problematic. Instead, the problem here is the actual fetishization. . . . It's not the relationships we should call into question, [but] rather this disturbing trend of fetishization. . . . But how are these distinguished? . . . There exists a very fine line between being attracted to a certain aesthetic and . . . actual fetishization. (Lee and Chaddha 2000)

Given the constitutive nature of racialization for "the practices of the world,"[13] though, we can agree that it is fantastic to assert the possibility of colorblindness, of not seeing race while "being attracted to a certain aesthetic," as it were, and by extension, of desiring, *purely*, some elemental personality lodged beneath the appearances of social identity. But, if exposing the fallacy of colorblindness affords no answer to the question of distinction that inhibits our thinking about "this disturbing trend of fetishization," then how do we avoid merely replicating the uncertainty, repeating it ad infinitum, amplifying its anxiety? There is another approach, but it yields a perhaps more disturbing conclusion: *there is no interracial relationship that is not implicated in the obscene fantasy* that taints the reputation of more valid romantic arrangements. This is not to say all implication is identical or equivalent in its political and historical significance. It is to state that the ethical question is not *whether* or *to what extent* a relationship is implicated in this fantasy but rather *how* and *to what effect?* Not a question of whether is one inside or outside the domain but rather of how one inhabits an unavoidably corrupted context for which there is no outside.

> The public authority maintains a civilized, gentle appearance, whereas beneath it there is a shadowy realm in which the brutal exercise of power is itself sexualized. And the crucial point, of course, is that this obscene shadowy realm, far from undermining the civilized semblance of the public power, serves as its inherent support. (Žižek 1996a, 100)

What disturbs the discourse of multiracialism is its inability to escape the association between its official discourse and political mobilization and the more disreputable articulations of sex across racial boundaries. How is it, for example, that both the mail-order bride industry and the multiracial movement can claim the same subversive, progressive potential in this post–civil rights era?[14] Why is multiracialism maddened by the whole panoply of racist sexual stereotypes if they simply do not apply?

Noted historian Gary Nash (1999) traces the story of how "Americans built racial classifications and how some Americans have defied the way society defined them and dared to dream of a mixed-race nation. Their lives show that the blending of races is not un-American; it is being American." For him, this study "is about insistent boundary patrollers and daring boundary crossers" (vii–viii). This is an important work not so much for its subtlety and detail (it is pitched as a monograph for young adult readers) as for the attention it brings to a history of political discourse that prefigures much in the contemporary debates about race mixture in the present. There are interesting historical parallels, for example, between advocates of the multiracial movement today and the abolitionist proponents of amalgamation in the mid-nineteenth century, especially between the fantasies of national redemption and regeneration that animate both. What is most telling, however, is the rather strange convergence of interests that the various "daring boundary crossers" seem to enjoy in Nash's account. While all of his examples are not collapsed into a singular political trajectory, there is a sense in which an abolitionist like Frederick Douglass is rendered equivalent to a colonialist like John Rolfe, simply because they both crossed boundaries of race and sex. Or, as per our discussion in the previous chapter, a comparison between these two historic figures and white male slaveholders who systematically raped enslaved black females for their own pleasure and profit. What they have in common, Nash argues, is their opposition to the maintenance of strict sexual boundaries between racial groups in the antebellum United States.

While this is not the place to conduct sustained critique of Nash's study, we notice similar problems with regard to analyses of the contemporary situation. What multiracialism has in common with its disavowed contaminants is, quite simply, a desire to affirm the progressive character of racial border crossing. They both proclaim the righteousness of a multiracial presence *in and of itself* to the shoring up of a "remixed" U.S. national identity. This national potential is cited in both instances as the untapped reserve of American exceptionalism, a moral example that could and should be given to the world, as the United States is encouraged to improve upon the historic examples of Latin American "racial democracy" or Hawaiian "racial paradise" or, as Charles Byrd would have it, South African apartheid! Yet, to the extent that nothing further is offered by way of critique, there can be no space of disagreement between these ostensibly divergent political tendencies. It should be clear by now that there is nothing inherently progressive about border crossing, that it can and has been articulated to a whole range of political projects right, left, and center, and the same can and should be said of constructing and maintaining social boundaries as well. The dialogic relation between a sexuality of the heights and a sexuality of the depths turns on their agreement that *sexual drives can be socially determined,* that these tendencies can be engineered to the greatest end.

> Anti-pornography activists [like multiracial activists] ironically share with "sex radicals" [and many pornographers] the utopian project of a "redemptive reinvention of sex," a denial of the ways in which sexual desire is unavoidably anti-communal, anti-egalitarian, anti-nurturing, anti-loving. . . . The fantasy of instantaneous and total self-realization via sexual satisfaction offered alike by sex radicals and by commercial pornography finds its perfect mirror in the fantasy of an eroticism free of power and oppression purveyed by anti-pornography crusaders. (Shaviro 1993, 160–61)

Neither a sexuality of the depths nor a sexuality of the heights offers a liberating option. Less because sexual desire inevitably contains elements of both height and depth than because both height and depth rely upon a *fantasy of the sexual relationship*—a ruse that is affirmed and celebrated on the one hand (depth) and disowned and purged on the other (height), but posited nonetheless by both. In order to parse the defect congenital to this stance, let us consider a third time why "there is no interracial sexual relationship."

Sexuation I Racialization

At this point, we can make provisional sense of this chapter's title, taken from Lacan's famous aphorism regarding the impossibility of the sexual relation.[15] In citing Lacan on this score, I am not denying the intercourse, interpenetration, or mingling of bodies. The crucial point of this assertion—"there is no sexual relation"—is the difference it marks between bodily contact and a proper, intersubjective relationship, a difference formulated otherwise than the conservative morality of multiracialism and its interlocutors. That is to say, every attempt at forging a sexual relation is, for Lacan, structured by an *internal* limitation, an irreducible gap foreclosing the possibility of resolving the antinomy of sexual difference through the communion of bodies. What Lacan renders shorthand in this deceptive one-liner is a very longhand demonstration of how accession to language bars the possibility of sexual relation. The masculine and feminine positions—the *psychoanalytic* rather than the *sociological* categories of "man" and "woman"—represent an asymmetric grid of subject formation, a binary matrix of psychic orientation that Lacan refers to as "sexuation." These two positions encompass the only ways in which to assume "the cut of symbolization," the means through which the social bond is *psychically* inhabited amidst the alienating effects of our insertion in discourse. This is also to say that sexual difference concerns how one takes up a relation to *jouissance*—the insufferable tension of enjoyment, the ineffable, pulsating force of prelinguistic Being left over by our "symbolic castration": sexuation involves choosing sides in a discrepancy between modes of enjoyment. Of course, as psychoanalytic experience has shown, whether one takes up the masculine or feminine position cannot be determined by recourse to any biological data or social convention. This positioning is a choice, but not in the sense of something freely willed or consciously intended. It is, instead, an unconscious "forced choice" that transforms contingency into a necessity of our psychic reality (Salecl 2000).

The relation between sexual positions is supplementary, rather than complementary. Bruce Fink (1995), the leading English-language translator of Lacan's work, has rendered the statement as "there is no such thing as a relation between the sexes" (98). In his view, this translation lends an apt emphasis to the problem of sexual difference and avoids the tendency to read Lacan naïvely, or insidiously, as an argument against the range of sexual practices or realities of patriarchal domination (for which some other concept of "sexual relation" is required).[16] For Lacan, the masculine and feminine structures cannot attain union, there is no union in reality (in the Symbolic), though bodies really interact (in the Real). The antagonistic structure of sexual difference remains irresolvable on the social plane. Not simply a sociological problem to overcome or an egalitarian political project to fulfill, sexual difference in the Lacanian schema does not coincide with the social production of gender, nor is its consideration reducible to the concerns of feminist critique. Rather, sexual difference is both constitutive of and constituted by the symbolic order. That is to say, the speaking-being is "sexed" by (its relation to) language and language is riddled by sexual difference whose impasse provides an in-built turbulence.

In pursuing the critique of multiracialism, we might be tempted to elaborate "formulae of racialization" in an extension of Lacan's enterprise for theorizing interrelations of race, sex, and sexuality as a formal logic. In lieu of such theoretical developments,[17] we limit our interests to the looser interpretation of Lacan's adage, bearing in mind Fink's cautionary note. Discussing Lacan in order to challenge the fantasy of union between the *sexes* may seem to miss the target somewhat, given that the emblem of the multiracialism is a union of *races*—always gendered because it is imagined heterosexually, but without particular respect for the sex ratio of intimates or the gender of the multiracial person in question. And, as noted previously, the neuter tone of multiracial discourse interacts with processes of desexualization, a desire to disconnect race and sexuality in order to rearticulate them in attenuated form. But if multiracialism attempts to remedy racial antagonism through a muted affirmation of interracial sexuality—an interracial union of the sexes—then it might provoke new directions for political and intellectual practice if this complacent relation were upset.

If Lacan's (1998) most extensive discussion of sexuation is, in part, a response to certain tendencies within French feminism (Marini 1993), he is engaged there in an implicit critique of the contemporaneous movement for sexual liberation as well. As the passage from Shaviro suggests, "the fantasy of . . . eroticism free of power and oppression" or the "redemptive reinvention of sex" misses something crucial to the operations of sexuality and its antagonistic relation to the social. Lacan will agree, but for another reason: sex acts never entail an encounter with the real other. Rather, "the 'real' body of the other serves only as a support for our phantasmatic projections" (Žižek 1994, 2). Thus, Lacan offers an important point about the discrepancy between the intermingling of bodies and the heterogeneous psychic register of fantasy, that is, about the "otherness of the body" within the intersubjective relation (Andre 1994). This is relevant to the discourse of multiracialism to the extent that it operates from an assumption regarding the isomorphism of bodily interaction (i.e., interracial biological mixture) and symbolic reconfiguration (i.e., interracial political accord). What drops out of consideration here is the intermediary register of fantasy running between these two domains: fantasy as the imaginary scenario in which the subject stages a relation to the object of desire. The tension between race and sexuality reemerges at this point of analysis with more clarity. On the one hand, we can grant that each subject takes up its relation to fantasy in a singular way. On the other, we note that the preconscious materials of such fantasies will be mediated by the culture of racialization.[18] Lacan is insistent on this point: the Imaginary is coextensive with, perhaps overdetermined by, the Symbolic. But is the sexual relation therefore symbolic?

In *Seminar XX*, Lacan (1998) states that "the sexual relationship drops into the abyss of nonsense," but adds straightaway that this fact "doesn't in any way diminish the interest we must have in the Other" (87). The obligatory "interest we must have in the Other" refers both to the attention we necessarily lend to the intersubjective dimension of our relationships with others and to our dependence upon the Symbolic as a defense against the overwhelming experience of the Real. In other words, the *jouissance* of "the 'real' body" would be unbearable were it not for the symbolic mediation of desire. Our insertion in language, our suturing in the order of signification, is precisely what enables any relationship whatsoever to persist in the face of this intrinsic obstruction, over and against the irruptive presence of that which remains unintelligible by definition. Joan Copjec

(1994) puts a finer point on it when she writes that there is "*a radical antagonism between sex and sense.* . . . Sex is the stumbling block of sense. . . . Sex is produced by the internal limit, the failure of signification" (204). In this sense, sex is an effect of the Real ("produced by . . . the failure of signification") and sexual difference is, as a result, understood as a *real* difference. Racial difference, on the other hand, would seem to present itself as a *symbolic* difference, what Foucault might call the functional effects of a discursive regime. Here is Stuart Hall (1996a) in that vein:

> It is not the status of racist discourse as "scientific" but the fact that its elements function *discursively* which enables it to have "real effects." They can only carry meaning because they signify, through a process of displacement, further along the chain of equivalences. . . . That is, because their arrangement within a discursive chain enables physiological signs to function as signifiers, to stand for and be "read" further up the chain. (21)

Thus, we have a structural incompatibility between the strictly meaningless sexual relation and the political attempt to commute the symbolic differences that articulate racial hierarchy. In fact, the elements of "racist discourse" would seem to be produced in the very moment that meaning wards against the encroachments of sex, making some provisional sense of things through an effective and affective *binding*, a desexualization of speech that is never far from the accumulation of power.[19] Given such cross-purposes, we can recognize that even if racial difference is interrupted by sex and cannot avoid stumbling over this radical antagonism, it is not therefore broached or banished sexually, and beliefs to the contrary obtain only in fantasy. But the fantasmatic structure of the interracial sexual relation is interesting not only for what it suggests for the theorization of race and sexuality. More immediate is what it reveals about the function of fantasy in the formation of social relations. Surely, interracial sexual relations are structured fantasmatically at the intersubjective scale, but what do we make of the political claims that multiracialism can bridge the racial divide by removing limits to "the good we could do in making our world a better place for all" (Mathabane and Mathabane 1992, 262)?[20] Are we not here facing a desire for real encounter with the other that produces relations of social harmony, the aim of the sexual relationship elevated to the national scale, perhaps even a fantasy of planetary love?

In his gloss of Lacan's maxim, Dylan Evans (1996) notes, "Love is an illusory fantasy of fusion with the beloved which makes up for the absence of any sexual relationship" (103). That is to say, love covers over the fundamental gap, "the abyss of nonsense," that separates subjects from one another—and divides them from themselves—insofar as they inhabit the symbolic order, that is, insofar as they are "speaking-beings" alienated in the signifier. Following Žižek, we see that fantasy serves as a screen against the traumatic encounter with the Real, the deadlock of symbolization that grounds the contingencies of the social. This deadlock is itself the Real, the constitutive antagonism about which Ernesto Laclau and Chantal Mouffe (1985) assert, "Society does not exist." Society's symbolic identity, in other words, cannot simply coincide with some preexistent material reality. Signifiers represent a subject for another signifier, as Lacan often remarked, and no less so for the signifier of Society itself. What we run up against is the signifier's inability to overcome its disjuncture from the signified that slides beneath it, the structural failure of representation. The ideological function of social fantasy is to mask the impossibility of its own actualization, to calibrate the subject's relation to that master signifier (the nation, democracy, love, etc.) that stops the endless slide of signification.[21] However, the social fantasy operates in another, more troublesome way: the ideological fantasy accounts for its own impossibility in advance, preempting potential counterresponses (Žižek 1989, 127). How, then, does this mechanism play out in regard to multiracialism?

The structural impossibility of "multiracial America" is evaded in the discourse through systematic externalization. This is not to deny actually existing external barriers to anything approaching democracy—liberal, radical or otherwise—and their formidableness is exactly what lends them their power as alibis. Rather, it is to call attention to the ways that ideology critique requires revision. The critique of multiracialism must consist of two moves. In the first move, we would identify the ways in which the official discourse functions as a symbolic act in Jameson's sense: "an ideological act . . . with the function of inventing imaginary or formal 'solutions' to unresolvable social contradictions" (1981, 79). Here, we would historicize those contingent factors that are reified and decontextualized in the service of an anticritical political project. Departing from Jameson, the second move would be to discern the ways in which this imaginary engagement with historical formations avoids the transhistorical encounter with the Real of social antagonism. In other words, what is presupposed to be a strictly external obstacle, a function of objective conditions (i.e., reigning social mores or even enduring structural inequalities), is revealed to be an internal structural limit, a necessary impossibility. Positing the presupposition in this manner is an attempt at "explaining away a structural impediment as the result of unfortunate concrete circumstances" (Žižek 1996c, 235). What is explained away is the impossible sexual relation, Society's nonexistence, signification's failure, and "such an inversion of impossibility into prohibition-exclusion *occults the inherent deadlock of the Real*" (Žižek 1995, 129).

All of this is not to relegate multiracialism to mere instrumentality, a veil for the reproduction of the status quo. Jameson's elaboration on the work of Karl Mannheim reminds us that every text has both its ideological function and, embedded within that function, a utopian, transideological impulse (Jameson 1981). Failing to recognize either dimension produces, for Jameson, an acute theoretical shortsightedness. But Žižek performs another turn of the screw. He agrees that "in every ideological edifice, there is a kind of 'trans-ideological' kernel"; however, it is precisely the utopian aspect of the ideological edifice that makes it efficacious:

> An ideological identification exerts a true hold on us precisely when we maintain an awareness that we are not fully identical to it, that there is a rich human person beneath it: "not all is ideology, beneath the ideological mask, I am also a human person" is the very form of ideology, of its "practical efficiency." (1997, 21)

Is not a version of this statement—I am irreducible to racial designation or I live and love with a "humanity beyond race"—the sine qua non of multiracial discourse, its ambivalent signature?[22] How might multiracialism account for its complicity in the ideological fantasies of white supremacy and antiblackness, the ways in which it participates in and identifies with the very regime it officially seeks to subvert? This interrogation does not call for the banishing of enjoyment from the political frame any more than it entails a blind faith in the unyielding righteousness of "true love." The critical distance toward fantasy that it encourages is not a flight from enjoyment but rather a reinvestment.

> The foremost problem is not how to denounce and rationally defeat the enemy—a task that can easily result in strengthening its hold upon us—but how to break its (phantasmatic) spell upon us. The point of [traversing the fantasy] is not to get rid of jouissance (in the mode of the old leftist Puritanism): the distance toward fantasy means, rather, that I as it were "unhook" jouissance from its phantasmatic frame and acknowledge it as that which is properly undecidable, as the indivisible remainder that is neither inherently "reactionary," the support of historical inertia, nor the liberating force that enables us to undermine the constraint of the existing order. (Žižek 1996a, 118)

Were multiracialism to relinquish the negative ideal of freedom from blackness, it could proceed only through a divestment of the fantasy of social harmony qua racial fusion. But is this divestment possible *within* the cul-de-sac of a sexuality of the heights and its perennial battle with the depths? A more adequate—and more ethical—response would consist in abandoning the whole of the multiracial project, not simply renovating its current modus operandi. In fact, there is no way to recuperate the quest for hale and hearty multiracial identities and upright interracial relationships, not only because the criteria of judgment are unsound or because the endeavor reifies racial difference and elides the disjuncture between the Real and the Symbolic. Each of these is sufficient reason to suspend the collective effort, and yet we can pursue an even more radical displacement. Beyond the arguments already offered, the interracial sexual relationship is impossible most fundamentally because *the bodies in question do not exist as such*. Not only do they irrevocably fail to serve as representatives of racial difference, intelligible to and commensurate with consciousness. Much more importantly, they do not exist *as bodies*, organic entities exhibiting an unfaltering integrity and contained in the self-unity of its parts. They are, in the least, not reducible to such necessary fictions. Rather, they are warped by the "palpitation of *jouissance*," traversed by the circuits of the drives, subject to a "psychoanalytical anatomy," a confounding topology of psychic energies that undoes the body's solidity and upsets its coherence for conscious apprehension (Morel 2000; Soler 2000). From the vantage of this *libidinal* economy, how can boundaries be transgressed that never finally exist or only ever finely exist? In other words, what fantasy of the border—the contact zone—is required for the celebration or abhorrence of its breakdown?

> It is clear that there has never been nor ever will be such a *dissolution* for the good reason that there has never been nor ever will be such a body bound up in its unity and identity, that this body is a phantasy, itself fairly libidinal . . . and that it is by contrast with this phantasy that all alienation is thought and *resented*. . . . There is no whole body. (Lyotard 1993, 112)

We discuss Lyotard further in the following chapter. Suffice it to say for now that we entertain his principle thesis: "There is no whole body" except in the register of fantasy, an imaginary wholeness against which a discourse of personal fragmentation and social division can be put forth. It is only through maintenance of a fantasy of the body as this indivisible property of self, nation, or race that the politics of multiracialism becomes conceivable. However, the fantasy founders endemically as multiracialism pursues its perpetual restoration, setting off down the hard road to renewal, accumulating points of conflict, recuperating intensity, discharging energies—strung between the insecurity of whiteness and the fact of blackness.

In this light, a multiracial challenge to white supremacy and antiblackness seems unlikely so long as it is approached in terms of the mixture of supposedly fixed and stable bodies, in terms of bodies believed to support or embody actually existing races, antiessentialist disclaimers notwithstanding.

If it is to do justice, the challenge can be executed only through the decon-struction of race, the traversal of the fantasy of interracial sexual union, and finally, the rearticulation of the concept of the body itself—an embod-iment not exhausted by its biological title (Miles 1996), one that is atten-tive to its excess and indifference, to the *multiplication* of its powers. We might yet invent a racialized sexuality neither of the depths nor of the heights, but rather of the *surfaces*—critical but not utopian, planned but not programmatic, indeterminate but not irresponsible, deliberate but not definitive. This is less an ethics than an *ars vitae*: "one in which we would be the artists and not the propagators, the adventurers and not the theo-reticians, the hypothesizers and not the censors" (Lyotard 1993, 11).

CHAPTER 4

The Consequence of Race Mixture

A political criticism must not take its object for granted: in a
specific sense, the object is not there in the first place, for its
condition is that it is marked by an interior historicity which
subjects it to constant modification, constant shifting. The proper
"object" of the critic who is aware of the materiality of history is,
paradoxically, an object conditioned not by its appearance relative to
a covert essence, but rather an object conditioned precisely by its
temporal disappearance or "immaterialization."

—Thomas Docherty, *Alterities: Criticism, History, Representation*

The object of desire itself coincides with the force that prevents
its attainment—in a way, the object "is" its own withdrawal,
its own retraction.

—Slavoj Žižek, *The Metastases of Enjoyment:*
Sex Essays on Woman and Causality

The Body of Whiteness

The epigraphs for this chapter dispute the multiracial project by remarking
the destabilization of political criticism by the temporal force of historicity and the peculiar display of desire revealed by the structural dynamics
of psychoanalytic experience. Insofar as multiracialism speaks of "the end
of race," the multiracial personality prides itself on causing trouble for the
white supremacist rage for order, an ostensible violation of racial discipline, a threat to enshrined notions of racial purity. Multiracial identity is
elusive and cannot be fixed, captured, or tethered. However, a troublesome, fugitive presence has its consequences. For Linda Alcoff (1995), "A
self that is internally heterogeneous beyond repair or resolution becomes

a candidate for pathology in a society where the integration of self is taken to be necessary for mental health" (261). The multiracial is convoluted by internal heterogeneity—"beyond repair or resolution"—but pathologizing the radical otherness of "micro-diversity" (Zack 1995a) has always required the political labor of articulation. That link can be broken and reworked if the criteria of well-being are sufficiently scrutinized, or it can be affirmed and upheld by a scripted debate *within* the prevailing terms of "mental health," driven by a conservative desire for repair and resolution. As we have seen, multiracialism is defined by the latter approach, a decision that ramifies on some of the largest political questions of the present moment. The constituency of the multiracial "occupies quite literally a 'pre-post'-erous space where it has to actualize, enfranchise, and empower its own 'identity' *and* coextensively engage in the deconstruction of the very logic of 'identity' and its binary and exclusionary politics." The abdication of this *double* duty promises that multiracialism will "result in the formation of . . . yet another 'identical' and hegemonic structure" (Radikrishnan 1990, 50). As we have seen, the empowerment of multiracial identity intensifies anti-black racism to the extent that it retrenches concepts of biological race, espouses the social value of nonblackness, and normalizes the field of sexuality—all to suggest the recent emergence of "oppressive black power." Pressing the multiracial project on some of its most basic tenets, then, may complicate its heroic search-and-rescue mission.

In *Libidinal Economy*, Jean-François Lyotard (1993) asserts, amid an extended analysis of historical capitalism, the following provocation: "capital cannot form a body." The upshot of capital's unformed, misshapen body—its lack of bodily integrity being no less than the proliferating bodies whose unending labor constitutes its "nontotalized system"—is the production of "two divergent movements always associated in a single vertigo." They are distinguished as, on the one hand, "a movement of flight, of plunging into the bodiless, and thus of continual invention, of expansive additions or affirmations of new pieces . . . a movement of tension" and, on the other, "a movement of institution of an organism, of an organization and of organs of totalization and unification—a movement of reason." The crucial point, for Lyotard, is that "both kinds of movement are there, effects as force in the *non-finito* . . . of capitalism" (102). The obvious parallels between Lyotard's schematization of capital's "divergent movements" and Gilles Delueze and Félix Guattari's (1987a, 1987b) heterodox theorization of capital's "schizophrenia"—its simultaneous production of deterritorialization and reterritorialization, decoding and recoding, and so on—is deliberate insofar as the former book is offered as an affirmative elaboration of the latter's earlier intervention. I draw from each the attention they bring to this double movement of dispersion and regulation, but with more specific respect to the system of global white supremacy (Mills 1998) or what is better described as the antiblack world (Gordon 1995a), both being inextricable from but irreducible to the history of capitalism. In its attention to racial formation in the United States, the critique of multiracialism proceeds from an understanding of antimiscegenation as a fundamental feature of antiblackness. The following comments are offered as a rejoinder to the clichés of racism against which the multiracial movement and the field of multiracial studies currently stage their political and intellectual battles. My contention is that multiracialism fails to appreciate, or refuses to acknowledge, the suppleness of racial whiteness—its elasticity and expansiveness; its affinity for ambiguity, impurity, and complexity; its vital dependence on the transgression of borders, continual alteration, and the incorporation of novel elements. This has been the historical case, but its implications have become ever more apparent with the reconfiguration of the color line in the post–civil rights era: from white/nonwhite to black/nonblack.

I begin by rephrasing Lyotard's maxim this way: *whiteness cannot form a body.* Despite this inability, or perhaps because of it, it continually attempts to do so. In a sense, whiteness is the very attempt to form this body, to manufacture a particular type of delimited body. Racial whiteness can be understood as "a means for mastering the trauma of an experience without categories and without unity, which has no positive content" (Shaviro 1990, 3), a traumatically uncategorized, incoherent experience that I call "the event of miscegenation"—an abject scene of excessive passion and violent upheaval operating beyond or beneath the semblance of racialized order. We feel its pressure dimly as the *outside* of racialization: a pure exteriority, "a movement of flight . . . a movement of tension," the unbinding force of schizophrenia, the peregrinations of desire. It is a trauma wrought by the sense that "we are all of mixed origin" well before any empiricist tabulations about the sameness of humanity, the knowledge that categories of racial difference obtain only in the force of convention, a pernicious and deadly cover story for the formation of power. The event of miscegenation highlights the fundamental insecurity of racist reasoning and indicates the centrality of its restriction for the preeminent fictions of Western modernity (Memmi 1999).[1]

Some qualifications to bear in mind as we proceed: miscegenation as *event* should not be confused with miscegenation as *interracial sex acts* or *the presence of multiracial people*. The latter are lures produced as components of the fiction of racial whiteness—refractions of a restricted economy—terms that are mirrored and reinforced by multiracialism's loyal opposition. Miscegenation as event is what cannot be represented, conceptualized, or apprehended in either the interracial sexual encounter or the multiracial personality, but rather is that which prevents either appearance from attaining a discernible image or a fixed and stable meaning, whether as object of desire or aggression or both. I am attempting to supplement commonplace understandings of race as a social category that, however unsuspectingly, reassert the myth of race as biology. I am not interested in how the empirical history of sex across the color line or the demographic profile of multiracial people might somehow trouble naïve fantasies of racial purity or the social recognition of discrete racial categories. That framing of the debate merely extends the interlocutory life of racist reason without undercutting its presumptions or dislodging its principles of organization. I am talking in a more radical sense about what undermines or dislodges the fantasy of interracial sexual transgression and the attendant fantasy of the subversive multiracial. I am interested in what wards against our thinking of interracial sex or multiracial people as *things in and of themselves*. In discussing miscegenation and antimiscegenation under such revised terms, I am objecting to that "psychological phenomenon that consists in the belief that the world will open to the extent to which frontiers are broken down" (Fanon 1967, 21).

In *Black Skin, White Masks,* Fanon (1967) makes two fascinating statements about the construction of racial categories and the existential phenomenology of the bodies supposed to represent those categories. He says first, "In the white world, the man of color [sic] encounters difficulties in the development of his bodily schema. Consciousness of the body is solely a negating activity" (110). This argument from the famous fifth chapter, "The Lived Experience of the Black," is only mistakenly familiar. Many read Fanon's observation as a straightforward (and easily translatable) lament about the deprivations of colonial domination: the pain of a denial of access to the idealized self-images enjoyed by the white world, of having to identify instead with images of monstrosity, incompleteness, and lack. Certainly, there are passages in Fanon that would support this reading. For example, his dramatization of the psychic violence he experiences when arrested by the look given him by the young, white, French girl who utters those searing, infamous words: "Look, a Negro!" The language of castration is profuse:

> The corporeal schema crumbled, its place taken by a racial epidermal schema. . . . I was given not one but two, three places . . . I existed triply: I occupied space. I moved toward the other . . . and the evanescent other, hostile but not opaque, transparent, not there, disappeared. Nausea. . . . What else could it be for me but an amputation, an excision, a hemorrhage that spattered my whole body with black blood? . . . My body was given back to me sprawled out, distorted, re-colored, clad in mourning on that white winter day. (112)

Fanon goes on to speak of a desire to refuse this disassembling force of the white look, to avoid the mournful shroud of blackness, a conservative desire for repair or resolution. "I did not want this revision," he says. "All I wanted was to be a man among other men." That is, to participate in the honorable world of whiteness, to not be deemed animal, bad, mean, or ugly. A desire to not be slashed, dissected, cut to slices.

But just as it seems Fanon is situating whiteness on the side of plentitude, wholeness, security, and integrity, he offers a second qualifying statement: "At the extreme, I should say that the Negro, because of his body, impedes the closing of the postural schema of the white man—at the point, naturally, at which the black man makes his entry into the phenomenal world of the white man" (160). The white man too has trouble with the solidity of his body, the demarcation of its boundaries of inside and outside. Whereas the white look tears the black body apart, the lacerated black body, in turn, intrudes upon the corporeal territory of whiteness, disturbing its function, throwing its coordinates out of alignment— "at the extreme." What are we to make of this bizarre scenario of interpenetration? How are we to think of the white look as both dissecting and, as Fanon suggests, as fixing, as both scattering and imprisoning, dislocating and objectifying? How to contain a body, an object, that is flung about, ripped to shreds, existing in triplicate? Within the universe of antiblackness, the social and historical forces that materially and symbolically invent the black body also seek to destroy it. The forces that seek to destroy the black body also seek to maintain it, to insist that it be there in its place. As Fanon says, "within bounds . . . classified . . . tucked away." The very thing that grants whiteness its social existence, blackness, is the very thing that— at the extreme, the edge, the verge of race—prevents it from enjoying a stable life, that "gives . . . its classification as seeming."[2]

In light of even a cursory history of racial formation in the United States, it goes without saying that, as Cornel West (1990) writes: "'Whiteness' is a politically constructed category parasitic on 'Blackness'" (29). The material and symbolic elaboration of racial whiteness as a cultural formation and a historic bloc is based firmly upon the domination—precisely, the *captivity*—enforced through racial blackness. It is rooted in the maintenance of blacks in the "position of the unthought," fungible objects of accumulation and exchange, socially excluded but symbolically central (Hartman 2003). That said, we restate that whiteness does not and cannot exist in its own right; it cannot form a body. There is no concept of whiteness that is calm, fully present, and self-referential; there are no positive qualities of whiteness, only differences *between* whiteness and its racial others, blackness in the paramount case. As Jacques Derrida's (1984) much-cited essay has it,

> One is but the other different and deferred, one differing and deferring the other. One is the other in *différance*, one is the *différance* of the other. This is why every apparently rigorous and irreducible *opposition* . . . comes to be qualified at one moment of another, as a "theoretical fiction." (18)

Perhaps Fanon prefigures this insight about the indeterminate play of racial difference in his own analysis when he warns: "We shall go very slowly, for there are two camps: the white and the black. Stubbornly we shall investigate both metaphysics and we shall find that they are often quite fluid" (1967, 8). However, there are a number of ways to specify the often fluid metaphysics of race within the Manichaean delirium of the antiblack world. Again, it is not my desire to rehearse axioms of deconstruction. Such sensibility is necessary but insufficient to a social theory of racialization, and I believe Fanon points a way forward, contrary to reductive images of his work as exhausted by the rhetoric of binary conflict. Despite decontextualized glosses on fantasies of violent reversal ascribed to Fanon (and recall here that he is often accused of prescribing such when he is attempting to describe *and* to critique various political tendencies), he is among those thinkers who help us to understand the complex entanglement of terms in any seeming opposition. "In an age when skeptical doubt has taken root in the world," he writes, "when . . . it is no longer possible to find the sense of non-sense, it becomes harder to penetrate to a level where the categories of sense and non-sense are not yet invoked" (9).

We must attend precisely to this level of analysis—discerning "the sense of non-sense"—if we are to unhook ourselves from the oppositional dynamics of the law and a transgression that remains passionately attached to it.[3] In order to map out the countervailing forces of antiblackness, we must traverse an *affective* terrain ontologically prior to the *conceptual* dichotomy, before the either-or distinction, where there are not yet objects, only processes that produce the one in the other. We must, to mention Deleuze and Guattari again, seek out the traces of multiplicity, the smooth spaces of *becoming* that antiblackness "striates" in attempts to capture the social forces of desiring-production, instituting race as an order of *being*.[4] To this end, I discuss the following points: first, the law of antimiscegenation as the founding gesture of racial whiteness; second, the complicit transgression of this law, referred to alternately as multiracialism, *mestizaje*, or "anti-antimiscegenation"; and third, the event of miscegenation as that which enables and exceeds both antimiscegenation and the political project of multiracialism.

The Law of Antimiscegenation

We are told that one of the most fundamental oppositions in the global racial formation is that between the doctrine of race purity characteristic of North American white supremacy and some other arrangement that challenges that position by tolerating, embracing, or even promoting the consequence of race mixture. F. James Davis (1995), for instance, identifies this other arrangement as the "Hawaiian alternative to the one drop rule" in a treatment that represents Hawaii as a laboratory for successful management of racial difference rather than a colonial possession of the United States for which the incidence of intermixture in no way mitigates the contravention of native sovereignty (Halualani 2002; Trask 1999) or even prevents the reproduction of racial hierarchies among settler classes (Coffman 2003). More notable is the writing of José Vasconcelos, who, in his influential 1925 essay "La raza cósmica," describes an epochal battle between "Anglo-Saxonism" and "Latinism." Where the former "wants exclusive domination by the Whites" the latter "is shaping a new race, a synthetic race that aspires to engulf and to express everything human in forms of constant improvement" (19). Some sixty years later, Gloria Anzaldúa (1999) would evoke Vasconcelos in order to elaborate the concept of *mestizaje* in her classic *Borderlands/La frontera*, a text that looms large in the formation of multiracial discourse, providing it elements of both meditation and manifesto.[5] Her intellectual debt to Vasconcelos is expressed in the following passage:

> José Vasconcelos, Mexican philosopher, envisaged *una raza mestiza, una mezcla de razas afines, una raza de color—la primera raza síntesis del globo*. He called

it a cosmic race, *la raza cósmica*, a fifth race embracing the four major races of the world. Opposite to the theory of the pure Aryan, and to the policy of racial purity that white America practices, his theory is one of inclusivity. At the confluence of two or more genetic streams, with chromosomes constantly "crossing over," this mixture of races, rather than resulting in an inferior being, provides hybrid progeny, a mutable, more malleable species with a rich gene pool. From this racial, ideological, cultural and biological cross-pollinization, an "alien" consciousness is presently in the making—a new *mestiza* consciousness, *una conciencia de mujer.* It is a consciousness of the Borderlands. (99).

It would require deliberate misreading to collapse distinctions between Anzaldúa and Vasconcelos and conflate their political visions. Yet, one cannot help wondering about this particular gesture of homage. In the space of a paragraph, we span a half-century divide without comment, bypassing the mid-century ferment of black political activity, the whole range of social and political transformations of the civil rights era, transformations which both enabled and inspired the Chicana feminism for which Anzaldúa would become so important an intellectual and artistic force (García 1997). Moreover, this unelaborated citation glosses over both the liberalism of the earlier text—reformist, modernizing tendencies that would later yield a turn to the political right despite official support for the revolutionary elite of the era—and its seduction by the reigning culture of eugenics (Miller 2004). *Mestizaje* is recruited from its early twentieth-century career as Latin American state ideology and nation-building doctrine (rather than, say, its advancement, to varied effect, by the *independistas* Simón Bolívar and José Martí in the nineteenth century)[6] and pressed into service as the progressive consciousness of the Borderlands in the late twentieth-century twilight of the cold war. "The new *mestiza*" is rendered as the echo, or perhaps the offspring, of this earlier dream of unequivocally *hierarchical* global integration, the renovated product of its restricted imaginative labor. Like her avowed predecessor, Anzaldúa opposes race mixture to the doctrine of race purity, countering the image of the Aryan with the image of the new *mestiza*. However, it is important to consult the earlier text, less to sketch the structuring presumptions of nation, class, gender and sexuality in "La raza cósmica" that Anzaldúa rightly contests than to ascertain the racial politics it advocates, examining the lines of contradistinction it draws in order to envision its ideal. For Vasconcelos, the work of hemispheric cross-pollination is more than a corrective to the devastating policies of Anglo-Saxon racial ideology or an antidote to Yankee imperialism. In fact, what we find is a protest less against the genocidal *objectives* of Anglo white supremacy than the inefficiency of unrestrained violence as the *means* of its accomplishment.

> The lower types of the species will be absorbed by the superior type. In this manner, for example, the black could be redeemed, and step by step, by voluntary extinction, the uglier stocks will give way to the more handsome. Inferior races, upon being educated, would become less prolific, and the better specimens would go on ascending a scale of ethnic improvement, whose maximum type is not precisely white, but that new race to which the white himself will have to aspire with the object of conquering the synthesis. The Indian, by grafting onto the related race, would take the jump of millions of years that separate [him] from our times, and in a few decades of aesthetic eugenics, the black may disappear. . . . In this manner, a selection of taste would take effect, much more efficiently than the brutal Darwinist selection. . . . [It would be] a mixture no longer accomplished by violence, nor by reason of necessity, but by the selection founded on the dazzling produced by beauty and confirmed by the pathos of love. (Vasconcelos 1997, 32–33).

In this fantasy, the black's disappearance remains imperative, but because it proceeds by "voluntary extinction," it is now redemptive. The black's redemption is found only in disappearance, a redemptive self-annihilation enjoyed in absentia, which is to say it is impossible. The sterilization of the black population, barring the reproduction of its ugliness and inferiority, is engineered for Vasconcelos through an aesthetic pedagogy promoting the dazzle of loving human beautification. The black simply has to be educated as to her unsightliness, an unambiguous point with which she will eventually agree, for her to refrain and "give way to the more handsome."

No longer proceeding by imposition or assault, no longer demanding "the brutal Darwinist selection," the focused and deliberate depopulation of blacks becomes a welcome mission dutifully executed by its victims. The "synthesis" born of "ethnic improvement" is not white supremacist because it does not elevate whiteness to its apex or "maximum type." The doctrine of white supremacy is dethroned as a "new race" supersedes, presenting itself as that select taste toward which even the former masters of the universe would aspire: "not *precisely* white," but "roughly" white, "approximately" white, "almost" white, but not quite. This new, multiracial summit of humanity, fostered by the euthanasia of *mestizaje* and improved by the measured incorporation of nonblack otherness ("the Indian . . . grafting onto the related race" while "the black may disappear"), is ranked *higher* than the old.

What the difference is between Anglo-Saxonism and Latinism probably depends on who you're asking. What is salutary for Vasconcelos about the emergence of this new race—what Anzaldúa calls the fruit of "racial, ideological, cultural and biological cross-pollination"—is that it is accomplished by a selection "founded on the dazzling produced by beauty" in an *aesthetic* resolution of conflict. Beyond the ravages of organized, state-sanctioned violence and the machinations of instrumental reason, there lies the cosmic force of love, the benevolent prime mover of global integration. The mode of hierarchical race mixture changes, but the aims remain intact. In fact, they are *enhanced*—"a selection . . . would take place, *much more efficiently.*" Less carnage, less coercion, and less political capital, this is evolution at a discount. The Indian must modernize, must undergo a formal disappearance; the black, being incapable of modernization, must disappear, root and branch, a casualty of her *constitutional* deficiency. The aesthetic of *mestizaje* is inscribed with the traces of this double life and its ethical duplicity. Its eugenicist impulses and implications are unavoidable, casting long shadows over whatever limited threats it presents to the "ethnic absolutism"[7] of Anglo-Saxon white supremacy. It seeks to abolish the reign of whiteness but only to challenge the supremacy of those deemed *precisely* white. It condemns the existence of those "uglier stocks," "uneducated," "inferior races" in a funereal makeover that is also a final farewell: adios, adeus, au revoir, and good riddance. Perhaps it cannot help itself.

For the sake of consistency with its own idealization and the dubious mantle it assumes from its vanquished rival, it must integrate everything, everyone—*"la primera raza síntesis del globo."* The actualization, empowerment, and enfranchisement of this emergent multiracial identity demands categories of human sacrifice in the historic instance, and it transfers this exigency as the half-hidden expense of its contemporary efforts.

Recognizing the anthological work of Maria Root (1992a, 1996b) and Naomi Zack (1995a) and the seminal writings of Anzaldúa as key influences, Gary Nash (1999) has more recently authored *Forbidden Love*, a book about "the secret history of mixed-race America," a historical account of the "America that could have been." Early on, he attempts to locate the Archimedean point of an unborn America's self-betrayal, the forfeiture of its own historical potential. Without noticeable compunction, he speculates that "the union of [John] Rolfe and Pocahontas could have become the beginning of an openly *mestizo*—or racially intermixed—United States" (8). It did not become that beginning, of course, as the ensuing three-hundred-year history of formal antimiscegenation attests. Not unexpectedly, Nash fails to *begin* the conversation in the crucible of gross asymmetry or to suffuse his investigation with critical attention to the animating spirit of conquest. He does not observe the displacement between the thwarted affiliation at the site of encounter between European colonists and the indigenous peoples of the eastern seaboard and the genesis of the "American" credo in the colonists' anxious regulation of sexual contact between enslaved Africans and *everyone else.* That is to say, in order for Nash to wax nostalgic about the distortions of desire between whites and Indians (the affirmation of which would be called *mestizaje* in the Spanish-dominated territories to the south, *mestiçagem* for the Portuguese, *métissage* for the French), his conceptual framing must commit two delicate operations: first, it must render equivalent and isometric the position of blacks and Indians in the libidinal and political economies of white supremacy; second, it must absorb the particular history of negrophobia (antimiscegenation as constructed explicitly about the black body, antimiscegenation *as* antiblackness) into a generalized racial purism in Anglo-Saxon society. En route, what is diminished are not only *variations* in the development and deployment of antimiscegenation (i.e., where it is constant and pervasive with respect to blacks, it ebbs and flows with respect to other nonwhites), but also stark *oppositions* in its logic (i.e., where blacks are subject uniquely to the one-drop rule, other nonwhites are subject to its *inverse*) (Bardaglio 1999; Moran 2001; Pascoe 1999). More importantly, Nash must foreclose consideration of contemporary implications stemming from qualitative differences between blacks and other nonwhites in the trajectories of intermixture, the lopsided geometry of interracial sexuality (Foner and Fredrickson 2004).

The future of an inchoate nation that would not politically consolidate for another two centuries somehow hangs in the balance of a highly symbolic *marriage*. Departing from this mythologized first moment of New World contract, Nash's essay goes on to chronicle the stories of relatively "anonymous Americans [who] have taken history into their own hands and have defied the official racial ideology" (19). He dichotomizes thusly: "Some Americans built racial classifications and . . . some Americans have defied the way society defined them and dared to dream of a mixed-race nation" (viii). According to this logic, we defy official racial ideology (a separatist ideology supposed "to keep people apart") by joining "a long line of rebels and idealists," by becoming "daring boundary crossers," by "daring to dream."

This conceptual distinction stands as a widespread frame of intelligibility for thinking racial difference in the United States, to say nothing of the West more generally: border policing versus border crossing, the rigid obsessions of race purity versus the flexible tolerance of *mestizaje*, hateful prohibition versus the defiance of "forbidden love" (Kaup and Rosenthal 2002). It takes on renewed urgency in the postwar era in the wake of Nazism's military defeat and the advent of the *Pax Americana* and encodes itself in later fabrications of global community.[8] We find articulations of this heuristic in the political rhetoric of the modern civil rights movement as well, though the latter insurgency is extremely circumspect in its advocacy, minding the fine line between "desegregation" and "integration," the razor's edge noted in the last chapter between "political equality" and "social equality." We can note its traces in the discourse of contemporary multiracialism as well, particularly insofar as it envisions itself as an extension of the struggle for civil rights, taking the previous generation's last stand as its front line. The hegemonic conception of white supremacy in the United States remains some version of "the racial divide," a division figured as "a crisis of national identity" where the proposed solution is, accordingly, "a closer drawing together of the . . . races in America," a propinquity meant to resolve—psychologically, through "mental health"—the unceasing political predicament. In this way, the postwar, post–civil rights era United States is imagined as the land of the cosmic race and not the outmoded white ethnic "melting pot." The title has been usurped, as is the case with so much else, from Latin America. In the present moment, this drawing together for national restoration entails an explicit recognition of multiracial people and an open tolerance of, if not a celebration of, interracial dating and marriage as the signs of historical *triumph* over the racism of old. "Those who have looked to America as a place of freedom and opportunity can see the rise of the *idea* of a mixed-race America where interraciality is becoming something to regard as a national strength" (Nash 1999, 183). Yet, in typical fashion, the author is compelled to moderate his statement: "Few argue that universal intermarriage is needed to bring us together." One wonders what proportion of which populations will do the trick.

Where "freedom and opportunity" (rather than "freedom, justice, and equality") pass through the fantasy of race mixture, the ideology of progress lacks novelty beyond the province, if not the provincialism, of the United States. Even within its borders, there were as far back as the early nineteenth century, radical "amalgamationists" who agitated for the abolition of slavery while proposing "universal intermarriage" as the gateway to "biracial democracy" (Nash 1999, 84–89). Nearly a century later, prominent scholars associated with the distinguished Chicago School of Sociology, including founder Robert Park and Vasconcelos himself (who enjoyed a stint at the university as a scholar-in-residence at Park's invitation), insisted that racism would exist so long as visible markers of a supposed racial difference persisted. Rose Hum Lee, the first woman and first Chinese American to head a sociology department in a U.S. university, was one of the most insistent on this point. A proponent of "complete integration" in the face of virulent white racism, she claimed that "the final objective of integration is a culturally homogenous population." Yet, "the barrier to complete integration is racial distinctiveness" (Lee 1960, 406). Today, as Nash's comments suggest, those writing within the field of multiracial studies assume a more restrained position. Nonetheless, most do agree that increases in the rates of interracial marriage indicate the erosion of racial barriers and a waning of racist sentiments. Even the Office of the President of the United States has claimed this to be an encouraging symbol of national progress. In his 1997 commencement address to the University of California at San Diego, Bill Clinton flattered the multiracial population for moving toward the goal of "Building One America for the Twenty-First Century." All of this optimism, however cautious it may be, would imply that racism is measured in relation to the degrees of permissible race mixture: its status and significance, its frequency and magnitude. This approach installs interracial sexuality as the final frontier, the last hurdle in the race for freedom, justice, and equality ("justice and equality" trading places with "opportunity"). The "multiracial question," in other words, is at the heart of the matter.

In his contribution to a recent collection of essays on Fanon, Kobena Mercer (1994) refers to "sexual politics as the Achilles heel of black liberation." As he puts it, "My sense is that questions of sexuality have come to mark the interior limits of decolonisation, where the utopian project of liberation has come to grief" (116). Among these questions of sexuality, the figure of the interracial holds an integral place.[9] This is so not only because, especially in the Anglophone world, whites (and other nonblacks) have been profoundly repulsed by and, for the same reasons, alternately, attracted to the idea of intimate relations with blacks but also because, as Mercer's statement reminds us, the final frontier of white supremacy overlaps in peculiar ways with the interior limits of black liberation. More than ten years after Fanon first published *Black Skin, White Masks*, the text which provides the center of attention for Mercer's critical meditation, Calvin Hernton (1988) penned a controversial, best-selling book of essays bearing remarkable similarity to the earlier text. Hernton's *Sex and Racism in America*, published originally in 1965 at the zenith of the civil rights movement, became an instant classic, eventually being translated into a half dozen languages and reprinted on more than one occasion. While his academic treatise is laced with polemical commentary, towering literary personalities the likes of Langston Hughes, Poet Laureate of Black America, raved that Hernton possessed an unparalleled temerity to "frankly tackle that old bugaboo S-E-X as it relates to life, liberty, and the pursuit of integration." In what came to be known as his founding scholarly achievement, Hernton claimed to explicate the fundamental relation of race and sexuality in the United States. He dubbed his conceptual centerpiece "sexual racism," the sentiment of antimiscegenation.

Doubtless, none would dispute his central thesis, "that all race relations tend to be, however subtle, *sex* relations," that "the race problem is inextricably connected with sex" (1988, 6). We take for granted by this point that race always involves a sexual politics and that, concomitantly, sexualities in the modern world are always-already racialized. But for our present purposes, it is necessary to do more than reiterate theoretical and historical insights that are, pace James Weldon Johnson, nearly a century old.[10] These deep connections have been established in broad strokes, but I want now to focus upon one particular aspect of Hernton's work, understood as part of a larger effort to illuminate this subtle entanglement of race and sexuality. Although Hernton is quite sure that race relations are always also sex relations, the precise relation between these relations presents itself as an enigma. So much is the case for Fanon before him and Johnson before Fanon. Hernton describes the sexual involvement of white and black people in the U.S. as "at once real and vicarious . . . so immaculate and yet so perverse, so ethereal and yet so concrete" (6). He marvels at this strange implication, an apparition that mediates the sacred and the profane, the virtual and the actual. It is this powerful, mysterious involvement, this secret and hidden history, a relation that "is not always recognized when it shows at the surface," that constitutes the paradoxical object of sexual racism. As material as the bodies in question and intangible as a spook, the interracial occultation gives the lie to the certainty of the color line, to the boundaries demarcating inside from out. It prompts, in Mercer's words, "a recognition of sexuality as a point of access to complexity—in the sense that *eros* arises from chaos . . . sexuality as that which constantly worries and troubles anything supposedly fixed as an identity" (1994, 119). As noted earlier, Hernton describes sexual racism as involving "the most degenerate and perverse form of sexual turn-on" (1988, xiii). It is, as he has it, "distorted desire." One cannot help but hear echoes of the Fanon who described racism as "anomalies of affect," the Fanon who wrote, "I believe in the possibility of love; that is why I endeavor to trace its imperfections, its perversions" (1967, 42). The imperiled possibility of interracial love, its fragile balance, its potential perfection, squares off against the degenerate forces of racism and sexual perversion—racism *as* sexual perversion. "If one wants to understand the racial situation psychoanalytically," says Fanon, "considerable importance must be given to sexual phenomena" (160).

Abby Ferber (1998) has observed, "White supremacist discourse is obsessed with interracial sexuality. . . . This point cannot be overemphasized" (86). The contemporary literature of North American white supremacist organizations, much like their transnational counterparts in the United Kingdom and Australia, abounds with pornographic imagery about the monstrosity of interracial sexuality, a horror that achieves its richest textual composition and its greatest libidinal energy from the supposed hyperactivity of preternatural black sexuality (Daniels 1996). It is often written there that black people have access to, or create, sui generis, experiences of sensuous enjoyment straddling the ecstatic limits of life and death. An ambivalent intensity, an oscillation between fear and desire, attends the look driven by obsession or curiosity about black bodies.[11] This is most certainly the case with contemporary Far-Right discourse, but it is also a constant in the broader intellectual, political, and popular culture throughout the history of the United States (Fredrickson 1987; Jordan 1977; Takaki 1990).

Closely associated in the discourse of white supremacy with an overwhelming, pulsating black corporeality, the purported locus and source of race mixing, is the beguiling figure of the multiracial. However, it is the *ambiguity* of this association between interracial sexuality and multiracial people that presents so many conceptual and political problems. Fugitive, illegitimate, marginalized, stigmatized, and pathological, the mulatto emerges as a threat to the categorical differences that ground the racial project. The ostensible danger of the black is the black's absolute difference from all others. That of the mulatto (still irredeemably a black in this formation—irredeemable so long as she is black) is to reveal that absolute difference as tenuous and permeable, to dramatize the impossibility of its permanent maintenance. This is a compounded danger, a doubling of the danger and excitement of racialized difference both across and within the established categories, marking an estrangement from or inhospitableness toward—or an enviable freedom from—racial categories as such.

Thus, the paranoid fantasy of white genocide so prevalent in the literature and often echoed in muted form in polite society takes the multiracial as its death sign. Robert Young (1995), for instance, concludes in a study of British colonial racial ideology: "None was so demonized as those of mixed race" (180). U.S. white supremacy, in its permutation of the British imperial racial formation, is similarly mortified by this overriding production of racial confusion, blurred indefinite bodies. However, this "swarming horde of indifferent, mulatto zombies" (Ferber 1998) must be understood, strictly, as *a retroactive projection*. That is to say, it ventures a desperate attempt to locate and capture the moment of racial annihilation via contact with blackness in the scenario of the interracial sexual encounter—"It is too late!" This is where it happens, where it has come to pass, the dissolution of the collective body of racial whiteness, the scattering of the genetic reserve, an unaccountable expenditure without return. Not simply a castration or amputation, race mixture signifies a process that tears the white racial corpus apart, exploding it from within by *insinuation*. If the so-called mongrel is the sign of race mixing par excellence, this unstable figure can only ever serve as the troubled embodiment of an interracial sexual encounter that *will have been*. In short, the mulatto is not the mixing itself but the always-already mixed race, a consequence, a multiracial trace of the "distorted desire" to transgress the color line.

The displacement is duly noted, even if it is not well understood. Tracing the normative assumptions of the prophylactic logic, we can chart the syllogism readily: heterosexual acts produce children and children inherit the race of their parents; hence, heterosexual contact between members of different races produces multiracial children. This much is elementary, but we must examine more closely the slippage that obtains between the consequence of the interracial sex act and the consequence of multiracial people. To wit: if the horror of interracial sexual encounter is the specter of multiracial offspring ("What about the kids?"), what is so unsettling about multiracial people themselves once they arrive on the scene ("We're here, we're healthy, get used to it")? Is the nightmare of the white supremacist imagination the multiplication of a few isolated multiracial people into a full-fledged population, his or her transformation from an aberrant fugitive into a social class that might displace and consume whites in the process—the *insatiable* cosmic race? If the impetus for antimiscegenation is the prevention of interracial *reproduction*, then why make a fuss about interracial *sexuality?* Why the legend and lore about inconceivable orgies, overdeveloped sex organs, inhuman sexual stamina, or bestial pleasures of the flesh? Does it really matter that "mongrels" are produced in a context of intense enjoyment, or is it not enough that they are produced at all? Why the incessant, vitriolic inquisition: "Did you like it?!"

Hughes issued a provocative phrase in review of Hernton's book: "life, liberty and the pursuit of *integration.*" But, to read Hughes and Hernton together, the notion of integration we muster from this blackened perspective seems relatively unconcerned about the creation of "indifferent, mulatto zombies." In fact, in Hernton there is no mention at all of multiracial people except as those light-skinned blacks *already existing* in the community as a result, we are told, of the legacy of sexual coercion endemic to the slave estate. Here Hernton differs from Fanon. Where the former does not consider at any length the question of the Negro's "whitening"— hallucinatory or otherwise—the latter takes it to be one of his primary tasks. Hernton's preoccupation, not unlike Fanon's, lies with questions of interracial desire, interracial intimacy, and interracial sexual relations. The question that drives his book is, beyond the guarantee of formal liberties, how can true interracial love and companionship be achieved in the United States? However, the urgency of his commentary is fueled less by a faith in the redemptive qualities of the multiracial than by the unspecified connection he reads between the psychosexual and the political economic spheres. In other words, the issue of sexual liberty is, for Hernton, bound up with, perhaps even ancillary to, the struggle for social, political, and economic justice. As he writes, "The racism of sex in the United States is but another aspect of the unequal political and economic relations that exist between the races in the American democracy" (1988, 179).

If black people did not grasp Lyotard's (1993) maxim in principle—"every political economy is libidinal"—it was certainly clarified in practice, crystallized in the postbellum legal edifice of Jim Crow and the extralegal institution of lynching. It was extended again by the reactionary campaign of "massive resistance" to the Supreme Court decision in *Brown v. Board of Education* and the emergence of the civil rights movement in the mid-1950s. The logic of white supremacy, then and now, construes "any attempt to increase racial or gender equality as a direct threat to the white race: not only to white power and hegemony, but to the very existence of the white race. . . . Desegregation becomes an attempt to increase interracial sexuality, to produce sameness" (Ferber 1998, 87–88). The leadership of the civil rights movement obliged to the exigency to introduce distance toward the issue of interracial sexuality in what was, in large part, a gesture of reassurance to the dominant order.

As Hernton (1988) notes, many believed that because "the sex issue is so explosive, and the segregationists use this issue to their advantage," a certain interracial intimacy should be avoided "because it will 'hurt the movement for civil rights'" (71–72). This is simply to say that the postwar white liberal consensus supported black freedom struggle to the extent that it did not exceed the purported boundaries of the public sphere, the legitimate terms of political struggle, and invade the private and quotidian. To push the issue of sexual freedom, mounting a political and moral defense of people's right to (let alone desire for) interracial relationships would be to court a measure of violence deemed, at best, strategically unwise and, at worst, suicidal. On the issue of "miscegenation" with blacks, it was understood that the political distinctions between whites as a whole were, and continue to be, effaced by a collective pull to the right.

Bill Condon's film *White Lie* (1991) offers a good illustration of this confluence. Leonard Madison (Gregory Hines), a black man working as an aide to the mayor of New York City, believed for the better part of his life that his father died in an accident when he was a young boy. He later discovers that his father was actually lynched for allegedly raping a prominent white woman in an unnamed state of the Deep South. (We later find that his father was falsely accused and was, in fact, having a consensual affair.) David Lester (Gregg Henry) is the son of the allegedly raped white woman and a Clintonesque Southern Democratic running for governor. Not coincidentally, young David was a witness to and participant in the lynching. Now he is running on a neoliberal agenda of slow progress against the coded racism of his ultraconservative opponent, David Cambio, a former Klansman à la David Duke. The tense parallels between the three Davids are evident, and Cambio's surname—from the Latin *cambiare*, meaning to change or exchange—suggests the chameleonlike quality of post–civil rights racism. In a revealing moment during which the local sheriff tries to convince Madison that there is a bright side to the neoliberal over the barely disguised Klansmen, Madison replies, "Well, right now, I'm having a hard time telling the two apart." The ever-present violence that structures this white closing-of-ranks should be highlighted. One black civil rights activist captures it well: "Defend interracial marriage on principle! Principle costs too much. . . . [If we did that] there would be no integrated swimming pools, no mixed schools, no public accommodations. . . . *Only* the burning cross. *Only* the rope" (quoted in Zimmerman 1999, 516; emphasis added).

The Right collapsed the historic battle against segregation with the pursuit of interracial sex, particularly sex between black men and white women (Hodes 1997; Robinson 2003). Like their terrorized black counterparts, though for different reasons and entirely different stakes, the white liberal consensus, even when sympathetic to a circumscribed civil rights platform, attempted to maintain a meticulous separation between that project and the interracial "bugaboo." Nonetheless, the question of race mixing surfaced regularly, both from without, as accusations from the Right, and from within liberal social circles, as the limit-test of political will and intent, "the 'ultimate expression' of . . . integrationist ideology" (Zimmerman 1999, 516). While no self-respecting white liberal would stand to be called a hypocrite or closet racist for tarrying on the issue of interracial sexuality (at least for others or in some distant future), none wanted to be found guilty of "nigger-loving" either. In order to legitimize their political demands under white supremacy, activists who were struggling side by side for social justice publicly declared that they were not, certainly not *primarily*, interested in being sexually involved with one another. Struggling side by side, that is, but not too closely, minding the interior limits of the movement. Hernton writes, "Since sex is automatically imagined and projected onto any and all interracial associations, both whites and blacks, including many liberals, wish that integration was not necessary to foster racial equality and justice" (1988, xvii). It goes without saying that this collective wish to desexualize the political struggle for racial equality produced material effects, structuring the shape of the movement, its demands, its organizational arrangements, and its composition. Hence, Andrew Weinberger (1964), in a contribution to Ashley Montagu's landmark *Man's Most Dangerous Myth*, observes, "Of all discriminations practiced against Negroes, Orientals, Indians, and other ethnic minorities, the prohibition against intermarriage is the one which the minority groups are least interested in abolishing. . . . There has been no effort whatever favoring intermarriage" (405–6).

Weinberger's defense of the civil rights movement goes further in its conscious rebuttal to Gunnar Myrdal's (1962) "White Man's Rank Order of Discrimination." He notes that blacks and other nonwhites do, in fact, "understandably find statutes repugnant which classify them as inferior and unfit to marry persons they may choose" (Weinberger 1964, 406). However, this repugnance is qualified in ways that recall Hernton. It is not simply that blacks and other nonwhites defend their legal right to marry a white person. They are also, perhaps more importantly, concerned about the ways in which legal prohibitions against intermarriage can and do cause "substantial injury to *more tangible* interests" such as tax status, legal incrimination, and prospects for upward mobility. Antimiscegenation is thus subsumed under supposedly more pressing and fundamental issues of political disenfranchisement and economic disadvantage. In this light, consider liberal essayist and World War II veteran Spencer Logan's exemplary comments:

> One barrier to a closer drawing together of the white and Negro races in America has been the misconception on the part of many whites that the Negro desires amalgamation. . . . Speaking as a Negro, I know that most Negroes do not desire sexual relationships with white women. . . . Negro men resent the mingling of white men and Negro women as much as white men fear miscegenation of white women and Negro men. (Logan 1946, 27)

This notion of drawing closer without amalgamating, mingling, or sexual contact is a perplexing thing. Apparently, one must not confuse political freedoms and economic gains with such offensive intimate liaisons. White America is assured that black people have no desire for interracial sex, that the repulsion is mutual, and not surprisingly, that the proprietary sensibilities of men toward women transcend the color line—biracial patriarchy in a strained homosocial dialogue. But let us think for a moment about the phrasing of this disclaimer. This is a step beyond Weinberger's qualification, one that simply relegated the fight to decriminalize racial intermarriage to the lowest priority. Logan asserts, "Most Negroes do not desire . . . Negro men resent . . . as much as . . . white men fear" (1946, 27). However, the certainty with which Logan declares the reciprocal, equivalent fear/resentment of white and black men is belied by the qualification that "*most* Negroes do not desire," implying as it does that *some* actually do. Is it implied that those few Negroes who "desire sexual relationships with white women" are, as it were, beyond the pale of the (political) community that Logan claims to represent? And is black men's resentment toward black women's desire for white men and white men's fear of white women's copulation with black men not deeply related to that proportion of each—the "some" within themselves—that cannot be counted on?

Hernton, despite the sluggishness of his growing solidarity with black feminism, expands this position beyond the precinct of Logan's masculinist pronouncement, beyond his uncanny, patriarchal mirroring across the racial divide. For the objection or caveat is not simply that black men resent the mingling of white men and, it is implied, *their* Negro women, but also (as supported by Logan's account) the mingling of black men with white women. "There is no doubt that the sexual aspect is as much a 'thorn in the side' to blacks as it is to whites. Both groups, for their own special reasons, are hideously concerned about it" (Hernton 1988, 2). By "hideously concerned," Hernton means that like white people who are, at the extreme, "obsessed with interracial sexuality," paranoiac about the prospects of miscegenation, disgusted by a supposedly engulfing black corporeality, "many blacks cannot bear the presence of whites."

> The very idea of interracial sex irritates these blacks, and they cannot discuss it for long without "blowing up." The sight of interracial couples makes them nauseous, and they feel as though they will "go crazy." Consequently, they experience hurt. . . . Ultimately, like whites, the vast majority of blacks really feel deep down inside that sex across the color line is morally wrong and somehow sinful. (xvi–xvii)

Yet, how is it that blacks and whites each have their own "special reasons" for being "hideously concerned" about interracial sex, but *ultimately* end up being "like" in their moral judgment about sex across the color line? Are there not qualitative differences in their madness, their pain, and their aversion; differences issuing from the pertinent political antagonism? Why does it seem that the discursive chain from interracial couples to interracial sex and, beyond that, to multiracial people binds these terms so closely? Why does the very idea of interracial sex always become "the sight of interracial couples," an image or a scene? Our collective feelings about sex across the color line, our judgment is, despite the ranting, still only vague, "somehow sinful," as Hernton says. We experience a sense of irritation, objection, even hurt that remains perplexing and unspecified, almost ambient. That is, until it explodes before a vision.

The real or imagined appearance of interracial intimacy was a liability to the movement for civil rights and, before that, the campaign for the abolition of slavery. Weinberger's disclaimer and Logan's defense find themselves echoing the sentiments of William Lloyd Garrison, the famous white abolitionist who pronounced in the mid-nineteenth century that "the blacks are not so enamored of white skins, as some editors imagine," and David Ruggles, a prominent black activist in 1830s New York, who "pointed out acidly that neither he nor 'any colored man or woman of [his] acquaintance' was eagerly pursuing cross-race marriage" (quoted in Nash 1999, 85). After the better part of two centuries, the sex that is "automatically imagined and projected onto any and all interracial associations" *remains* a liability for the articulation of multiracialism in the post–civil rights era. Although representing itself as the mobilization of a "biracial baby boom," the multiracial movement still refuses to announce the dreaded "national interracial orgy" as a condition of possibility. The post-*Loving* generation, coming of age in the political and economic spaces opened up by the new social movements of the 1950s and 1960s, effaces not only one likely outcome of its political activity ("that old bugaboo S-E-X") but also the modes and relations of reproduction that enable its discourse. In the current iteration, the disclaimer inhabits the other side of the formula: not an advance guarantee to do politics on good behavior but a willingness to conceal the itinerary of the current destination. The encumbrance of this contemporary "sexual hang-up," as Hernton would have it, is due less to the fact that whites still muse publicly about their own racial annihilation—though some are quite audible and many more do so behind closed doors (Ferber 1998)—than to the fact that the "superstitious imagining of the pornographic nature of interracial sex" has been commodified—which is to say *amplified*—as an item of late capitalist consumer culture.

While multiracialism's "quiet revolution" has established the psychological normality of multiracial people and "the validity of the majority of the relationships" (Root 1997) from which they issue, a multibillion dollar transnational industry has developed from the production of racially typed adult video, sex tourism, and mail-order bride services catering to the heteroclite sexual tastes of the global north (Altman 2001; Cornell 2000; Miller and Jayasundara 2001; Narayan 1995). Considering this broad historic convergence, we might wonder what the abundance of congratulatory attention lent to the progressive transformations of the biracial baby boom in the United States has to do with the dearth of critical energy directed toward the renewed commodification of interracial sexual encounter throughout the world. Because, in the latter case, we are dealing with a rate of growth outpacing any domestic increases in registered multiracial births or interracial marriages, the politicization of the biracial baby boom must muffle the register of its otherwise celebrated explosion of interracial sexual encounter in order to avoid guilt by association with the lucrative global traffic in "superstitious imagining of the pornographic nature of interracial sex." The "mini-revolutions" (Root 1992b) unfolding in respectable interracial relationships announce themselves quietly while reproaching their market-mediated counterparts with vehemence. In multiracial discourse, the image of the "indifferent, mulatto zombie" is countered by the recuperative image of the healthy multiracial person much like the image of pornographic interracial sex is countered with the gentrified image of the loving, multiracial family. In response to the disabling allegations leveled against them, multiracial advocates offer a certain pledge of allegiance to the terms of social respectability. This concession formalizes an agreement to dichotomize and to rank the political over the sexual, to sort out "legitimate" demands from the "depravities of human nature."[12] The sexual must be disallowed from political consideration because, when broaching matters of racial difference, especially regarding the welfare of blacks, it suggests motives that are not only ulterior to the stated agenda but also pathological: "the *most* degenerate and perverse form of sexual turn-on."

There is a triple structure of displacement and condensation at work here. Integration, or "social equality," is condensed with intermarriage figured as the sight of the heterosexual interracial couple (though there are interracial couples in many segregated spaces and an absence of such couples in many nominally integrated ones). The sight of the heterosexual interracial couple evokes the idea of interracial sex (though there are couples without sex and sex without couples per se). Interracial sex is reduced to potential interracial reproduction (though there is nonreproductive interracial sex and, as noted previously, "race mixture" that need not involve a sexual act in the conventional sense). Integration, intermarriage, interracial sexual reproduction, a "mongrel breed of citizens": all along a seemingly inexorable slope of consciousness. But despite the seeming clarity of this syllogism, we still cannot talk precisely about what it is that troubles us—in our ratios of race and gender—about the processes, terms, and figures that slip and slide around this conceptual nodal point: race mixture/mixed race. Where do we mark the arbitrary closure? Do we, following Hernton, concede that "when all is said and done about the reasons for opposing racial integration, the bottom line is invariably a superstitious imagining of the pornographic nature of interracial sex" (1988, xiv)? This much is supported by avowed white supremacists. A contributor to the *National Vanguard* opines, for example, "Civil rights . . . do not really mean equal employment opportunities; they mean equal *enjoyment* opportunities" (quoted in Ferber 1998).[13] Are we wiser to follow, instead, the advice of those scholars who find that the bottom line of antimiscegenation is a paranoid fantasy about white racial suicide, the so-called mongrelization of the white race?[14] Or is the opposition to "social equality"—integration cum intermarriage—only a red herring, a ruse for the defense of material interests, a strategy for maintaining the political economy of white supremacy?

The Event of Miscegenation

Let us turn the situation on its head. It is typically assumed that there are some primordial existing races and that these races then intermix at some later historical point. Even the critique of racial essentialism, not least that circulating in the literature in multiracial studies, falls prey to this theoretical faux pas. As noted in our discussion of Nathan Douglas in chapter 1, there is a world of difference between asserting, on the one hand, that human history is characterized by empirical incidences of racial intermixture and, on the other, claiming that there are not now and never were such things as human races. To make the former claim is to speak of the withering of racial difference, but for the latter claim, a different argument is required and a different set of questions emerges. Rather than ask after the causes of or barriers to racial intermixture in the past, present, or future, we would inquire instead, by what political mechanisms are races produced or reproduced in the first place? What, in fact, is "racialization," and how does it do its work?[15] As a first approach, let us posit miscegenation as something that *precedes* the demarcation of racial categories "in a pre-logical or pre-theoretical sense, as distinguished from a pre-ontological sense . . . but

[that] does not simply suspend the latter" (Plotnitski 1993, 22). Miscegenation is a precondition of racial categorization rather than the effect of its breakdown, as is typically assumed. But what would come *before* the racialization, and is this prior state captured absolutely by the imposition of racial order?[16]

First, there is miscegenation and then, in a moment of retroactivity—positing its presupposition—there is racialized difference. That is to say, the projected and reified racial difference supposed to be mortally threatened (for better or worse) by the prospect of subsequent interracial sex acts is itself produced, need we say *performatively*, in and through the apprehension of miscegenation. If, as Naomi Zack (1995b) rightly observes, "the term 'race' always connotes purity" (300), then impurity must serve as its definitional other. Racial discourse is thus always also a commentary on race *mixture*. However, returning to Deleuze and Guattari (1987b), we see that race is "defined not by its purity but rather by the impurity conferred upon it by a system of domination. Bastard and mixed blood are the true names of race" (379). This impurity is conferred by a system of domination, the refracted image of a restricted economy, but it is not simply controlled as a result. The general economy of race produces an excess within the political instrumentality of the interracial sexuality, an excess that provokes the demand for a domesticating scene, an image of race.[17] There are practices of desiring and identification, movements of social organization, and so on (what Deleuze and Guattari would term relations of "connectivity" and "disjuncture"), and objects of desire or socially legible identities are the imaginary precipitates or condensations of these complex psychic and social processes. Racial identities and the delimited bodies they attempt to signify are "moments of closure or conclusion" that must labor to maintain the appearance of an existence anterior to miscegenation. These appearances—these images of race—must deny their dependence upon the generative work of miscegenation, which is simply another name for what Homi Bhabha (1994) calls an "*inter*-subjective agency without subjectivity" (186).[18] No miscegenation, no racial identity; no purity without a prior mixture and not the other way around. How might we think differently, then, about the formation of racial difference in relation to the "absolute sexuality" of miscegenation?[19]

We might begin by thinking for a moment about the "consequence of race mixture" in a double sense, complicating the phrase that titles this chapter. Specifically, "we need, not surprisingly, to invoke both meanings of [the word *consequence*] and then to repeat the difference of the one in the other" (186). The consequence of race mixture is, in one sense, the significance of the interracial sex act, or more specifically, its proximity to the limits of signification, meaning, and value. This sense would indicate both the disjunction produced for any spatialized, coherent, and meaningful identity by the vertiginous rush of temporality and the disorientation produced by the mobility of affect.[20] At the same time, the consequence of race mixture is the domesticating boundary that establishes the spatialized, coherent, and meaningful identity, the manufactured effect of this libidinal play and dramatic action, its moment of conclusion in the image of the multiracial body. The consequence, then, is precisely "the kinetic tension that holds this double determination [of interracial sexuality and multiracial bodies] together and apart within discourse" (186). The terms of this double determination, whether antagonistic or convivial (or both), are produced performatively, which is only to say, the racializing project can never complete itself once and for all. Rather, it exists as a structured virtuality that materializes only in the performance of miscegenation as a form of value,[21] as an objectification of the absolute sexuality that opens up beside the interracial sex act or the appearance of the multiracial body. The absolute sexuality of miscegenation does not simply threaten the racial order, however; it rends the fabric of social reality itself. Antiblackness, as a matter of political ontology, materializes in the violent closure of the event of miscegenation, reifying it in a moment of conclusion that signifies miscegenation as concrete sex acts or forms of identity within a discursive chain that contributes to a frame of (particularly visual) intelligibility. It articulates miscegenation with other relations of meaning, makes sense of it, and, in the process, makes it appear as an effect of antimiscegenation.

This alternate perspective is noted in passing in most contemporary analyses of the social construction of race, but only to be subsequently disavowed, if not repressed altogether. Nash, to stay with a useful example, writes: "When you look at the so-called races, the categories crumble. . . .

Racial classifications are definitions placed on *already mixed populations* in an effort to give these highly diverse groups essential and binding characteristics. . . . Race is a myth . . . it has been socially constructed and historically shaped rather than biologically determined" (1999, viii; emphasis added). Yet, for all of the discussion about "the social construction of race," including the tendency toward an "essentialism of the social" that some critics have rightfully identified (Butler 1993), there is little mention of *what* is essentialized, constructed, or bound by imposed definitions of race. In other words, what are the raw materials of these social and historical processes, "the social construction of what" (Hacking 1999)? Is it the oneness of humanity that is disavowed, the overwhelming realization that we are, in fact, more similar than we have been led to believe? Or is it something else altogether?

In my view, the event of miscegenation—undecidability, excessive affect, crumbled categories—provides the ground for and generates the social and psychic power of racial difference. Racialization is not, as the popular mythology asserts, some superficial designation that somehow corrupts otherwise natural human relations, sexual or otherwise, from the outside. Quite the contrary, *miscegenation is the outside of racialization.* The event of miscegenation is, to evoke Derrida (1983) once again, the "dangerous supplement" of the racial formation, the intrusive remainder that founds the project from which it is disavowed. It founds a culture of antiblackness that alternately scorns the dangers and celebrates the potentials of miscegenation as a form of value, that is, as instrumental or interpretable acts of interracial sex or meaningful multiracial bodies, predicates of the sentence of racialization, images of race.

In relation to its racial terms, the event of miscegenation is "not something that is either absent or present, although it could be said to be absent on the condition that absence is not understood as a modification of presence, as an absent-presence."

> It is a non-dialectical middle, a structure of jointed predication, which cannot itself be comprehended by the [racialized] predicates it distributes. . . . Instead of being simply an opacity within the system of rationality, which

would thus be comprehensible by it, it is nonrational. . . . [Racial] reason is structurally incapable of comprehending its origin. . . . Not that this inability of [racial] reason to understand its origin shows a lack of power; rather this inability is constitutive of the very possibility of the logic of identity, and of what appears of necessity to [racial] reason, as its irrational Other according to that very logic. (Gasche 1986, 210)[22]

The event of miscegenation, the outside of racialization, cannot itself be comprehended by the racializing project. It can only appear as what is imagined about "the pornographic nature of interracial sex" or the zombie-like presence of multiracial people. The outside of racialization "cannot offer itself as a positive presence—as something inwardly illuminated by the certainty of its own existence—but only as an absence that pulls as far away from itself as possible, receding into the sign it makes to draw one toward it (as though it were possible to reach it)" (Foucault 1987, 28). Within the order of white supremacy, both its advocates and its opponents attempt to manipulate the receding sign of miscegenation, to disparage or valorize its objects, to tell a story about it, to bestow upon it a meaning, to define it, to construct it within a narrative.

Lyotard (1988) reminds us that "any narrative whatsoever begins in the middle of things and . . . its so-called 'end' is an arbitrary cut in the infinite sequence of data" (2), and this is no less true for the narratives of racial whiteness and racial blackness. "The middle of things" is a rich, multivalent phrase, and it is interesting to think of miscegenation according to it. It connotes, on the one hand, the *in-between space*, connective tissue that is itself productive of the social categories believed to be primordial and discrete. It suggests, on the other, *active processes*, in this case the practices of miscegenation which the reification of racial designations attempts to interrupt and interpolate, to capture in "a movement of [racial] reason." As noted, racial identities are the retroactive precipitates of miscegenation, or in Deleuze and Guattari's (1987a) terms, paranoid blockages of schizophrenic affective flows. This is not to posit, with Nash and others, an original, prelapsarian unity out of which "humanity" is, in a secondary manner, divided. In speaking of miscegenation prior to racialization, I am not referring to any neutral sameness or global commonality. To assert such would only recapitulate the common understanding of racism as the corruption of otherwise colorblind desires and identifications among members of the *human* race. In that respect, I am not making a humanist argument. However, in trying to articulate an alternative theoretical position, the effort is complicated by the fact that miscegenation, as we think of it now—the mixture of preconstituted races—is only intelligible from the perspective of a culture in which antimiscegenation is *already* constitutive. Whatever we imagine to happen before, beyond, beneath, or between meaningful categories of interracial sex or multiracial identity is *not* the event of miscegenation strictly speaking. Our retroactive projections, filtered through this lens, miss the point in the very attempt to grasp it.[23]

Antimiscegenation, then, is not simply the prohibition of interracial marriage or the punishment of sexual transgressions of the color line. Neither is it simply the derogation of multiracial people. Rather, antimiscegenation is more properly understood as the reactive quest for racial being, which is to say the performative reiteration of racial whiteness itself. Thus, there is antimiscegenation wherever there is whiteness and its correlatives, even, perhaps especially, in places where some version of *mestizaje* is recognized. This is so because whiteness qua antimiscegenation is about more than the empirical preservation of white racial purity. White racial purity is neither a necessary nor a sufficient condition of white supremacy. There can be whiteness without purity, and purity alone would not secure its status.[24] To insist that antimiscegenation is simply a defense of the category of whiteness from pollution vis-à-vis the production of multiracial bodies is to privilege only one dimension of its labor, the intergenerational conservation of the race.

Charles Mills (1998) reminds us, however, that "white supremacy will take different forms in different parts of the world [and transforms over time]—expropriation and enclosure on reservations here, slavery and colonial rule there, formal segregation and antimiscegenation laws in one place, mixing and intermarriage in another" (101). While there is a distinction between our different uses of the term *antimiscegenation*, the point can be granted that the fabrication of racial whiteness, a project that requires antimiscegenation as its founding gesture (and not simply as an auxiliary defense), is a strategy of power. Michel Foucault (1990) notes in his *History of Sexuality*, "There can exist different and even contradictory discourses within the same strategy; they can, on the contrary, circulate without changing their form from one strategy to another, opposing strategy" (102). In the history of white supremacy, we have seemingly contradictory discourses of antimiscegenation and anti-antimiscegenation, of white purity and *mestizaje*, Anglo-Saxonism and Latinism, inhabiting the same strategic integration. It is because the position of the multiracial does not break from the assumptive logic of antimiscegenation that it can be accommodated by white supremacy and antiblackness. It threatens the racial schema from within but does not seek to challenge the regime of definition that white Anglo racism paints in such bright lines. Multiracialism seeks merely to refine or reconfigure the apparatus, to establish a space for the full play of a multiracial identity or a race-transcendent humanity. It is, in other words, a battle within the bounds of the strategic field, contained by the fear of being undone by or losing itself in the struggle.[25]

Ultimately, white supremacists have good reason to insist that even the slightest racial mingling will lead swiftly to their total annihilation, and it is not found in the cognitive dissonance they experience between, say, actual rates of intermarriage and their own perception of its ubiquity. In other words, it is not a simple distortion between paranoid speculations about the numbers of whites that are "mixing it up" and the empirical truth of the matter. If this reassuring rationalist fantasy were to be the case, the still relatively low incidences of "race mixture," especially in the case of blacks, alongside repeated assurances that race mixing is of little interest to black people themselves, should soothe the uneasy conscience. Moreover, the historical examples of Latin America, Hawaii, and South Africa all serve as warranties that white supremacy and antiblackness can be maintained under conditions of "racial democracy," "racial paradise," or some tripartite racial scheme. Yet the paranoia remains, and not only because the data is disbelieved or discarded as propaganda of an ostensible Jewish conspiracy (Daniels 1996; Ferber 1998). Disavowal is at work, but it does not cover the entire field of antimiscegenation. Rather, antimiscegenation is an ideology that exceeds both its theory and its practice. Colette Guillaumin (1995) writes,

> Ideology, more diffuse but also more widespread, is the mode of apprehension of reality shared by a whole culture, to the point where it becomes omnipresent and, for that very reason, goes unrecognized. The ideology of race (racism) is a universe of signs . . . far more extensive than simply the "theory" into which it crystallized in the course of the nineteenth century. (35)

This "mode of apprehension" binds the positions of antimiscegenation and anti-antimiscegenation tightly into the imperatives of identity politics, an unyielding pact to either uphold or violate the law of the color line, both which positions maintain it.

If it is true that "no plot is trivial if it is performed according to the calling of law" (Lyotard 1988, 4), then it makes sense to think that the paranoia of white supremacy merely inflates the prevalence of race mixture as a rationalization for upholding the law of the color line. However, this self-validating instrumentality, raising the political stakes to vindicate the defensive law of race purity, actually conceals a much more frightening operation. The specter of miscegenation is threatening to white supremacy and antiblackness not only because it holds out the empirical possibility of thoroughly "mixing the blood" of whites with their racial others. Its power derives more fundamentally from its potential to undo the illusory coherence of racial identities tout court, to give the lie to the radical *indifference* of the groups in question, to expose the secret of whiteness: that it cannot control its own law, that it cannot even *know* its own law. Miscegenation tauntingly proclaims, in short, that "whiteness cannot form a body." The horror of the racial other is not its potential to subsume whiteness into the brown mire of racial sameness (what white supremacists refer to affectionately as "the mud"). In a more radical way, the horror is that *the other does not exist.* Instead, the mud exists as a condition of whiteness. The mud, the hotbed of miscegenation, the incoherent flux of bodies and pleasures are its raw materials.

Miscegenation intimates the irreducible failure of whiteness to maintain itself on its own account, its inability to totalize its reign over the multiplicity, the passion and excess of the outside. Thus, the old-fashioned specter of miscegenation as an external threat to whiteness is more accurately described as an objectification or projection of the internal structural barriers to the project of whiteness as securable identity. That is to say, to its apprehension as a stable and homogenous object of value. It is a defense against the immanence of the abject. It is a reactive movement of reason against the tension of "what disturbs identity, system, order. What does not respect borders, positions, rules. The in-between, the ambiguous, the [always-already] composite" (Kristeva 1982, 4). For the fate of racial whiteness, the force of the abject is much more ruinous than a battle with an opposable foe, a correlative, "which, providing me with someone or something else as support, would allow me to be more or less detached and autonomous."

> The abject has only one quality of the object—that of being opposed to I. . . . What is abject . . . is radically excluded and draws me toward the place where meaning collapses. . . . On the edge of non-existence and hallucination, of a reality that, if I acknowledge it, annihilates me. (1–2)

The edge of nonexistence is the threshold of the outside, where the dichotomies of sense and non-sense are not yet operative, where there is no-thing, only bodies and flows. This edge, the verge of race, is the absence of the interracial occult, the supplement that cannot be comprehended by racial reason. It is the "night in which the outline of the signified thing vanishes and where only the imponderable affect is carried out" (10).

If miscegenation is "what existed in the archaism of pre-objectal relationship, in the immemorial violence with which a body becomes separated from another body in order to be" (10), then it is not simply a potentiality or a possibility within the social field of white supremacy, an external obstacle. It is not a threat from the future, something that *could* change the mythically preconstituted faces of the earth, the purported dominion of white civilization. It is, rather, an archaic threat from the past, a perpetual, structural danger related to *the catastrophe of what has already taken place, what is always in excess,* the return of the repressed, or more radically, a mythic origin foreclosed from the Symbolic that returns in the Real. What this leads us to conclude is that, contrary to assurances offered to white supremacy by its loyal opposition, there is nothing for which to apologize. Whiteness cannot be annihilated. It can only be reminded of the oblivion from which it came, the insignificance from which it continues to construct itself by decree. The myth of "the black hole into which the non-'black' ancestors of these people get sucked" (quoted in Spencer 1999, 94) is a defense against the mystical foundations of this authority: a myth that inverts the structures of racial oppression, reverses the relations of captivity, and converts the external force of confinement into the self-generated force of gravity.

CHAPTER 5

The True Names of Race: Blackness and Antiblackness in Global Contexts

A stark evasion manifests itself in the face of the black body. The black body lives in what evinces itself as an anti-black world. In that world, it dwells as a form of absence of human presence.

—Lewis Gordon, "The Black and the Body Politic"

No industrialized nation has so large a percentage of its population in prison as does the United States. And no such nation is producing so many mixed race people. These two facts about the United States are not directly related. Yet they bear mention together because of the antithetical implications these two realities have for a postethnic America.

—David Hollinger, *Postethnic America: Beyond Multiculturalism*

The Specter of Multiracialism

If the discourse of multiracialism is troubled by its disavowal of interracial sexuality and that disavowal's origination is in a protective concession to negrophobia, then the global cultural imaginary, or rather *the cultural imaginary of the global*, is no less interrupted by a figure of race mixture, a scandal at the heart of the cultures of globalization. If the overlapping conceptions of "globalization," "globalism," and "globality" articulate a vast array of transformations and restructuring in political economy, social organization, cultural production, and law (Lechner and Boli 2003), they betray nonetheless a curious inability to formulate a coherent position regarding the fate of *race* insofar as it structures the field of sexual encounter and its inconsistent relation to "the work of reproduction" (Appadurai 1996). In order to find sustained treatment of racialized sexuality in the global age, one is forced to move beyond official accounts and the bulk of academic criticism of the "New World Order" to consult unseemly sources: the literature of transnational white supremacist networks and the marketing campaigns of the global sex industries (Ferber 1998, Kempadoo and Doezema 1998). The former exhibits its customarily paranoid rhetoric of annihilation, while the latter revels in the multibillion dollar windfall of commodified racial–sexual difference. The public sphere of the multiracial movement and the growing academic field of multiracial studies together constitute a third term of social commentary on such matters, steering a precarious path between the biopolitics of race and the realization/racialization of value, particularly with respect to the United States and other G-8 nations.

Although this new assemblage is grounded in the specificity of the North American instance and the parameters of the current study are established accordingly, one cannot reduce its significance to the supposedly domestic politics of white supremacy and antiblackness in the United States, any more than these domestic politics are reducible to their locality (Brock, Kelley, and Sotiropolous 2003). Multiracialism traverses bounds of nation, region, and hemisphere, due partly to a multidirectional dissemination by way of the Internet and the circuits of university and corporate press publications. But also because it emerges from the social conditions of contemporary mass immigration, most especially the demographic transfers from Latin America and Asia to the United States since the late 1960s. As well, the comparative sensibility brought to bear on racial formation in the United States (viz. Europe, Latin America, the Caribbean, the Pacific Islands, etc.) speaks to the expansive imaginative geography of its deliberations. In this way, linkages have cropped up between the so-called post-*Loving* generation of multiracial Americans and various multiracial populations across the globe: from South Africa, to Mexico, the Caribbean, Central and South America, to Canada, the United Kingdom, and the European continent, to various countries across Asia and the Pacific Islands (Christian 2000). Such connections register in the political pronouncements of local movements and have begun to take fledgling organizational form: witness, for instance, the International Interracial Association.[1]

However, it is apparent that regardless of the panoply of counterexamples that underwrite its global aspirations, multiracialism demonstrates lasting explanatory difficulty about the basis and longevity of a putatively exceptional one-drop rule of racial definition—that is to say, the persistence of a painfully discernible antiblackness in the birthplace of liberal democracy, epicenter of the "financialization of the globe" (Spivak 1999) that overdetermines the planetary movement of people, ideas, images, and things.

This difficulty is more properly understood as a quandary. Multiracialism establishes itself as a movement of opposition to or defiance of the one-drop rule, an injunction entirely *singular* to the historical construction of racial blackness in the North American instance. Yet, it reinforces the very same rule in its own political articulation: first, by issuing a constitutive exclusion of African Americans from its demographic on the specious claim that an intermingled genealogy is irrelevant to the extent that it is not immediate or "first-generation" (Spencer 1999); second, by issuing a constitutive denial of the societal derogation of blackness while highlighting, when not openly celebrating, the relative frequency, indeed the *normalization*, of intermixture among nonblack nonwhites. When pressed to contemplate the structural inequalities behind the empirical indicators, multiracial discourse must either take refuge in prevarication or reiterate the "reversal of gesture and intention," the "specific transvaluation of agency" that seem to characterize "the inverted projections of white paranoia" (Butler 1993, 16). In noting, say, the gross disparity of rates of intermarriage or strategies of multiracial identification (where sharp statistical variations indicate *qualitative* differences), multiracialism suggests, as I have shown, not that the world is particularly antiblack but that blacks are particularly antiworld.

In place of an analysis that would not only account for the emergence of the one-drop rule in the consolidation of racial slavery but also address its complexity, its multivalent character, its various articulations and appropriations, what we find, more or less, is a loquacious moral denunciation: sometimes clear and unequivocal ("the one-drop rule is simply stupid and anyone adhering to it is a racist"), sometimes oblique ("the one-drop rule, is archaic and its function in the present is merely the residuum of a past that we are transcending"), sometimes dissimulated ("the one-drop rule is a component of *racialism*, a complicated ideological formation against which we must continue to do battle"). What is avoided or minimized in each case is the marked discrepancy *internal* to "the multiracial experience," a radical discontinuity *within* the field of racialized sexuality and its hierarchical "matrices of value" (Gordon 1997). It is only by passing over this extreme incongruity that the vectors of association between native-born whites and nonwhite immigrant populations (typically coded "brown" in an unsurprising rhetorical excision of the "black immigrant") can be drawn into a chain of equivalence with the ongoing history of black–white encounter, sexual and otherwise—before and after the advent of European colonization, the dawn of revolution, the launch of westward expansion, the outbreak of civil war, the surge of industrialization, and the initiation of empire. Such equivalence is required of the comforting notion—the elementary covenant of multiracialism—that, with respect to "the multiracial experience," we are all in it together. It is also necessary to the position of condescension toward "black community in general and its political leadership specifically" (Byrd 1996) assumed by hardline advocates, those who would dismiss and deride rather than engage and examine the reigning sexual politics, practices of group definition, or popular conventions of judgment and adjudication.

What is most interesting about such political and intellectual developments is the epochal significance broadly attributed to increases in interracial sexual encounter in the contemporary global arena. Parker and Song (2000a) note: "Racial mixture is nothing new—it has been the history of the world. What stand out as novel are the forms of political contestation gathered around the topic of 'mixed race'" (1). When set against the monumental social, political, military, and economic conflicts defining the age of globalization, the rising tide of love across the color line, and the new multiracial consciousness it is said to nurture, are taken as bulwark against the harrowing countertendencies of fragmentation, dissension, or, worse, regression to the embattled reservoir of tradition (notorious, in the post-Enlightenment era, for its a priori authoritarianism). From this angle, within the multiracial imagined community, what the figure of race mixture signals and supports is the peaceful mediation of historical antagonism toward the goal of world-scale reconciliation or, at least, a modicum of functional tolerance in its systemic integration. With some notable exceptions, the discourse articulated by intellectuals, advocates, and artists from within this small but noteworthy transnational social movement tends not to call into question the axioms of the capitalist world-system or to contest the tenets of antiblackness.

On one level, there is some familiar variety of opinion within the multiracial camp, depending upon whether one emphasizes race mixture's empirical or symbolic purchase. For the latter, the vast majority of commentators, the prospect of race mixture is primarily pedagogic and provides the nascent global community with exemplars of interracial cooperation, understanding, and synthesis (Root 1992a, 1996b). For the former, the force of interracial desire promises to undermine the putative basis of racism itself, scrambling the bounds of race by redistributing, as it were, the traits of a formerly categorical bodily difference. Often, such assertions are found in composite and always in quite irresolvable tension with the partially incorporated antiessentialist insights of critical race theory. One sees quite easily the ways that this twin investment in multiracialism (the literal and the figurative) as a counter to racism works to entrench its pernicious ideologies—a paradox of the movement being, of course, the naturalization of the same categories it seeks to denaturalize, problematize, and challenge. This is only to restate what is, by now, a well-established critique. What has been more difficult to ascertain is the precise status of sexuality within the discourse of multiracialism: how it is or is not an object of thought and what figures stand in for its difficulty, and here lies the intimate discrepancy between multiracialism and those other, seedier globalizing domains of race and sexuality mentioned previously.

Globalization and Black Liberation

At the turn of the twenty-first century, Fredric Jameson (1998b) announced that "the state of things the word *globalization* attempts to designate will be with us for a long time to come; and . . . its theorization . . . will constitute the horizon of all theory in the years ahead" (xvi). It would thus seem that any intellectual project accompanying the historical movement of black liberation—whose intervention sustains the current position of enunciation—must take as central the series of questions posed by the term. We might posit the reverse as well: anyone thinking seriously about globalization, particularly those hoping to organize political resistance to it, cannot afford to elide the question of black liberation without missing something essential to its unfolding. It is my suspicion that this vital consideration, made only more pointed by the ambivalent rendering of race mixture, forces an uncanny encounter with the black body—its capacities, its energies, its appearance as well as its structured installation in the nexus of sexuality and violence. In each case noted previously (the white supremacist movement, the global sex industries, the discourse of multiracialism), it is the image of the black body that throws the apparatus of representation into unmitigated crisis.

"The history of racism is a narrative in which the congruency of micro- and macrocosm has been disrupted at the point of their analogical intersection: the human body" (Gilroy 1997, 192). This prescient point, offered by Paul Gilroy in his essay "Scales and Eyes," bears significantly on the present effort. The body presents a problem, a point of disruption, for the historical narrative of racism. It has failed to lend itself, once and for all, to a stable designation. As Gilroy asks, "Has anyone ever been able to say exactly how many 'races' there are, let alone how skin shade should correspond to them" (195)? Of course, the answer is no, but we have seen that the indeterminacy of race in "the order of active differentiation" (192) has not proved insurmountable, even if it is inescapable. Quite the contrary, this perennial difficulty has given rise to a frenetic succession of methods designed for specifying human difference that characterize the protean nature of modernity's "most pernicious signature" (192). In the current moment, we confront a novel question: "What does that trope 'race' mean in the age of molecular biology" (192)?

For Gilroy, we now inhabit "a space beyond comparative anatomy" where "the body and its obvious, functional components no longer delimit the scale upon which assessments of the unity and variation of the species are to be made" (194). Our collective estrangement from anatomical scale has rendered the eye inadequate, if it ever was, "to the tasks of evaluation and description demanded" by racial segregation. Thus, the ascendancy of what he terms "nanopolitics" "departs from the scalar assumptions associated with anatomical difference [and] accelerates [a] vertiginous, inward movement towards the explanatory power of ever-smaller scopic regimes" (193). Indeed, this one-way movement, "downwards and inwards," locks the racializing project into a perpetual search for the zero degree of difference. However, if racial difference "cannot be readily correlated with genetic variation" (194), the most basic level of differentiation known to date, at what level can it be asserted, maintained, legitimated? Or is it destined simply to remain anxious and uncertain, forever suspicious?

Gilroy is less than sanguine about these developments. Although skepticism about "the status of visible differences" is welcomed for the trouble it causes to the paradigm of comparative anatomy, there is no indication that the calibration of "human sameness" and "human diversity" will diminish in political importance. The frustration of this procedure at one scale does not prevent its seeking refuge by burrowing deeper into the flesh, the viscera, the blood, the DNA. Gilroy asks, "Can a different sense of scale and scaling form a counterweight to the appeal of absolute particularity celebrated under the sign of 'race'?" "Can it answer the seductions of self and kind projected onto the surface of the body?" Scarcely: the repudiation of surface-level sameness by "the proliferation of invisible differences" remains an object of aggravated fascination insofar as such differences are understood to "produce catastrophic consequences where people are not what they seem to be" (192). We are familiar with the vast literature regarding the thematic of racial passing in and beyond the United States, which often sensationally features the scandal of seeming to be white when one is, "in truth," something else (Ginsberg 1996; Sánchez and Schlossberg 2001). Today, the fear of invisible blackness commingles with the global traffic in hypervisible blackness, the premier consumer product. Across the globe, one can play at blackness, selectively appropriating "everything but the burden," to borrow Greg Tate's (2003) apt phrase. Yet, Gilroy's remarks on the crisis of *visible* difference invoke another catastrophic consequence not unrelated to an unsuspected or invisible blackness. Visible differences, he notes, not only prove unreliable in determinations of race, they also "do not . . . tell us everything we need to know about the health-status of the people we want to have sex with" (192). They really never did, of course, but Gilroy's comment here makes reference to another "catastrophic consequence" associated with the age of molecular biology: AIDS. He concludes his essay as follows:

> With the body figured an epiphenomenon of coded information, this aesthetics [of racial difference] is now residual. The skin may no longer be privileged as the threshold of identity. There are good reasons to suppose that the line between inside and outside now falls elsewhere. (196)

This other threshold of identity, this newly privileged "elsewhere" that now houses the persistent dividing line, is located *within* the body, tracking an invisible presence that demotes and denotes the significance of the bodily surface. It is, in effect, a displacement of the skin as the preeminent sign of race. Here we note a convergence with the project of multiracialism discussed at the outset: for different reasons, both developments portend the obstruction or unraveling of racialization in the field of vision—one betting on the increasing difficulty of making clear discriminations on the surface, the other devaluing the surface altogether. However, nothing in Gilroy's account alludes to the wholesale replacement of the surface by the interior, wherein the latter simply supplants the former. More likely, we have an augmentation of racial difference, an alloy of the inner and outer, by way of the discourses of biotechnology and genetic science. Similarly, the blurring of the color line prophesied by multiracialism provides the occasion, within the imagination of white supremacy and antiblackness, for a redoubled effort to police it. In this respect, the surface becomes a more intense object of observation precisely *because* it has become more unreliable as a sign of race.

Globalization and Antiblackness

As mentioned, the age of molecular biology is also the era of the AIDS pandemic and, as such, the pseudoscience of race (reenergized and refocused by the Human Diversity Genome Project) mingles with the "cultural pol-itics of 'curing' AIDS" (Erni 1994). This conflation is motivated not only by a coeval discursive production or contingent institutional links but also by more structural determinants. David McBride insists that "in the future, given the history and force of racial stratification in the United States, no Americans, regardless of color, will be able to approach the dynamics of racial discriminations and the AIDS [pandemic] as separable problems" (quoted in Haver 1996, 207n8). This is even more the case at the global scale. The empirical record regarding the incidence of HIV/AIDS among black populations in the United States, not to mention in the Caribbean and sub-Saharan Africa, even when taken very critically, is staggering (Irwin, Millen, and Fallows 2003). I will forego adding detail to the archive, but suffice it to say that one cannot rightly think about the global phenome-non called AIDS without thinking through the political, economic, and cultural locations of the black diaspora. As Cathy Cohen (1999) brilliantly demonstrates, the reverse is even more the case. Allowing ourselves an extrapolation from the U.S. context, we might say that the global impact of AIDS on black communities and their responses to it (or lack thereof) reveal both "the boundaries of blackness" (who's in, who's out) and the breaking point of black politics (what's possible, what's not). It is not over-stating the case to say that addressing the historic articulation of racial blackness and AIDS in the era of globalization may be decisive to the future possibility of political struggle as such.

Although Gilroy does not pursue the associations he draws between "the crisis of raciology" and the emergence of the AIDS pandemic, his passing reference is instructive nonetheless. The discourse of AIDS medi-ates between the political economy of globalization and the reconfigura-tion of global white supremacy as a cultural structure. Dennis Altman (2001) notes in his *Global Sex* that AIDS is both an effect and a cause of global-ization; proliferating along itineraries etched by flows of populations, images, commodities, and capital, AIDS simultaneously structures such flows while mechanisms of regulation and repression are established in re-sponse. The racial imaginary that accompanies these strategies of social control slates the black body as the primary source of danger to planetary public health (where "public health" is often enough shorthand or code-word for "national security" and "stable business environment"): what "the inner city" is to the U.S. national scene, "sub-Saharan Africa" and "the Caribbean" are to the world. In this sense, the well-heeled research agenda of the bourgeoning genomics industry and the tortured scientific and policy debates about the AIDS pandemic share a common ground of concern at the molecular scale. What is race, and where is race to be located in the body? What is AIDS, and where is it to be located in the body? How do they work, and what can be said about them in the name of science? These sets of questions gain urgency from the figures of blackness that make them *socially* intelligible. Frantz Fanon (1967) writes in *Black Skin, White Masks* that, in the racist imaginary, "the Negro symbolizes the biological danger" (165). We might learn something from this prompt about the double economy of miscegenation that characterizes the modern world-system (Gruzinski 2002).

In his landmark essay "Concerning Violence," Fanon (1965) offers a crucial historical periodization of anticolonial struggle that is generally overlooked in the critical literature. In that opening chapter of his famous *Wretched of the Earth*, he asks, "What are the forces which in the colonial period open up new outlets and engender new aims for the violence of colonized peoples" (59)? He first criticizes "the political parties and the intellectual or commercial elites" whom, he notes, are characteristically troubled by the "savagery" of the masses, that is, their penchant to "destroy everything."

> For in fact they are not at all convinced that this impatient violence of the masses is the most efficient means of defending their own interests. More-over, there are some individuals who are convinced of the ineffectiveness of violent methods; for them, there is no doubt about it, every attempt to break colonial oppression by force is a hopeless effort, an attempt at suicide. (63)

However, Fanon is quick to rebut this conviction. He writes:

> The violence of the native is only hopeless if we compare it in the abstract to the military machine of the oppressor. On the other hand, if we situate

that violence in the dynamics of the international situation, we see at once that it constitutes a terrible menace for the oppressor. (79)

The international situation of which he speaks is, of course, the context of the cold war. "Each act of sedition in the Third World makes up part of a picture framed by the Cold War . . . an atmosphere of international stress . . . the atmosphere of doomsday" (75, 76, 81). The cold war, because it embroils the metropolitan powers in costly conflict with one another, renders the citadel of colonialism vulnerable "to knives and naked fists." This is why Fanon claims "a colonized people is not alone . . . the Third World is not cut off from the rest" (70, 76). Because, in the cold war context, "there is no colonial power . . . capable of adopting the only form of contest which has a chance of succeeding, namely, the prolonged establishment of large forces of occupation" (74), opportunities emerge for worldwide anticolonial struggle. The violence of rebellion is enabled by this epochal geopolitical dynamic. In fact, "that [the native] openly brandishes the threat of violence proves that he [or she] is conscious of the unusual character of the contemporary situation and that he means to profit by it" (74).

These comments do no justice to the complexity of Fanon's thinking on the topic. However, they should at least remind us of the haste with which many dismiss his commentary as simply outdated. On closer reading, one can appreciate the lucidity with which it offers critical examination of the emerging world order and speculation on the fate of the Third World therein. (Here one could productively read Fanon alongside Du Bois on "the problem of the color line.") Fanon forewarns: "The capitalist regime must not try to enlist the aid of the socialist regime over 'the fate of Europe' in the face of the starving multitudes of colored peoples" (105). In his view, the cold war has the auspicious capacity to turn over into a global redistribution of "the colonial inheritance," provided the forces of liberation win out. Entrenched resistance from the Western governments is to be expected. As such, "this huge task," according to Fanon, "will be carried out with the indispensable help of the European *people*. . . . [But] to achieve this, the European peoples must first decide to wake up and shake themselves, use their brains, and stop playing the stupid game of the Sleeping Beauty" (106). By "the European people," Fanon means, of course, *working* people, and much is riding on this dream of proletarian popular awakening, this postcolonial New International. Although the optimism of his will would not conscience a post–cold war rapprochement between the capitalist and socialist regimes, Fanon was keenly aware of its distinct possibility. As we have seen, the First World's enlistment of the Second World, its violent integration into what is now called the global North, is precisely what defines the era of globalization after the collapse of "the world power and the territorial empire of the USSR" (Ali 2000). To large degree, this uneasy and unequal coalition finds coherence in the legacies of global white supremacy, a point revealed plainly by the transatlantic victories of the New Right across the 1970s and 1980s (Chomsky 1991; Smith 1994), the consolidation of neoliberal consensus in the 1990s (Harvey 2005), and ascendant restrictions on postcolonial immigration (Cornelius et al. 2004)—aspects of a systemic backlash against the limited successes of the new social movements and the anticolonial struggles for national liberation.

Globalization erodes the horizon of capitalist expansion as it reworks the space of a transnational whiteness. Insofar as "the capitalist relation has colonized all of geographical and social space, *it has no inside* into which to integrate things" (Massumi 1993, 19).[2] This is the upshot of the real subsumption of society by capital. Encompassing the globe, capital turns inward toward an intensive expansion, an "endocolonization" of the last oases of the private domain (Massumi 2002, 132). It goes so far as to commodify as labor one's leisure, one's senses, even one's attention (Beller 1998). Downward and inward: like the gaze of the new raciology, like the science and cultural politics of "curing" AIDS, all enabled by new visual technologies: cinema, television, digital media, x-ray, magnetic resonance imaging, virtual reality, and so forth (Bolter and Grusin 2000). Sexuality emerges in this historic intersection as a term of political mobilization and theoretical activity, including its entanglement with the juridical apparatus. Locally, the legalization of a circumscribed interracial sexual encounter in the United States after 1967 signals this decisive moment, perhaps more so than the Civil Rights and Voting Rights Acts of 1964 and 1965. It is through the belated naming of the multiracial (a naming that becomes possible only as the end of the cold war is declared, "the end of History") that the historical force of miscegenation is put on display and concealed in the same gesture. That is to say, the site where the materiality of racialization is made most manifest—sexuality as a field where the pleasure and violence of difference converge—is "de-sublimated" (Stephens 1999) only to be banished more thoroughly from consideration. To my mind, it is this disavowal of racialized sexuality that feeds directly into the rejuvenation of white supremacist movements and the exploitation of exoticism in the global sex industries. It is a question, therefore, whether "whiteness as value" is a component of capital, or vice versa (Tadiar 2003).

Global Apartheid

The immanence of global capital in no way prevents the drawing of internal lines of exclusion. As Giovanni Arrighi (1995) states, "Entire communities, countries, even continents, as in the case of sub-Saharan Africa, have been declared 'redundant,' superfluous to the changing economy of capitalist accumulation on a world scale." In the wake of the cold war, "the unplugging of these 'redundant' communities and locales from the world supply system has triggered innumerable, mostly violent feuds . . . over the appropriation of resources that were made absolutely scarce by the unplugging" (330). Managing such feuds—fueling them and containing them in order to profit from them—has become a principal strategic concern of the new global hegemony and the indispensable underside of its political economic globalization (Bhattacharyya 2005). It is carried forward by means of a brutal geopolitics, at the heart of which lie black populations: north, south, east, and west. Achille Mbembe (1999) notes, for instance, that "the African experience shows that in the age of globalization bringing the world climate under control involves of necessity the forcible breaking-down of existing territorial frameworks . . . and the simultaneous erection of shifting areas and areas in which populations judged to be superfluous can be corralled and their mobility limited." For those consigned to decomposition "on the outskirts of the great technological changes going on today," deterritorialization "goes hand-in-hand with the setting up of a constraint economy, designed quite simply to get rid of their unwanted populations and exploit their resources in the raw state." "In these circumstances," after the breakdown of the "three worlds" heuristic, "war seen as a general economic system no longer necessarily pits those who have the weapons against each other. Preferably, it sets those who have weapons against those who have none" (Mbembe 1999). Weapons include not only structural adjustment policies (SAP) and increased militarization, recently known in the United States as "the prison-welfare-industrial complex" (Davis 2003; Wacquant 2005) but also, returning to our earlier point, the new forms of apartheid intended for the spatial containment of AIDS (Dean 2000).[3] *Immobilization and exclusion:* counterparts to the accelerated mobility and intercourse of people, goods, and information that typically register in descriptions of the new global context (Bauman 2000). From this vantage, it is imperative to recall that "the 'Grab for Africa' . . . was the high-water mark of European imperialism, and the frenzy for possessions was certainly underlain by the sense of the closing of the world." It was, in other words, "the great time of the 'tracing of lines' in the chancelleries of Europe" (Parker 1998, 24–25n4). We reencounter this rehabilitated geopolitical inscription today—still Eurocentric—but underlain now by the sense of the closing of the world of a qualitatively different order.

The effects of the consummate geography of capital on subjectivity are titanic. The catastrophic consequences described by Gilroy have now become generalized as the conditions of possibility for human being. "Capitalist power actualizes itself in a basically uninhabitable space of fear. That much is universal. The particulars of the uninhabitable landscape of fear in which a given body nevertheless dwells vary according to the socially valorized distinctions applied to it by selective mechanisms of power implanted throughout the social field" (Massumi 1993, 24). For Brian Massumi, the paradigmatic subject of this universal fear is white, bourgeois, metropolitan, and female; the paradigmatic source is public, unmediated, anonymous, and sexualized. "An urbanized North American woman dwells in the space of potential rape and battering. Her movements and emotions are controlled (filtered, channeled) by the immanence of sexual violence to every coordinate of her socio-geographical space-time." This image is deliberately evoked as a cliché. It is Massumi's point to demonstrate its iconic status, its readymade legibility, its status as an omnipresent screen of projection, circulating as ubiquitous collective fantasy in print media, television, and film culture. However, there is a twist to the trope of the imperiled white woman vulnerable to sexual violence. "Capitalist power determines being a woman as the future-past of male violence. . . . [Yet] the 'flow of stupidity' in contemporary society ['perception and intellection restricted to a recognition reflex'] consists in *the translation of the 'she' to the 'we,'* of everywoman to everyone: a *loss of the specificity* of the landscape of fear" (24; emphasis added).

Massumi writes at some length about the "fear-blur" produced in this situation, especially by the machinations of mass media. "It is vague by nature," he claims. "It is low-level fear. A kind of background radiation saturating existence. . . . It may be expressed as 'panic' or 'hysteria' or 'phobia' or 'anxiety.' But," he continues, "these are to low-level fear what 'HIV' is to AIDS: *signs* of subjectivity in capitalist crisis. The self, like AIDS, is a syndrome" (24–25): "a complex of effects coming from no single, isolatable place, without a linear history, and exhibiting no invariant characteristics" (11). The introduction of the concept of the syndrome marks out a requisite shift in analytical frameworks to the extent that syndromes, unlike symptoms, "mark the limit of causal analysis. They cannot be exhaustively *understood*—only pragmatically altered by experimental interventions operating in several spheres of activity at once" (31). To take up this challenge is to pursue a "syndromatic" analysis.[4]

Bearing in mind the difficulties for analysis engendered by the syndrome of capitalist subjectivity, the generalization of the white woman's fear of "potential rape and battering," we can still suppose that this ambient, low-level fear is overdetermined by what Fanon calls "the racial distribution of guilt" in the antiblack world (1967, 103). "Here the Negro is the master," he remarks sardonically. "He is the specialist of this matter: whoever says *rape* says *Negro*" (166). That AIDS, in its symbolic soldering to the black body, is widely considered to be "the privileged locus of bio-fear production" (Massumi 1993, vii) only compounds this atmospheric dread. If, as Baxandall (1995) suggests, "the fear of AIDS has made sexual contact increasingly stigmatized" (243), then this fear is amplified by the legacies of negrophobia in which, as noted previously, "the Negro symbolizes the biological danger" (Fanon 1967, 165). The contemporary fear of AIDS reinvigorates a longstanding premise of antimiscegenation: the fear that sexual contact with black bodies will turn over into violence, that such contact *in and of itself* constitutes violence, a site of brutality or morbid contamination or both.

To speak of the "fear" of AIDS is, of course, to understate the case, just as it is an understatement to speak "simply" of negrophobia. The loathing relative to AIDS is far more radical than the affective condition of fear suggests. We are facing, rather, what Dean (2000) describes as "wholesale repudiation by a society that refuses to admit a signifier for AIDS" (99).

> By persistently representing itself as having a "general population" that remains largely immune to incidence of AIDS, the United States [and global civil society] pushes AIDS—and the social groups seen as representing AIDS—to the outside of its psychic and social economies, treating them exactly like shit. (99)

The fate of AIDS and the fate of the black are fundamentally intertwined: rendered in the symbolic order as abject, fecal objects. Symbolizing the danger faced by the body in the throes of globalization, the confusion of boundaries marking inside from out, and a crisis in the scale of cognitive mapping (Jameson 1998b); shuttled between disciplined mobility and the lethal economy of constraint; AIDS, like blackness, should be understood "as a condition of the body, an index of the body's vulnerability" (Dean 2000, 98). The constitutive outside of society's political and libidinal economies is, of course, located differently across the globe. In the deindustrialized urban areas of the North, particularly in the United States, it is operated most prominently by the practices of policing and crystallized in the overt use of the racial profile. It is put into effect much more powerfully by the virtual expulsion of sub-Saharan Africa from the global political economy, a structural exile beneath what we might call "the arc of the global South." This continental prohibition, a demarcation *internal* to the underdeveloped regions, may require reconfiguration of the global imaginary—and the nomenclature of theory, culture, and politics—away from the present North–South axis, useful as it may be in some respects, toward an uneven East–West partnership as the definitive vector in the movement of globalization.

In the United States, a fractal reflection of the "global racial formation" (Winant 2001) is observable. Pierre Bourdieu notes, for instance,

> The "Charitable State," founded on the moralizing conception of poverty, tends to bifurcate into a Social State which assures minimal guarantees of security for the middle classes, and an increasingly repressive state counteracting the effects of violence which results from the increasingly precarious condition of the large mass of the population, notably the black (quoted in Bauman 2000, 103).

I will only mention the litany of social indicators for this "increasingly precarious condition": unparalleled rates of residential and educational segregation (Massey and Denton 1998), unemployment (Wilson 1996), premature death by preventable disease and toxic environments (Bullard 1994; Semmes 1996), homicide (Hutchinson 2002), imprisonment and surveillance (Mauer 1999), and so forth. Within the politics of multiracialism, the isolation and criminalization of blackness is transmuted into a concern for the unwillingness of the black population to participate in "the browning of America" (Root 1995).[5] Conservative critics cite the clannishness of black community, its atavistic investment in notions of black pride and the reproduction of the one-drop rule, that is, the internalization of racist rules of identification that make blacks, at worst, "more separatist inspired than . . . the long-standing white power structure" (Byrd 1996). Liberal critics, in turn, bemoan the tenacity of attitudinal barriers to intimate relations between blacks and nonblacks, but only to advance their forced assimilation in the name of national unity (Lind 1998). This mainstream apprehension finds its alter ego in the unwavering theater of panic staged in explicit white supremacist discourse. If, as Ferber (1998) says, "it is an understatement to claim that white supremacy is obsessed with interracial sexuality," then that compulsion to repeat finds its firmest moorings in the idea of the sex/violence of blacks. It is here that we find ourselves undergoing a globalization without Africa, a multiracialism without blacks, a world community in which the color line becomes etched more deeply even as it is, in some quarters, dissolved.

Relocating the Color Line

In "The Negro and Psychopathology," Fanon (1967) writes pointedly, "There is nothing ontological about segregation. Enough of this rubbish" (186). Surely, there is nothing ontological about the chain of equivalence that links racial blackness to sexual violence (or to sexuality *as* violence) and again to the pandemic called AIDS. There is nothing ontological about the construction in society and culture of the black as phobic object par excellence. There is nothing ontological about the wholesale repudiation of the black at work in the political and libidinal economies of the present historical conjuncture. Nothing which *requires*, once and for all, that we have no language, no image, no idea of—much less a means to redress—the grammar of suffering that underlies the condition of those faces at the bottom of the well; those millions now warehoused behind bars, subject to the ravages of starvation, disease, or armed conflict financed by the managers of global power and wealth; those whose recent circulation among the various middle strata of class societies serves mainly to multiply the apparatuses of policing, even for those symbolically enriching for the corridors of the elite; those relegated to object-status regardless of any willingness to fulfill the social contract, incarnating the status of anti-value in every corner of state and civil society, perennial harbingers of the downward trend; those, in other words, whose human being is put permanently in question.

And yet, the foreclosure of blackness from the prospects and preoccupations of the modern world, the constitutive exclusion of blacks from the realm of "humanity," hierarchies and all, can certainly be thought in ontological terms. Perhaps its structural manifestations should at least be considered *quasi-ontological*. This nomination would have to do with both the breathtaking historical longevity of antiblackness—whether one dates its emergence proper in the eighteenth century, the sixteenth century, or the thirteenth century—and its basic coextension with the culture and politics of modernity (Barrett 2002). Notwithstanding differences in the respective theoretical frameworks, one can read traces of this deduction in the phrasing of Derrick Bell (1992), preeminent black legal scholar and founding figure of critical race theory, regarding what he takes to be "the permanence of racism." We recall that contest about this claim is at the heart of the politics of multiracialism: hence the systemic disfiguring of slavery and its afterlife in the new multiracial histories, the inversions of extant political realities in the rhetoric of the multiracial movement, the displacements of antiblackness in the academic literature of multiracial studies. Multiracialism cuts its teeth on the denial of this fundamental social truth: not simply that antiblackness is longstanding and ongoing but also that it is unlike other forms of racial oppression in qualitative ways— differences of kind, rather than degree, a structural singularity rather than an empirical anomaly.

But all of this is not to mark difference for difference sake, much less to participate in the ranked determination of suffering. It is, instead, to properly locate the political dynamics and to outline the ethical stakes at hand. Antiblackness is not only unique (something rightly ascribed to any number of political histories). My argument turns on the further point that it is both historically and ontologically prior to, thereby enabling, the range of racial inequalities against which the multiracial Left does battle,[6] just as it subtends the formations of globalizing capital (Wilderson 2003) and thoroughly conditions the elaborations of gender power and the regulations of sexuality (Jackson 2003). This is why the idea of a new racism in the United States, or the pluralizing concept of *racisms*, indexes the centralization of a politics of immigration across the global North (a process we might think of as the political "Europeanization" of the United States, where race talk is exhausted by concern for the discriminations of immigration policy, the dangers of xenophobia, and the legacies of colonialism; in another register, we could speak of the debilitating leveling effects of Third World-ism or the disabling fallout of the "people of color" heading). This is also why introducing questions about antiblackness, prompted often enough by the mere entrance of black people to multiracial spaces of intellectual inquiry or political activism, throws the discussion into disarray. The politics of multiracialism provides an object lesson in this governing tendency.

On this last note, let us again consider the concept of the color line, the self-proclaimed territory of the multiracial experience—"racial borders as the new frontier," to cite Root's (1996b) awkward metaphor. It has become a defining characteristic of post–civil rights era United States to demand paradigm shift with respect to racial theory and the politics of antiracism. The enjoinder resonates in the ivory towers of academe, in the pages of the mass media outlets and the alternative press, and in the policy papers and strategic deliberations of progressive nonprofit institutes and community-based organizations. We are told, in a variety of tone and tenor, that race matters are no longer, if ever they were, "simply black and white." At the least, the focus of such dualistic analysis is deemed inadequate to apprehending the current and historical reality of U.S. racial formation (to say nothing of the Americas more generally or other regions of the world). At its worst, this apparently Procrustean dichotomy is rendered as politically stunting insofar as it effectively precludes "discussion of the colors in the middle, now inexorable parts of the Black/white spectrum" (Cho 1993, 205). Indeed, we now enjoy a vast literature in the social sciences and humanities that details the vexed position (or positions) *between* the black and the white. "Neither black nor white" (Sollors, 1997) indicates today not only the articulation of emergent mixed-race identity claims, as per the focus of the present study, but also the contemporary reformulations of critique and political mobilization among Asian Americans, Pacific Islanders, Latina/os, and American Indians (Gracia and De Greiff 2000; Jaimes 1991; Wu 2001).[7]

However, the notion of an endemic black–white model of race, much like the caricature of the one-drop rule, is something of a theoretical fiction deployed for a wide range of purposes. In examining attempts to displace it, then, we do well to recognize its designation as a rather recent emergence, presenting itself as a sort of imaginary lure that indicates more about the preoccupations of state and civil society than it does about the blind insistence of black scholars, activists, or communities.[8] When perusing the critical literature a propos of the "explanatory difficulty" (Omi and Winant 1993, 111) of present-day racial politics—including multiracial studies as component of the broader field of comparative ethnic studies—one frequently wonders exactly to whom the demand to go "beyond black and white" is being issued. Also puzzling is the persistently incoherent reasoning exhibited in most contemporary race talk. One regularly encounters a compelling litany of complicating factors and sorely neglected subjects, accompanied by a failure to offer any cogent account of the *implications* of this newfound or rediscovered complexity. Taken together, these ambiguities beg a key question: what economies of enunciation are involved in this broadly patterned discursive gesture, the popular demand to put an end to "biracial theorizing" (Omi and Winant 1994, 154)?

What we have broached here indicates a structural antagonism between black studies and ethnic studies, or between black politics and the multiracial coalition, now reflected within the discourse of race mixture itself. That is to say, the protocols of valuation and devaluation attendant to the social formation of white supremacy insofar as white supremacy is supposed to be the true enemy of racial justice. The undertheorized ramifications of *differential* and *hierarchical* collective positioning have returned with a vengeance in the form of a multiracial subject who, it is assumed, must negotiate such conflicts in the most intense and personal ways. This observation cuts across the grain of the received wisdom of the post–civil rights era which would warn against the dangers of playing at "Oppression Olympics" (Martínez 1998), the seedy competition to be considered the most despised and downtrodden population in the United States. Such ecumenical sentiment was forged in the strategic alliances of the new social movements, among them the Third World Strikes at San Francisco State University and the University of California–Berkeley that ushered in some of the earliest ethnic studies programs in the country. By now, however, the blanket injunction against situating multiple forms of oppression has become articulated with the neoliberal containment strategies of multiculturalism, wherein cultural diversity is managed as a depoliticized term of experience.[9]

The most pertinent dimension of this tension between black studies and ethnic studies makes itself felt in the continuing pressure to produce comparative analyses without benefit of any viable methodological or analytic frameworks to ground such comparisons. How, after all, does one draw comparisons without occluding not only important contrasts, but also incommensurable differences in the respective formations? It is out of this inability or unwillingness to address "difference in and as hierarchy" (Spillers 2003) that the persistent return of differential value issues forth, spotted now and again in the disclaimers and complications that pepper multiracial discourse but that have yet to fundamentally alter its assumptive logic. A pretense of concern is granted to the fact that one cannot, for instance, assume "all mixes are on equal terms, the product of a harmonious balance between the mixing elements," that "the reasons for, and consequences of, the 'mixture' cannot be reduced to a universally positive designation" (Parker and Song 2000a, 9). However, when it comes time to elaborate "the specific power relations and historical influences shaping this 'mixture,'" analyses of the multiracial experience fail to deliver.

Katya Azoulay's *Black, Jewish and Interracial* (1997) is one of the rare exceptions. She echoes our concern for particularity when she writes, "Although issues of interethnic identities include any combination, the Black/white theme has a dominance that eclipses other racial combinations." This historical legacy is one of the reasons that "Black students [often] insist on focusing on the specificity of the African American experience with interracial liaisons" (4). The historical character of this insistence is emphasized in order to counter the tendency to assign mental pathology or atavistic fixation to black people's difficult questioning of both interracial sexuality and multiracial identity politics. The ethical compromise of multiracialism obtains in proponents' desire to move "beyond the black–white binary" in order to ignore its *centrality* to racial formation. To do more than pay lip service to a foundational antiblackness, that is, to *theorize* its centrality, both to the overall figuration of race mixture and to the constitution of the entire field of ethnic studies (multiracial studies included), seems an unconscionable capitulation to an outdated model. It is to take up residence in the camp of the unenlightened, the backward-looking, the narrow-minded, the plain and the simple.[10]

On this point, the full range of the multiracialism gains consistency, where multiracial studies and the fields of Asian American and Chicano/ Latino studies—and their counterparts in the political domain proper— find common ground. This presumptive distinction is found in the now obligatory claims that one "complicate," "update," and "expand" upon the limited capacities of the black–white binary model. In its more dramatic moments, the multiracial scholar-activist must work to "escape"; she must struggle "to move away from the Black–White racial binary that prevails in a majority of U.S. discourse," for such a binary, at a basic level, "problematizes the multiracial community's existence as [a] . . . collective social movement." Suggestions for doing so are typically nondescript save the rather unimaginative calls for new subject matter or new focus. But as Spencer (1999) reminds us, the black–white binary is neither dismantled nor superseded by the mere addition of other racialized groups:

> The traditional racial groups in the United States . . . are, in . . . descending order: whites, Asians, Native Americans, and blacks. In the United States, blacks and whites are in a binary opposition *even when the other racial groups are recognized,* since the American racial construct is a hierarchical scale, with whites most valued at the one end and blacks least valued at the other. (23; emphasis added)

At a loss about what else to do in the face of this living legacy, the editors of a special "multiracial issue" of *Amerasia Journal* go so far as to propose that "an interdisciplinary approach" would do the trick, thereby ascribing to the black–white binary yet another theoretical shortcoming, the stricture of a single-discipline approach (Houston and Williams 1997, xi).

By assembling these distinct strains of thought, I am drawing attention to a broad-based grievance with a rhetorical figure that remains vague by definition but that has nonetheless become a popular trope in recent years: the black–white, monochrome analysis of race. In the mass media, a recent *Newsweek* article boldly announces that the color line in the post– civil rights United States is "not just a matter of black and white anymore; the *nuances* of brown and yellow and red mean more—and less—than ever"

(Meacham 2000). This headline marks in shorthand the convergence of several trends, all of which bear directly on the politics of multiracialism under critique in this study. First, the decentering of blackness: a shift in focus from the conditions of black people as the metonym of domestic "race relations" to a supposedly more encompassing, indeed, more *nuanced*, commentary on nonblack nonwhites (described earlier by Cho (1993) as "the colors in the middle"). This shift was at the forefront of controversy regarding President Clinton's hackneyed 1997 Initiative on Race, in which the chair, esteemed black historian John Hope Franklin, offered at the inaugural meeting that the United States "cut its eye teeth on racism in the black/white sphere." "A brief debate ensued among the panelists. Linda Chavez-Thompson argued that the 'American dilemma' had become a proliferation of racial and ethnic dilemmas. Angela Oh [who also suggested the Initiative 'dump unusual concepts like race'] argued that the national conversation needed to move beyond discussions of racism as solely directed at Blacks. . . . Although the Board members subsequently downplayed their differences, their distinct perspectives continued to provoke debate within academic, policy, and community activist settings regarding the Black–White race paradigm" (Omi 2001, 250).[11]

In fact, Oh, a noted Korean American attorney, self-described liberal feminist, member of the Los Angeles City Human Relations Commission, and former Special Counsel to the California Assembly Special Committee on the Los Angeles Crisis (i.e., the 1992 LA uprising), rebuffed Franklin's claim in a subsequent interview in the *Los Angeles Times* with comments that would be baffling were they not so noticeably instrumental to the moral and conceptual grounds of her stance: "Asian-Americans because of how we look. . . . Our susceptibility or vulnerability to being called foreigner is never going to go away. I have had people ask me, 'How does it feel to always be viewed as a foreigner?' African-Americans actually have said to me, 'At least we know we belong here. . . .' That is a very unsettling question when it is put to you. African-Americans are never told, 'Go back to your own country'" (Yoshihara 1997, 3). This contention, that Asian Americans in particular (and other immigrants of color), are faced with a qualitatively different and, as it is usually implied, *additional* form of racism (e.g., nativism or xenophobia) from that faced by native-born blacks, is a popular position in the formation of Asian American identity per se. It is found throughout the field of Asian American studies and is particularly acute in the field of Asian American jurisprudence (Han 2006). However, it is an assertion that can only be maintained (like the imaginary correlative of a black who knows he or she "belongs here") against the full force of history, the continuing and palpable construction of blacks as "foreigners within" or "intimate enemies" of U.S. culture and society, and the quotidian regularity with which blacks are told to "go back to Africa" without so much as the privilege of deportation or repatriation to a specified country—any African country whatsoever will do.

Second, the decentering of race more generally, a trend marked by the ascendancy of antiessentialist critique and the development of intersectional analyses of race, nation, class, gender, and sexuality. (It entails as well the more disconcerting rise of colorblindness and/as "class-not-race" analyses [Doane and Bonilla-Silva 2003], both of which perspectives can be found readily in multiracial discourse.) These theoretical innovations— a certain deconstruction of race and the multiplication of analytic dimensions—are, in turn, closely associated with the blurring of racial categories supposed by the multiracial subject (even as multiracialism reinforces notions of race purity unavoidably, implicitly, perhaps insidiously). Some even imagine multiracial studies to be avant-garde in this respect:

> [In multiracial studies,] notions of boundary-creation, boundary-busting, and boundary-expansion have been explored; and the deeply personal and highly political nature of "identity" has thus been articulated. As the discourse on multiple identities expands to include class, language, gender, sexuality, and body, along with race, ethnicity, and nation, multiracial individuals and their identity formation remain theoretically and experientially *cutting edge*. (Houston and Williams 1997, ix–x; emphasis added)

I have no quarrels with either of these trends per se, and it should be said that both antiessentialist critique and intersectional analyses have enriched the field of black studies (they have often been pioneered by black intellectuals) and expanded our understanding of antiblackness immensely. As well, it is quite clear that the appropriations of these critical approaches within multiracial discourse often fail to do justice to their animating political projects. What concerns me in the articulation of these various developments within the horizon of the multiracial—pointing toward both racial multiplicity and racial mixture—is their common point of reference, their common antagonism with a figure of blackness supposed to stand in the way of future progress, silencing the expression of much needed voices on the political and intellectual scene.

On this score, we might bear in mind a provocative thought recently offered by Mari Matsuda (2002) during a 1997 symposium on critical race theory at the Yale Law School:

> When we say we need to move beyond Black and white, this is what a whole lot of people say or feel or think: "Thank goodness we can get off that paradigm, because those Black people made me feel so uncomfortable. I know all about Blacks, but I really don't know anything about Asians, and while we're deconstructing that Black–white paradigm, we also need to reconsider the category of race altogether, since race, as you know, is a constructed category, and thank god I don't have to take those angry black people seriously anymore." (395)

Importantly, the above comment is drawn from an otherwise sympathetic meditation on the need for more adequate models of racial analysis and innovative strategies of multiracial coalition building, not to mention the indispensability of global perspectives on race matters. What Matsuda signals, and what we have been tracking implicitly throughout our examination of multiracialism, is a particular danger attendant to the often unexamined *desire* for new analyses and the often anxious *drive* for political alliance.[12] Although her comments here are speculative and her concern is to suggest how it is that the oppression of nonblack people of color under white supremacy is framed by or shot through with antiblackness, Matsuda's interrogative gambit—calling to question the motive force of a nominally critical intervention on the "Black–white paradigm"—nevertheless resonates with the present endeavor. That is to say, the stark ambivalence of critical thinking about "bipolar conceptions of race" also structures the generally tense and conflicted relations, political and otherwise, between communities of color, whether between blacks and immigrants or between blacks and the multiracial contingent. The force of antiblackness consistently troubles the myriad efforts at mediation and melioration among the nonwhite. If one of the ostensible benefits of a reconstructed racial theory, one that adequately addresses itself to "the increasing complexity of racial politics and racial identity today" (Omi and Winant 1994, 152), is its capacity to enable a grasp of "antagonisms and alliances *among* racially defined minority groups" (154), then that intellectual and political enterprise is not, for all that, without its pitfalls.

Samira Kawash sharpens the issues in her challenging and important work, *Dislocating the Color Line* (1997):

> It is true that multiplication of racializing discourses since the 1960s [including multiracial discourse] and the successive waves of immigration from places other than Europe [which developed alongside and fueled the 'biracial baby boom'] has compounded and complicated the work of racial distinction and racist discrimination. But, somehow, in spite of the fact that empirically (from the perspective of multiple ethnic groups or census categories) it makes little sense to think of the United States as a nation divided into black and white, this racialized opposition persists in both explicit and subtle ways. Indeed, in the past decade, questions of binarizing boundaries have increasingly become *the medium of politics*. (6–7; emphasis added)

The medium of politics, the new frontier: could it really be that the centering of black freedom struggle was no more than a narrow fixation, or merely the effect of an underdeveloped consciousness, and that the displacement or dislodging of this unfolding history from the forefront of political and ethical consideration is a progressive development in the movement for social justice, a radicalization of antiracism?[13] How is black politics in the historic instance considered by any number of leftist enterprises to be at once instructive or inspiring or enabling—if not vanguard—and, *for the same reasons*, hindering or prohibiting or exclusive? Could it be that the interventions of nonblack people of color in theory, culture, and politics have rightly illuminated the existence of many color lines, disclosing a situation in which not only is racial oppression more variegated than once thought but also in which people of color stand in relation to one another, alternately, as victims and as *victimizers?* One should not be misled by references to the supposed fluidity of power relations in the literature under review. When read against the general movement of the discourse of multiracialism, it seems clear that such arguments are, for all intents and purposes, intended to render legitimate claims that *blacks can victimize.* I say this because, while it is noted that multiracial people may hold objectionable views of blacks, may sometimes betray a desire with great historical precedent to distance themselves from blackness, and even commit occasional acts of political aggression against them (e.g., the dismantling of affirmative action programs and antidiscrimination law), all of the authors considered for this study maintain that blacks are mistaken in thinking that multiracialism victimizes them in any structural way.

For multiracialism, we have seen that the residue of racism is encapsulated in the one-drop rule of hypodescent. The last real effect of racism, or at least the one of greatest concern, is the enforcement of this rule of definition. The tragedy, more specifically, is that multiracial people are "made to be black." As such, they are denied "the dignity of self-definition." Nancy Brown and Ramona Douglass (1996), in an exemplary passage, claim that "what was originally enacted by European Americans to ensure the racial 'purity' of the 'haves' versus the 'have nots' has recently been embraced by some segments of the oppressed [black] culture as a . . . badge of courage or a sign of . . . loyalty" (325). Are we to assume by this account that white society no longer enforces this rule, or that the only racial "policing" is done by black people themselves and not, pace Hollinger, the local, state, and federal police? Are we to assume further that the contemporary employment of the one-drop rule is a mere extension or, worse, a replacement of its historical institution under slavery?

In "Making the Invisible Visible," Brown and Douglass claim to bring to light the "quiet revolution" about which Root (2001) has written at length. Upon closer scrutiny, however, the invisible element being made

visible is, in fact, nonblack heritage. The problem, they claim, is "the negation, obliteration, or deprecation of any other racial/ethnic strain that a
multiracial child might lay claim to" (Brown and Douglass 1996, 325) aside
from blackness. As a result, the reclamation of those other nonblack racial/
ethnic strains becomes the key to multiracial dignity. And the stakes run
high: as a result of the erasure of mixture (previously a white thing, now
a black thing), "interracial families, and multiracial individuals specifically
. . . developed a shame-based perception of self." The acceptance or endorsement of the one-drop rule, or self-identification as black, is posited as the
outcome of internalized "negative self-concepts" and thereby produces "a
sense of powerlessness and invisibility" (326). All of this makes life with a
black identity a rather miserable affair. One wonders, of course, whether
the difficulties of black identity are considered inherent to its social position or simply an effect of the supposed inaccuracy or dishonesty of claiming it when one is "in truth" something else.

This much is left unquestioned but appears to be of no consequence
simply because it refers to days gone past. Out of this dark history emerges
the new moment: multiracial people, empowered by the civil rights movement and the ideal of Black Pride, can now claim their "rightful heritage."
What are the effects of the reclamation? Brown and Douglass cite two major
benefits: first, greater physical and psychological comfort for the multiracial
person, and second, an improved capability to navigate the social terrain.
Escaping the one-drop rule, becoming unshackled from its restrictions is
salutary. Once free, the multiracial person and the interracial family can
find community and "an atmosphere of health and safety." By contrast, to
the extent that the rule is enforced, these same groups will find themselves
at risk and endangered. Thus, for those traditional civil rights organizations who oppose the alteration of the federal racial/ethnic classification
schema, for example, the charges are more than academic. They decide
the multiracial person's right to life, liberty, and the pursuit of happiness.

Let us return here to Michael Lind's 1998 *New York Times Magazine*
article, published barely one year after the initial resolution of the federal
racial classification debates of the mid-1990s. In his meditation on "the
blending of the races in America," Lind writes, "Shifting patterns of racial

intermarriage suggest that the next century may see the replacement of the historic white–black dichotomy in America with a troubling new division, one between beige and black" (38).[14] That is, where the color line once suggested a division between the white and the nonwhite, it is now moving steadily toward a fundamental division between the black and the non-black. For Lind, "beige" signifies "the mostly-white mixed race majority" whose emergence he predicts as an effect of the relatively high rates of interracial marriage, dating, and mixed-race births for Asian Americans, Latinos, and American Indians. This new majority, while experiencing increasing *internal* intermixture (despite conflicts and the maintenance of minor hierarchies of race, ethnicity, and color), will remain well segregated from the black minority on pivotal matters of housing, education, and employment. Moreover, the various groups comprising this majority will maintain social distance toward blacks and spurn interracial intimacy due to pervasive "anti-black prejudice—the most enduring feature of the eroding American caste system" (38), a factor that accounts, in large part, for comparatively low rates of black out-marriage to date.

Like the proponents of multiracialism, Lind recognizes a certain dislocation of the black–white binary, but he does so without entirely losing sight of the implications it holds for the social, economic, and political positioning of blacks in the coming century. Insofar as the position of blacks is at stake, the move beyond the black–white binary and toward a black–nonblack binary is no improvement. In fact, it portends an intensification of antiblack racism rather than its mitigation. Herbert Gans (2004), in presentation of supporting research, states, "The hierarchy is new only insofar as the old white–nonwhite dichotomy may be replaced by a non-black–black one, but *it is hardly new for blacks*, who are likely to remain at the bottom once again" (589; emphasis added).[15] Lind attributes this development in part to a cynical "mixed-race majority, [that] even if it were predominantly European in ancestry, probably would not be moved by appeals to white guilt." "Some of the new multiracial Americans," he continues, "might disingenuously invoke an Asian or Hispanic grandparent to include themselves among the victims rather than the victimizers." But this much is more than probable. Insofar as antiblackness is mystified as an affliction exclusive to whites, it is easily disowned by nonblack people of color. What Lind does not see, but that our investigation of multiracialism makes known, is that "the new multiracial Americans" have already done more than cast themselves as common victims of white racism. Much more disturbing is the attempt to construct multiracial people, like the white constituency of neoconservatism, as the *victims of black people*, the construction of "black racism" as a most dangerous amalgam of thought and practice—oppressive black power. Rather than a defensive declaration of similarity or shared ground, what we have is an aggressive and delirious accusation in which the world is upside down.

There is a way out of this racial wonderland, and it returns us to arguments from Gordon (1997) cited at various points earlier in this chapter:

> There is no way to reject the thesis that there is something wrong with being black beyond the willingness to "be" black—not in terms of convenient fads of playing blackness, but by paying the social costs of anti-blackness on a global scale. . . . Racism cannot be rejected without a dialectic in which humanity experiences a blackened world. (67)

That is to say, a willingness to affirm the absolute vulnerability that historically structures "existence in black" (Gordon 2000) "on a *global scale*." Neither acceptance nor celebration, such affirmation promises something more than resignation or despair, more than the hopeless "attempt at suicide" that Fanon's detractors would have defeat the wretched of the earth in advance. This affirmation unfolds in the space between worlds, the Old and the New, in the time between what has been and what will be—a derelict nonplace, a distorted space-time, anticipating *what will have been.* Affirming the derangement of hierarchical social distinctions—of class, gender, sexuality, nationality—all of the official terms of dignity foreclosed by our massive arrest, our eviction from History. In this uninterrupted state of confinement, we might, following Spillers (2003), claim the "monstrosity" of a prerogative to name not only the structures of kinship whose perpetual disallowance provides the conditions of possibility for all other's claims to the universal and the particular, but also the outrage of personhood that remains the founding anathema of a global civil society.

"The semi-illiteracy of conventional rhetoric shaping the dominant discourse on 'race'" encourages our "severing racism from its logical culmination in genocide" (James 1996a, 115), misrecognizing its origination in the violent formation of the modern commodity-form. It encourages as well our forgetting about its embedment in the seizure and theft of body whose anxious figure opened our considerations and whose effacement, in the first and last instance, makes possible the historical sensibility of the emergent multiracial imagined community: the dispossessed black female confronted, invented, by the slave estate and its undead symbolic mechanisms. That is to say, finally, that the critical gesture under pursuit seeks no more, and no less, than the potential legibility unleashed by the project of a radical black feminism, the insurgent ground of a political movement that "might rewrite after all a radically different text for female empowerment" (Spillers 2003, 229). A project that, because of that, provides the only viable—that is to say, ethically consistent—means of unraveling that "single bundle of nerves" in which the violence of race, nation, class, gender, and sexuality "does not bear distinction" (330). Risk incurs here not to the humiliation of dismissal but to the exhilarating possibility that we may be taken seriously, not least by an intramural engagement. The political task that remains is neither a restoration nor a restitution, but a creative destruction.[16]

Notes

Introduction

1. My use of the term *racial blackness* is encouraged by my reading of Barrett (1999): "If the material economic transaction [i.e., 'the exchange of African bodies'] produces racial blackness as a phenotypical and commodifiable essence, the related transaction [i.e., 'efforts to determine African American consciousness'] aims at producing blackness as a negative discursive, cultural, and psychological essence. . . . In a phrase, the New World arena of value, in both its materialist and idealist transactions, depends upon the expenditure of blackness. To expend the 'humanity' of Africans in the profitable cultivation of staple crops (or other commodities) as well as the political and psychological contours of a privileged whiteness (defined foremost as Anglo or Western European) remains a fundamental element and an enduring legacy of the New World arena of value" (Barrett 1999, 56). It should be noted that my use of that term may differ in significant ways from Barrett's very sophisticated deployment and that, like Barrett, I often use "racial blackness" and "blackness" interchangeably.

2. Although the history of hypodescent is considerably more complex than common references to the "one-drop rule" allow (Zackodnik 2001), we can note nonetheless the clear political and economic interests involved in the seventeenth-century codification of *partus sequitur ventrem*, the principle by which children followed "the condition of the mother" (literally, "offspring follow the womb") regarding their legal status as enslaved or free. For a case study of the law, see Curtis (1999). Interestingly, given the considerable gender imbalances of interracial dating and marriage in the post–civil rights era, most of those born of black–white

interracial couplings today follow the condition of the father insofar as they self-identify as black or African American: *partus sequitur patrias*.

3. The term *miscegenation* was coined in 1863 by anonymous pamphleteers (later revealed to be the Democratic Congressman Samuel Cox and *New York Tribune* editor Horace Greeley) as a political hoax meant to slander the Republican Party (and eventually the Union) by painting the prospect of abolition with the brush of "amalgamation" or "race mixing." For an extended discussion, see Kaplan (1949).

4. This point holds whether one is thinking here of the "new Latin Americanism" (Moreiras 2001), largely inspired by revision of José Martí's famous *nuestra América*, Anzaldúa's (1999) earlier queer feminist appropriations of José Vasconcellos's *raza cósmica*, or a more long-standing sociocultural "Latin Americanization of the United States" (Goldman 1998).

5. The official conflation of "social equality" with "amalgamation of race" is censured by W. E. B. Du Bois (1987) in a 1921 contribution to *The Crisis* titled "President Harding and Social Equality," a pointed response to an address given by the conservative Republican in Birmingham, Alabama, in October of that year. In clear endorsement of the prevailing sentiments of antimiscegenation, Harding's speech followed postbellum conventions of public discourse by splitting the difference between "political equality" (extension and defense of civil rights and liberties to blacks), considered to be worthy of at least limited debate under terms of "the Negro Problem," and "social equality" (private association across the color line), considered to be simply beyond the pale. For Du Bois, this ambiguously phrased executive declaration—"Racial amalgamation there cannot be"—was pivotal: "For fifty years we who, *pro* and *con*, have discussed the Negro Problem, have been skulking behind a phrase—'Social Equality.' Today President Harding's speech, like sudden thunder in blue skies, ends the hiding and drives us all into the clear light of truth" (1188).

6. The phrase "Building One America for the Twenty-First Century" is generally associated with the discourse of the Clinton administration of the 1990s and refers specifically to the former President's ill-fated and ineffectual Initiative on Race.

7. This work is already well in progress, and it is as much critical of as concordant with Fanon. For an excellent discussion of the nonnormative sexuality of African Americans generally, see Ferguson (2003). Ferguson's work is a very rich example of larger developments in black queer studies (Alexander 2000) and the gathering intellectual force of arguments made concisely by Barrett (1997): "Race,

since it is not a genetic reality, might be more assuredly characterized as a series of prohibitions on social desire and sexual practice. . . . Race amounts foremost to a set of fundamental prohibitions on the discharge of sexual energies. . . . If race proves, at bottom, a set of practices worrying over the coding and dissemination of visible but unstable physical traits, then it is ineluctably insinuated into the notion of heterosexual domestication itself" (110). Doubtless, current trends in "queer of color critique" are especially indebted to the pioneering work of radical black lesbian feminism, especially from the 1970s to the present. See the following note.

8. The literature here is vast, but one could consult, for instance, Constantine-Simms (2001), Crenshaw (1995), Ferguson (2003), Hull (1986), Moraga and Anzaldúa (1984), Moten (2003), Muñoz (1999), Smith (1983), and Somerville (2000).

9. Harper (1994) also captures this sensibility aptly when he writes: "One can never predict in advance desire's object or the nature of its manifestation" (147).

10. For an extended discussion of the decentering of the subject of history, see Macksey and Donato (1972). We should note the historical coincidence of the emergence of structuralist thought in the United States (commemorated by the famous 1966 Johns Hopkins University conference) and the rescinding of legal antimiscegenation (formalized in the U.S. Supreme Court decision in *Loving v. Virginia* in 1967). Daniel (2001) attempts to make these connections explicit; however, his treatment of postcolonial and postmodern theorizations are unfortunately imprecise.

11. Racialization has divergent significations, but its genealogy can plausibly be traced to Fanon (1967), who "contrasted 'to racialize' with 'to humanize'" (Goldberg 2002, 12). I retain that sense of the term even as I invoke a more commonly understood definition from Small (1994), who writes of racialization as the general notion that "social structures, social ideologies, and attitudes have been imbued with 'racial' meaning, that such meanings are contingent and contested, and that they are shaped by a multitude of other variables, economic, political, religious" (36).

12. It should also be noted that the emergence of what is now known as "identity politics," particularly after the civil rights movement, has intensified the anxiety of the body vis-à-vis social categories of race, gender, class, and sexuality (S. Robinson 2000).

13. Fink (1995), to cite another source, describes the fundamental fantasy

as "that which underlies [a subject's] various individual fantasies and constitutes the subject's most profound relation to the Other's desire" (62).

14. Miller writes: "Suture names the relation of the subject to the chain of its discourse: we shall see that I figures there as the element which is lacking, in the form of a stand-in. For, while there lacking, it is not purely and simply absent. Suture, by extension—the general relation of the lack to the structure—of which it is an element, inasmuch as it implies position of a taking-the place-of" (quoted in Heath 1985, 84).

15. "The binary machine is an important component in apparatuses of power. So many dichotomies will be established that there will be enough for everyone to be pinned to the wall, sunk in a hole. Even the divergences of deviancy will be measured according to the degree of binary choice; you are neither white nor black, Arab then? Or half-breed? You are neither man nor woman, transvestite then? This is the white wall/black hole system. And it is not surprising that the face has such importance in this system: you must have the face of your role" (Deleuze and Parnet 1987, 21).

16. The *American Heritage Dictionary* defines the verge as both "the extreme edge or margin; a border" and "the point beyond which an action, state, or condition is likely to begin or occur; the brink." I like the double sense of the term because it suggests both the border work of racialization at the site of the interracial, its productivity, and the anticipation and teetering that characterize the domain of sexuality.

17. It should be noted that Spurr (1993) is critical of this perspective and only seeks to document its circulation in Western writing on the colonized world.

18. Althusser and Balibar (1997) define a problematic as "the horizon of a definite theoretical structure" and argue that it "constitutes its absolute and definite condition of possibility, and hence the absolute determination of *the forms in which all problems must be posed*, at any given moment" (25). The translator's glossary adds that a problematic is "the theoretical or ideological framework in which [a word or concept] is used." Importantly, he adds, "the problematic is *not* a worldview. It is not the essence of the thought of an individual or epoch which can be deduced from a body of texts by an empirical, generalizing reading; it is centered on the *absence* of problems and concepts within the problematic as much as their presence; it can therefore only be reached by a symptomatic reading" (316). It is this understanding of problematic that inspires the readings found in the following chapters.

19. "[Biological concepts of race] reinforced the notion of the inescapable corporeality of non-white peoples, while leaving the corporeality of whites less certain, something that fed into the function of non-white, especially black, people in representation of being a kind of definite thereness by means of which white people can gain a grounding in materiality and 'know who they are'" (Dyer 1997, 24).

20. The literature on chaos theory and complexity is vast. For general introductions, see Briggs (1990), Gleick (1988), and Waldrop (1992). Although the influence may be oblique, it seems that the work of Deleuze and Guattari (1987a, 1987b) anticipates the recent turn of the human sciences toward nonlinearity, chaos, and complexity (Kiel and Elliott 1997).

21. In recasting racism this way, Memmi calls into question both the source and the aim of its unfolding. One cannot help but notice the implicit reference here to Freud's four basic elements of the drive: source, aim, object, and force (or impetus). Although Memmi seems to have a sense of racism's aim and object—to inferiorize its victim—he is at a loss to understand its source and force except to locate each in the realm of affect.

22. The notion of racism as seesaw resonates interestingly with Lacan's discussion of the imaginary relation in his early seminar lectures (Lacan 1991).

23. Memmi, despite his criticisms of the latter, is echoing comments made earlier by Fanon (1967), who describes racism as, among other things, "anomalies of affect."

24. This point echoes arguments made apropos of "the Law" by Foucault (1987).

25. In this respect, Memmi's work can be considered of a kind with more recent theorists like Young (1996a). She writes: "It is impossible to produce a neat, seamless explanation for the maintenance of racist ideologies and their absorption into the fabric of this society. Racism is not attributable to a single factor such as capitalism, the colonial enterprise or personal prejudice. It appears to be a complex inter-weaving of all these factors, in a continual state of flux and subject to the political, social and economic imperatives of the particular moment" (40). However, this account, while an advance over more reductive models, still seems to think in an additive or even intersectional ("inter-weaving") way about white supremacy. Although it is a more complex rendition of racism, it still elides the question of its formation.

26. This historical equation of "race" with "blackness" should be kept in mind throughout the following chapters. Understanding this conceptual relation

in no way diminishes or denies the racialization of whites or other people of color in the United States and beyond. It only posits that racialization takes place *through* blackness as its matrix or schema.

27. Although it is well beyond the scope of this study, it seems possible to think about the economy of race (its production and circulation as value) together with the historical development of a money economy conventionally understood. A diacritical reading of, for example, Leyshon and Thrift (1996) with Lott (1999) might prove fruitful.

28. I am reminded here of Jameson's arguments vis-à-vis "the visual" in his *Signatures of the Visible* (1992b), from which this phrase is cited. His well-known opening claims: "The visual is *essentially* pornographic, which is to say that it has its end in rapt, mindless fascination; thinking about its attributes becomes an adjunct to that, if it is unwilling to betray its object. . . . Pornographic films are thus only the potentiation of films in general, which ask us to stare at the world as though it were a naked body" (1). It goes without saying that the logic of race is overwhelmingly, though by no means exclusively, visual and, where the visual provokes thinking only in those moments when "it is unwilling to betray its object," we might readily sense the particular echo of the racial image. If race is what goes without saying—the "rapt, mindless fascination" of our common sense—we become most aware of it not simply in the experience of reified racial difference but precisely in moments of a (naked?) body's inscrutability. Hence: "One of the first things we notice [without always noticing that we notice] about people when we meet them (along with their sex) is their race. We utilize race to provide clues about *who* a person is. This fact is made painfully obvious when we encounter someone whom we cannot conveniently racially categorize—someone who is, for example, racially 'mixed' or of an ethnic/racial group we are not familiar with. Such an encounter becomes a source of discomfort and momentarily a crisis of racial meaning" (Omi and Winant 1994, 59). It becomes as well the occasion for "thinking about its attributes." What this crisis betrays, however, is not simply the apparent unfamiliarity of racial "mixture" or a particular "ethnic/racial group." More importantly, it reveals the (unconscious) crisis management that subtends the entire process of racialization, a project that attempts to comfort itself with a minimally necessary racial knowledge of visually recognizable groups. It is, in other words, anchored epistemologically and perceptually in the appearance of black skin, and yet the visual unfailingly gives way to the authority of the invisible, that which eludes the visual epistemology, the unseen ground of an extrapolated logic of race that is more than skin deep.

29. This question is a rephrasing of that which Cutrone (2000) uses to open his provocative (and problematic) essay: "The first question should be, why address the sex between black and white men in America as a social, political, aesthetic or other category" (249).

1. Beyond the Event Horizon

1. I refer to the resolution as provisional because although the multiple check option addressed the concerns of both multiracial advocates and civil rights groups, it did not and could not put to rest the matter of classifying and tabulating the resultant census data. The chapters collected in Perlmann and Waters (2002) detail this ongoing challenge.

2. Of course, this sanction is both limited and problematic, pertaining as it does to the legalization of heterosexual interracial marriage and, presumably, to the selective decriminalization of heterosexual interracial relationships without the institution of marriage.

3. *Interracial Voice* founding editor, Charles Byrd, offered the following summation in his remarks at the Los Angeles-based Multiracial Solidarity March II in August 1997: "All along, there were two main reasons why I advocated for a multiracial census category, and neither involved establishing yet another special-interest group looking for its own set of entitlement programs or its own *protected status* [emphasis in original]. (1) Otherwise self-determined individuals should have the ability to self-identify, since Census forms are supposed to be based upon self-identification. There's so much at stake here that goes to the heart of one's self-esteem and to one's basic right to free association. Though there is no factual foundation for race, racial pressures of all kinds—particularly where people have to choose one part of their heritage and deny the other—are harmful to psychological health, especially for children. (2) Mixed-race is a repudiation of the notion of racial purity. This discussion of racial identity is already blowing the lid off most people's perceptions of race, and that's good. Eventually, we should scrap all racial classifications. Until that day comes, a multiracial category would be a good first step along the way to 'racial sanity.' Accordingly, for some of us, the 'check-all-that-apply' scheme proposed by the government simply is not good enough. Not only is there no consideration or understanding that some of us do not recognize the existing racial groups as valid in terms of identity and affiliation, there is no symbol or icon—specifically a multiracial header—representative of a self-determined, integral being who self-identifies other than monoracially." The précis of the

multiracial category proposal offered here is deceptively complex, and we will attempt to unpack its various points of argument as we proceed.

4. Spencer's analysis is also at pains to dispel the idea that there are legitimate health-related concerns attached to multiracialism. That is, he challenges the sense that there may be health concerns specific to multiracial populations as an extension of the already flawed uses of racial data in medical research to date.

5. For more on these organizations and their affiliates, see the official Web sites: http://www.ameasite.org and http://www.hif.org.

6. Charles Byrd, for instance, did not shy away from good old-fashioned red-baiting, accusing the AMEA and HIF of forming a "federación socialista" with the NAACP on this count. For more on these organizations, see the official Web sites: http://www.projectrace.com, http://www.aplaceforusnational.com, http://www.webcom.com/~intvoice/, and http://www.multiracial.com. At the time of this writing, the contingent also includes the National American Metis Association (http://www.americanmetis.org), the Center for the Study of Biracial Children (http://www.csbc.cncfamily.com), and the Interracial Women's Political Consortium, among others.

7. At the 1996 Multiracial Solidarity March, Byrd phrased the multiracial ideal as "a future of racelessness through assimilation into the American mainstream" insofar as "the multiracial identifier [is] one to which the vast majority of Americans could eventually drift, effectively neutralizing the concept of race." More about this historic event and Byrd's central role there appears later in this chapter. An archive of selected speeches displaying a more or less consistent roll-call of conservative commentary is available online at http://www.webcom.com/~intvoice/speech.html.

8. Gingrich's letter of endorsement is posted on *The Multiracial Activist* Web site: http://www.multiracial.com/site/content/view/975/29/. In it he glosses the party line of the right-wing coterie of the multiracial movement identified earlier (Project RACE, A Place for Us National, *Interracial Voice, The Multiracial Activist*): "I believe that we can begin to address the country's racial divide by adding a multiracial category to federal forms and the United States Census while simultaneously phasing out the outdated, divisive and rigid classification of Americans."

9. Of course, the entanglement with the census debates is structurally inescapable precisely because the historical development of racial taxonomy and classification is coeval with the formation of the modern state (Goldberg 2002; Perlmann and Waters 2002).

10. In his 1997 congressional testimony, Nathan Douglas of the Interracial Family Circle describes opposition to the multiracial movement in the following terms: "No organization or individual has the moral authority to impose racial patriotism over others. Some of our opponents appear to have commissioned themselves as members of a 'racial border patrol.' They dutifully stand guard over America's imaginary borders between the races, scanning the horizon for 'illegal racial immigrants.' And when they see one, they swoop down with all their might and unrighteous indignation" (quoted in Douglas 2003). Notwithstanding the fantastic metaphorical figure involved in lending federal police power (imposing "racial patriotism" with "all their might") to the very communities most directly subjected to it, one wonders which "America" Douglas has in mind here, given the dreadful popularity that patrolling "America's imaginary borders" enjoys at present (Sadowski-Smith 2002).

11. For discussion of the concept of the racial state, see Goldberg (2002) and Omi and Winant (1994), especially chapter 5.

12. Multiracial advocates often claim that Asian American or Latino or even Native American communities—though the latter cannot be considered in the same light as the former two—do not typically evince the characteristics that would qualify black communities as a threat to multiracialism: they do not, in the main, apply correspondingly "rigid rules of membership"; they are not defined historically by a one-drop rule that might then be internalized and imposed on others, quite the contrary, in fact; and they all exhibit relatively high rates of intermarriage with whites, as much as four times the rate of blacks at present (Hollinger 1995; Root 1992a, 1996b; Stephens 1999). A. D. Powell, a regular contributor to *Interracial Voice* and *The Multiracial Activist*, writes, for instance: "American Indians, Asian-Americans and others might inappropriately claim some mixed people but they do not generally go into a towering rage over the thought of losing the 'blood' of their 'white' rivals" (quoted in Byrd 1996). We revisit this last quote in greater length later in the chapter.

13. *Monoracial* is a term used widely in the essays collected by Root (1992a, 1996b). Like Spencer (1999), I take it as a terminological indicator of the disavowed reassertion of racial purity that characterizes the academic literature on people of mixed race to date.

14. Root frames this idea of an oppressive "squeeze" by way of a gross misappropriation of the work of Chela Sandoval. Root quotes Sandoval's discussion of "the hierarchical interpretation of difference" (Root's phrase) under the dominance

of a white, capitalist, and male "power nodule" (Sandoval's phrase) in order to sit-
uate "racially mixed men and women" within this schema. For Sandoval, there are
four hierarchically arrayed categories of intersecting racial/gender oppression
(class becomes analytically muted at this point of discussion), and they run, from
top to bottom, as follows: (1) white males, (2) white women, (3) men of color, and
(4) women of color. Whatever faults one may find with Sandoval's schema (and
mine lie beyond the scope of the present study), it is abundantly clear that her overriding concern is to diagram the relational operations of *power*, and her attempts
to differentiate the often contradictory and countervailing effects of the intersections of race/gender/class are meant to lend greater subtlety to our understanding
of the dynamics of *oppression*. Root, in her turn, disavows (because she notes it but
then proceeds as if she has not just noted it) Sandoval's strict attention to *hierarchy*
in favor of a mystifying discussion of rigid and dichotomous *difference* without
respect to the specific relations of power within which such difference is produced
and reproduced. That is, Root disarticulates—separates and confuses—the critical
conjunction of difference *and* power that underwrites Sandoval's political and intellectual project. Root's rewriting thus proceeds by syllogism: "*Extending this model*,
racially mixed men and women would occupy the fifth and sixth tiers in this model,
respectively, *because of* the rigidity of the dichotomy between White and non-White.
Subsequently, multiracial people experience a 'squeeze' of oppression *as* people of
color and *by* people of color" (Root 1992b, 5; emphasis added). The claim that the
"squeeze of oppression" experienced by multiracial people is an "extension" of
Sandoval's model is unfounded—not only because it is not argued at sufficient length
but also because the "argument" put forward ("because of the rigidity of the
dichotomy between White and non-White") is a non sequitur. In fact, the white–
nonwhite dichotomy to which Root refers is, in Sandoval's model, a hierarchy and
so would more likely find "racially mixed men and women" situated below "white
males" and "white women" but *above* "men of color" and "women of color." Root's
assertion that "racially mixed men and women" would, for some reason, occupy
lower positions in the hierarchy is not an extension of Sandoval's model but a radical
departure from it. This equivocation about relations of power is found more clearly
in another of the oft-cited theoretical resources of multiracial studies, Gloria
Anzaldúa's *Borderlands/La frontera* (1999). Indeed, Root formulates her most basic
ideas about "rigid rules of belonging" from her reading of the following passage
in Anzaldúa: "The internalization of negative images of ourselves, our self-hatred,
poor self-esteem, makes our own people the *Other*. We shun the white-looking

Indian, the 'high yellow' Black woman, the Asian with the white lover, the Native woman who brings her white girl friend to the Pow Wow, the Chicana who doesn't speak Spanish, the academic, the uneducated. Her difference makes her a person we can't trust. Para que sea 'legal,' she must pass the ethnic legitimacy test we have devised. And it is exactly your internalized whiteness that desperately wants boundary lines (this part of me is Mexican, this part Indian) marked out and woe to any sister or any part of us that steps out of our assigned places" (quoted in Root 1992b, 5). While Anzaldúa may pursue a critique of power elsewhere in her text, the arguments presented here—at least as they are excerpted—dispense with questions of power. How, we must ask, is it that those among "our own people" who exhibit various indices of racial/class privilege (e.g., "white-looking," "high yellow," "white lover," "white girl friend," English-language proficiency, professional employment— the inclusion of "uneducated" at the end of this string is a curious and telling supplement, an attempt to render privilege as privation!) are "shunned" (i.e., avoided, expelled, banished) by those among "our own people" who do not enjoy the same proximity to power, by what institutional mechanisms, by what political means? And what is the cost to those so shunned? Are they, by this calculus, thereby more oppressed, as Root goes on to suggest, or rather less so? More to the point, Anzaldúa misattributes what could more reasonably be considered resistance to or disidentification from whiteness (hostility, skepticism, or suspicion in the face of markers of whiteness) as an internalization of or identification with whiteness. This misattribution is accompanied by a rhetorical disidentification by the author from the reading audience (marked by "self-hatred" and "poor self-esteem") that she identified herself with in the immediately preceding sentences. Shifting register from the first-person plural personal "we" and the first-person plural possessive "our" to the second-person plural possessive "you," she declares: "it is exactly *your* internalized whiteness." She is able to do this only because she (1) disassociates the critical voice from the pathological internalization of whiteness in the same gesture by which she defends that voice's social proximity to whiteness and (2) reductively defines whiteness, from within the logic of her guiding metaphor (i.e., the border), as a desperate want for boundary lines. Are there not, however, boundary lines that are *worth* desperately wanting, that are perhaps even *vital* to maintain—for instance, the boundary lines of one's bodily integrity or one's ability to consent to or to refuse sex? The connection between the discourse of "border-crossing" and the ongoing contention about sexual violence—in particular, the structural foreclosure of consent under the regime of racial slavery—is explored further in chapter 2.

15. Anticipating arguments made later in this chapter regarding the force of negrophobia in the formation of multiracialism, it is not difficult to see how what, in the field of politics, I call a "purely formal negation of blackness," or in the fantasy of blackness, "oppressive black power," is plausibly animated by phobic affects and structured as a social relation to a collective phobic object. Fanon (1967) writes of the phobic, "The choice of the phobic object is . . . *overdetermined.* The object does not come at random out of the void of Nothingness; in some situation it has previously evoked an affect in the patient. His [or her] phobia is the latent presence of this affect [an 'anxious fear' derived from 'subjective insecurity'] at the root [or foundation] of his [or her] world *[le fond de monde du sujet];* there is an organization that has been given a form [or, better, a format—*il y a organization, mise en forme*]. For the object, naturally, need not be there, it is enough that somewhere it *exist:* It is a possibility. This object is endowed with evil [or malicious] intentions *[d'intentions méchantes]* and with all the attributes of malefic [force or] power *[d'une force maléfique].* In the phobic, affect has a priority that defies all rational thinking. As we can see, the phobic is a person who is governed by the laws of rational prelogic and affective prelogic: methods of thinking and feeling that go back to the age at which he [or she] experienced the event that impaired his [or her] security" (Fanon 1967, 155). Fanon continues, in accord with the major currents of psychoanalytic theory of his time, "If an extremely frightening object, such as a more or less imaginary attacker, arouses terror, this is also . . . and especially, a terror mixed with sexual revulsion [or horror—*d'horreur sexuelle*]" (155). However, Fanon will determine, in a certain revision of psychoanalytic theory, that there need not be some discrete event that impairs the subjective security of the phobic, since it is sufficient that the culture identify an imago, a mythological object, as "phobogenic" for it to occupy an etiological place for any given subject. "There is a constellation of postulates, a series of propositions that slowly and subtly—with the help of books, newspapers, schools and their texts, advertisements, films, radio [what Fanon elsewhere calls 'a thousand details, anecdotes, stories']—work their way into one's mind and shape [the] view of the world of the group to which one belongs" (152). For Fanon, the black is the archetypal object of this process (188–90). Importantly, when Fanon invokes Jung's collective unconscious, he is at pains to disabuse the notion from any biological association: "Jung locates the collective unconscious in the inherited cerebral matter. But the collective unconscious, without our having to fall back on the genes, is purely and simply the sum of prejudices, myths, collective attitudes of a given group . . . the collective unconscious is cultural, which means

acquired. . . . The collective unconscious is not dependent on cerebral heredity; it is the result of what I shall call the un-reflected imposition of a culture" (188, 191). And it is in this precise sense that he offers his famous claim: "The Negro is a phobogenic object, a stimulus to anxiety *[Le nègre est un objet phobogène, anxiogène]*" (151). We should also note that Fanon does not rest with the suggestion that negrophobia is a straightforward aversion toward the black but argues, in another vein, that it represents the "denegation," "the complete inversion" of a repressed desire for the black. We return to this very complicated point in later chapters.

16. While it is true that segregation is a problem faced by blacks, Latinos, and many Asian American populations in common, the discrepancy between such rates is also quite stark. So much so that we can reasonably point to qualitative differences in the sorts of segregation experienced by blacks and that experienced by Latinos and, to lesser extent, by Asian Americans. In other words, blacks are the only group to face what Massey and Denton (1998) refer to as "hypersegregation." Massey (2000) has demonstrated the seriousness of this divide among people of color, a situation aptly captured by the fact that even the most segregated of Asian Americans in poverty, including many Southeast Asian refugees, are more integrated than the most "integrated" middle-class blacks. Similarly, for Latinos, issues of segregation seem to be class bound, except for those Latinos of discernible African descent (i.e., Afro-Latinos). For blacks, segregation is a cross-class, racially bound phenomenon.

17. Pascoe (1999) defines racialism as "an ideological complex that other historians often describe with the terms 'race' or 'racist.' I intend the term *racialism* to be broad enough to cover a wide range of nineteenth-century ideas, from the biologically marked categories scientific racists employed to the more amorphous ideas George M. Fredrickson has so aptly called 'romantic racialism.' Used in this way, 'racialism' helps counter the tendency of twentieth-century observers to perceive nineteenth-century ideas as biologically 'determinist' in some simple sense. To racialists (including scientific racists), the important point was not that biology determined culture (indeed, the split between the two was only dimly perceived), but that race, understood as an indivisible essence that included not only biology but also culture, morality, and intelligence, was a compellingly significant factor in history and society" (467). The critique of racialism asserts that race is (or at least should be) an *insignificant* factor in history and society but often does so by problematically describing race as superficial or "merely skin deep," thereby reinforcing the notion of race as biology.

18. In this sense, the multiracial movement participates in civil rights discourse as a political domestication of the movement from which it historically departs. On the distinction between "civil rights discourse" and the "civil rights movement," see Crenshaw and others (1995), especially the introduction.

19. The one-drop rule or hypodescent rule refers to the (sometimes codified) convention of defining a person as racially black if he or she has any known African ancestry or at least "one-drop of black blood." Under this rule, people of mixed race with some discernible African ancestry would thereby be designated as black. As Daniel (2001) notes, "Most people are unaware that the one-drop rule is unique to the United States and applies specifically to Americans of African descent"(xi). Davis (1991) gives an earlier and more comprehensive account of the phenomenon. Others have noted that the rules of racial definition for nonblack people of color, such as Native Americans and Asian Americans, diverged from this convention and sometimes operated inversely (Jaimes 1995; Yu 2002). I hasten to add, again, that hypodescent is not reducible to the one-drop rule (not even for the definition of racial blackness in the historic instance), since one can be defined by hypodescent according to proportionally higher minimum criteria ("one quarter" or "one half" rather than "one drop"). That multiracialism takes aim at the one-drop rule in particular—the only form of hypodescent applied exclusively to racial blackness—is further evidence that it is singularly interested in contesting the terms of black identity as they have developed under the regimes of racial slavery and Jim Crow segregation.

20. This is not to suggest, against Byrd's repeated denials, that multiracial advocates are simply "running away from [their] blackness," whatever that allegation might mean in this context. Rather, it is to observe that multiracial advocates cannot avoid claiming that they are de facto (though, since 1997, no longer de jure) subsumed by an unwanted association with racial blackness. Given the state of the union, then, to claim that "mixed-race" is *not* a "subset" of "blackness" (an insistence that, as noted, renders blackness as a term of racial purity), that multiracial experience is *not* a mere local instance of a larger (federal) black experience, the quest for multiracial self-determination via self-identification must cut a border between "black" and "multiracial," must, in other words, separate itself and declare "racial independence" (Douglas 1997) from the former. The allusion to the Confederacy and to states' rights discourse, especially its grounding principle of "nullification," is, I think, more fitting to the political project of multiracialism than the evocation of the American Revolution preferred by many multiracial

proponents. The multiracial movement can be institutionally linked to the mobilization of white supremacist "neo-Confederates" by one degree of separation, with noted neoconservative organizations like Ward Connerly's American Civil Rights Institute—whose initiatives are regularly endorsed in the pages of *Interracial Voice* and *The Multiracial Activist*—as intermediary between multiracial groups and white supremacist organizations like the Council of Conservative Citizens and Ku Klux Klan. Though multiracial spokespeople often perfunctorily denounce the Far Right for its promotion of antimiscegenation, both movements display an unqualified opposition toward federally sponsored remedies for persistent *racial* inequality (especially those linked to the redress of slavery) and both offer strikingly similar "arguments" to that effect. Moreover, a number of regular contributors to multiracial publications like *Interracial Voice* frequently diminish the political significance of the white supremacist movement and even go so far as to represent its resurgence as a by-product of self-serving but ultimately moribund black identity politics (Winkel 2001). This point hopefully becomes clearer in the immediate discussion. For more on Ward Connerly's role in the Republican Party's national antiaffirmative action campaign and its links to Far-Right political groups, see Hansen (2006).

21. Byrd continues: "After the assassinations of Malik El-Shabazz and Martin Luther King Jr., the black community took the wrong fork in the road, particularly forgoing the transcendent nature of King's movement which pointed to the equality of human beings as the benchmark for social justice and which was evolving into a grassroots movement that included whites as soldiers in the cause of justice for black Americans. Afrocentric nationalism polarized and hurt the civil rights movement, replacing effective strategy with empty shouting and posturing of the sort that allowed America the opportunity to avoid both identification with black people and the job of bettering this nation. My friends, replacing a white ideal with a black ideal doesn't improve things, it just *reverses* them" (emphasis added).

22. This phrase is an obvious reference to the title of the famous 1959 CBS report on the Nation of Islam, the media event that launched Malcolm X to national prominence as an unflinching critic of the gradualism and reformism of the mainstream civil rights organizations of the time. It was this penchant for compelling and highly stylized radical political critique that eventually enshrined him as the patron saint of Black Power in the wake of his assassination (Van Deberg 1992).

23. This is why Byrd (1996) can suggest that "The turn towards Afrocentric nationalism by the black community coupled with the 1967 Supreme Court decision overthrowing the remaining antimiscegenation laws in this country, are *the*

two most important factors in the genesis of the multiracial 'movement'" (emphasis added).

24. The work of the latter contingent is discussed at length in chapter 2.

25. For another, very thorough review of the various aspects of antiblackness in multiracial discourse, see Makalani (2001). I build on such points in this chapter.

26. Several multiracial organizations, including the HIF and the AMEA, were vocal in their opposition to Proposition 54 (Welland 2003), but their belated opposition to the right-wing political tendencies of their erstwhile allies seems to me more an attempt to shake their shadow, as it were, than an effort to pursue a substantive political divergence from the tenets of multiracialism.

27. For further evidence of this structural contempt for black politics within the province of multiracialism, see the conclusion to Winters and Debose (2003).

28. For an extended discussion of a nonessentialist, postnationalist elaboration of black solidarity, see Shelby (2005).

29. Assertions about the "natural" centrality of multiracial people to the "critique" of race—whether as its muses, its authors, or more grandly, its fulfillment—are reiterated ad infinitum across the literature of multiracial studies (Root 1992a, 1996b; Winters and DeBose 2002; and Zack 1995a) despite the exceptions registered by those critical voices that have attempted to intervene (Brunsma 2006; Christian 2000; Dalmage 2004; Parker and Song 2002b; Spencer 2006; see also the essays by Ferber and Goldberg in Zack 1995a). The tension between an active and passive critique identified here echoes, I think, a more profound ambivalence in multiracial discourse about the nature of (interracial) desire: is it responsive to and, moreover, does it require some affirmative action—a positive social engineering to counteract the intraracial inertia of a centuries-long regulation of intimacy—or does it operate on the model of free love, spontaneously and without prejudice, once it is liberated from the external constraints of antimiscegenation in law and culture? What, precisely, are the politics of interracial desire, and how is such desire entwined with the psychic life of power? As we shall see in later chapters, the popular notion of "free love" circulated in multiracial discourse draws quite directly from the early twentieth-century writings of the famous Mexican philosopher José Vasconcelos (1997), specifically his essay "La raza cósmica." In much the same way that Spencer (1999) details the unacknowledged influence in contemporary multiracialism of the deeply problematic sociological studies of Edward Byron Reuter, I suggest that Vasconcelos exerts a lasting intellectual influence as well,

including the reactionary resonances of his most famous thesis. Both Root's description of the rise in interracial marriage rates as "love's revolution" (2001) and the concomitant "biracial [or multiracial] baby boom" as a "quiet revolution" (1996a) are indebted to the three-stage schema of historical development found in Vasconcelos. For Vasconcelos, the twentieth century would bear witness to the advent of the Spiritual or Aesthetic Era (following the passage of the Materialistic or Warring Era and the Intellectual or Political Era) "in which creative imagination and fantasy would supplant the rule of expediency and reason [and] mankind's [sic] behavior would be determined by the pathos of aesthetic emotion" (MacKenzie 1983, 305). Most important, according to the description of the text offered by Johns Hopkins University Press on the back cover of its 1997 reprint, "marriages would no longer be dictated by necessity or convenience, but by love and beauty; ethnic obstacles [or rather racial barriers], already in the process of being broken down, especially in Latin America, would disappear altogether, giving birth to a fully mixed race, a 'cosmic race,' in which *all the better qualities of each race would persist by the natural selection of love*" (emphasis added). This last phrase should be read with the full connotation of its evolutionist rhetoric, a rhetoric (and conceptual framework) that brings Vasconcelos into proximity with then-prevailing social Darwinist and eugenicist thought.

30. For a broad historical overview of the nineteenth-century monogenesis/polygenesis debates with which this contemporary conceptual waffling interacts, see Goldberg (1993).

31. The idea that one's race should not function as a determinate factor in one's social identity has a long and problematic history in the United States. See, for example, Pascoe's (1999) excellent discussion of what she calls "modernist racial ideology." She explains how such "culturalist" critiques of racialism found themselves caught in a contradiction: arguing, on the one hand, that race does not exist (as a biological category) and, on the other, arguing that race (as a set of superficial traits, "mere biology") should not decide one's life chances. As she puts it: "Culturalists set these two seemingly contradictory depictions of race—the argument that biological race was nonsense and the argument that race was merely biology—right beside each other. *The contradiction mattered little to them*" (471; emphasis added). This contradiction reemerges in the discourse of multiracialism with important consequences.

32. The question that begs to be asked is, of course, who requires such absolution in the first place? Whose "ancestors or contemporaries" have committed

such "sins"? It might be fitting here to contemplate briefly a statement made by Gordon (1995b): "The crisis of European man emerges . . . as a problem that goes deeper than most of us—white, brown, or black—may be willing to admit. To be black may mean to suffer, literally and figuratively, on an everyday basis, but to be white may ultimately mean—at least when moral reflection is permitted to enter— to be condemned" (26).

33. I want to add one interesting point of reference about Root's rhetoric of revolution, specifically her designation of the "biracial baby boom" as a "quiet revolution." One cannot miss the allusion here to the famous 1960s "Quiet Revolution" in Québec, with its consolidation of a leftist Francophone nationalism (including an armed radical sovereignty movement pursuing socialist revolutionary aims, e.g., *Front de liberation du Québec*) working in opposition to a staunchly conservative Catholic provincial regime beholden to the interests of the Anglophone Canadian Confederation and responsible for a host of sweeping progressive social, political, and economic reforms under the administration of Jean Lasage (1960–1966). At the level of identity politics, this period also produced a popular shift in nomenclature among the residents of Québec from the traditionally accommodating "French Canadian" to the overtly politicized "Québécois." What is most remarkable about this oblique genealogy is that the nationalist sentiment there entailed strong political identifications with the grassroots mobilization, public protests, and direct-action campaigns of the U.S. civil rights movement and, more pointedly, with the revolutionary nationalism of Black Power (including its use of defensive and offensive political violence—the FLQ is reputed to have carried out over two hundred bombings, various bank robberies to finance its operations, and most famously, the 1970 kidnapping and ransom of British and Canadian political officials known popularly as the "October Crisis"). Root's citation of the "quiet revolution" in this context is one that purges it of its progressive political effects and the violent conflagrations of its radical history.

34. This founding statement was first presented by Root as part of her keynote address to a multiracial conference at San Francisco State University in March 1993. It is reprinted in a slightly different form in Root (1996b).

35. It is significant that the issue of loyalty is articulated in the terms of *ethnicity* within a document written explicitly for multi*racial* people. Root (1992b) makes this slip only *after* distinguishing race from ethnicity several years earlier: "Whereas race can contribute to ethnicity, it is neither a sufficient nor necessary condition for assuming one's ethnicity, particularly with multiracial populations"

(4). This common transposition of terms is, in my view, an attempt to contain the destabilizing force of racial antagonism, an evasion of history and material context. See following note.

36. I want to emphasize the notion of objective interests here as a way to highlight the general elision of structural analysis within the domain of multiracial scholarship. As a result, processes of racialization, wherein all manner of material and symbolic violence is deployed, are gentrified. Moreover, a political critique that might reveal the intrinsic antagonism between the collective interests of differently racialized groups is foreclosed. Instead, analysis is pitched at another level such that structures of violence are rendered as instances of misunderstanding, social distance, or a lack of exposure—in other words, problems of experience. For a discussion of conflicts along lines of race, class, and gender, see Wolfenstein (1993), especially chapter 8, "Lordship and Bondage." Of course, to speak of objective conflicts of interest does not require reifying the concept of race. Indeed, it must be understood as dynamic and relational precisely because of the conflicts of interest it articulates.

37. In the second version of the Bill of Rights, the address of the declaration shifts from "WE HAVE THE RIGHT . . ." to "I have the right. . . ." So it seems that even within an already individualized movement, the scope of politics has narrowed. A semantic shift that is symptomatic of a general orientation in the movement which, to invert the feminist maxim, believes "the political is personal."

38. I am echoing Sharpley-Whiting (1996) on this point insofar as she criticizes multiracialism less for attempting to articulate a multiracial identity than for what she sees as their "desire for an identity that is somehow perceived as *better* than a culturally degraded black one, while whiteness remains normative" (162n2; emphasis added).

39. Spencer's explanation here is perhaps somewhat reductive and overly confident—"this is no doubt the reason"—but it suffices to establish the *politics* of the one-drop rule in a way that refutes the tendency to address it as an unconsidered attachment, a "fixation" or "hang-up," on the part of blacks that, in one way or another, affirm it.

40. "Although the mechanics of racism seem to start with those in power, the system is also maintained by the oppressed's internalization of the mechanics. . . . This internalization of the mechanics of oppression is a version of the hostage syndrome observed in prisoners of war. Prisoners take on characteristics of their captors and even defend their behaviors as their plight and ability to make sense out of an irrational reality are integrally linked with survival" (Root 1996a, 5).

41. Fanon (1967) reminds us that "when a story flourishes in the heart of a folklore, it is because in one way or another it expresses an aspect of 'the spirit of the group'" (64).

2. Scales of Coercion and Consent

1. This sanguine and passing assessment of the state of the union (and the world) with regard to white supremacy and antiblackness is among the most dubious and unsubstantiated points reasserted across the literature of multiracial studies. Historian Gary Nash (1999), whose work we consider later in the chapter, writes, for example, "The tide of American sentiment is shifting toward viewing skin color and 'race' as irrelevant to the issue of love and marriage." As a result, the problem is only one of facing down "tide pools of old-fashioned racism" (181). There is simply too vast a library and too persuasive a counter-consensus across the human sciences regarding the persistence and reconfiguration of racism and white supremacy—including the racialization of sexuality—in the post–civil rights era to take the claims of the multiracial project as anything but wishful. On this score, see even the largely sympathetic (to the multiracial movement) work of Moran (2001). Indeed, Stephens's self-characterization writes itself as "optimistic," the posture of a detached observer confident that the forces of change are inevitable.

2. It is important that Stephens characterizes this so-called pessimism as "a reactionary position quite similar to white supremacist thought" and not simply as "racialism," which, even by his own definition (and certainly those of the theorists he cites—Appiah, Sollors, Gilroy—as well as the historical figures he examines—Douglass, Ellison, Marley), is not identical in its various forms. This is a slippage that occurs frequently throughout his text and betrays a confusion about whether his project is to identify structural similarities in seemingly opposed schools of thought—at the level of ideas—or to contest the formation of actual structures of political, economic, social, and cultural supremacy, that is to say, the construction of hierarchy and the relations of power that underwrite it. These are quite distinct points to make even if they are inextricable at some level. One can, for instance, track the ways that ideologies (and movements) of resistance, as it were, appropriate (to varying degrees) the terms of dominance toward other ends and, as a result, operate with dimensions of complicity with that which they seek to challenge, transform, or overthrow. However, one must make additional theoretical moves—and often stretch logic or make quick use of the evidence at hand—to identify that complicity (which is not in itself contemptible, for even "the critique of

the critique" recognizes its own implications) with an incipient inversion (or unthinking defense) of the status quo.

3. This suggests something more complex than notions of "internalized racism." It is to recognize the ways in which white supremacy is *constitutive* (not merely contingent) not only to whiteness and something called white racial identity but also for the subjectivity of blacks. Frantz Fanon stands as the most well-known theorist in this regard, but see also more recent departures from his and other work in Marriott (2000).

4. One should not be distracted by Stephens's use of qualifiers like "almost always" when describing the "unequal power relations" obtaining between blacks and whites in the antebellum United States. He is uninterested in those exceptional cases of interracial relationships that he would suggest unfolded on terms of equality. His point, like those of authors discussed later, is to argue that "unequal power relations" are ultimately inconsequential to the politics of interracial intimacy.

5. Interestingly, the "usual suspects" of Afrocentrism (e.g., Molefi Asante, Leonard Jeffries) are not criticized in Stephens's study. In fact, they are not mentioned at all. They have only a spectral presence superimposed on those black scholars he seeks to discredit by proxy.

6. Kennedy states at another point that "the evidentiary record has been perhaps irredeemably stunted by the illiteracy of victims and, more decisively, the indifference, if not hostility, of authorities to whom black female suffering was a relatively trivial concern" (2003, 175).

7. "How does seduction uphold perfect submission and, at the same time, assert the alluring, if not endangering, agency of the dominated? It does so by forwarding the strength of weakness. As a theory of power, seduction contends that there is an ostensible equality between the dominant and the dominated. The dominated acquire power based upon the identification of force and feeling. . . . The artifice of weakness not only provides seduction with its power but also defines its essential character, for the enactment of weakness and the 'impenetrable obscurity' of femininity and blackness harbor a conspiracy of power. The dominated catalyze reversals of power, not by challenges presented to the system but by succumbing to the system's logic. Thus power comes to be defined not by domination but by the manipulations of the dominated. The reversibility of power and the play of the dominated discredit the force of violence through the assertion of reciprocal and intimate relations. In this regard, recognition of the agency of the dominated and

the power of the weak secures the fetters of subjection, while proclaiming the power and influence of those shackled and tethered" (Hartman 1997, 88–89).

8. For an excellent critique of the notion that records of manumission or interracial transfers of wealth constitute evidence of "romantic ruptures in the racist fabric of southern enslavement," see Davis (1999). She demonstrates that, far from effecting the sort of subversion romantically projected onto them today, such exceptional cases, as they actually unfolded, were "fully consonant with the sexual economy" of the antebellum south (268). More to the point, she cautions that "relying on records [as do Stephens and Kennedy] to attribute affection may yield distorted histories as the legal records and many of the other formal documents were recorded by the slaveholding class" (230).

9. Davis (1999) is again insightful. Aside from the obvious problems Kennedy (and others) experiences in matching his claims to the evidence at hand, there are much less contingent troubles to the effort: "The rhetoric of filial bonds [evoked so clearly in the multiracial project] directs attention away from the sexual *economy* that produced the relationships. It erases the presence and effects of the sexual and racial *norms* that make enslaved women's sexuality available for consumption, with or without affection and commitment on the part of the men. Filial obligation projects the benevolence of slavery . . . drawing on its imagery of paternalism and patriarchal domesticity. . . . It obscures all of the emancipations that didn't happen [while projecting] . . . a powerful image of interracial family undistorted by the sexual exploitation and abuse *endemic* to slavery" (259; emphasis added).

10. For a sustained and trenchant critique of Genovese on interracial sexuality under slavery, see Sommerville (2004).

11. I am, of course, aware of the historical specificity of Gramsci's elaboration on the concept of hegemony, that is, its emergence as a form of rule within advanced industrial societies (Grossberg 1996). However, the fact remains that the authors in question here are in search of consent in the sexual field as a means of establishing a broader commentary on the nature of coercion/consent under the regime of slavery, articulating discrepant discourses regardless of whether hegemony provides a (flawed) conceptual frame of their endeavors. The point of their historical musings is, again, to assert points about the nature of power on the contemporary scene.

12. The paradoxical phrase "the manufacture of consent" was coined in 1921 by the famous liberal journalist Walter Lippmann to indicate the role of the intellectual elite in governing the potential disorder of a general public prone to

stereotypical thinking and unable to contemplate critically the events of the broader world. Lippmann was, not coincidentally, also a noted anticommunist and presidential advisor to the Progressive-Era Democrat Woodrow Wilson regarding the formulation of Wilson's Fourteen Points, one basis of the Treaty of Versailles and the germinal statement of the failed League of Nations. Lippmann popularized the term "cold war" just after the end of the Second World War in a book of the same title. Lippmann's earlier phrase was appropriated by radical critics Edward Herman and Noam Chomsky, whose book, *Manufacturing Consent* (1988), explored the functions of propaganda in the political economy of contemporary U.S. mass media, or what the authors also term the production and dissemination of "necessary illusions"—thought control—for preventing the rise of radical democratic alternatives to late capitalism without resort to totalitarian state repression. "Historical engineering" was, according to Herman and Chomsky, a term used by Wilson-era historians willing to spin the historical record in ways that supported the current policy regime, notably U.S. involvement in the First World War.

13. The full quote reads: "Moving as such testimony doubtless is, what does it *really* tell us about the incidence of rape under slavery? In a society numbering in the millions, ten, twenty, fifty, or even a hundred anecdotes by themselves can *provide little basis for determining* whether the events they describe were representative or idiosyncratic. That fact is, *no one knows for sure*—or can even offer a rigorous quantitative estimate of—the extent to which whites sexually coerced blacks during the slavery era. . . . The reality was complex—probably more complicated than we will ever be able to appreciate satisfactorily. After all, the very meaning of the words we use to organize our perceptions—key words such as 'rape'—change over time and continue to spur and reflect sharp conflicts. Moreover, as previously noted, the evidentiary record has been perhaps irredeemably stunted by the illiteracy of victims and, more decisively, the indifference, if not hostility, of authorities to whom black female suffering was a relatively trivial concern" (175; emphasis added). Its is curious, to say the least, that Kennedy will declare, repeatedly, for the "extreme vulnerability" of black women and the likelihood that white-on-black rape (defined in the narrow sense of "personal" sexual violence) was prevalent under slavery but maintain, nonetheless, that it is perhaps *equally plausible* that sexual assault of black women was "representative *or* idiosyncratic," normative *or* exceptional. The move toward an impossible (in Kennedy's terms) and, I would add unnecessary, "rigorous quantitative estimate" is a typical displacement of the *structural* arguments made by black women, then and now, about the sexual politics of enslavement. It

presents itself as a silencing gesture meant mostly to dampen the tone and tenor of an impassioned historical memory and to attenuate the horror of the institution of slavery and its still unfolding legacies.

14. For a discussion of black women's complicated relationships to law enforcement in cases of their victimization, sexual or otherwise, by black men, see Richie (1996).

15. We recall that Kennedy consistently hedges any such acknowledgment—handling black women's slave narratives with suspicion about their value as primary sources (and not simply "anecdotes") and all but dismissing the work of contemporary black feminist writers—and he broaches no discussion of what might begin to constitute redress, legal or otherwise, for this centuries-long legacy of sexual violence. On that score, he only encourages black women to take it to court from here on out—against black men, that is, since he fails to make any explicit statement about prosecuting white men for sexual violence against black women in the present.

16. I believe this to be the case with Kennedy's discussion of the welfare of parentless children as well, whose perilous fate in the obviously dysfunctional adoption–foster care system is often exacerbated by the contradictory concerns of black and white social workers. There he proceeds to discredit the arguments of the National Association of Black Social Workers (NABSW), though he fails to adequately address the historical questions and political concerns from which they arise. Moreover, though he admits that the situation of black parentless children will not substantially improve with the meager policy changes he proposes (i.e., a move to colorblind placements), and that there are structural factors regarding the problem of care for black children that no adoption policy can properly address, he nonetheless limits his intervention to this domain. A full discussion of Kennedy's arguments on this count is beyond the scope of the present work, but suffice it to say that the critical protocol would be analogous. See chapters 9, 10, and 11 in Kennedy (2003).

17. It is interesting that Kennedy would invoke the Mau Mau Uprising (1952–1960) against British colonialism in Kenya, given that, despite the unquestionable importance of the movement for anticolonial struggle in Africa and beyond, the nearly 12,000 casualties sustained during this period were borne almost exclusively by Kenyans, not the militarily victorious British colonial administration.

18. Civil death is a legal status entailing the loss of most or all civil rights, typically though not exclusively due to conviction of a felony offense.

19. While Spencer (1999) has rightly noted this general reversal of polarity, he does not go on to identify the particular threats that blacks are said to pose to state and civil society, particularly the sexual nature of this supposed threat. See subsequent text for more on this point.

20. Lubiano (1993) writes that questions of black cultural "ownership" arise in and reflect contexts of hierarchical appropriation, which is to say relations "structured in dominance."

21. The passage reads as follows: "*The black American has been mostly freed from one part of being black in America: coercion.* That coercion does come into play when a security guard follows her around a department store for no good reason; or when a real estate agent fails to show her houses in a certain neighborhood; or when he seeks a job as a head coach in the NFL or a governorship or promotion in a modern company with old-boy cabals; or when a black friend criticizes him for dating a white woman or listening to *Carmen* instead of Luther. Increasingly, African Americans live in a world of post-black possibility. The details of his or her life are often black; but his mind is free to flash between black and mulatto and white and Latino shades. *Choice has defeated coercion*" (239; emphasis added). One cannot help but notice the typical bundling together of recognizable racial discrimination (e.g., police harassment, denial of employment, political exclusion) with the new "discrimination" that blacks impose on one another (or anyone else) when they do not measure up to their "rigid rules of belonging" (Root 1992b, 5).

22. This is similar to the maneuvers of the antiaffirmative action campaign that proposes a replacement of race-conscious policies with policies that explicitly target class inequities but that fails (or refuses) to develop the alternative platform (Crenshaw 2003).

3. There Is No (Interracial) Sexual Relationship

1. For an excellent critical survey of this tendency within the movement, see Spencer (1999), chapter 3.

2. Project RACE, A Place for Us National, *Interracial Voice*, and *The Multiracial Activist* are the most vocal proponents of this line of argumentation. However, the efforts of the liberal MAVIN Foundation—especially its national "Match-Maker Bone Marrow Project"—are also exemplary. For more on this front, see the official Web site: http://www.mavinfoundation.org. For a critique of the very idea of multiracial public health policy, see Spencer (1999).

3. On this score, the following comment from Hernton (1988): "Bad feelings

and bad acts against interracial associations are part and parcel of the sundry acts of terror and violence that are presently perpetrated against black people in our cities and suburbs and on our college campuses. This violence is but a blatant manifestation of the more "hidden" racism that seethes just beneath the surface of contemporary American society and pervades every institution and every facet of our world" (xii).

4. See, for example, the definition in Gaskins (1999): "Monoracial: A so-called racially 'pure' person; someone who identifies himself or herself as white, black, or Asian/Pacific Islander, for example" (12). The notion of racial purity, while admitted here to be conventional, constructed, and "so-called," is nonetheless *absolutely necessary* to the possibility of conceptualizing a mixed-race project.

5. Multiracial discourse responds differently to different formulations of antimiscegenation, as we will see in this chapter. The affirmation of multiracial health and well-being engages the concerns about the decline of civilization due to "mongrelization." The purified, desexualized image of interracial relationships responds, in turn, to the distinct but related moral panic about the perversity of interracial sex as such.

6. These terms are drawn from Root (1992b, 1996a).

7. See comments by Shaviro (1993) later in this chapter.

8. Within the parameters of racist culture, to move away from the low areas of the body and the carnality of desire is also to move away from racialized blackness. See Frantz Fanon's prescient commentary throughout *Black Skin, White Masks* (New York: Grove Press, 1967). See also the extended quote from Hernton that follows.

9. Here Jameson's (1981) critique of immanence is instructive insofar as we can determine that the multiracial movement operates within a model of immanence in its production of discourse about the multiracial experience: "that is to say, the phenomenological ideal—that of some ideal unity of consciousness or thinking and experience or the 'objective' fact . . . the vision of a moment in which the individual subject would be somehow fully conscious of his or her determination by class [race, gender, etc.] and would be able to square the circle of ideological conditioning by sheer lucidity and the taking of thought" (282–83).

10. In this passage, Fanon is discussing why it is important to critique the psychic mechanisms behind the persistent stereotypes of black sexuality, especially those that give rise to an image of the black body in the first place. His entire book is, of course, an effort toward that end.

11. http://www.asianwhite.org/.

12. I am strongly suggesting that in order for a relationship to be considered interracial, especially in the U.S. context, it must involve a black person. This is not always the case, of course, and there are myriad historical examples of hysteria prompted by the prospect of sexual encounter between whites and nonblack people of color. What I sense, however, is that within the racist imagination, relationships with blacks, whether the other is white or a nonblack person of color, constitute interracial relationships par excellence. A pedestrian, though not insignificant, index of this tendency is found in the taxonomic practices of commercial pornography. Until recently, to label pornographic films "interracial" in the United States meant it featured sex between blacks and some other racial group, usually whites. The presence of Asian or Latino actors (nearly all of whom would be paired with white actors) would either leave the racial designation unchanged or move it into an ethnic-specific label, such as Asian, Oriental, Hispanic, Spanish, Latin. Black films, in contrast, were those that starred *only* blacks.

13. See Omi and Winant (1994), especially chapter 4, and Winant (2001), especially Part I. See also Dyer (1997), where he writes: "Racial imagery is central to the organization of the modern world. At what cost regions and countries export their goods, whose voices are listened to at international gatherings, who bombs and who is bombed, who gets what jobs, housing, access to health care and education, what cultural activities are subsidized and sold, in what terms they are validated—these are all largely inextricable from racial imagery. The myriad minute decisions that constitute the practices of the world are at every point informed by judgments about people's capacities and worth, judgments based on what they look like, where they come from, how they speak, even what they eat, that is, racial judgments. Race is not the only factor governing these things and people of goodwill everywhere struggle to overcome the prejudices and barriers of race, but *it is never not a factor, never not in play*" (1; emphasis added).

14. Many mail-order industries claim to be bridges between nations and cultures in much the same way that most multiracial advocates and scholars do. For example, see http://www.planet-love.com.

15. See Lacan (1998), especially chapter 6, "God and ~~Woman's~~ Jouissance." There he states: "There's no such thing as a sexual relationship" (71). See also Žižek (1996c).

16. Evans (1996) echoes this point and translates the phrase in the same way. He writes: "The formula might better be rendered 'there is no relation between

the sexes,' thus emphasizing that it is not primarily the act of sexual intercourse that Lacan is referring to but the question of the relation between the masculine sexual position and the feminine sexual position" (181).

17. See, for instance, Abel, Christian, and Moglen (1997); Cheng (2000); Eng (2001); Lane (1998); and Seshadri-Crooks (2000).

18. Fanon (1967) writes that the other, the white man had "woven me out of a thousand details, anecdotes, stores" (111). Or again, "there were legends, stories, history" (112).

19. The point at which the movement of signification is arbitrarily brought to closure is decided as an effect of power when the determination of race is at stake. In the case of racial blackness in particular, the inscription is a matter of direct relations of force: "If African-Americans have been taught anything under the regimes of New World domination, it adheres in the very close analogy between dominant behavior and the shape of the information in which it is conveyed. If I am captive and under dominance, there can be no doubt of this reading in the woundings and rendings of my flesh" (Spillers 2003, 272).

20. Williams (2004) observes the discrepancy between the official message of the multiracial movement—that multiracialism can and will bridge the racial divide—and the opinions of leaders and members stated privately in the interview setting. The latter betrays a deep reticence, and for some a sizeable opposition, to the notion of race mixture as conduit of reconciliation.

21. Žižek (1989) provides an excellent exposition of this process in chapter 3.

22. This ambivalence is marked by the other major tendency in multiracial discourse, namely, that which insists on the identity between one's self and one's racial designation, so long as it is *multiracial*.

4. The Consequence of Race Mixture

1. We recall Memmi's (1999) passage from chapter 3: "There are no pure races, nor are there even homogenous biological groups. Were there any, they would not be biologically superior. Were they biologically superior, they would not necessarily be superlatively endowed or culturally more advanced than others. Were they that, they would not have any God-given right to eat more than others, to be better housed, or to travel in better conditions. They could certainly decree such conditions for themselves, and impose them, but then neither justice nor equality would be found among them. . . . In short, racist reasoning has no secure foundation, is incoherent in its development, and is unjustified in its conclusions" (19).

2. The phrase is from Kristeva (1982) and is discussed in more detail later in this chapter.

3. See Brown (1995) for a critique of political strategies of opposition that both entrench and foster (psychic, political, discursive) dependence on the contested structures of power.

4. On the capture of desiring-production and the "striation" of smooth space, see Deleuze and Guattari (1987b), especially chapter 12, "1440: The Smooth and the Striated." See also Massumi (1992).

5. This is not to say that those who, like Root, popularize or appropriate Anzaldúa for the discourse of multiracialism necessarily do justice to the complexity, artistry, or political impetus of her work. However, something in her critique of dualistic or binary thinking provides a point of entry through which a more problematic enmity toward blackness enters the scene. In this way, we might say that the repressed historical and conceptual elements of the *mestizaje* advanced in *Borderlands/La frontera* return to commandeer and displace the critical project from which her thinking emerges and to which it seeks to contribute. See the discussion of the relation between Anzaldúa and Vasconcelos in this chapter.

6. Even these articulations are not without their problems. For an excellent engagement with Martí, especially as regards the history of racial slavery in the Americas, see Spillers (2003), chapter 13, "Who Cuts the Border? Some Readings on America."

7. This term is borrowed from Gilroy (1991). He describes it as an understanding of cultures "as fixed, mutually impermeable expressions of racial and national identity" (61).

8. McLuhan's (1962) foundational discussion of the "Global Village" informs much succeeding discourse on forms of global community, especially in the post–cold war era. Speaking principally of the evolution of electronic media technologies like radio and telephone (his attention to visual-based technologies like film, television, and computers would come later), McLuhan was at least ambivalent about the emergence of what he called "total interdependence" and "superimposed coexistence," and he offered a cautionary tale about its profoundly repressive tendencies and capacities. For an overview of his thinking and its impact in various fields, see Marchessault (2004).

9. It must be said that Mercer's principle concern in reading Fanon's sexual politics is to critique the homophobic implications and heteronormative presumptions operative in *Black Skin, White Masks*. However, it is possible, without losing

the specificity of his intervention, to understand the prohibitions and derision produced about the gender of object-choice as one of several primary regulations of
sexuality meant to manage and allay the anxiety and consternation of normative
identities along the color line. A number of nonblack feminist critics have attempted
to explore these interconnections (Chow 1998; Doane 1991; Fuss 1995). For an important black feminist riposte to these treatments of Fanon, see Sharpley-Whiting
(1996).

10. Hernton notes that a statement by Johnson provided the inspiration for
his own studies in *Sex and Racism*. The epigraph is from Johnson's autobiography,
Along This Way: "Through it all I discerned one clear and certain truth: in the core
of the heart of the American race problem the sex factor is rooted, rooted so deeply
that it is not always recognized when it shows at the surface. Other factors are obvious and are the ones we care to deal with; but regardless of how we deal with these,
the race situation will continue to be acute as long as the sex factor persists. . . . It
may be innate; I do not know. But I do know it is strong and bitter" (quoted in
Hernton 1988, xxi).

11. For a compelling account of this psychosexual dynamic, racism as cultural discourse, see Yaba Badoe's excellent documentary film *I Want Your Sex* (1991).

12. This phrase was made famous in the United States by Thomas Jefferson,
who used it to denounce what he saw as the corrupting influence of Wall Street
financiers upon the republican values of the American Revolution. The ascendance
of financial capital in the business capital of the postrevolutionary era prompted
Jefferson to describe New York City as "a cloacina [sewer] of all the depravities of
human nature." In Roman mythology, Cloacina was the goddess of the ancient
Roman sewer system, but, interestingly, her personality was appropriated from earlier Estruscan mythology in which she was considered to be the protector of sexual intercourse in marriage, perhaps filtering "waste" away from its vicinity.

13. Of course, there is an important slippage to this statement. Enjoyment
here could be read in two different ways. It could be understood that black people
(assumed to be men), in advocating civil rights, simply want to experience (sexual)
enjoyment in the same ways that whites do, that is, by having sex with white women.
In this case, we have to wonder what precisely is pornographic or superstitious about
such sex. After all, white men as a group should know as well as anyone what it's
like to have sex with white women. Are they simply coveting a scene that is already
pornographic? Or does the fact that black men are enjoying women that are not
rightfully accessible to them render such obscene? For an interesting discussion

of the latter proposition, see Stember (1976). However, enjoyment could also be read simply as partaking in the institutions of the state and civil society, enjoying the same (group) rights and privileges as white people. Although there we tend to confine enjoyment to the sexual and, further, to reduce the sexual to sex acts, we must remember that enjoyment spreads out across the entire social field, it metastasizes. As such, we should note that, potentially, any practice or activity is capable of being eroticized. It should also be noted that this sexualizing of black political rights is long-standing in the United States, dating from at least the postbellum era. For example, in the scene depicting the fictional black-dominated South Carolina legislature in D. W. Griffith's infamous film *Birth of a Nation* (1915), the newly empowered politicians hang a placard that reads: "Equality. Equal Rights. Equal Politics. Equal Marriage." Rogin (1987) discusses *Birth* at length.

14. The fantasy of white genocide as racial suicide might be mistaken as the inverse of Vasconcelos's projections of "voluntary annihilation," but it is more accurately understood as the involution of white supremacy and antiblackness, the power politics of domination. This is so because, despite the usage of the term *suicide*, white supremacists understand such a nightmare to be a form of race murder. That is, even those white "race traitors" who earn the enmity of "self-respecting" white supremacists are considered to have been coerced at some level: ensnared, shamed, guilt-tripped, brainwashed by blacks.

15. This is in no way a new question, and the theoretical genealogy of racialization goes all the way back to Fanon (1967). The concept has been developed subsequently by Martinot (2002), Miles (1989), Omi and Winant (1994), and Small (1994), among others.

16. This question is meant to recall the discussion of general and restricted economies outlined in the introduction to the present study.

17. Kristeva writes of the powers of containment and defense attributed to the image: "Specular fascination captures terror and restores it to the symbolic order. . . . Calm reigns before a vision of hell framed in an image" (quoted in Burgin 1996, 191).

18. See chapter 9 in Bhabha (1994) for a discussion of this very rich, difficult concept.

19. What I am calling an absolute sexuality, or miscegenation of a different order, is drawn from Kawash's (1999) discussion of absolute violence in the writings of Fanon. She writes: "Fanon's violence of decolonization . . . is always in excess and elsewhere to the instrumental violence of the colonized in struggle. And it is this

excess—which is not reducible to or identifiable as particular violent acts—that portends the decolonization that will be a rupture with, rather than a re-formation of, the colonial past. . . . The violence of decolonization appears as another order of violence altogether. . . . Instrumental violence and absolute violence are two ways in which violence emerges into and operates on a reality that is always constituted and conceived discursively. . . . Instrumental violence in Fanon's text is the violence of revolt and reversal, the violence whereby the colonized challenge and attempt to upend the domination that has oppressed them. At the same time, another violence (perhaps alongside or unleashed by instrumental acts of violence) emerges as the world-shattering violence of decolonization" (237). I am aware of the strained comparison drawn between organized violence in the context of anticolonial struggle and interracial sex in various contexts. However, without insisting on any identity between the two, we can see the rich suggestiveness of a distinction between miscegenation as interracial sex acts—an instrumental sexuality—and miscegenation as an event that undermines "the value and distinction of means and ends" (238)—an absolute sexuality. It is the latter order of sexuality, akin perhaps to Deleuze and Guattari's (1987a) "desiring-production," that I am arguing precedes and exceeds the reach of racialization as a practice of signification and social structural organization.

20. I draw this distinction from Docherty (1996). His comments regarding the philosophy of identity for the practice of aesthetic criticism are valid for our critique of racialization as a mode of apprehension (perhaps a popular aesthetic practice): "The dominant mode of criticism is to console the Subject (either a psychoanalytic Subject or a historical Subject and political agent) in the face of her or his anxiety that the world and its aesthetic practices [and, we might add, its social, political, economic, and cultural processes] may be evading our conscious control or apprehension." That is, "the threatening possibility that the world may not be 'there' *for* a Subject of consciousness," that the world may be "of a fundamentally *different* order of being from that which is already known to and by consciousness" (vii). For a discussion of the disruptive effects of temporality on spatialization—including the space of identity formation or imaging—see especially chapter 7 in Docherty (1996).

21. Barrett (1998) writes of the production of value as form: "No matter how overwhelmingly value seems to impose itself as a normative design, a non-contingent form, a singular objective validity, it nonetheless reserves for itself an Other—a negative resource—and, from the perspective of the reserved Other, the force and

promiscuity of value are, with equal invariability, dis-covered. Invariably and para-doxically, value reserves for itself an Other perspective from which 'value as form' bursts forth as 'value as force'. . . . Value is [thus] a twofold action or structure, a presentation and representation, a performance riddled by the dialectic nature of its coming into being and, more than merely dialectic, categorically disjunctive in its binarism. . . . Always inherent in value is the trace of an original, violent expen-diture. Value is violence and, more to the point, value is violence disguised or dis-figured" (27–28). Or again: "Value is violence, then it is not. Value is violence, then it is form. Value courts violence, then, in an immediate second appearance court-ing form, tries to belie its Other and Othering past" (33).

22. I was drawn to this quote by its citation in Bhabha (1994, 180).

23. Deleuze (1986) makes a similar point: "The model would be rather a state of things which would constantly change, a flowing-matter in which no point of anchorage nor center of reference would be assignable. On the basis of this state of things it would be necessary to show how, at any point, centers can be formed which would impose fixed instantaneous views. It would therefore be a question of 'deducing' conscious, natural . . . perception" (57–58).

24. On the instability of definitions of whiteness, its flexibility regarding the purity requirement, see Zackodnik (2001). In this historic instance, it seems that one need not be white absolutely, but only white enough.

25. Though making a slightly different point, Spencer (1999) notes the ret-icence or inability of the multiracial movement to apprehend the critical poten-tial of the questions it sets loose or reanimates on the social landscape.

5. The True Names of Race

1. For more on the history and politics of this organization, see its official Web site: http://www.i3n.net.

2. "[Capital] has become an unbounded space—in other words, a space co-extensive with its own inside and outside. It has become a field of immanence. The crisis of production has been made productive by inventing ways in which the circu-lation of capital can create surplus value. No longer is Keynes's goal of 'protecting the present from the future' of catastrophe the guiding principle of economics. The trick is instead to figure out 'how to make money off the crisis.' The classical prob-lem of the capitalist cycle, or the inevitability of periodic economic collapse, has been solved by eternalizing crisis without sacrificing profits. The future-past of the catastrophe has become the dizzying ever-presence of crisis" (Massumi 1993, 19).

3. See especially chapter 3: "Emphasis has been placed not on care (who tends their shit?), but on properly identifying the 'outside'—hence calls for mandatory HIV testing—so that it may be excluded all the more thoroughly—hence calls to quarantine all persons who test positive for HIV antibodies" (Dean 2000, 99).

4. Massumi (1993) gestures in this direction: "The idea of causality needs work. Recursivity and cocausality (multifactor analysis) may be beginnings. But in the end, the very concept of the cause may have to go, in favor of effects and their interweavings (syndromes). Syndromes mark the limit of causal analysis. They cannot be exhaustively understood—only pragmatically altered by experimental interventions operating in several spheres of activity at once" (31).

5. Root (1995) employs this phrase to refer both to the growth of nonblack nonwhite immigrant groups and domestic minorities and to the increasing numbers of self-identified people of mixed racial descent.

6. As Spencer (1999) has argued, "Race in America is and has always been, from the earliest period of the invasion of the Americas by Europeans, primarily a hierarchical binary opposition between white and black. . . . I contend that these two perceived extremes make each other possible, and in turn make the American racial paradigm possible" (8). He makes this point even more clearly in another passage: "From the perspective of the overall social schema in America, what matters most is neither mixture among non-white groups nor mixture between whites and Asians or Native Americans (although these mixtures may certainly prove problematic in the first and immediately succeeding generations); rather, what is crucial is that whiteness not include any trace of African ancestry" (16).

7. Although I refer to the post–civil rights proliferation of multiracial identity politics alongside the contemporary emergence of nonblack people of color in theory, research, and political organization, I would not conflate their historical significance. That is to say, while these various racial projects may share a certain desire, at times bordering on a passion, to decenter the black–white binary, they do so in contradictory ways. This is especially the case for American Indian political and intellectual formations. It goes without saying that questions of Indian sovereignty sit in deep tension, if not direct conflict, with the claims of immigrants to the United States (I would not say the same of black freedom struggles). This point need not be diminished or glossed over to recognize that despite this unending discrepancy, the rights claims of these respective nonblack groups are dependent upon the exclusion of blackness from the qualifying criteria of citizenship, whether of the nation-state or the tribal government respectively.

8. The casting of racial politics in black–white terms is, in part, an effect of the postwar race relations industry in the United States as it developed around the emergence of the modern black civil rights movement and its radicalization as Black Power. Perhaps the most well-known document in that vein remains the *Report of the National Advisory Commission on Civil Disorders* (1968), a.k.a. the Kerner Commission, in which was coined the infamous phrase "two societies, one black, one white—separate and unequal." This report provides the title for Hacker (1992), whose work serves as a frequent example of the paradigm in question. The black civil rights struggle—dating back to at least 1787—has, however, consistently understood itself not in isolation but in relation to other oppressed peoples around the world. On this, see Birnbaum and Taylor (2000). That being said, the compulsive return to the binary model, which is to say the return to discussion of the lived reality of the black, must be explained otherwise, an exercise that would reveal that it is not only overdetermined but also entirely warranted.

9. This is no less the case among intellectuals and activists on the Left. The discourse of "conflict" between blacks and immigrants (whether from Asia or Latin America) is saturated by anecdotal testimony about the experience of encounter, invariably evoking incidents of interpersonal or even mob violence committed by blacks against nonblacks. To my knowledge, all such discussions either ignore or soft-pedal questions of social structure and political economy, historical and contemporary, by quarantining slavery as a thing of the past or rendering equivalent slavery and other forms of oppression. As a result, the literature of contemporary multiracial coalition building seeks a blend of mutual understanding through attitude adjustment and prejudice reduction and the establishment of common cause through joint business venture or collaborative development projects. See, for instance, Chang and Diaz-Viezades (1999).

10. The special "multiracial issue" of *Amerasia Journal*, discussed later in the chapter, provides a good example. The editors note: "The product of the interracial union is that apocalyptic monster about which the protectors of traditional racial classification warned their followers, those who clung to the belief that race is Black or White, that race can be pure; that, in order to be racially correct and socially acceptable, one must run from the monster, demand conformity, and keep difference in the closet. That product is considered even more frightening if its multiracial composition includes African ancestry" (Houston and Williams 1997, vii). At this late point in our discussion, it should hardly seem peculiar that the authors would refer generically to "protectors of traditional racial classification" rather than

to the specific historical formation of white society or even the white ruling elite. Note also that the protectors of traditional racial classifications are described as being in a common defensive position. They do not actively forge and construct race, they are not ensconced in its politics, but rather inherit and defend an established tradition, something that can be discarded or divested if so chosen. The invention of race in relation to structures of domination is erased from the account. These protectors are simply leaders of a devout following ("the protectors . . . warned their followers . . . who clung to the belief") and without question the flock was misled, frightened, extorted into an avoidance of difference, a difference that would spoil the coveted belief in racial purity. Lest we confuse this for a critique of white supremacy and antiblackness in its reliance upon the white purity concept, we are reminded that any of those who believe that race is "either Black or White" are, as it were, closeting difference, repressing the truth of the interracial (Stephens 1999). As we have seen in detail, multiracialism asserts that in the post–civil rights era, black people are clinging most desperately to the belief that "race is black."

11. The article from which this passage is drawn represents an updated iteration of the critique of the black–white binary found in Omi and Winant (1993, 1994) in which the authors note the empirical register of racial multiplicity and racial mixture without subsequent theoretical advancement in the understanding of the logic of race and racism.

12. The multiracial movement is split on the issue: whereas hardline conservatives in the movement want to dismantle the basis of black politics, the liberal faction seeks a working relationship with the traditional civil rights establishment, even amid their disagreements.

13. I am expanding in this question a point made by Han (2006) in a discussion of the racial politics of immigration rights and its legal claims to the institution of U.S. citizenship: "The putatively expanded frame of racial politics today qua non-white immigration is, contrary to the common sense, a legal *narrowing* of the possibilities for racial justice, a scenario in which we can discern a sequestering of the historic demands of black freedom struggle."

14. For Lind (1998), former conservative turned neoliberal, to make such predictions could be read in various ways. It could, for example, be aligned with the scathing projections of right-wing pundits like David Horowitz (2000), who denounces the reparations for slavery movement in the United States, citing "ten reasons why reparations for slavery are a bad idea for black people." The reparations movement, he contends, will only "provide black leaders with a platform from which

to complain about all the negative aspects of black life—to emphasize inner-city pathologies and failures, and to blame whites, Hispanics and Asians for causing them. How is this going to impress other communities? It's really just a prescription for sowing more racial resentment and creating even greater antagonism" between blacks and the rest of the U.S. population. The paroxysms of his supposedly regretful and "painfully honest" article are shot through with a desire to see his predictions for more resentment and antagonism come true. As such, it should be considered a recruitment effort for nonblack people of color to the side of anti-black racism under the guise of responding to so-called black anti-Americanism. I am inclined to rearticulate Lind's statement as a diluted, journalistic account of a dynamic analyzed by Gordon (2000), who writes a propos of mixed-race identity: "The individual who is a mixture of white and black finds himself . . . in more than a construction of mixture by itself. He finds himself facing a mixture of clearly unequal terms. He is thus simultaneously less and more of an animal, in the American (and global) racial hierarchy of evolutionary humanoids. His choice of identity, then, functions in relation to blackness in dual forms of denial: affirmation of whiteness is a rejection of base blackness, but so too is affirmation of being *mixed*, since in either formulation the black stands as a point at which both white and mixed race designations will stand, like a renaissance humanity that reaches at the gods in a flight from the animal kingdom, in a world 'above.' It is not that one is less of an animal in the extent to which one is a human being, but that one is less of an animal in the extent to which one is *white*" (104). The ramifications of this schematic for the designations of other nonblack people of color (Latinos, Asians, American Indians, Arabs, Persians, etc.) should be of concern as well. Considering the hegemony of this global racial hierarchy, it is actually quite conceivable that the black–nonblack dichotomy so feared as historical possibility by white liberals and conservatives alike will have been, in fact, the more fundamental color line.

15. Charles Gallagher (2004) corroborates such findings: "The Multiracial Movement has raised public awareness that millions of individuals with mixed-race backgrounds do not fit into the racial categories established by the government. What this movement has ignored, however, are the ways in which existing categories expand to incorporate groups once considered outside of a particular racial category. The social and physical markers that define whiteness are constantly in a state of flux, shifting in response to sociohistoric conditions. Groups once on the margins of whiteness, such as Italians and the Irish, are now part of the dominant group. National survey data and my interviews with whites suggest

a process similar to the incorporation of Southern and Eastern Europeans into the 'white' race is taking place among certain parts of the Asian and Latino populations in the United States. I argue that the racial category 'white' is expanding to include those ethnic and racial groups who are recognized as being socially, culturally, and physically similar to the dominant group" (59–60). See also Yancey (2003).

16. The phrasing here is drawn from Wall (1999), who writes in a quite different context: "The political task that remains is destruction" (155). It should be noted that we are inflecting such statements in distinct ways and I do not mean to represent a necessary correspondence on this point. That being said, his very rich study of "radical passivity" has not failed to influence my thinking in productive ways.

Works Cited

Abel, Elizabeth, Barbara Christian, and Helene Moglen, eds. 1997. *Female Subject in Black and White: Race, Psychoanalysis, Feminism.* Berkeley: University of California Press.

Alcoff, Linda. 1995. "Mestizo Identity." In Naomi Zack (ed.), *American Mixed Race: The Culture of Microdiversity.* New York: Rowman and Littlefield.

Alexander, Bryant Keith. 2000. "Reflections, Riffs and Remembrances: The Black Queer Studies in the Millennium Conference (2000)." *Calalloo* 23, no. 4: 1285–305.

Ali, Tariq, ed. 2000. *Masters of the Universe: NATO's Balkan Crusade.* New York: Verso.

Allen, Theodore. 1994. *The Invention of the White Race.* Vol. 1, *Racial Oppression and Social Control.* New York: Verso.

———. 1997. *The Invention of the White Race.* Vol. 2, *The Origin of Racial Oppression in Anglo-America.* New York: Verso.

Allman, Karen. 1996. "(Un)Natural Boundaries: Mixed Race, Gender, and Sexuality." In Maria Root (ed.), *The Multiracial Experience: Racial Borders as the New Frontier.* Thousand Oaks, Calif.: Sage.

Althusser, Louis, and Étienne Balibar. 1997. *Reading Capital.* Trans. Ben Brewster. New York: Verso.

Altman, Dennis. 2001. *Global Sex.* Chicago: University of Chicago Press.

Andre, Sergé. 1994. "The Otherness of the Body." In Mark Bracher, Marshall Alcorn, Ron Corthell, and Franciose Massardier-Kenney (eds.), *Lacanian Theory of Discourse: Subject, Structure, and Society.* New York: New York University Press.

Anzaldúa, Gloria. 1999. *Borderlands/La frontera: The New Mestiza*. San Francisco: Aunt Lute Books.

Appadurai, Arjun. 1996. *Modernity at Large: Cultural Dimensions of Globalization*. Minneapolis: University of Minnesota Press.

Appelbaum, Nancy, Anne Macpherson, and Karin Alejandra Rosemblatt, eds. 2003. *Race and Nation in Modern Latin America*. Chapel Hill: University of North Carolina Press.

Appiah, Kwame Anthony. 1993. *In My Father's House: Africa in the Philosophy of Culture*. New York: Oxford University Press.

Arboleda, Teja. 1998. *In the Shadow of Race: Growing Up as a Multiethnic, Multicultural and "Multiracial" American*. London: Lawrence Erlbaum.

Arrighi, Giovanni. 1995. *The Long 20th Century: Money, Power, and the Origins of Our Times*. New York: Verso.

Awkward, Michael. 1995. *Negotiation Difference: Race, Gender, and the Politics of Positionality*. Chicago: University of Chicago Press.

Azoulay, Katya. 1997. *Black, Jewish, and Interracial: It's Not the Color of Your Skin but the Race of Your Kin and Other Myths of Identity*. Durham, N.C.: Duke University Press.

Baldwin, James. 1985. *The Price of the Ticket: Collected Nonfiction, 1948–1985*. New York: St. Martin's.

Barad, Karen. 1998. "Getting Real: Technoscientific Practices and the Materialization of Reality." *differences* 10, no. 2 (Summer): 87–128.

Bardaglio, Peter. 1999. "'Shameful Matches': The Regulation of Interracial Sex and Marriage in the South before 1900." In Martha Hodes (ed.), *Sex, Love, Race: Crossing Boundaries in North American History*. New York: New York University Press.

Barrett, Lindon. 1997. "Black Men in the Mix: Badboys, Heroes, Sequins, and Dennis Rodman." *Calalloo* 20, no. 1 (Winter): 106–26.

———. 1998. *Blackness and Value: Seeing Double*. Cambridge: Cambridge University Press.

———. 1999. *Blackness and Value: Seeing Double*. Cambridge: Cambridge University Press.

———. 2002. "The 'I' of the Beholder: The Modern Subject and the African Diaspora." Paper presented at "Blackness in Global Contexts." University of California, Davis (March).

Barrymoore, Vincent. n.d. "Spice vs. Soup." Asiaphile home page at http://www.asianwhite.org/afwm/#anchor1241913.

Bauman, Zygmunt. 2000. *Globalization: The Human Consequences.* New York: Columbia University Press.

Baxandall, Rosalyn. 1995. "Marxism and Sexuality." In Antonio Callari, Stephen Cullenberg, and Carole Biewener (eds.), *Marxism in the Postmodern Age: Confronting the New World Order.* New York: Guilford.

Bell, Derrick. 1992. *Faces at the Bottom of the Well: The Permanence of Racism.* New York: Basic

———. 2000. *Race, Racism, and American Law.* New York: Aspen.

Beller, Jonathan. 1998. "Cinema/Capital." In Eleanor Kauffman and Kevin Jon Heller (eds.), *Deleuze and Guattari: New Mappings in Politics, Philosophy, and Culture.* Minneapolis: University of Minnesota Press.

Benjamin, Walter. 1969. *Illuminations.* New York: Shocken.

Berlant, Lauren. 1997. *The Queen of America Goes to Washington City: Essays on Sex and Citizenship.* Durham, N.C.: Duke University Press.

Bernal, Martin. 2001. *Black Athena Writes Back: Martin Bernal Responds to His Critics.* Durham, N.C.: Duke University Press.

Bhabha, Homi. 1994. *The Location of Culture.* New York: Routledge.

Bhattacharyya, Gargi. 2002. *Sexuality and Society: An Introduction.* New York: Routledge.

———. 2005. *Traffick: The Illicit Movement of People and Things.* London: Pluto Press.

Birnbaum, Jonathan, and Clarence Taylor. 2000. *Civil Rights since 1787: A Reader in the Black Struggle.* New York: New York University Press.

Bittker, Boris. 2003. *The Case for Black Reparations.* New York: Beacon Press.

Black Public Sphere Collective, eds. 1995. *The Black Public Sphere: A Public Culture Book.* Chicago: University of Chicago Press.

Blackburn, Robin. 1998. *The Making of New World Slavery: From the Baroque to the Modern, 1492–1800.* New York: Verso.

Block, Sharon. 1999. "Lines of Color, Sex, and Service: Comparative Sexual Coercion in Early America." Martha Hodes (ed.), *Sex, Love, Race: Crossing Boundaries in North American History.* New York: New York University Press.

Boas, Franz. 1987. *Anthropology and Modern Life.* New York: Dover Publications.

Bolter, Jay David, and Richard Grusin. 2000. *Remediation: Understanding New Media.* Cambridge, Mass.: MIT Press.

Bonilla-Silva, Eduardo. 2003. *Racism without Racists: Colorblind Racism and the Persistence of Racial Inequality in the United States*. New York: Rowman and Littlefield.

———. 2004. "From Biracial to Tri-Racial: The Emergence of a New Racial Stratification System in the United States." In Cedric Herring, Verna M. Keith, and Hayward Derrick Horton (eds.), *Skin/Deep: How Race and Complexion Matter in the "Color-Blind" Era*. Chicago: University of Illinois Press.

Bost, Suzanne. 2003. *Mulattas and Mestizas: Representing Mixed Identities in the Americas, 1850–2000*. Athens: University of Georgia Press.

Brah, Avtar, and Annie Coombes, eds. 2000. *Hybridity and Its Discontents: Politics, Science, Culture*. New York: Routledge.

Branch, Taylor. 1989. *Parting the Waters: America in the King Years, 1954–63*. New York: Touchstone.

Brennan, Teresa. 1993. *History after Lacan*. New York: Routledge.

Briggs, John. 1990. *The Turbulent Mirror: An Illustrated Guide to Chaos Theory and the Science of Wholeness*. New York: Harper Collins.

Brock, Lisa, Robin D. G. Kelley, and Karen Sotiropoulos, eds. 2003. "Transnational Black Studies." *Radical History Review* 87 (Fall): 1–3.

Brooks, Peter, and Alex Woloch, eds. 2000. *Whose Freud? The Place of Psychoanalysis in Contemporary Culture*. New Haven, Conn.: Yale University Press.

Brown, Nancy, and Ramona Douglass. 1996. "Making the Invisible Visible: The Growth of Community Network Organizations." In Maria Root (ed.), *The Multiracial Experience: Racial Borders as the New Frontier*. Thousand Oaks, Calif.: Sage.

Brown, Wendy. 1995. *States of Injury: Power and Freedom in Late Modernity*. Princeton, N.J.: Princeton University Press.

Brunsma, David, ed. 2006. *Mixed Messages: Multiracial Identities in the "Color-Blind" Era*. Boulder, Colo.: Lynn Reinner.

Bullard, Robert. 1994. *Dumping in Dixie: Race, Class, and Environmental Quality*. Boulder, Colo.: Westview.

Burgin, Victor. 1996. *In/Different Spaces: Place and Memory in Visual Culture*. Berkeley: University of California Press.

Buscaglia-Salgado, José. 2003. *Undoing Empire: Race and Nation in the Mulatto Caribbean*. Minneapolis: University of Minnesota Press.

Butler, Johnnella, ed. 2001. *Color Line to Borderlands: The Matrix of American Ethnic Studies*. Seattle: University of Washington Press.

Butler, Judith. 1993. *Bodies That Matter: On the Discursive Limits of Sex*. New York: Routledge.

Byrd, Charles Michael. 1996. Speech. Multiracial Solidarity March I, Washington, D.C. (July 20). *Interracial Voice*. http://www.webcom.com/intvoice/speech1.html.

———. 1997. Speech. Multiracial Solidarity March II , Los Angeles (August 9). *Interracial Voice*. http://www.webcom.com/intvoice/speech2.html.

———. 2002. *Beyond Race: The Bhagavad-Gita in Black and White*. Philadelphia: Xlibris Press.

Camper, Carol, ed. 1998. *Miscegenation Blues: Voices of Mixed Race Women*. Toronto: Sister Vision Press.

Caper, Robert. 2000. *Immaterial Facts: Freud's Discovery of Psychic Reality and Klein's Development of His Work*. New York: Routledge.

Carby, Hazel. 2000. *Race Men*. Cambridge, Mass.: Harvard University Press.

Chandler, Nahum. 2000. "Originary Displacement." *boundary 2* 27, no. 3: 249–86.

Chang, Edward, and Jeannette Diaz-Veizades. 1999. *Ethnic Peace in the American City: Building Community in Los Angeles and Beyond*. New York: New York University Press.

Cheng, Anne. 2000. *The Melancholy of Race: Psychoanalysis, Assimilation, and Hidden Grief*. New York: Oxford University Press.

Cho, Sumi. 1993. "Korean Americans vs. African Americans: Conflict and Construction." In Robert Gooding-Williams (ed.), *Reading Rodney King/Reading Urban Uprising*. New York: Routledge.

Chomsky, Noam. 1991. *Deterring Democracy*. New York: Verso.

Chow, Rey. 1998. "The Politics of Admittance: Female Sexual Agency, Miscegenation, and the Formation of Community in Frantz Fanon." In *Ethics After Idealism: Theory-Culture-Ethnicity-Reading*. Bloomington: Indiana University Press.

Christian, Mark. 2000. *Multiracial Identity: An International Perspective*. New York: Palgrave Macmillan.

Churchill, Ward. 1997. *A Little Matter of Genocide: Holocaust and Denial in the Americas, 1492 to the Present*. San Francisco: City Lights Books.

Churchill, Ward, and Jim Vander Wall. 2002. *Agents of Repression: The FBI's Secret War against the Black Panther Party and the American Indian Movement*. Boston: South End Press.

Coffman, Tom. 2003. *The Island Edge of America: A Political History of Hawai'i*. Honolulu: University of Hawai'i Press.

Cohen, Cathy. 1999. *The Boundaries of Blackness: AIDS and the Breakdown of Black Politics.* Chicago: University of Chicago Press.

Constantine-Simms, Delroy, ed. 2001. *The Greatest Taboo: Homosexuality in Black Communities.* Los Angeles: Alyson Publications.

Copjec, Joan. 1994. *Read My Desire: Lacan against the Historicists.* Cambridge: MIT Press.

Cornelius, Wayne, Takeyuki Tsuda, Philip L. Martin, and James F. Hollifield, eds. 2004. *Controlling Immigration: A Global Perspective.* Stanford, Calif.: Stanford University Press.

Cornell, Drucilla, ed. 2000. *Feminism and Pornography.* New York: Oxford University Press.

Courtney, Susan. 2004. *Hollywood's Fantasies of Miscegenation: Spectacular Narratives of Gender and Race, 1903–1967.* Princeton, N.J.: Princeton University Press.

Crenshaw, Kimberlé. 1988. "Race Reform, Retrenchment: Transformation and Legitimation in Anti-Discrimination Law." *Harvard Law Review* 101: 1331–87.

———. 1995. "Mapping the Margins: Intersectionality, Identity Politics, and Violence Against Women of Color." In Kimberlé Crenshaw et al. (eds.), *Critical Race Theory: The Key Writings That Formed the Movement.* New York: New Press.

———. 2003. "Beyond Affirmative Action: The Twenty-Five Year Détente." *TomPaine.com,* July 10. http://tompaine.com/scontent/8322.html.

Crenshaw, Kimberlé, Neil T. Gotanda, Gary Peller, and Kendall Thomas, eds. 1995. *Critical Race Theory: The Key Writings That Formed the Movement.* New York: New Press.

Curtis, Christopher. 1999. "*Partus Sequitur Ventrem:* Slavery, Property Rights, and the Language of Republicanism in Virginia's House of Delegates, 1831–1832." Paper delivered at the 18th Annual Conference of the Australian and New Zealand Law and History Society, July. http://www.newcastle.edu.au/centre/cispr/conferences/land/curtispaper.pdf.

Cutrone, Chris. 2000. "The Child with a Lion: The Utopia of Interracial Intimacy." *GLQ: A Journal of Gay and Lesbian Studies* 6, no. 2 (Spring): 249–85.

DaCosta, Kimberly. 2000. "Remaking the Color Line: Social Bases and Implications of the Multiracial Movement." Ph.D. diss., University of California, Berkeley.

———. 2002. "Multiracial Identity: From Personal Problem to Public Issues." In

Loretta Winters and Herman DeBose (eds.), *New Faces in a Changing America: Multiracial Identity in the 21st Century*. London: Sage.

———. 2004. "All in the Family: The Familial Roots of Racial Division." In Heather Dalmage (ed.), *The Politics of Multiracialism: Challenging Racial Thinking*. Albany: State University of New York Press.

Dalmage, Heather, ed. 2004. *The Politics of Multiracialism: Challenging Racial Thinking*. Albany: State University of New York Press.

Daniel, G. Reginald. 2001. *More Than Black? Multiracial Identity and the New Racial Order*. Philadelphia: Temple University Press.

Daniels, Jessie. 1996. *White Lies: Race, Class, Gender, and Sexuality in White Supremacist Discourse*. New York: Routledge.

Davis, Adrienne. 1999. "The Private Law of Race and Sex." In *Stanford Law Review* 51, no. 2: 221–88.

Davis, Angela Y. 1981. *Women, Race, and Class*. New York: Vintage.

———. 2003. *Are Prisons Obsolete?* New York: Seven Stories Press.

Davis, David Brion. 1986. *Slavery and Human Progress*. New York: Oxford University Press.

Davis, F. James. 1991. *Who Is Black? One Nation's Definition*. College Station: Penn State University Press.

———. 1995. "The Hawaiian Alternative to the One Drop Rule." In Naomi Zack (ed.), *American Mixed Race: The Culture of Microdiversity*. New York: Rowman and Littlefield.

Dean, Tim. 2000. *Beyond Sexuality*. Chicago: University of Chicago Press.

Deleuze, Gilles. 1986. *Cinema 1: The Movement-Image*. Trans. Hugh Tomlinson and Barbara Habberjam. Minneapolis: University of Minnesota Press.

Deleuze, Gilles, and Claire Parnet. 1987. *Dialogues*. Trans. Elion Albert and Hugh Tomlinson. New York: Columbia University Press.

Deleuze, Gilles, and Félix Guattari. 1987a. *Anti-Oedipus: Capitalism and Schizophrenia*. Vol. 1. Trans. Robert Hurley. Minneapolis: University of Minnesota Press.

———. 1987b. *A Thousand Plateaus: Capitalism and Schizophrenia*. Vol. 2. Trans. Brian Massumi. Minneapolis: University of Minnesota Press.

Delgado, Richard, and Jean Stefancic, eds. 1999. *Critical Race Theory: The Cutting Edge*. Philadelphia: Temple University Press.

Dent, Gina, ed. 1992. *Black Popular Culture*. Seattle, Wash.: Bay Press.

Derrida, Jacques. 1970. "Structure, Sign, and Play in the Discourse of the Human

Sciences." Trans. Alan Bass. In Richard Macksey and Eugenio Donato (eds.), *The Structuralist Controversy*. Baltimore, Md.: Johns Hopkins University Press.

———. 1983. *Dissemination*. Trans. Barbara Johnson. Chicago: University of Chicago Press.

———. 1984. "Différance." In *Margins of Philosophy*. Trans. Alan Bass. Chicago: University of Chicago Press.

———. 1986. "But beyond . . . (Open Letter to Anne McClintock and Rob Nixon)." In Henry Louis Gates, Jr. (ed.), *"Race," Writing, and Difference*. Chicago: University of Chicago Press.

———. 1997. *Of Grammatology*. Trans. Gayatri Spivak. Baltimore, Md.: Johns Hopkins University Press.

Doane, Ashley, and Eduardo Bonilla-Silva, eds. 2003. *White Out: The Continuing Significance of Racism*. New York: Routledge.

Doane, Mary Ann. 1991. "Dark Continents: Epistemologies of Racial and Sexual Difference in Psychoanalysis and Cinema." In *Femme Fatales: Feminism, Film Theory, Psychoanalysis*. New York: Routledge.

Docherty, Thomas. 1996. *Alterities: Criticism, History, Representation*. New York: Clarendon Press.

"Don't you dare list them as 'other.'" 1996. *U.S. News and World Report*, April 8.

Doty, Roxanne Lynn. 1996. *Imperial Encounters: The Politics of Representation in North–South Relations*. Minneapolis: University of Minnesota Press.

Douglas, Nathan. 1997. "Declaration of Racial Independence." *Interracial Voice*. http://www.webcom.com/~intvoice/natdoug2.html.

———. 2003. "The Multiracial Movement: An Uncomfortable Political Fit." *The Multiracial Activist*, October/November. http://www.multiracial.com/site/content/view/414/27/.

Du Bois, W. E. B. 1968. *Dusk of Dawn: An Essay toward the Autobiography of a Race Concept*. New York: Shocken.

———. 1987. "President Harding and Social Equality." In Nathan Huggins (ed.), *W. E. B. Du Bois: Writings*. New York: Library of America.

Dyer, Richard. 1997. *White*. New York: Routledge.

Eng, David. 2001. *Racial Castration: Managing Masculinity in Asian America*. Durham, N.C.: Duke University Press.

Erni, John. 1994. *Unstable Frontiers: The Cultural Politics of "Curing" AIDS*. Minneapolis: University of Minnesota Press.

Esteva-Fabregat, Claudio. 1995. *Mestizaje in Ibero-America*. Trans. John Wheat. Tucson: University of Arizona Press.

Evans, Dylan. 1996. *Introductory Dictionary of Lacanian Psychoanalysis*. New York: Routledge.

Fanon, Frantz. 1963. *The Wretched of the Earth*. Trans. Constance Farrington. New York: Grove.

———. 1967. *Black Skin, White Masks*. Trans. Charles Markmann. New York: Grove Press.

Feagin, Joe. 2006. *Systemic Racism: A Theory of Oppression*. New York: Routledge.

Ferber, Abby. 1995. "Exploring the Social Construction of Race." In Naomi Zack (ed.), *American Mixed Race: The Culture of Microdiversity*. New York: Rowman and Littlefield.

———. 1998. *White Man Falling: Race, Gender, and White Supremacy*. New York: Rowman and Littlefield.

Ferguson, Roderick. 2003. *Aberrations in Black: Toward a Queer of Color Critique*. Minneapolis: University of Minnesota Press.

Fink, Bruce. 1995. *The Lacanian Subject: Between Language and Jouissance*. Princeton, N.J.: Princeton University Press.

Foner, Nancy, and George Fredrickson, eds. 2004. *Not Just Black and White: Historical and Contemporary Perspectives on Immigration, Race, and Ethnicity in the United States*. New York: Russell Sage Foundation.

Foucault, Michel. 1987. "Maurice Blanchot: The Thought from the Outside." In *Foucault/Blanchot*, trans. Jeffrey Mehlman and Brian Massumi. New York: Zone Books.

———. 1990. *The History of Sexuality: An Introduction*. Vol. 1. Trans. Robert Hurley. New York: Vintage.

Frankenberg, Erica, and Chungmei Lee. 2002. *Race in American Public Schools: Rapidly Resegregating School Districts*. Cambridge, Mass.: Civil Rights Project.

Fredrickson, George. 1981. *White Supremacy: A Comparative Study in American and South African History*. New York: Oxford University Press.

———. 1987. *The Black Image in White Mind: The Debate on Afro-American Character and Destiny, 1817–1914*. Hanover: Wesleyan University Press.

Freud, Sigmund. 1990. "Screen Memories." In *The Standard Edition of the Complete Psychological Works of Sigmund Freud*. Vol. 3, trans. James Strachey. New York: W. W. Norton.

Fundeburg, Lise, ed. 1994. *Black, White, Other: Biracial Americans Talk about Race and Identity.* New York: Harper Collins.

Fung, Richard. 1991. "Looking for My Penis: The Eroticized Asian in Gay Video Porn." In Bad Object-Choices (ed.), *How Do I Look?* Seattle, Wash.: Bay Press.

Furedi, Frank. 1999. *The Silent War: Imperialism and the Changing Perception of Race.* New Brunswick, N.J.: Rutgers University Press, 1999.

Fuss, Diana. 1995. "Interior Colonies: Frantz Fanon and the Politics of Identification." In *Identification Papers.* New York: Routledge.

Gallagher, Charles. 2004. "Racial Redistricting: Expanding the Boundaries of Whiteness." In Heather Dalmage (ed.), *The Politics of Multiracialism: Challenging Racial Thinking.* Albany: State University of New York Press.

Gans, Herbert. 2004. "The Possibility of a New Racial Hierarchy in the Twenty-First-Century United States." In Charles Gallagher (ed.), *Rethinking the Color Line: Readings in Race and Ethnicity.* New York: McGraw Hill.

García, Alma, ed. 1997. *Chicana Feminist Thought: The Basic Historical Writings.* New York: Routledge.

Gasche, Rodolphe. 1986. *The Tain of the Mirror.* Cambridge, Mass.: Harvard University Press.

Gaskins, Pearl Fuyo, ed. 1999. *What Are You? Voices of Mixed-Race Young People.* New York: Henry Holt.

Genovese, Eugene. 1976. *Roll, Jordan, Roll: The World the Slaves Made.* New York: Vintage.

Gibson, Nigel. 2003. *Fanon: The Postcolonial Imagination.* London: Polity Press.

Gil, José. 1998. *Metamorphoses of the Body.* Trans. Stephen Muecke. Minneapolis: University of Minnesota Press.

Gilanshah, Bijan. 1993. "Multiracial Minorities: Erasing the Color Line." *Law and Inequality: A Journal of Theory and Practice* 12, no. 1 (Winter): 183–90.

Gilroy, Paul. 1991. *Ain't No Black in the Union Jack: The Cultural Politics of Race and Nation.* Chicago: University of Chicago Press.

———. 1997. "Scales and Eyes: 'Race' Making Difference." In Sue Golding (ed.), *The Eight Technologies of Otherness.* New York: Routledge.

———. 2000. *Against Race: Imagining Politic Culture beyond the Color Line.* Cambridge, Mass.: Harvard University Press, Belknap Press.

Ginsberg, Elaine, ed. 1996. *Passing and the Fictions of Identity.* Durham, N.C.: Duke University Press.

Gleick, James. 1988. *Chaos: Making a New Science.* New York: Penguin.

Goldberg, David Theo. 1993. *Racist Culture: Philosophy and the Politics of Meaning.* New York: Blackwell.

———. 1995. "Made in the USA." In Naomi Zack (ed.), *American Mixed Race: The Culture of Microdiversity.* New York: Rowman and Littlefield.

———. 1997. *Racial Subjects: Writing on Race in America.* New York: Routledge.

———. 2002. *The Racial State.* New York: Blackwell.

Goldman, Shifra. 1998. "The Latin Americanization of the United States." *Art Nexus* 29 (August–October): 80–84.

Goodchild, Philip. 1996. *Deleuze and Guattari.* London: Sage.

Gordon, Lewis. 1995a. *Bad Faith and Anti-black Racism.* New York: Prometheus.

———. 1995b. *Fanon and the Crisis of European Man: An Essay on Philosophy and the Human Sciences.* New York: Routledge.

———. 1996a. "The Black and the Body Politic: Fanon's Existential Phenomenological Critique of Psychoanalysis." In Lewis R. Gordon, T. Denean Sharpley-Whiting, and Renée T. White (eds.), *Fanon: A Critical Reader.* Oxford, U.K.: Blackwell.

———. 1996b. "Race, Sex, and Matrices of Desire in an Antiblack World: An Essay in Phenomenology and Social Role." In Naomi Zack (ed.), *Race/Sex: The Sameness, Difference, and Interplay.* New York: Routledge.

———. 1997. *Her Majesty's Other Children: Sketches of Racism from a Neocolonial Age.* New York: Rowman and Littlefield.

———. 2000. *Existentia Africana: Understanding Africana Existential Thought.* New York: Routledge.

Gossett, Thomas. 1997. *Race: The History of an Idea in America.* New York: Oxford University Press.

Gracia, Jorge, and Pablo De Greiff, eds. 2000. *Hispanics/Latinos in the United States: Ethnicity, Race, and Rights.* New York: Routledge.

Graham, Richard, ed. 1990. *The Idea of Race in Latin America: 1870–1940.* Austin: University of Texas Press.

Green, Charles, ed. 1997. *Globalization and Survival in the Black Diaspora: The New Urban Challenge.* New York: State University of New York Press.

Grier, William, and Price Cobbs. 1968. *Black Rage.* New York: Harper Collins.

Grossberg, Lawrence. 1992. *We Gotta Get Out of This Place: Popular Conservatism and Postmodern Culture.* New York: Routledge.

———. 1996. "History, Politics and Postmodernism: Stuart Hall and Cultural

Studies." In David Morley and Kuan-Hsing Chen (eds.), *Stuart Hall: Critical Dialogues in Cultural Studies*. New York: Routledge.

Grosz, Elizabeth. 1990. *Jacques Lacan: A Feminist Introduction*. New York: Routledge.

Grunzinski. 2002. *The Mestizo Mind: The Intellectual Dynamics of Colonization and Globalization*. New York: Routledge.

Guattari, Félix. 1996. *Soft Subversions*. Trans. Sylvere Lotringer. New York: Semiotext(e).

Guillaumin, Colette. 1995. *Racism, Sexism, Power, Ideology*. New York: Routledge.

Hacker, Andrew. 1992. *Two Nations: Black and White, Separate, Hostile, Unequal*. New York: Macmillan.

Hacking, Ian. 1999. *The Social Construction of What?* Cambridge, Mass.: Harvard University Press.

Haizlip, Shirlee Taylor. 1994. *The Sweeter the Juice: A Family Memoir in Black and White*. New York: Simon and Schuster.

Hall, Stuart. 1996a. "The After-life of Frantz Fanon." In Alan Read (ed.), *The Fact of Blackness: Frantz Fanon and Visual Representation*. Seattle, Wash.: Bay Press.

———. 1996b. "Race, Articulation, and Societies Structured in Dominance." In Houston Baker, Manthia Diawara, and Ruth Lindeborg (eds.), *Black British Cultural Studies: A Reader*. Chicago: University of Chicago Press.

———. 1998. "Subjects in History." In Wahneema Lubiano (ed.), *The House That Race Built*. New York: Vintage.

Halualani, Rona Tamiko. 2002. *In the Name of Hawaiians: Native Identities and Cultural Politics*. Minneapolis: University of Minnesota Press.

Han, Sora Y. 2006. "The Politics of Race in Asian American Jurisprudence." *UCLA Asian Pacific American Law Journal*, 11, no. 1: 1–40.

Hannaford, Ivan. 1996. *Race: The History of an Idea in the West*. Princeton, N.J.: Woodrow Wilson Center.

Hansen, Ronald. 2006. "KKK Backing Welcomed." *Detroit News*, November 4. http://www.detnews.com/apps/pbcs.dll/article?AID=/20061104/POLITICS01/611040362/1022/POLITICS.

Harper, Phillip Brian. 1994. "Walk-On Parts and Speaking Subjects: Screen Representations of Black Gay Men." In Thelma Golden (ed.), *Black Male*. New York: Whitney Museum.

———. 1996. *Are We Not Men? Masculine Anxiety and the Problem of African American Identity*. New York: Oxford University Press.

Harris, David. 2002. *Profiles in Injustice: Why Racial Profiling Cannot Work*. New York: New Press.

Hartman, Saidiya. 1997. *Scenes of Subjection: Terror, Slavery, and Self-Making in Nineteenth-Century America*. New York: Oxford University Press.

——. 2003. "The Position of the Unthought: An Interview by Frank B. Wilderson, III." *Qui Parle: Literature, Philosophy, Visual Arts, History* 13, no. 2 (Spring/Summer): 183–201.

Harvey, David. 2005. *A Brief History of Neoliberalism*. New York: Oxford University Press.

Haver, William. 1996. *The Body of this Death: Historicity and Sociality in the Time of AIDS*. Stanford: Stanford University Press.

Heath, Stephen. 1985. *Questions of Cinema*. Bloomington: Indiana University Press.

Hennessey, Rosemary. 2000. *Profit and Pleasure: Sexual Identities in Late Capitalism*. New York: Routledge.

Herman, Edward, and Noam Chomsky. 1988. *Manufacturing Consent: The Political Economy of the Mass Media*. New York: Pantheon.

Hernandez, Tanya Kateri. 1998. "'Multiracial' Discourse: Racial Classifications in an Era of Color-Blind Jurisprudence." *Maryland Law Review* 57: 97–173.

Hernton, Calvin. 1988. *Sex and Racism in America*. New York: Grove.

Hill-Collins, Patricia. 1990. *Black Feminist Thought: Knowledge, Consciousness, and the Politics of Empowerment*. New York: Routledge.

——. 1998. *Fighting Words: Black Women and the Search for Justice*. Minneapolis: University of Minnesota Press.

Hodes, Martha. 1997. *White Women, Black Men: Illicit Sex in the Nineteenth-Century South*. New Haven, Conn.: Yale University Press.

——, ed. 1999. *Sex, Love, Race: Crossing Boundaries in North American History*. New York: New York University Press.

Hollinger, David. 1995. *Postethnic America: Beyond Multiculturalism*. New York: Basic Books.

——. 2000. *Postethnic America: Beyond Multiculturalism*. New York: Basic Books.

hooks, bell. 1990. *Yearning: Race, Gender, and Cultural Politics*. Boston: South End Press.

——. 1992. *Black Looks: Race and Representation*. Boston: South End Press.

Horowitz, David. 2000. "The Latest Civil Rights Disaster." *Salon.com*, May 30. http://archive.salon.com/news/col/horo/2000/05/30/reparations/index.html.

Houston, Velina Hasu, and Teresa Kay Williams, eds. 1997. *No Passing Zone: Voices of Asian-Descent Multiracials.* Los Angeles: UCLA Asian American Studies Center Press.

Hull, Gloria T., ed. 1986. *But Some of Us Are Brave: Black Women's Studies.* New York: City University of New York Press.

Hunter, Tera. 1997. *To Joy My Freedom: Southern Black Women's Lives and Labors after the Civil War.* Cambridge, Mass.: Harvard University Press.

Hutchinson, Earl Ofari. 2002. "Why Black Murder Rates Remain So High." *Znet,* August 9. http://www.zmag.org/content/Race/hutchbmurder.cfm.

Illouz, Eva. 1997. *Consuming the Romantic Utopia: Love and the Cultural Contradictions of Capitalism.* Berkeley: University of California Press.

Irwin, Alexander, Joyce Millen, and Dorothy Fallows. 2003. *Global AIDS: Myths and Facts, Tools for Fighting the AIDS Pandemic.* Boston: South End Press.

Jackson, Zakiyyah. 2003. "Gender Profiling: A Discourse of Marginalization and Displacement of People of Color." *Objector: A Magazine of Conscience and Resistance* (Summer): 15–17.

Jaimes, M. Annette, ed. 1991. *The State of Native America: Genocide, Colonization, and Resistance.* Boston: South End Press.

———. 1995. "Some Kind of Indian: On Race, Eugenics and Mixed-Bloods." In Naomi Zack (ed.), *American Mixed Race: The Culture of Microdiversity.* New York: Rowman and Littlefield.

James, Joy. 1996a. *Resisting State Violence: Radicalism, Gender, and Race in U.S. Culture.* Minneapolis: University of Minnesota Press.

———. 1996b. *Transcending the Talented Tenth: Race Leaders and American Intellectualism.* New York: Routledge.

Jameson, Fredric. 1981. *The Political Unconscious.* Ithaca, N.Y.: Cornell University Press.

———. 1992a. *Postmodernism, or The Cultural Logic of Late Capitalism.* Durham, N.C.: Duke University Press.

———. 1992b. *Signatures of the Visible.* New York: Routledge.

———. 1998a. *The Cultural Turn: Selected Essays on the Postmodern, 1983–1998.* Durham, N.C.: Duke University Press.

———. 1998b. "Notes on Globalization as a Philosophical Issue." In Fredric Jameson and Miyoshi (eds.), *The Cultures of Globalization.* Durham, N.C.: Duke University Press.

Jameson, Fredric, and Masao Miyoshi, eds. 1998. *The Cultures of Globalization.* Durham, N.C.: Duke University Press.

JanMohamed, Abdul. 1992. "Sexuality on/of the Racial Border." In Domna Stanton (ed.), *Discourses of Sexuality.* Ann Arbor: University of Michigan Press.

Jay, Martin. 1994. *Downcast Eyes: The Denigration of Vision in Twentieth-Century French Thought.* Berkeley: University of California Press.

Jaynes, Gerald, ed. 2000. *Immigration and Race: New Challenges for American Democracy.* New Haven, Conn.: Yale University Press.

Johnson, Kevin, ed. 2003. *Mixed Race America and the Law: A Reader.* New York: New York University Press.

Jones, Lisa. 1994. *Bulletproof Diva: Tales of Race, Sex, and Hair.* New York: Doubleday.

Jordan, Winthrop. 1977. *White over Black: American Attitudes toward the Negro, 1550–1812.* New York: W. W. Norton.

Judy, Ronald. 1993. *(Dis)Forming the American Canon: African-Arabic Slave Narratives and the Vernacular.* Minneapolis: University of Minnesota Press.

Kaplan, Sidney. 1949. "The Miscegenation Issue in the Election of 1864." *Journal of Negro History* 34, no. 3 (July): 274–343.

Kaup, Monika, and Debra Rosenthal, eds. 2002. *Mixing Race, Mixing Culture: Inter-American Literary Dialogues.* Austin: University of Texas Press.

Kawash, Samira. 1997. *Dislocating the Color Line: Identity, Hybridity, and Singularity in African American Narrative.* Stanford, Calif.: Stanford University Press.

———. 1999. "Terrorists and Vampires." In Anthony Alessandrini (ed.), *Frantz Fanon: Critical Perspectives.* New York: Routledge.

Keeling, Kara. 2001. "Dig If You Will a Picture." Ph.D. diss., University of Pittsburgh.

———. 2003. "'In the Interval': Frantz Fanon and the 'Problems' of Visual Representation." *Qui Parle: Literature, Philosophy, Visual Arts, History* 13, no. 2 (Spring/Summer): 91–117.

Kelley, Robin D. G. 2003. *Freedom Dreams: The Black Radical Imagination.* New York: Beacon Press.

Kempadoo, Kamala, and Jo Doezema, eds. 1998. *Global Sex Workers: Rights, Resistance, and Redefinition.* New York: Routledge.

Kennedy, Randall. 1998. *Race, Crime, and the Law.* New York: Vintage.

———. 2003. *Interracial Intimacies: Sex, Marriage, Identity, and Adoption.* New York: Pantheon.

Kiel, L. Douglas, and Euel Elliott, eds. 1997. *Chaos Theory in the Social Sciences.* Ann Arbor: University of Michigan Press.

Kirby, Vicky. 1997. *Telling Flesh: The Substance of the Corporeal.* New York: Routledge.

Korgen, Kathleen. 1999. *From Black to Biracial: Transforming Racial Identity among Americans.* Westport, Conn.: Greenwood.

Kovel, Joel. 1984. *White Racism: A Psychohistory.* New York: Columbia University Press.

Kristeva, Julia. 1982. *Powers of Horror.* New York: Columbia University Press.

Lacan, Jacques. 1972. "Of Structure as an Inmixing of an Otherness Prerequisite to Any Subject Whatever." In Richard Macksey and Eugenio Donato (eds.), *The Structuralist Controversy.* Baltimore, Md.: Johns Hopkins University Press.

———. 1991. *Seminar I: Freud's Papers on Technique.* Trans. John Forrester. New York: W. W. Norton.

———. 1997. *Seminar VII: The Ethics of Psychoanalysis.* Trans. Dennis Porter. New York: W. W. Norton.

———. 1998. *Encore: The Seminar of Jacques Lacan. Book XX: On Feminine Sexuality: The Limits of Love and Knowledge, 1972–1973.* Trans. Bruce Fink. New York: W. W. Norton.

Laclau, Ernesto, and Chantal Mouffe. 1985. *Hegemony and Socialist Strategy: Towards a Radical Democratic Politics.* New York: Verso.

Lane, Christopher, ed. 1998. *The Psychoanalysis of Race.* New York: Columbia University Press.

Lawrence, Cecile. 1995. "Racelessness." In Naomi Zack (ed.), *American Mixed Race: The Culture of Microdiversity.* New York: Rowman and Littlefield.

Lazarre, Jane. 1997. *Beyond the Whiteness of Whiteness: Memoir of a White Mother of Black Sons.* Durham, N.C.: Duke University Press.

Lebeau, Vicky. 1998. "Psychopolitics: Frantz Fanon's *Black Skin, White Masks.*" In Jan Campbell and Janet Harbord (eds.), *Psycho-politics and Cultural Desires.* London: University College London Press.

Lechner, Frank, and John Boli, eds. 2003. *The Globalization Reader.* New York: Blackwell.

Lee, Donna R. 1998. "Mail Fantasy: Global Sexual Exploitation in the Mail-Order Bride Industry and Proposed Legal Solutions." *Asian Law Journal* 5, no. 1 (May): 139–79.

Lee, Liz, and Anmol Chaddha. 2000. "Fetishes!" *Hardboiled* 3.5, April. http://www.ocf.berkeley.edu/~hboiled/issue3.5/index.html.

Lee, Rose Hum. 1960. *The Chinese in the United States of America*. Hong Kong: Hong Kong University Press.

Lewis, Elliott. 2006. *Fade: My Journeys in Multiracial America*. New York: Carroll and Graf.

Leyshon, Andrew, and Nigel Thrift. 1996. *Money/Space: Geographies of Monetary Transformation*. New York: Routledge.

Lind, Michael. 1998. "The Beige and the Black." *New York Times Magazine*, August 16.

Logan, John. 2002. *Choosing Segregation: Racial Imbalance in American Public Schools, 1990–2000*. Albany, N.Y.: Lewis Mumford Center.

Logan, Spencer. 1946. *A Negro's Faith in America*. New York: Macmillan.

Lorde, Audre. 1984. *Sister Outsider: Essays and Speeches*. New York: Crossing Press.

Lott, Tommy. 1999. *The Invention of Race: Black Culture and the Politics of Representation*. New York: Blackwell.

Lowe, David. 1995. *The Body in Late Capitalist USA*. Durham, N.C.: Duke University Press.

Lubiano, Wahneema. 1993. "Foreword." In Ronald A. T. Judy, *(Dis)Forming the American Canon: African-Arabic Slave Narratives and the Vernacular*. Minneapolis: University of Minnesota Press.

———. 1998. "Black Nationalism and Black Common Sense: Policing Ourselves and Others." In Wahneema Lubiano (ed.), *The House That Race Built*. New York: Vintage.

Lyotard, Jean-François. 1988. *Peregrinations*. New York: Columbia University Press.

———. 1992. *The Inhuman*. Trans. Rachel Bowlby and Geoffrey Bennington. Stanford, Calif.: Stanford University Press.

———. 1993. *Libidinal Economy*. Trans. Ian Hamilton Grant. Bloomington: Indiana University Press.

MacKenzie, Malcolm. 1983. "Book Review: *The Cosmic Race/La raza cósmica*." *Hispania* 66 (2 May): 304–5.

Macksey, Richard, and Eugenio Donato, eds. 1972. *The Structuralist Controversy*. Baltimore, Md.: Johns Hopkins University Press.

Makalani, Minkah. 2001. "A Biracial Identity or a New Race? The Historical Limitations and Political Implications of a Biracial Identity for People with One Black and One White Parent." *Souls: A Critical Journal of Black Politics, Culture, and Society* 3, no. 2 (Fall): 73–102.

Marchessault, Janine. 2004. *Marshall McLuhan*. London: Sage.

Marini, Marcelle. 1993. *Jacques Lacan: The French Context*. Trans. Anne Tomichi. New Brunswick, N. J.: Rutgers University Press.

Marriott, David. 2000. *On Black Men*. New York: Columbia University Press.

Martí, José. 2002. *Selected Writings*. New York: Penguin.

Martinez, Elizabeth. 1998. *De Colores Means All of Us: Latina Views for a Multi-Colored Century*. Boston: South End Press.

Martinot, Steve. 2002. *The Rule of Racialization: Class, Identity, Governance*. Philadelphia: Temple University Press.

Massey, Douglas. 2000. "The Residential Segregation of Blacks, Hispanics, and Asians, 1970–1990." In Gerald Jaynes (ed.), *Immigration and Race: New Challenges for American Democracy*. New Haven, Conn.: Yale University Press.

Massey, Douglas, and Nancy Denton. 1998. *American Apartheid: Segregation and the Making of the Underclass*. Cambridge, Mass.: Harvard University Press.

Massumi, Brian. 1992. *A User's Guide to Capitalism and Schizophrenia: Deviations from Deleuze and Guattari*. Cambridge, Mass.: MIT Press.

———. 1993. "Everywhere You Want to Be: Introduction to the Politics of Everyday Fear." In Brian Massumi (ed.), *The Politics of Everyday Fear*. Minneapolis: University of Minnesota Press.

———. 2002. *Parables for the Virtual: Movement, Affect, Sensation*. Durham, N.C.: Duke University Press.

Mathabane, Mark, and Gail Mathabane. 1992. *Love in Black and White: The Triumph of Love over Prejudice and Taboo*. New York: Harper Collins.

Matsuda, Mari. 2002. "Beyond, and Not Beyond, Black and White: Deconstruction Has a Politics." In Francisco Valdes, Jerome McCristal Culp, and Angela Harris (eds.), *Crossroads, Directions, and a New Critical Race Theory*. Philadelphia: Temple University Press.

Mauer, Marc. 1999. *The Race to Incarcerate*. New York: New Press.

Mbembe, Achille. 1999. "Migration of Peoples, Disintegration of State: Africa's Frontiers in Flux." *Le Monde diplomatique*, November. http://www.en.monde -diplomatique.fr/1999/11/12africa.

———. 2000. *On the Postcolony*. Berkeley: University of California Press.

McBride, James. 1996. *The Color of Water: A Black Man's Tribute to His White Mother*. New York: Riverhead Books.

McCulloch, Richard. 1994. "The Racial Golden Rule." *The Racial Compact: A Call for Racial Preservation, Racial Independence, Racial Rights and Racial Good Will*. http://www.racialcompact.com/racialgoldenrule.html.

McGreal, Chris. 2001. "Africans Back Down at UN Race Talks." *Guardian*, September 9. http://www.guardian.co.uk/unracism/story/0,1099,548954,00.html.

McLuhan, Marshall. 1962. *The Gutenberg Galaxy: The Making of Typographic Man*. Toronto: University of Toronto Press.

Meacham, Jon. 2000. "The New Face of Race." *Newsweek*, September 18. http://www.msnbc.msn.com/id/4387275/.

Melville, Stephen. 1986. *Philosophy beside Itself: On Deconstruction and Modernity*. Minneapolis: University of Minnesota Press.

Memmi, Albert. 1999. *Racism*. Trans. Steve Martinot. Minneapolis: University of Minnesota Press.

Meng, Eddy. 1994. "Mail-Order Brides: Gilded Prostitution and the Legal Response." *University of Michigan Journal of Law* 28 (Fall): 197–247.

Mercer, Kobena. 1994. *Welcome to the Jungle: New Positions in Black Cultural Studies*. New York: Routledge.

———. 1996. "Decolonisation and Disappointment: Reading Fanon's Sexual Politics." In Alan Read (ed.), *The Fact of Blackness: Frantz Fanon and Visual Representation*. Seattle, Wash.: Bay Press.

Mignolo, Walter. 2000. *Local Histories/Global Designs: Coloniality, Subaltern Knowledges, and Border Thinking*. Princeton, N.J.: Princeton University Press.

Miklitsch, Robert. 1998. *Psycho-Marxism: Marxism and Psychoanalysis Late in the Twentieth Century*. Durham, N.C.: Duke University Press.

Miles, Kevin. 1996. "Body Badges: Race and Sex." In Naomi Zack (ed.), *Race/Sex: Their Sameness, Difference, and Interplay*. New York: Routledge.

Miles, Robert. 1989. *Racism*. New York: Routledge.

Miller, Jacques-Alain Miller. 1977. "Suture: Elements of the Logic of the Signifier." *Screen* 18, no. 4 (Winter): 24–34.

Miller, Jody, and Dasheeshana Jayasundara. 2001. "Prostitution, the Sex Industry, and Sex Tourism." In Claire M. Renzetti, Jeffrey L. Edleson, and Raquel Kennedy Bergen (eds.), *Sourcebook on Violence against Women*. Thousand Oaks, Calif.: Sage.

Miller, Marilyn Grace. 2004. *The Rise and Fall of the Cosmic Race: The Cult of "Mestizaje" in Latin America*. Austin: University of Texas Press.

Mills, Charles. 1998. *Blackness Visible: Essays on Philosophy and Race*. Ithaca, N.Y.: Cornell University Press.

Minority Rights Group, ed. 1995. *No Longer Invisible: Afro-Latin Americans Today*. London: Minority Rights Group Publications.

Moraga, Cherríe, and Gloria Anzaldúa, eds. 1984. *This Bridge Called My Back: Writings by Radical Women of Color.* New York: Kitchen Table Press.

Moran, Rachel. 2001. *Interracial Intimacy: The Regulation of Race and Romance.* Chicago: University of Chicago Press.

Moreiras, Alberto. 2001. *The Exhaustion of Difference: The Politics of Latin American Cultural Studies.* Durham, N.C.: Duke University Press.

Morel, Geneviève. 2000. "Psychoanalytical Anatomy." In Renata Salecl (ed.), *Sexuation.* Durham, N.C.: Duke University Press.

Morrison, Toni. 1992. *Playing in the Dark: Whiteness and the Literary Imagination.* Cambridge, Mass.: Harvard University Press.

Moten, Fred. 2003. *In the Break: The Aesthetics of the Black Radical Tradition.* Minneapolis: University of Minnesota Press.

Muñoz, José Esteban. 1999. *Disidentifications: Queers of Color and the Performance of Politics.* Minneapolis: University of Minnesota Press.

Myrdal, Gunnar. 1962. *An American Dilemma: The Negro Problem and Modern Democracy.* New York: Harper Collins.

Narayan, Uma. 1995. "'Male-Order' Brides: Immigrant Women, Domestic Violence, and Immigration Law." *Hypatia* 10, no. 1 (Winter): 104–19.

Nash, Gary. 1999. *Forbidden Love: The Hidden History of Mixed-Race America.* New York: Henry Holt.

Nelson, William Javier. 1982. *Racial Definition Handbook.* Minneapolis: Burgess.

Njeri, Itabari. 1997. *The Last Plantation: Color, Conflict, and Identity: Reflections of a New World Black.* New York: Houghton Mifflin.

O'Hearn, Claudine, ed. 1998. *Half and Half: Writers on Growing Up Biracial and Bicultural.* New York: Pantheon.

Omi, Michael. 2001. "The Changing Meaning of Race." In Neil Smelser, William Julius Wilson, and Faith Mitchell (eds.), *America Becoming: Racial Trends and Their Consequences.* Washington, D.C.: National Academies Press.

Omi, Michael, and Howard Winant. 1993. "The Los Angeles 'Race Riot' and Contemporary U.S. Politics." In Robert Gooding-Williams (ed.), *Reading Rodney King/Reading Urban Uprising.* New York: Routledge.

———. 1994. *Racial Formation in the United States: From the 1960s to the 1990s.* New York: Routledge.

Ore, Tracy, ed. 2003. *The Social Construction of Difference and Inequality: Race, Class, Gender, and Sexuality.* New York: McGraw-Hill.

Palumbo-Liu, David. 1999. *Asian/American: Historical Crossings of a Racial Frontier.* Stanford, Calif.: Stanford University Press.

Parenti, Christian. 2000. *Lockdown America: Police and Prisons in the Age of Crisis.* New York: Verso.

Park, Robert. 1928. "Human Migration and the Marginal Man." *American Journal of Sociology* 33, no. 6: 881–93.

Parker, David, and Miri Song. 2002a. "Introduction: Rethinking 'Mixed Race.'" In David Parker and Miri Song (eds.), *Rethinking "Mixed Race."* London: Pluto.

———. 2002b. *Rethinking "Mixed Race."* London: Pluto.

Parker, Geoffrey. 1998. *Geopolitics.* London: Pinter.

Pascoe, Peggy. 1999. "Miscegenation Law, Court Cases, and Ideologies of 'Race' in the Twentieth Century." In Martha Hodes (ed.), *Sex, Love, Race: Crossing Boundaries in North American History.* New York: New York University Press.

Peiss, Kathy, and Helen Horowitz, eds. 1996. *Love across the Color Line: The Letters of Alice Hanley to Channing Lewis.* Amherst: University of Massachusetts Press.

Penn, William, ed. 1998. *As We Are Now: Mixblood Essays on Race and Identity.* Berkeley: University of California Press.

Perlmann, Joel, and Mary Waters, eds. 2002. *The New Race Question: How the Census Counts Multiracial Individuals.* New York: Russell Sage Foundation.

Plotnitski, Arkady. 1993. *Reconfigurations: Critical Theory and General Economy.* Gainesville: University of Florida Press.

Post, Robert, and Michael Rogin, eds. 1998. *Race and Representation: Affirmative Action.* New York: Zone Books.

Prashad, Vijay. 2002. *Fat Cats and Running Dogs: The Enron Stage of Capitalism.* Monroe, Maite: Common Courage Press.

Radikrishnan, R. 1990. "Ethnic Identity and the Post-Structuralist Différance." In Abdul JanMohamed and David Lloyd (eds.), *The Nature and Context of Minority Discourse.* New York: Oxford University Press.

Rapaport, Herman. 2001. *The Theory Mess: Deconstruction in Eclipse.* New York: Columbia University Press.

Reddy, Maureen. 1996. *Crossing the Color Line: Race, Parenting, and Culture.* New Brunswick, N.J.: Rutgers University Press.

Reed, Ishmael, ed. 1997. *Multi-America: Essays on Cultural Wars and Cultural Peace.* New York: Viking.

Reid-Pharr, Robert. 2001. *Black, Gay, Man: Essays.* New York: New York University Press.

Reuter, Edward. 1918. *The Mulatto in the United States.* Boston: Gorham Press.

Richie, Beth. 1996. *Compelled to Crime: The Gender Entrapment of Black Battered Women.* New York: Routledge.

Roberts, Dorothy. 1998. *Killing the Black Body: Race, Reproduction, and the Meaning of Liberty.* New York: Vintage.

Robinson, Cedric. 1997. *Black Movements in America.* New York: Routledge.

———. 2000. *Black Marxism: The Making of the Black Radical Tradition.* Chapel Hill: University of North Carolina Press.

Robinson, Charles F. 2003. *Dangerous Liaisons: Sex and Love in the Segregated South.* Fayetteville: University of Arkansas Press.

Robinson, Randall. 2000. *The Debt: What America Owes to Blacks.* New York: Plume.

Robinson, Sally. 2000. *Marked Men: White Masculinity in Crisis.* New York: Columbia University Press.

Rockquemore, Kerry Ann. 2004. "Deconstructing Tiger Woods: The Promise and Pitfalls of Multiracial Identity." In Heather Dalmage (ed.), *The Politics of Multiracialism: Challenging Racial Thinking.* Albany: State University of New York Press.

Rockquemore, Kerry Ann, and David Brunsma. 2002. *Beyond Black: Biracial Identity in America.* London: Sage.

Roediger, David. 1991. *The Wages of Whiteness: Race and the Making of the American Working Class.* New York: Verso, 1991.

Rogin, Michael. 1987. *Ronald Reagan, the Movie: And Other Episodes of Political Demonology.* Berkeley: University of California Press.

Romano, Renee. 2003. *Race Mixing: Black–White Marriage in Postwar America.* Cambridge, Mass.: Harvard University Press.

Root, Maria, ed. 1992a. *Racially Mixed People in America.* Newbury Park, Calif.: Sage.

———. 1992b. "Within, Between, and Beyond Race." In Maria Root (ed.), *Racially Mixed People in America*, 3–11. Newbury Park, Calif.: Sage Publications.

———. 1995. "The Multiracial Contribution to the Psychological Browning of America." In Naomi Zack (ed.), *American Mixed Race: The Culture of Microdiversity.* New York: Rowman and Littlefield.

———. 1996a. "A Bill of Rights for Racially Mixed People." In Maria Root (ed.), *The Multiracial Experience: Racial Borders as the New Frontier.* Thousand Oaks, Calif.: Sage.

————, ed. 1996b. *The Multiracial Experience: Racial Borders as the New Frontier.* Thousand Oaks, Calif.: Sage.

————. 1997. "Contemporary Mixed-Heritage Filipino Americans: Fighting Colonized Identities." In Maria Root (ed.), *Filipino Americans: Transformation and Identity.* Thousand Oaks, Calif.: Sage.

————. 2001. *Love's Revolution: Interracial Marriage.* Philadelphia: Temple University Press.

Roy, Arundati. 2004. "Project for a New American Century." *Nation,* January 22.

Sadowski-Smith, Claudia, ed. 2002. *Globalization on the Line: Culture, Capital, and Citizenship at U.S. Borders.* New York: Palgrave Macmillan.

Saks, Eva. 2000. "Representing Miscegenation Law." In Werner Sollors (ed.), *Interracialism: Black–White Intermarriage in American History, Literature, and Law.* New York: Oxford University Press.

Salecl, Renata, ed. 2000. *Sexuation.* Durham, N.C.: Duke University Press.

Sánchez, Maria Carla, and Linda Schlossberg, eds. 2001. *Passing: Identity and Interpretation in Sexuality, Race, and Religion.* New York: New York University Press.

Saulny, Susan. 2002. "Convictions and Charges Voided in '89 Central Park Jogger Attack." *New York Times,* Sec. A, p. 1, col. 4.

Scales-Trent, Judy. 1995. *Notes of a White Black Woman.* University Park: Penn State University Press.

Semmes, Clovis. 1996. *Racism, Health, and Post-Industrialism: A Theory of African-American Health.* Westport, Conn.: Praeger.

Senna, Danzy. 1998. *Caucasia.* New York: Riverhead Books.

Seshadri-Crooks, Kalpana. 2000. *Desiring Whiteness: A Lacanian Analysis of Race.* New York: Routledge.

Sharpe, Jenny. 1993. *Allegories of Empire: The Figure of Woman in the Colonial Text.* Minneapolis: University of Minnesota Press.

Sharpley-Whiting, T. Denean. 1996. "Engaging Fanon to Reread Capecia." In Lewis Gordon, T. Denean Sharpley-Whiting, and Renée T. White (eds.), *Fanon: A Critical Reader.* New York: Blackwell.

Shaviro, Steve. 1990. *Passion and Excess: Blanchot, Bataille, and Literary Theory.* Tallahassee: Florida State University Press.

————. 1993. *The Cinematic Body.* Minneapolis: University of Minnesota Press.

Shelby, Tommie. 2005. *We Who Are Dark: The Philosophical Foundations of Black Solidarity.* Cambridge, Mass.: Harvard University Press.

Shepherdson, Charles. 1998. "Human Diversity and the Sexual Relation." In Christopher Lane (ed.), *The Psychoanalysis of Race*. New York: Columbia University Press.

———. 2000. *Vital Signs: Nature, Culture, Psychoanalysis*. New York: Routledge.

Shor, Ira. 1992. *Culture Wars: School and Society in the Conservative Restoration, 1969–1984*. Chicago: University of Chicago Press.

Silverman, Kaja. 1983. *The Subject of Semiotics*. New York: Oxford University Press.

Skerry, Peter. 2000. *Counting on the Census? Race, Group Identity, and the Evasion of Politics*. New York: Brookings Institution Press.

Small, Stephen. 1994. *Racialized Barriers: The Black Experience in the United States and England in the 1980s*. New York: Routledge.

Smith, Ann Marie. 1994. *New Right Discourse on Race and Sexuality: Great Britain, 1968–1990*. New York: Cambridge University Press.

Smith, Barbara, ed. 1983. *Home Girls: A Black Feminist Anthology*. New York: Kitchen Table Press.

———. 2000. *The Truth That Never Hurts: Writings on Race, Gender, and Freedom*. New Brunswick, N.J.: Rutgers University Press.

Smith, Valerie. 1998. *Not Just Race, Not Just Gender: Black Feminist Readings*. New York: Routledge.

Smith, Zadie. 2001. *White Teeth: A Novel*. New York: Vintage.

Soler, Colette. 2000. "The Curse on Sex." In Renata Salecl (ed.), *Sexuation*. Durham, N.C.: Duke University Press.

Sollors, Werner. 1997. *Neither White nor Black Yet Both: Thematic Explorations of Interracial Literature*. Cambridge, Mass.: Harvard University Press.

Somerville, Siobhan. 2000. *Queering the Color Line: Race and the Invention of Homosexuality in American Culture*. Durham, N.C.: Duke University Press.

Sommerville, Diane Miller. 2004. "Moonlight, Magnolias, and Brigadoon, or 'Almost Like Being in Love': Mastery and Sexual Exploitation in Eugene D. Genovese's Plantation South." *Radical History Review* 88 (Winter): 68–82.

Spencer, Jon Michael. 1997. *The New Colored People: The Mixed-Race Movement in America*. New York: New York University Press.

Spencer, Rainier. 1999. *Spurious Issues: Race and Multiracial Identity Politics in the United States*. New York: Westview.

———. 2004. "Beyond Pathology and Cheerleading: Insurgency, Dissolution, and Complicity in the Multiracial Idea." In Heather Dalmage (ed.), *The Politics of Multiracialism: Challenging Racial Thinking.* Albany: State University of New York Press.

———. 2006. *Challenging Multiracial Identity.* Boulder, Colo.: Lynn Reinner.

Spickard, Paul. 1991. *Mixed Blood: Intermarriage and Ethnic Identity in Twentieth Century America.* Madison: University of Wisconsin Press.

Spillers, Hortense. 1994. "The Crisis of the Negro Intellectual: A Post-Date." *boundary 2* 21, no. 3 (Autumn): 65–116.

———. 2003. *Black, White, and in Color: Essays on American Literature and Culture.* Chicago: University of Chicago Press.

Spivak, Gayatri. 1988. "Can the Subaltern Speak?" In Cary Nelson and Lawrence Grossberg (eds.), *Marxism and the Interpretation of Culture.* Chicago: University of Illinois Press.

———. 1999. *A Critique of Postcolonial Reason: Toward a History of the Vanishing Present.* Cambridge, Mass.: Harvard University Press.

Spurr, David. 1993. *The Rhetoric of Empire: Colonial Discourse in Journalism, Travel Writing, and Imperial Administration.* Durham, N.C.: Duke University Press.

Stember, Charles. 1976. *Sexual Racism: The Emotional Barrier to an Integrated Society.* New York: Harper and Row.

Stephens, Gregory. 1999. *On Racial Frontiers: The New Culture of Fredrick Douglass, Ralph Ellison, and Bob Marley.* Cambridge: Cambridge University Press.

Stoler, Ann Laura. 1995. *Race and the Education of Desire: Foucault's "History of Sexuality" and the Colonial Order of Things.* Durham, N.C.: Duke University Press.

———. 2002. *Carnal Knowledge and Imperial Power: Race and the Intimate in Colonial Rule.* Berkeley: University of California Press.

Stonequist, Everett. 1937. *The Marginal Man: A Study in Personality and Culture.* New York: Charles Scribner's Sons.

Streeter, Caroline. 1996. "Ambiguous Bodies: Locating Black/White Women in Cultural Representations." In Maria Root (ed.), *The Multiracial Experience: Racial Borders as the New Frontier.* Thousand Oaks, Calif.: Sage.

Tadiar, Neferti. 2003. "In the Face of Whiteness as Value." *Qui Parle: Literature, Philosophy, Visual Arts, History* 13, no. 2 (Spring/Summer): 143–82.

Takaki, Ronald. 1990. *Iron Cages: Race and Culture in 19th-Century America.* New York: Oxford University Press.

Talty, Stephen. 2003. *Mulatto America: At the Crossroads of Black and White Culture—A Social History.* New York: Harper Collins.

Tate, Greg. 2003. *Everything but the Burden: What White People Are Taking from Black Culture*. New York: Broadway.

Taylor, Mark C. 1997. *Hiding*. Chicago: University of Chicago Press.

Trask, Haunani-Kay. 1999. *From a Native Daughter: Colonialism and Sovereignty in Hawai'i*. Honolulu: University of Hawai'i Press.

Twine, Frances Winddance. 1996. "Heterosexual Alliances: The Romantic Management of Racial Identity." In Maria Root (ed.), *The Multiracial Experience: Racial Borders as the New Frontier*. Thousand Oaks, Calif.: Sage.

Van Deberg, William. 1992. *New Day in Babylon: The Black Power Movement and American Culture, 1965–1975*. Chicago: University of Chicago Press.

Vasconcelos, José. 1997. *The Cosmic Race/La raza cósmica: A Bilingual Edition*. Trans. Didier Jaén. Baltimore, Md.: Johns Hopkins University Press.

Wacquant, Loic. 2005. *Deadly Symbiosis: Race and the Rise of Neoliberal Penality*. London: Polity Press.

Wade, Peter. 1997. *Race and Ethnicity in Latin America*. London: Pluto.

Waldrop, M. Mitchell. 1992. *Complexity: The Emerging Science at the Edge of Order and Chaos*. New York: Touchstone.

Walker, Rebecca. 2001. *Black, White, and Jewish: Autobiography of a Shifting Self*. New York: Riverhead Books.

Wall, Thomas Carl. 1999. *Radical Passivity: Levinas, Blanchot, and Agamben*. Albany: State University of New York Press.

Wallace, Michelle. 1990a. *Black Macho and the Myth of the Superwoman*. New York: Verso.

———. 1990b. *Invisibility Blues: From Pop to Theory*. New York: Verso.

Wallenstein, Peter. 2002. *Tell the Court I Love My Wife: Race, Marriage, and Law— An American History*. New York: Palgrave Macmillan.

Warner, Michael, ed. 1993. *Fear of a Queer Planet: Queer Politics and Social Theory*. Minneapolis: University of Minnesota Press.

———. 1999. *The Trouble with Normal: Sex, Politics, and the Ethics of Queer Life*. New York: Free Press.

Warren, Jonathan, and France Winddance Twine. 1997. "White Americans, the New Minority?" *Journal of Black Studies* 28, no. 2 (November): 200–18.

Weinberger, Andrew. 1964. "A Reappraisal of the Constitutionality of 'Miscegenation' Statutes." In Ashley Montagu, *Man's Most Dangerous Myth*. New York: Meridian Books.

Welland, Sasha. 2003. "Being Between: Can Multiracial Americans Form a Cohesive

Anti-Racist Movement Beyond Identity Politics and Tiger Woods Chic?" *ColorLines: Race, Culture, Action* 6, no. 2: 31–33.

Werbner, Pnina, and Tariq Modood, eds. 1997. *Debating Cultural Hybridity: Multi-Cultural Identities and the Politics of Anti-Racism*. London: Zed.

West, Cornel. 1994. *Race Matters*. New York: Vintage.

West, Cornel. 1990. "The New Cultural Politics of Difference." In Russell Ferguson, Martha Gever, Trinh T. Minh-ha, and Cornel West (eds.), *Out There: Marginalization and Contemporary Cultures*. Cambridge, Mass.: MIT Press.

White Lie. 1991. Directed by Bill Condon. Universal City: Calif.: Alan Barnette Productions.

Whitten, Norman, and Arlene Torres, eds. 1998. *Blackness in Latin America and the Caribbean: Social Dynamics and Cultural Transformations*. Bloomington: Indiana University Press.

Wiegman, Robyn. 1995. *American Anatomies: Theorizing Race and Gender*. Durham, N.C.: Duke University Press.

Wilderson, Frank. 2003. "Gramsci's Black Marx: Whither the Slave in Civil Society?" *Social Identities: Journal for the Study of Race, Nation and Culture* 9, no. 2 (June): 225–40.

Williams, Eric. 1994. *Capitalism and Slavery*. Chapel Hill: University of North Carolina Press.

Williams, Gregory. 1995. *Life on the Color Line: The True Story of a White Boy Who Discovered He Was Black*. New York: Dutton.

Williams, Kim. 2004. "Linking the Civil Rights and Multiracial Movements." In Heather Dalmage (ed.), *The Politics of Multiracialism: Challenging Racial Thinking*. Albany: State University of New York Press.

Williams, Patrick, and Nahem Yousaf. 1999. "Colonial Discourse/Postcolonial Theory." In *The Year's Work in Critical and Cultural Theory*. Vol. 6. London: Blackwell.

Williams-Leon, Teresa, and Cynthia Nakashima, eds. 2001. *The Sum of Our Parts: Mixed-Heritage Asian Americans*. Philadelphia: Temple University Press.

Williamson, Joel. 1984. *New People: Miscegenation and Mulattoes in the United States*. New York: New York University Press.

———. 1986. *A Rage for Order: Black–White Relations in the American South since Emancipation*. New York: Oxford University Press.

Wilson, William Julius. 1996. *When Work Disappears: The World of the New Urban Poor*. New York: Vintage.

Winant, Howard. 2001. *The World Is a Ghetto: Race and Democracy since World War II*. New York: Basic Books.

Winkel, Gregory. 2001. "On Rejecting Identity Politics." *Interracial Voice*. http://www.webcom.com/~intvoice/gwinkel.html.

Winters, Loretta, and Herman DeBose, eds. 2002. *New Faces in a Changing America: Multiracial Identity in the 21st Century*. London: Sage.

Wolfenstein, Eugene. 1993. *Psychoanalytic Marxism: Groundwork*. New York: Guilford Press.

Wu, Frank. 2001. *Yellow: Race in America beyond Black and White*. New York: Basic Books.

Wynter, Leon. 2002. *American Skin: Pop Culture, Big Business, and the End of White America*. New York: Crown.

Yancey, George. 2003. *Who Is White? Latinos, Asians, and the New Black/Nonblack Divide*. Boulder, Colo.: Lynne Rienner.

Yancey, George, and Sherelyn Whittum Yancey, eds. 2003. *Just Don't Marry One: Interracial Dating, Marriage, and Parenting*. Valley Forge, Pa.: Judson Press.

Yoshihara, Nancy. 1997. "Angela Oh: Adding an Asian American Voice to the Race Debate." *Los Angeles Times*, July 13, sec. M, p. 3.

Young, Lola. 1996a. *Fear of the Dark: 'Race,' Gender, and Sexuality in Cinema*. New York: Routledge.

———. 1996b. "Missing Persons." In Alan Read (ed.), *The Fact of Blackness: Frantz Fanon and Visual Representation*. Seattle, Wash.: Bay Press.

Young, Robert. 1995. *Colonial Desire: Hybridity in Theory, Culture, and Race*. New York: Routledge.

Yu, Henry. 1999. "Mixing Bodies and Cultures: The Meaning of America's Fascination with Sex Between 'Orientals' and Whites." In Martha Hodes (ed.), *Sex, Love, Race: Crossing Boundaries in North American History*. New York: New York University Press.

———. 2002. *Thinking Orientals: Migration, Contact, and Exoticism in Modern America*. New York: Oxford University Press.

Zack, Naomi. 1993. *Race and Mixed Race*. Philadelphia: Temple University Press.

———, ed. 1995a. *American Mixed Race: The Culture of Microdiversity*. New York: Rowman and Littlefield.

———. 1995b. "Life after Race." In Naomi Zack (ed.), *American Mixed Race: The Culture of Microdiversity*. New York: Rowman and Littlefield.

Zackodnik, Teresa. 2001. "Fixing the Color Line: The Mulatto, the Southern

Courts, and Racial Identity." *American Quarterly* 53, no. 3 (September): 420–51.

Zantop, Suzanne. 1997. *Colonial Fantasies: Conquest, Family, and Nation in Precolonial Germany, 1770–1870.* Durham, N.C.: Duke University Press.

Zimmerman, Jonathan. 1999. "Crossing Oceans, Crossing Colors: Black Peace Corps Volunteers and Interracial Love in Africa, 1961–1971." In Martha Hodes (ed.), *Sex, Love, Race: Crossing Boundaries in North American History.* New York: New York University Press.

Žižek, Slavoj. 1989. *The Sublime Object of Ideology.* New York: Verso.

———. 1992. *Looking Awry: An Introduction to Jacques Lacan through Popular Culture.* Cambridge: MIT Press.

———. 1994. "Introduction." In Slavoj Žižek (ed.), *Mapping Ideology.* New York: Verso.

———. 1995. *Tarrying with the Negative: Kant, Hegel, and the Critique of Ideology.* Durham, N.C.: Duke University Press.

———. 1996a. "I Hear You with My Eyes." In Renata Salecl and Slavoj Žižek (eds.), *Gaze and Voice as Love Objects.* Durham, N.C.: Duke University Press.

———. 1996b. *The Metastases of Enjoyment: Sex Essays on Woman and Causality.* New York: Verso.

———. 1996c. "There Is No Sexual Relationship." In Renata Salecl and Slavoj Žižek (eds.), *Gaze and Voice as Love Objects.* Durham, N.C.: Duke University Press.

———. 1997. *The Plague of Fantasies.* New York: Verso.

Index

Created by Denise E. Carlson

Uniform Code of Military Justice,
136, 143
United Nations' World Conference
Against Racism (2001), 3
United States: AIDS in, 236, 242; Bill
of Rights, 77–78, 277n37; black
population of, 40–41; Europeanization of, 245; hegemony of, 3; immigrants to, 228, 294n13; interracial
sexuality in, 31–35, 238; Latin
Americanization of, 260n4; mixed
race in, 6, 55, 68, 179–80, 202,
203–5, 227, 243; multiracialism in,
4, 11, 185–86; national identity of,
97–98, 134; nation-building by, 87;
post–civil rights era, 246–47, 249;
race in, 48, 61, 75, 292n6, 293n8;
racial formation in, 6, 150, 193,
196, 228, 235, 243, 249; racism in,
13, 50–51, 57–58, 172, 245; white
supremacy in, 78, 204, 207–8. *See
also* census classification debates;
civil rights movement; Peace
Corps: interracial relationships in
"unity-in-diversity," 32

value, 290n21
Vasconcelos, José, 198–201, 204,
260n4, 274n29, 289n14
victimization, 98–99, 154, 254, 257
violence, 4, 195, 258, 277n36, 279n7;
black, 162, 244; mass, 236–37; of
miscegenation, 100, 239, 289n19;
racial, 151, 258; sexual, 9, 11, 12,
35–37, 60–62, 92, 113, 135–45, 147,
173, 232, 240–42, 244, 269n14,

282n15; state-sanctioned, 104,
200–201. *See also* rape; slavery
Voting Rights Act of 1965, 238

Walker, Alice, 137
Wall, Thomas Carl, 296n16
war, 240
Wardle, Francis, 80
Weinberger, Andrew, 212, 214
West, Cornel, 196
White Lie (Condon), 210–11
white men, 64, 122, 139–40, 144,
286n18; interracial sexual encounters, 178, 213–14; sexual violence
by, 137, 138, 147, 282n15. *See also*
slavery: sexual coercion under
white–nonwhite binary, 229–30, 256,
268n14
whites, 170, 276n32; interracial
sexuality and, 133, 202, 267n12;
perceived threats to, 210, 215;
racialization of, 52, 264n26. *See
also* black–white binary; racial
whiteness
white supremacy, 210, 232; animus of,
75–76; antiblackness and, 18, 36,
51, 174, 192, 252–53, 294n10;
antimiscegenation and, 21–22,
25–26, 98–99, 107, 222; criminal
justice system under, 139, 141; discourse of, 7, 134, 294n10; economy
of, 28, 202; final frontier of, 205;
global, 5, 50–51, 193, 228, 235,
238; history of, 147, 222–23; interracial sexuality and, 20, 23, 31–35,
85, 92, 159, 170–72, 207–9, 214,

Jared Sexton is associate professor of African American studies and film and media studies at the University of California, Irvine, where he is associated with the Critical Theory Institute and the Center in Law, Culture, and Society.